Vol. 20 No. 1
February 1978

# JOURNAL OF INTERAMERICAN STUDIES

# and WORLD AFFAIRS

A Publication of the Center for Advanced International Studies,

The University of Miami

SAGE PUBLICATIONS

*Journal of INTERAMERICAN STUDIES*
*and WORLD AFFAIRS*



The editors and publisher wish to acknowledge with gratitude the assistance and encouragement of the Center for Advanced International Studies, University of Miami, in providing ancillary services and support for this journal.

*Journal of*
INTERAMERICAN
STUDIES
*and* WORLD AFFAIRS

Vol. 20
No. 1
February
1978

# CONTENTS



*Power and Politics in Peronist Trade Unions*
DANIEL JAMES 3

*Diplomatic Protection of Foreign Economic Interests: The Changing Structure of International Law in the New International Economic Order*
BENOIT OTIS BROOKENS 37

*Toward a Reinterpretation of Political Change in Peru During the First Century of Independence*
RONALD H. BERG
FREDERICK STIRTON WEAVER 69

**REVIEW ESSAYS**

*Mexico's Foreign Policy—Indeed a Foreign Policy?*
WOLF GRABENDORFF 85

*On the Virtues of Total Submersion: An Essay on the Trials and Tribulations of Development Literature Through the Bright Light of a New Product*
ARPAD VON LAZAR 93

BOOKS RECEIVED 99

SAGE PUBLICATIONS / *Beverly Hills* *London*

**POLICY: THE JOURNAL OF INTERAMERICAN STUDIES AND WORLD AFFAIRS** reflects the interests of the scholarly community and interested public concerned with the social, economic, political, and cultural aspects of life in Latin America (including the Caribbean); particularly in those instances where the subject is of concern to more than one of the traditional disciplines. As these concerns change, so will the content of the journal.

**ARTICLES** which have special relevance for interrelationships between American nations and of those nations with the rest of the world will be given special consideration. An effort will be made to include occasional articles that state an unusual or even discordant position on a subject of broad interest to be supplemented by critical comments of authorities representing differing positions on the topic. The editors continue to welcome articles by scholars from all parts of the world.

**MANUSCRIPTS** should be submitted in duplicate to: Editor, JOURNAL OF INTERAMERICAN STUDIES AND WORLD AFFAIRS, Box 24-8134, University of Miami, Coral Gables, Florida 33124. Manuscripts should be typewritten, double-spaced, with footnotes, references, tables, and charts on separate pages, and should follow the current journal style. A brief biographical paragraph describing each author's current affiliation, research interests, and recent publications should accompany the manuscript.

**CORRESPONDENCE** regarding book reviews should be sent directly to: Book Review Editor, JOURNAL OF INTERAMERICAN STUDIES AND WORLD AFFAIRS, Box 24-8134, University of Miami, Coral Gables, Florida 33124.

---

**JOURNAL OF INTERAMERICAN STUDIES AND WORLD AFFAIRS** is published four times annually—in February, May, August, and November. 

**Subscriptions:** Regular institutional rate $26.00. Individuals may subscribe at a one-year rate of $15.00. Add $1.00 per year for subscriptions outside the United States. Orders from U.K., Europe, the Middle East, and Africa should be sent to the London office (address below). Noninstitutional orders **must** be paid by personal check.

Second-class postage paid at Beverly Hills, California.

**Inquiries:** Address all correspondence and permissions requests to SAGE PUBLICATIONS, INC., 275 South Beverly Drive, Beverly Hills, California 90212. Inquiries and subscriptions from U.K., Europe, the Middle East, and Africa should be sent to SAGE PUBLICATIONS LTD, 28 Banner Street, London EC1Y 8QE, England. Other orders should be sent to the Beverly Hills office.

**Advertising:** Current rates and specifications may be obtained by writing to the Advertising Manager at the Beverly Hills office (address above).

This journal is abstracted or indexed in **Historical Abstracts, Human Resources Abstracts, Sage Urban Studies Abstracts, International Political Science Abstracts, Public Affairs Information Service, Current Contents, Social Sciences Citation Index, Social Sciences Index, ABC POL SCI** and **United States Political Science Documents.**

**Back Issues:** Information about availability and prices of back issues may be obtained from the publisher's order department (address above). Write to London office for sterling prices.

**Claims for undelivered copies** must be made no later than three months following month of publication. The publisher will supply missing copies when losses have been sustained in transit and where the reserve stock will permit.

**Change of Address:** Six weeks' advance notice must be given when notifying of change of address. Please send old address label along with the new address to insure proper identification. Please specify name of journal.

**DANIEL JAMES**
*Centre for Latin American Studies*
*University of Cambridge*
*Cambridge, England*

# *POWER AND POLITICS IN PERONIST TRADE UNIONS*

The subject of this article is the Peronist union leadership in the period from the fall of Perón in 1955 until the elections of March 1973, which heralded the return of Peronism to power. The first section examines this leadership mainly in terms of its internal power base, especially vis-à-vis its membership. This involves primarily an examination of internal union government, union elections, and potential limitations of leadership power by the rank and file. The second part looks at the union leadership in terms of its power as a political force bargaining on behalf of the Peronist movement. This will also involve a brief look at the union leadership's relationship with Perón himself. Finally, the third section attempts to suggest an explanatory framework within which to situate the development of this union leadership's power.

A brief case study will provide a useful point of entry for a discussion of both the internal power base of the union leadership and some of the ramifications of this power in the wider society. The case study is that of the 1970 elections in the Unión Obrera Metalúrgica, the most powerful union in the country and the traditional center of Peronist union power. In the wake of the assassination of Augusto Vandor, who had controlled the union and dominated the entire union scene throughout the 1960s, there developed two chief contenders for the elections to

AUTHOR'S NOTE: Field research for this article was made possible by a grant from the Foreign Area Fellowships Programme. The author would like to express his thanks to Jorge Di Pasquale and Alberto Belloni for their great help and patience.

Journal of Interamerican Studies and World Affairs, Vol. 20 No. 1, February 1978

be held in March 1970: Lorenzo Miguel, the treasurer of the national organization, and Avelino Fernández, the leader of the *lista azul*, Vandor's group which had its power in the Federal Capital branch, the largest in the union. Both had been loyal followers of Vandor for over a decade, but in the period since his death Miguel had become known as a "blando," more open to negotiate with the government, and Fernández as a "duro," more faithful to the letter of Perón's instructions, which at that time were calling for intransigence toward the military government. Around the two main contenders revolved a number of lesser stars. Chief of them were Luis Guerrero, Secretario Adjunto of the National Organization and chief of the Avellaneda section, and Victorio Calabro, from Vicente López, another important branch in the industrial belt around the capital. Both of them were allies of Miguel and faced strong challenges from Fernández's followers. Beyond them in more distant orbit were a number of minor provincial leaders waiting to see which way the wind was blowing before making a definite decision to back one contender or the other.

The growing tension between the rival groups exploded in late January 1970, with a shoot-out outside the Federal Capital headquarters of the union which left two dead and at least three wounded (from *Periscopio,* Feb. 3, 1970). Somewhat startled by the repercussions of this and following what were reported to be strong hints from Perón to patch up the quarrel, an agreement was reached whereby the two agreed to put forward a joint list of candidates with Miguel having one more place on the list than Fernández. But by mid-February, it was becoming obvious that Miguel, through his control of the central apparatus of the union, would have control of the election machinery and hence the election results. Fernández was now offered only three places on the list, which he rejected. He decided to fight the election with a new union grouping, the *Azul y Blanco,* but it was a losing battle. Even Paladino, Perón's personal delegate and an erstwhile supporter, was reported to be ready to accept the inevitability of Miguel's victory (from *Periscopio*, Mar. 10, 1970). In early March, the Fernandez group was declared unable to present its list of candidates by the Junta Electoral because it had in some way infringed the statutes of the union. No further clarification was given. Fernández appealed to the Labor Secretariat where his case was duly dismissed—a foregone conclusion, since it had been a much commented fact that Secretary of Labor San Sebastián was personally interested in Miguel's victory. In the elections, Miguel's allies duly won in the different regions, with loud cries of fraud from the opposition. The official and only list in the Federal Capital was returned with about 7 percent participation of the membership in the elections (from *Periscopio,* Mar. 17, 1970).

The sequel to the story is of relevance too. Those who had known how to pick the winner were duly rewarded. Calabró was to become, with Miguel's patronage, the vice-governor of Buenos Aires province in the 1973 elections, and later in 1974, the governor. Ricardo Otero, a rather lesser figure in the U.O.M. hierarchy, was given the Ministry of Labor in 1973. José Rucci, a long-standing trouble-shooter for the central leadership, became Secretary-General of the labor central, the C.G.T., in 1970. Miguel himself, although formally holding no government post, was to be a key figure during the government of both Perón and his widow. Luis Guerrero—to look on the darker side—was killed by sub-machine guns in late 1972, while driving to union headquarters in Avellaneda. José Rucci suffered a similar fate nine months later. Avelino Fernández was expelled from the union in 1972 with about two hundred of his followers.

In some ways the story is a microcosm of Peronist trade unionism. It certainly conveys the prevalent tone, the flavor of union power in Argentina—a curious mixture of organized gangsterism, *el "far west sindical"* as one writer called it (from *Confirmado,* Feb. 4, 1970), and the highest political maneuvering, bargaining and, ultimately, participating in power. More specifically for our immediate discussion, it shows the power of an already ensconced leadership in relation to potential opposition within the union. And it is this power that needs to be looked at now.

## *The Basis of the Peronist Union Leaders' Internal Power and Some Limitations*

It starts at a very basic level, for example, through control of the interpretation of unions' statutes. Most Argentine unions have statutes that contain disciplinary clauses so elastic that virtually anyone could be found guilty of breaching them at one time or another. Clauses abound which prohibit the "provocation of disorders," "notorious malconduct," or the even vaguer "*conducta indecorosa.*" Article 9 of the metalworkers statutes states that a cause for expulsion of a delegate will be "the undue use, to the detriment of the organization, of the representation and faculties granted to him." It was this clause that was used to expel Fernández and his followers in 1972. The central council of a union is generally empowered to judge on infringements of these articles, and although there may be an appeal procedure, this too is usually controlled by the central leadership. The same Article 9 of the metalworkers' statutes also empowered the leadership to expel an affiliate by simple resolution of the central committee without any calling of an assembly.

The general structure of trade unions plays its part, too. Although Argentine labor law allowed for either a federative structure or the more centralized, concentrated union structure, among the largest and most important unions in the country, the nonfederative structure predominates. Unions in engineering, railway, textile, and construction industries, as well as the major white-collar unions, all have highly centralized structures that concentrate power in a central leadership elected by the national membership. It should be borne in mind, too, that although there are also many federations representing local unions in one industry, this is in no way synonymous with real freedom from centralized control. Most federations have their offices in Buenos Aires and are inevitably dominated by the Federal Capital union which, of course, usually dominates in terms of number of members.[1] In addition, many federations have in their statutes the power to severely discipline member unions and strictly limit their independent activities. Thus, for example, Article 59 of the statutes of the Federation of Petrol Workers' Unions lays down that the affiliate unions are obliged "to respect the resolutions adopted by the National Secretariat and Central Directive Committee of the Federation." Article 60 states that in no case can the local unions "pursue, at a local level, problems of a general character, nor take up positions which might compromise the opinion of the Federation."

This prevalent type of structure is particularly important for what it meant in financial terms. It meant on a very basic level that in the major industrial and white-collar unions, the membership dues of the metal worker from Córdoba, the textile worker from Rosario, or the railroad worker from Tucumán were paid directly into the respective bank accounts of the central union in Buenos Aires.[2] The sums were large by any standards. It has been calculated that the U.O.M. was receiving 650 million pesos a year in 1966 from this source alone (Primera Plana, 1966: No. 168). But even larger are the sums accruing from the percentage of every negotiated wage increase that the union was entitled to retain. This percentage was usually equivalent to about 2 percent of a month's wage, and the retention applied to both union and nonunion members in the industry in which the union operated. In addition, it has become more frequent for union leaders to ask governments for the right to deduct extraordinary "descuentos por única vez." Usually this would be the whole of the first month's increase from a new contract. In 1971 this meant a sum of 750 million pesos for the construction union, 800 million pesos for the garment workers, and 420 million for the textile workers' union (Correa, 1972: 48). Such huge sums were, of course, an important explanatory factor in themselves of the gangsterism and violence associated with Peronist unions, as well as of the personal corruption that has been an increasingly common trait. Stories abound of the diversion of these funds to the private profit of individual union leaders. But more important than this, given the concentrated centralism of most unions, these sums provided a huge source of patronage and pressure for the union leaderships (Correa, 1972: 43-65). They were the bedrock on which negotiations between different factions of the bureaucracy could take place, or the carrot that could be dangled before the eyes of any waverers. And they were important not merely for what they represented in pure money terms, but also for what they represented in terms of jobs, influence, and prestige. The patronage system was built on a complex pyramid of interlocking interests both within individual unions and within the movement as a whole, with the most powerful unions at the apex of the pyramid. Gazzera (1970: 116), a close collaborator of Vandor's for many years, has given an insight into what this could mean for a man of Vandor's stature:

> They used to buzz around him ceaselessly, waiting for his favour to convert them into leaders. They were at his disposal because they needed inspectors from the Secretary of Labour who would be partial in their decisions, or they wanted the U.O.M. printing press to print propaganda for their union elections. Or they wanted Vandor "to persuade" some rival leader of theirs to give way.

The methods of "persuasion" could vary. It could be physical intimidation of individuals or, for a particularly recalcitrant union section, it could mean the complete drying up of funds from the center, a delay in the building of a union health clinic, or the withdrawing of a branch's quota for the union holiday hotels in Mar del Plata or Córdoba.

Yet even more important than the power accruing from union funds and patronage was the ability to control the election procedure, to head off challenges from the internal union opposition. This could be done most easily by making it difficult to present lists of candidates for the elections. Requirements that had to be fulfilled for a list to be presented were laid down in union statutes. It has been a common trend over the last ten years in Argentine unions for these requirements to get even more difficult. The statutes have been changed. In the Auto Workers Union a new statute of September 1968 stipulated that 2,000 signatures now had to be collected for the list to stand. In the Construction Workers' Union a new statute laid down that a candidate had to have been at least a previous member of his local regional executive committee and that his list needed the signatures of at least 30 percent of the active delegates in the entire union. The Textile Union in 1967 changed its old requirements, which had been the presentation of 700 signatures, to now demand the signed support of 10 percent of members (this in a union of about 100,000 members). The result has been an increasing number of noncontested elections. The U.O.M. has had single list elections now in many of its main sections for the last four consecutive elections. Figures based on a Ministry of Labor study show that between 1964 and 1968 well over half of all union elections were single list elections, the best year being 1964 with 55.6 percent of elections unopposed and the worst being 1967 with 76.1 percent (Torre, 1974a: 7).

The central leadership's control of the Junta Electoral is also a vital weapon, since this controls the actual running of the elections and the vote counting. Opportunities for fraud are numerous and, of course, it is impossible to assess empirically the extent to which it exists. But there are enough proven examples of disappearing ballot boxes, false voting lists, and the like for it to be assumed that fraud is very common (Correa, 1972: 84-90). A leaflet issued by the opposition after the U.O.M. election of 1961 listed some of the different frauds that could be practiced by a union leadership:

> With only 48 hours to go to the elections the places where the voting boxes were to be placed were unknown, together with the days on which they would be placed in the work places; something which the official candidates were, of course, not ignorant of, given that the election committees were not composed of people from the rival lists, but only of those from the official one. . . .The electoral list of the Federal Capital branch, a branch with 65,000 members, showed 95,000 eligible to vote. . . .No list that did not dispose of the money of the official organization, like Vandor's did, could hope to have so many activists available for electioneering with expenses paid. . . .The Junta Electoral prevented the election monitors of the non-official lists from checking the details of the factory at which a voter worked, nor would they

> allow them to inspect in detail the membership cards [*see Palabra Obrera,* Jan. 12, 1961].[3]

Moreover, once elected, the leadership had no worries of having its work overseen by the opposition. There was no provision for minority representation except in very exceptional circumstances, and the list that had the majority took complete control of the union even if it had a minority of votes cast overall.[4]

All these factors helped give a union leadership, once elected, a considerable power in terms of control of its own internal power base. But as the example of the U.O.M. election cited at the beginning also makes clear, this was a fundamentally ambiguous power, for the whole key to the operation as far as Miguel and his supporters who controlled the central apparatus of the union were concerned was the acquiescence of the secretary of labor to their control of the Junta Electoral and the subsequent banning of Fernández's list. Argentine labor law gave a government potential control of most areas of a union's internal affairs. A union's very ability to bargain collectively with employers was dependent on its being granted "*personería,*" legal recognition that it was the sole labor body able to represent a certain industry. Without *personería* the union lost its raison d'être. Labor law laid down stipulations covering everything from internal democracy and the running of elections to the keeping of adequate records of where the unions' funds go. The secretary of labor had power to oversee the entire election procedure, checking the list of those eligible to vote, appointing inspectors to check the polling on election day. He also had great power to check all financial matters—where the funds went, how they were collected. The law also regulated the frequency of general assemblies, who was eligible to be a delegate, how much notice of the holding of such an assembly had to be given.[5]

The precise use made of all this power by the secretary of labor did, of course, vary and was itself the basis of negotiations and bargains between governments and unions. It could be a subtle, negative use, as in the U.O.M. case cited earlier—the turning of a blind eye. Or it could be more direct. Given the wide area that labor regulations covered, very few unions could claim to adhere to the letter of the law in all matters, and the secretary of labor could usually find one such lapse when pressure needed to be brought on a particular union leadership. In August 1962, to give an example, a fairly minor breach of regulations by the textile union, then the leader of the union opposition to the government, was used as a pretext for the government's withdrawing the union's *personería*." This meant that for six months the union was unable to start negotiations on a new wage agreement. It also meant that the union received no funds since the employers, in spite of having by law to stop dues from members' wage packets, did not now have to pass the money on to the union. This hit both the union social services and basic administration, since they were unable to pay professional staff. In addition, grievances which were normally dealt with by the labor ministry's conciliation department now had to go to the labor section of the Justice Department where they could take many months to be dealt with (see A.O.T., Órgana de la Asociación Obrera Textil, July 1963 and Primera Plana, 1962: Nov. 27). Ultimately, of course, the ministry could "intervene" a union completely—that is, hand over the running of the union to a government-appointed administrator—until it could arrange for a compliant leadership. In the same year as the U.O.M. elections of 1970, "acceptable" leaderships were obtained by direct government intervention in the shopworkers', bank clerks', chemical workers', civil servants' and railway workers' union (see *Review of River Plate,* Mar. 31, 1970). The fact that so much of a union's normal functioning was subject to such tight potential supervision by the government of the day—that so much of what Landsberger has called the "locus of decision-making" was outside the orbit of direct union control—inevitably led to an increasing "politicization" of union affairs in Argentina, regardless of the specific ideology of the union leadership (Landsberger, 1967: 290). Union leaders had to be interested in the complexion of national government—its potential hostility or friendliness toward them—whether they liked it or not. However, the *specific* political role assumed by the Peronist union leadership does also need examination.

*The Advantages and Disadvantages of Playing Politics*

We now turn to this second aspect of union power—the political role of Peronist unions as the chief organizing force of the Peronist movement—what Carri has called the "*juego doble*" of representing the working class in its struggle for economic demands and representing the Peronist movement in its conflicts and maneuverings with other political forces in Argentine society (Carri, 1973: 5). It was a role that turned union leaders into national political figures and gave them power beyond that of a normal union leader. Yet this, too, was an ambiguous power.

Their political role was an advantage in several ways. The very fact of being those on the ground in Argentina charged with the day-to-day negotiation and running of the movement, the distribution of Perón's political patronage—and with a base of power in the unions relatively free from his direct control—helped to enhance the union leaders' authority. Moreover, their ability to mobilize the working class in the name of Perón was an important weapon which could be used to pressure a government for concrete economic gains. Out of the sustained mobilization of the Semana de Protesta, 1963, the Plan de Lucha of 1964, and the mobilization during the De Gaulle visit, concessions such as the Minimum Wage Law were obtained from the radical government of Illia (see Carri, 1967: 115-125; Rotundaro, 1972: 291-313). Or again, the whole operation mounted by the unions for the return of Perón at the end of 1964 can be seen partly as a means of maintaining that pressure, with the more concrete political demand for Perón's return of relatively secondary importance.

Also, it should be noted that being the chief political representative of Perón vis-à-vis the Peronista rank and file gave them a certain authority and a basic reservoir of support that failures in the economic field might otherwise have denied them: every visit to Madrid or letter from Perón could be used to offset a strike lost or a bad wage agreement signed. On one level this could be regarded as no more than a specific Argentine twist to a common practice of trade union leaderships—the "selling" of collective agreements and leadership decisions. In this sense their political role helped the Peronist union leadership to maintain what one writer has described as the "illusion of achievement" (Allen, 1971: 53). But it is also important to realize that this was not simply a question of a convenient means of making the unpalatable acceptable, a useful "packaging" device; it also reflected an ideological assumption common to both the union leadership and the rank and file—namely, that the role of the trade union went beyond the basic process of wage bargaining. This assumption evidently had its roots in the working class experience during the 1946-1955 period, particularly in the vital role played by the unions in the government coalition (Little, 1973). In the post-1955 period the Peronist leaders deliberately fostered an image of the extensive functions of trade unions based on their previous experience under Perón, with all the implications this had of wider political activity. It was an image that found a ready response in their membership, particularly since it was confirmed by the "golden age" experienced by the working class prior to 1955 and symbolized thereafter in the exiled figure of Perón. But also political mobilization in the post-1955 period could give an embattled working class hope and a realizable substitute for victories in the economic arena. In the generally unfavorable economic climate in this period, union leaders often emphasized the difficulty of making gains in the purely collective bargaining field and directed their membership's attention to the need to seek a solution to their demands in the wider field of political action. They spoke to them as both union and political leaders, and the latter undoubtedly helped to bolster up the former.

Andrés Framini, the textile workers' leader, amply demonstrated this curious amalgam of the pragmatic "selling" of a bad contract and the shared ideological belief in his speech to the Eighth National Congress of the Textile Union in December 1961. After starting with a lament that "the material conditions have made this unequal struggle of ours unsuccessful," he went on to contrast this with the experience under the government of Perón: "For ten years we had a government which allowed the working class to obtain its just demands and place itself above all other sections of society." He ended with the exhortation to his members to realize that "the union also must serve for other things of great importance, which involve action far beyond the daily struggle that we carry on within trade unionism. . . .We have to convince ourselves once and for all that we will not be able to help ourselves even as textile workers if we don't aim much higher, because if we don't, we won't achieve even our limited immediate ends" (A.O.T., Organo de la Asociación Obrera Textil, December 1961). A writer on the European trade union movement has stated that "the socio-political identity of the European working class is first and foremost incarnate in its trade unions (Anderson, 1967: 274), and I would suggest that very much the same was true in Argentina and that this was a powerful factor in enabling the union leadership to maintain strength in what otherwise were, on many occasions, highly unfavorable situations.

It was a situation Vandor exploited with great skill in an attempt to create a union bureaucracy whose position was relatively independent of Perón and which sought political alliances with other social sectors and with governments, and it was based not entirely on the cynical opportunism of *real-politik*. The whole history of the political alliances and maneuverings of the union bureaucracy since the fall of Perón is often analyzed in this way, particularly by the Personist left (James, 1976). It would, of course, be naïve to deny the opportunism and power politicking of someone like Vandor, but it would also be wrong to ignore the fact that this opportunism had a firm ideological underpinning with at least as respectable a Peronist pedigree as the Peronist left had. The seeking of a modus vivendi with Frondizi, the proscribed Frente Nacional of 1963, the support for Onganía, and the support for the alliance which won the elections of 1973 all testify to the fact that the union bureaucracy did have a long-term political objective and that was to re-create the coalition on which Peronism was founded. This was the way they interpreted their function as the political representatives of the Peronist working class (Portantiero, 1974: 112). And while this objective was being pursued, life went on, and day-to-day compromise with governments had to be found (O'Donnell, 1976).

Ultimately, however, the seemingly independent political power of the trade unions was very limited. First, because in a political framework dominated by the Perón/anti-Perón dichotomy, there was always a limit as to how far the unions could push the bargaining threat of Peronist mobilization, participation in elections, and the like before the army said enough and stepped in, doing away, albeit temporarily, with the process of threat and counterthreat.

The Frondizi episode well illustrated the limits and dangers of the game. For four years Frondizi used the threat that if the unions pressed too hard, struck too often, or participated victoriously in elections, there would be a coup against him which would lead to a far tougher antiunion regime. The threat, naturally enough, worked both ways and much of the modus vivendi with Frondizi and the unions was due to the recognition of this fact. The Peronist participation in the elections of March 1962 showed that Frondizi had been right, for the Guido government made life more difficult for the unions, especially in regard to the total recuperation of the C.G.T. which had been arranged with Frondizi.[6] Likewise, the union-organized Peronist victory in the 1965 elections and the probable victory in 1967 were important factors in the calculations of those who carried out the June 1966 coup. It was, in other words, the "*juego imposible*" that the Peronist unions could not win through the very fact of being Perón's chief political expression (O'Donnell, 1972).

It is also important to realize that their power of bargaining politically came more from being Perón's political representatives before the masses than from the independent bargaining power they derived from the trade union field and was, ultimately at least, dependent on the prestige of Perón's name. As pointed out above, this was a source of power, but it was also a source of a fundamental weakness in their political activity, since their chief bargaining weapon was, in the last resort, not entirely theirs to control. The use of the *camiseta* did give them considerable room for maneuver and some independence in their relations with Perón and with governments, but it was not the same as if they had been bargaining politically from a position of independent trade union strength.

Perón, in fact, did allow the union leadership very considerable freedom of action in their role as his political representatives and very rarely interfered in their specifically trade union dealings. Partly this reluctance to interfere was due simply to realism on his part. From the other side of the Atlantic he could not hope to control the day-to-day details concerning the movement in Argentina.[7] He was, moreover, aware of the power of a union leadership, its capacity to control the union machinery and the potential dangers of weakening what was after all the vertebral column of the movement. As he explained to a correspondent who had questioned his failure to curb Vandor's independence earlier:

> If the U.O.M., as a Peronist organization, names its secretary general, we can do nothing else but accept it, especially when it is the case of Vandor who has always been a Peronist. To do otherwise would imply the expulsion of the union from the Peronist movement which would be inconceivable because the metalworkers are all Peronists. As you can see, the problem seen from the point of view of the leadership of the movement, is not as simple as it seems. [letter to Dr. Don Antonio Caparros, July 1969]

Moreover, Perón was, in general, very cautious about siding with one wing or another of the movement and this was not merely due to pragmatic realism. It also reflected a recognition on his part of the contradictory amalgam of forces which he considered one of the movement's essential strengths. As he explained to one interviewer when asked about the conflict between Vandor and Framini, the leader in the early and mid-1960s of the most militant wing of the movement:

> Within the Justicialist score I wanted to call upon the different melodies. . . .I assigned to Vandor the leadership of the conservative, evolutionary currents, which were the only ones the regime

> would tolerate; Framini on the other hand assumed the leadership of the revolutionary, aggressive wing, that of permanent rupture with the system. . . .Both came to correspond to the different aspects and currents which to make up the national, Christian content of our labouring masses. [interview with Enrique Pavón Pereyra, end of 1968, appeared in *Sieta Días,* No. 312, 1973]

He preferred to act as final arbiter of conflict, and direct intervention on one side or another was only a very last resort.[8]

However, it remained true that while the *camiseta* did give them considerable room for maneuver and a fair measure of independence in their relations with Perón and with governments, it was not the same as if they were bargaining politically from a position of completely independent trade union strength.[9] Vandor's reported remark that "if I abandoned the *camiseta,* I would lose the union in a week" (Walsh, 1969: 171), is a realistic recognition of this fact. When the union leaders' independence became too great and they started to use their power in ways Perón disapproved of, he could remind them of the relative nature of that power. The most spectacular example of this was the Mendoza election of March 1966, when Perón's personal candidate defeated the Vandorista candidate and sank any plans Vandor might have had to create a union-based party with Perón being relegated to a mere figurehead (Gazzera, 1970: 135-138).[10] Indeed, the history of post-1955 Peronism contains many examples of Perón deliberately preventing the organization of any institutionalized union domination of his movement. In 1958, after the union-organized vote for Frondizi, and again in 1962, after the March elections, coordinating councils of the Peronist movement were set up totally dominated by union leaders, on both occasions to be replaced within months by more reliable figures from the far more docile political wing of the movement.

## *Some Elements of an Explanatory Framework*

Up to now, the picture that has emerged has tended to verify the generally accepted image of a highly oligarchic union leadership with great powers vis-à-vis its rank and file controlling large sums of money and sources of patronage. Its power was also reinforced by its peculiar political role as the chief political negotiator of Peronism. As has been mentioned, this power was fundamentally ambiguous, but still the dominant picture is one of a largely unrestrained, oligarchic leadership. Yet an adequate explanatory framework is still largely missing. Some of the elements of a strongly based union bureaucracy have been described, but in themselves they are not a sufficient explanation of the power of such a leadership or its survival over an 18-year period. Certainly any explanatory framework that looked primarily to the existence of fraud, corruption, intrigue, and force for its key elements would be partial at best, since while being important *aspects* of leadership power and control they do not alone and in themselves explain *why* this power existed and endured. They are, I will argue, themselves part of, and explained by, a more profound social process. Another line of approach, with its intellectual parentage in the work of Michels (1958), can also be taken. This regards bureaucracy and oligarchy as an inevitable development and often, indeed, as a welcome sign of maturity. The integrating effect of an advanced society on the individual union leaders is often emphasized in this approach, as is the growing dominance of the institutional needs of the union over the more emotional wishes of the membership. This results in what José Luis de Imaz has described as a situation where "functional criteria prevail over ideological passions" (1970: 220). Imaz saw this process as a reflection of the growing status aspirations of both the union leaders and their constituents in an increasingly socially mobile society.

Similar aspects have been highlighted by much of the literature on the sociology of trade unionism in both Western Europe and the United States (Hyman, 1971a, 1971b; Bell, 1956: 208-221). There is no doubt that up to a point there is much to be said for a view that stops treating Peronist unionism as an exception and starts regarding it as more akin to the rule. After all, in a highly urbanized and industrialized country with mass unionization where the rate of unionization at 25-30 percent is one of the highest in the world (Torre, 1972; Zorilla, 1974) and with a complex system of labor relations (see Alexander, 1962; Rotundaro, 1972), it is at least arguable that bureaucracy, a growing dominance of a union hierarchy over its members, is not only inevitable, but necessary. It is evident, for example, that what have been described as the "socializing influences" at work on union leaders (Allen, 1966: 26) played an important role in Argentina, too. Constant bargaining with employers and discussions with governments inevitably had a "corrupting" effect in terms of fostering a tendency to consider the point of view of authority rather than of their members, as well as of pandering to the status yearnings of working class leaders. This could be reflected in their acquisition of fast cars, *barrio norte* apartments, and invitations to the dinner parties of the oligarchy, but in general it was usually reflected in a more subtle change of temperament and of attitude (for example, Gazzera, 1970: 185-188). Likewise, the growing tendency noted by many sociologists for unions in advanced industrial society to act as regulators of social conflict and for labor leaders to become what Mills described as "managers of discontent" (Mills, 1948: 9) with all that implies for leadership control over its members, can also be observed in the development of Peronist trade unionism. In this sense, the answer to the question of why the power of such a union leadership endured for the 18-year period we are interested in is unexceptionable and in line with sociological orthodoxy; despite an often hostile environment, the Peronist union leaders' power survived because they performed a very functional and important role within the social system.

But such an approach, while containing important elements for analysis of union leadership power in Argentina, must be placed within the context of the specific historical development of the Peronist union leadership. For it is important to note that the power of such a leadership is not the result of a self-contained, inevitable process, but is itself a result of the wider history and development of the Argentine working class. In particular, I want to suggest that its roots lie in the experience of a demobilized and at least partially defeated working class, a demobilization whose origins can be located more precisely in the period of the Frondizi government from 1958 to 1962.

The Argentine working class emerged from the period that is known as the Resistance to the Aramburu government and its anti-Peronist and antiunion policies with great confidence. They had successfully resisted the "de-Peronization" of the unions and the attempt, in 1957, to create a union central dominated by anti-Peronist union figures. Much of the sclerosis that had afflicted Peronist trade unionism under Perón had de facto disappeared with the discrediting of the old union leadership and the government's prohibition of its participation in union affairs (Carri, 1967: 65-87; Senen González, 1971: 14-21). With the unions formally intervened by military and anti-Peronist figures the initiative naturally tended to pass to the rank and file. This, together with the fact that there was no formalized bureaucratic structure to be used, led to a greatly increased closeness between the rank and file and the new leaders that emerged in these years. Leader and follower shared a common vilification. This led in turn to a far greater involvement of the rank and file in the day-to-day struggles and to a consequently far greater degree of democratization in Peronist working class practice. In fact, much of the resistance to the military government was spontaneous, involving rank and file militants acting locally rather than obeying any overall plan. The metal workers' strike of 1956, for example, which lasted for over a month despite intense repression and which was a turning point in the struggle against Aramburu, was run and organized by a national congress of elected rank and file delegates (see *Unidad Obrera* for December 1956). Even when the military government began to give way to this working class pressure in 1957 and accept the failure of this "de-Peronization" program and to allow the Peronists to organize more formally and contest some elections this democratization process persisted. The newly elected Peronist leadership in those unions where free elections had been allowed still, in general, maintained the close relationship with their members. The plenary meetings of the sixty-two organizations—the coordinating body of Peronist unionism set up after the failed C.G.T. Congress of 1957—were, in fact, in 1957 and 1958 largely composed of rank and file factory delegates and were open to any union member, Peronist or not. Meetings often went on all night and the public gallery—*la barra,* as it was called—played a vociferous and influential part in the proceedings.[11]

It was, therefore, an extremely combative and confident working class that emerged from the period of the Aramburu government. The strike statistics for these years show a wave of militancy unparalleled in Argentine labor history with over 5 million days lost in strikes in 1956, over 3.6 million in 1957, and over 6 million in 1958—this in the Federal Capital alone (Ministerio de Trabajo, 1972). The confidence and power of this working class were demonstrated and reinforced by the organized Peronist vote that gave Frondizi the presidency in 1958. It was a confidence and militancy that was to lead them into a series of massive struggles in 1959 to defend their living standards and organization against a concerted attack from the Frondizi government. In January 1959, the plan to hand back to private ownership the Lisandro de la Torree *frigorífico* led to the occupation of the plant and a virtually spontaneous general strike throughout the country that reached near insurrectional proportions in some areas. In May an extended bank strike began, and in late August a six-week strike in the engineering and steel making industries began, to be followed by a month-long textile workers' strike. In the course of the year there were also eight days lost owing to three general strikes. Again, the strike statistics speak for themselves: over 11 million days lost in the Federal Capital, with 2.5 million workers involved.

Every one of these major conflicts was either lost, or at best resulted in a bad compromise for the unions. The Lisandro de la Torre *frigorífico* was handed back to private ownership, the general strike called in solidarity with the workers was abandoned, and the major unions involved were intervened for several months (Perón-Cooke, 1972: 139-152; interview with Sebastián

Borro, En Lucha, Organo del Movimiento Revolucionario, 17 de Octubre, February, 1974). The bank workers were isolated, many were arrested, and finally they were driven back to work. The metal workers finally settled for an emergency increase that did not even apply to the bonus system. The textile workers, after four weeks of strikes, ended up discussing the original management offer based on the acceptance of rationalization. With the resistance of the most powerful sectors of the organized working class broken, in particular the metal workers and textile workers, less powerful sectors fell into line and Frondizi's economic offensive went ahead. The meat workers, for example, who in January had struck for a minimum increase of 1,500 pesos, in December accepted 800 and did not even try to get this formalized in a collective wage agreement (from *Palabra Obrera,* December 17, 1959). Indeed, both they and the rubber workers union publicly stated that they had accepted bad offers because, if after many weeks of struggle the textile and metal workers had done so badly, they could not possibly hope to do better (from *La Razón*, December 15, 1959).

These defeats marked the turning of the tide as far as working class mobilization and confidence were concerned. Some of what this meant can be gleaned from the strike statistics themselves. From over 10 million days lost in 1959, there was a decline to just over 1.5 million in 1960 and 1961, plummeting finally to 268,000 in 1962. But this was only part of its significance. In far less easily quantifiable terms, it represented the beginning of a process of demobilization and demoralization—the falling out from active militancy and participation of thousands of rank and file and middle-ranking activists who had been the core of the post-1955 resistance and renaissance of Peronist trade unionism. Partly, this was the result of simple state and managerial repression. Thousands of Peronist militants were arrested under the state security provisions brought in by the Frondizi government. The blacklist was rampant in industry, too. Sebastián Borro, the leader of the Lisandro de la Torre occupation and a hero of the resistance, was never again to work in the meatpacking industry (interview with Sebastián Borro, January 14,

1974). He was symbolic of many thousands of other militants. The economic crisis of 1962 was the culmination of this process of victimization. By June 1962 over 40,000 metal workers alone were either suspended or permanently dismissed as Argentina entered one of the severest cyclical crises of the entire period. Over 20,000 of these were metal workers in the Federal Capital and Avellaneda (see Servicio de Documentación e Información Laboral of June 1962). The situation in textiles was even more desperate. Employers, at times in collaboration with union leaderships, took advantage of this situation to rid themselves of many well-known activists in their factories.

But this demobilization and falling out from active militancy reflected to a considerable extent a gradual, if reluctant, acceptance by many of the middle-rank activists of the fruitlessness of continued intransigent opposition to both government and management. After the prolonged militancy of the 1956-1959 period, the defeats of 1959, coupled with the repression and economic crisis of the following years, did much to undermine their confidence and morale. Jorge Di Pasquale, a militant leader of the 62 organizations, had given an eloquent description of this process: "The hard struggle was wearing out many people. . . .The repression was ever more intense, the Plan Conintes was introduced and conditions got ever more difficult. There were many comrades who didn't want to continue along the path of confrontation and gradually we were losing them. . . . The majority began to separate themselves from combative positions and dedicate themselves exclusively to their own affairs" (En Lucha of February 1974). In May 1960, at a national congress of the 62 organizations, a meeting dominated by activists loyal to the most intransigent wing of the movement, speeches by the meatworkers' leader, Cardoso, and the petrol workers' leader, Gomis, both prominent proponents of conciliation with the government, in which they attacked extremism and argued the need to ally with other "factors of power," were greeted with an almost total lack of opposition. Only two delegates spoke against, both minor union figures. The silence of the great majority of delegates, who twelve months before at similar meetings had castigated the leaders of the big unions for what they considered the betrayal of the solidarity strike with the Lisandro de la Torre occupation, was testimony to the growing sense of confusion and the erosion of confidence (from *La Razón,* May 25, 1960).[12] The 62 organizations were to be less and less a forum for expressing rank and file views and more and more a part of the apparatus of power at the disposal of the Peronist union leadership.

Yet more fundamentally this process was based on a growing acceptance by the rank and file in general of the logic of a union leadership that increasingly negotiated independently of its members, that made deals with other "factors of power" and that was increasingly erecting and using the apparatus of internal power previously described. When Cardoso, himself one of the new generation of union leaders thrown up during the post-1955 period, announced at a meeting of *frigorífico* workers called to discuss how to fight the growing unemployment that it was "*la hora de la patronal,*" and that one had to be realistic and make unpleasant compromises, he was not speaking merely as the archetypal union boss making excuses for a bad deal, he was also touching a vein of shared experience in the entire working class movement (from *Palabra Obrera,* April 12, 1960). In the absence of counterexamples of victorious, militant methods, the rationale of institutional pragmatism which was increasingly used by union leaders was bound to win at least a passive acceptance by many of their members. An indicator of this admittedly reluctant acceptance can be found in the Federal Capital if one breaks down the voting figures of the ten major factories in the U.O.M. elections of 1961. These show that some 58.6 percent of the workers in these plants abstained from voting in the elections (from *Palabra Obrera,* February 9, 1961). All these factories had been overwhelmingly won by Vandor in the 1958 elections. Perhaps equally instructive is the fact that workers in these factories looked to abstention rather than voting for the rival antileadership candidates. This abstentionist vote, which one can see paralleled in other unions, reflected a growing rank and file fatalism and resignation.

It is in this context that the whole question of fraud, corruption, and internal domination by the union hierarchy needs to be situated. As a case in point, take the question of union elections and the lack of participation by the rank and file in official union elections. Taken in isolation, the available figures can lead to some confusion, since, even allowing for fraud by the entrenched leadership, they tend to show a level of membership involvement not at all inferior to the low levels normal in most advanced industrial countries—thus, Torre's elaboration of government figures for electoral participation rates for the major unions to be in the 20 to 40 percent range (1974a: 5). Even if one takes into account all the quite valid reservations that Torre makes concerning the relevance of elections as a valid mechanism in Argentina for the union membership to effect a change in their leaders (1974a: 17), it still remains to be explained why a not insignificant proportion of the membership of the unions *did* bother to participate in the electoral process. After all, even the figure of 7 percent participation of the metal workers in the 1970 elections in the Federal Capital in what was a one-horse race amid fairly obvious fraud with 7 percent the opposition's estimation of the figures, is on a par with figures for major British trade unions.[13]

Part of the explanation for these figures is probably to be found in the tendency, within certain limits, for any entrenched leadership to enjoy a degree of unquestioned authority. Even in a union as notoriously undemocratic as the East Coast Longshoremen in the United States, the bulk of the membership showed satisfaction with their leadership's running of the union (Bell, 1956: 186-187). Moreover, the figures are a reflection of the basic reservoir of support that had its roots in the process just described: the process of demobilization, resignation and, above all, *acceptance* of the style of union government and its content, regardless of what this meant in terms of formal union democracy. At the same time, however, the significance of the figures also lies in their *comparative* use—for although a figure like 7 percent may be respectable in international terms, in terms of its relation to the figures from the 1957-1960 period, it represents a considerable decline in membership involvement. Figures from this earlier period were sometimes extremely high—sometimes as high as 85 percent, as in the case of the 1957 textile workers' elections (de Imaz, 1970: 236).

A similar point could be made with regard to the other elements of union power, such as corruption and the use of violence. The leadership's domination was, of course, partly based on the persecution of those who might have opposed it, and violence and corruption have increasingly played their part, but its domination was not imposed on an entirely unwilling working class. It was also based on the acquiescence of the rank and file and in this sense the personal fallibilities of individual union leaders were of relative insignificance.

Another essential part of the context for the discussion of the domination of a union leadership over its membership—the nature of internal government and growing membership apathy—is the extent to which there were real possibilities for meaningful rank and file involvement at the most basic level of a union's activities, the factory floor. After all, it would be quite possible to have the most perfect, formal democratic mechanisms and still in practice have membership apathy. Indeed, this is likely to happen if the ordinary member perceives that, despite the formal democracy, his *actual* meaningful control over those areas of most immediate concern to him is virtually nonexistent.[14] The collective bargaining system in Argentina had a built-in bias against the involvement of the member in those areas of most immediate concern to him. Bargaining was done at the national level between the central union negotiators and the central employers' federation for the corresponding industry. The conditions and wages negotiated were applicable by law to all factories in the industry. The very most plant organization could do was to monitor the implementation of the central agreement.

In addition, the agreements signed always contained clauses that specified very strictly what the shop floor representative could and could not do, which laid down a detailed grievance procedure that was legally enforceable; procedures that a delegate must go through to call a meeting; and qualifications he must meet in order to become a delegate. The concept of wage drift built on a strong rank and file organization was obviously, in these conditions, unknown in Argentina. Even the most basic of shop floor functions was denied a delegate in that dues were automatically deducted from the workers' wages by the employer and then deposited by him in the central union account. There was not, therefore, even the minimum level of rank and file involvement, i.e., paying union dues to an elected representative. Meaningful shop floor organization was thus very difficult to sustain, since there was little concretely to center activity and interest around.

This has been made worse by the fact that control of any area of the productive process has been lost by Argentine unions. And again, this can be traced to the process of demobilization. A fair degree of ad hoc control inside the factory had been achieved in important areas during the Peronist government before 1955. This control began to be eroded somewhat in the 1955-1959 period, but it was really following the defeats of 1959 that the flood gates opened. It was precisely in the contracts signed immediately following the 1959 strikes that the major erosion started. The metal workers' contract of the following year contained in Clause 83 a total carte blanche for management in the field of production arrangements, the union renouncing any right to interfere in manning, speed, quality, control, or shift arrangements.

The 1959 contract contained for the first time the detailed limitations on shop steward activity. Within three years there was not a major industry without such contracts.[15] If one is to use Goodrich's metaphor (1974), the "frontiers of control" did not exist inside Argentine factories, for the frontier was firmly fixed at the factory gate and all territory beyond was strictly under management dominance.

The significance of this aspect for the discussion here is that it represented the development of what was virtually a system of institutionalized rank and file passivity which was independent of the specific antidemocratic machinations or actions of the

Peronista union leadership, but which evidently contributed greatly to the consolidation and maintenance of their power. Naturally enough, union bureaucracy could make use of specific statutes and the like to discipline shop floor representatives, but the *comisiones internas* were generally in a state of crisis for most of the 1960s anyway.

The point is of some importance, for once again we are dealing with the convergence of the subjective attitudes and actions of the union leaders and the objective process the unions are caught up in. Of course, there were attractions for the leadership in increased management control of the production process and of shop floor representatives. Life was easier all round. They could get on with the job of bargaining "responsibly," with management unhampered by rank and file representatives whose power was based on their independent strength on the shop floor. But this should not be explained solely in terms of leadership "betrayal." To a considerable extent, it was the result of the demoralization and downturn in militancy already discussed. As one textile militant expressed in [*Palabra Obrera*] of February 19, 1960:

> It's true that the national leadership have repeatedly declared that they are not going to sign any agreement based on rationalization. But in practice, these good intentions are nothing more than wishful thinking, since as the internal organization in the plants has run down since the last national strike, the bosses simply apply the new systems when and where they want.

There is also the point that, as a general rule, trade unions in most developed countries have tended to regard control issues as of secondary importance to straightforward economic gains. As one author of a recent comparative study of Western Europe and the United States put it:

> As trade unions are organized toward the attainment of economic bargaining gains, they tend in practice to lose sight of control issues. . . .Job control is viewed by the trade unions as something that can be exchanged periodically for economic rewards. . . .This preoccupation of trade unions with economism is not a mere case

> of betrayal by the leadership: it is rooted in the workers' very experience and he reinforces the unions' position. Normally, confronted by an employer who will budge on economic but not on control issues, the worker takes what he can easily get.[Mann, 1973: 21]

Evidently, the pressures on both leadership and membership to conform to such a tendency are greater, the more difficult the overall economic situation is. Thus, in Argentina in the period we are analyzing there was an added incentive to regard control issues as a luxury that could be bargained away, if necessary.

Finally, it is also important to look at the whole tradition of leadership in Peronist unionism. It would be fair to say that a tradition of union *caudillismo* was strongly embedded in the Peronista union tradition, what Turner has described as "popular bossdom" in another context (1962: 290). This was, of course, reflected in a dominant style of populist paternalism in union government.

Two points need to be made about this. First, it was a tradition, a style of union leadership, deeply embedded in the historical experience of the Peronist working class. It was not a false or artificially cultivated tradition. Historically, it had its roots in the pre-1955 Peronist movement—in the whole conception of a structured, controlled, hierarchical mobilization of the working class with its implied passivity of the ordinary member. More important for our discussion here, though, is the fact that the post-1955 Peronist union leadership, while often having an initial experience in the union movement prior to 1955, overwhelmingly owed its leadership position to its active participation in the working class mobilizations and experiences of the 1955-1959 period. It was voted into the leadership of the major unions in 1957 and 1958 precisely because of the reputation it had won in the resistance and as a reflection of the rank and file's rejection of the old guard Peronist leadership. Vandor, Cardoso, Rucci, Gomis, even Lorenzo Miguel, had all suffered terms of imprisonment in the post-1955 period. Armando Cabo, one of Vandor's closest collaborators in the U.O.M. and the man castigated by Walsh (1969) as one of the chief organizers of gangsterism in the union, was famed and admired as a participant in one of the biggest bombings to take place during the resistance. Vandor himself was known to have escaped from a clandestine meeting of the 62 organizations in 1959 by running across the roof tops.[16] All this was important in that it gave them a common background, a shared experience with their rank and file which was vital in the process of acceptance of such a style of leadership. "Popular bossdom" did have, to a certain extent, a genuine popular element to it. It was in some ways a genuinely responsive paternalism. The fact that for most of the 1960s virtually any rank and file worker could go to the U.O.M. headquarters and be personally attended to by Vandor should not be simply relegated to the realm of paternalistic anecdote. At the very least it led to an ambiguity on the part of many rank and file militants. Even when condemning the apparatus of domination he had erected, while attacking his bargaining with governments, there was usually at least a tacit, grudging recognition that Vandor had won his spurs as part of the same movement.

The second point is that it was a tradition as deeply embedded in left, militant Peronist unionism as in the more orthodox mainstream sectors. Andrés Framini, leader of the textile workers, long the leading figure of the *linea dura,* as well as one of the founders of the Revolutionary Peronist Movement, could—at the same time as he was issuing dire warnings that "there can be no solution within the capitalist system" in the early 1960s—preside over a union many of whose sections had been intervened to prevent them being won by militants opposed to his leadership. In one of the major textile plants of Buenos Aires, La Bernalesa, which had been Framini's traditional power base, there existed a situation where there were only ten delegates for 1,500 workers on the works committee (from *Palabra Obrera*, June 12, 1961). The rest had their credentials withdrawn for opposition activity. Textile workers' congresses in this period were as manipulated and managed as those of the well-known right-wing unions. *La máquina*, as it was known, was as much an essential part of Framini's style of union government as of any other Peronist union leader. This failure of the Peronist left to even recognize the issue meant that antibureaucracy movements, challenges on the issue of internal democracy, and, indeed, rank and file organizations in general, were deprived of what would otherwise have been their natural mode of expression. It is only since the Cordobazo of 1969, and more especially since 1973, that the question of limiting and controlling the elements of union leadership power has moved to the center of political union discourse and controversy.

## *Conclusion*

The main purpose of this article has been to detail some of the principal aspects of the Peronist union leadership's power, both in terms of its internal control and power over its membership, and in terms of its external power in the wider political context. In the first sections an attempt was made to demonstrate that this power was both considerable in extent and ambiguous in nature. The main burden of the argument of the second half of the article has been that the extent of this power, and the oligarchic and undemocratic nature of much of it, cannot be separated from the historical experience and development of the Argentine working class in the post-1955 period. They were not the result of an inexorable, predetermined bureaucratic process, nor of the personal wishes of individual union leaders. As Torre (1974b: 78) has perceptively noted, "the political space the official bureaucrats end up occupying vis-à-vis the workers is space yielded by the workers themselves." It is this process of "yielding" seen in its historical context that I have tried to sketch in the second half of the article. In particular, it has been argued that the "yielding" was part of the process of demobilization and demoralization which had its roots in the period of Frondizi's presidency from 1958 to 1962, and which must be seen in part at least as a reaction to a period of growing working class confidence and militancy in the preceding period.

Evidently, other aspects of the theme of the roots of power of the Peronist union leadership require attention, such as the precise nature of the ideology that linked union membership and union leaders. Similarly, the whole question of the economic performance of the union leaderships in terms of meeting their members' needs is obviously of great importance. However, the point remains that these variables must be analyzed within the context of the specific historical experience of the Peronist working class if we are to understand the complexity of the development of Peronism and its unions over the last twenty years.

## NOTES

1. The advantages of the federative structure in terms of the freedom it afforded from central union control have been emphasised by some authors. For instance, Zorilla (1974: 83) states, "This type of organization confers a great autonomy . . . especially on local units. . . .They can resist the decisions taken at a higher level." This is to take the theory of Argentine labor law for the reality. Even within a federation which granted such great powers of autonomy to its constituent unions as the Light and Power Workers' Federation where, indeed, local unions had full negotiating rights and had their own independent source of income, pressure could still be brought by the federation leadership in Buenos Aires. Thus, many of the local unions which had supported the militant wing of the Peronist unions under Raimundo Ongaro in 1968 were forced to withdraw when the federation withheld financial contributions to the local social services of these unions. Only the Córdoba union under Agustín Tosco had the strength to withstand this pressure.

2. There has been some confusion about union funds and dues. One author has maintained that union dues were compulsory for all workers in a particular industry whether they were union members or not (Correa, 1972: 47). This is not the case. For the perioa dealt with in this article, the basic union dues—the *"cuota sindical"*—were deducted only from union members. Indeed, it was precisely this that was altered by Law 20.615 of 1973 which replaced the Law of Professional Associations, 14.455 of 1958. Article 7 of the new law made both members and nonmembers liable to have the monthly union dues deducted from their wage packets. What were applicable to both members and nonmembers in the pre-1973 period were the extraordinary contributions written into the collective agreements signed every two years. This right had been granted the unions by Law 14.250 of 1953, which continued in force in the period with which we are dealing.

3. Torre gives similar details for the Textile Workers' Union (1974a: 38). It is worth noting too that the date of the election was early January, in the middle of the annual summer holiday period.

4. This itself was also a factor in the violence surrounding elections, since the list of candidates elected not only took over the posts contested in the election, but once

installed, with no opposition vigilance to worry about, it almost always proceeded to install its own supporters throughout the administrative apparatus of the union. A professional administrative apparatus independent of different union factions was thus difficult to maintain. The author well remembers working at the Petrol Workers' Union in 1973 at Buenos Aires. The secretary general of the union, Diego Ibañez, came from the Mar del Plata branch, and I was constantly amazed at the number of employees and minor functionaries working in central union headquarters who were from the same branch right down to the three doormen. This was obviously an example of the patronage powers just described, but it also added another dimension to the election process, since in addition to posts contested in the election, a whole network of employment opportunities was also at stake.

5. It should be noted that the powers at the disposal of secretaries of labor did in fact vary in this period, and the list presented here is a compilation of powers accruing from various acts passed in the 1955-1973 period. By far the most far-reaching measure was Decree 969 of 1966 regulating the Law of Professional Associations of 1958. Clause 6 contained very stringent guarantees for internal union democracy. There were also clauses aimed at increasing the local autonomy of unions. The military coup of 1966 meant that the decree was never implemented as originally intended, though it was kept as a threat to the union leaders. Decree 2477 of 1970 modified Decree 969 in some aspects, though keeping most of the guarantees concerning union democracy. The new law of 1973 specifically set out to free the union leadership from the overseeing power granted the secretary of labor by previous legislation.

6. Frondizi took a calculated risk with the March 1962 elections, estimating that the Peronists would either vote "en blanco" as they had consistently done, or that it would be possible to keep their gains from the elections within "acceptable" limits—acceptable to the military, that is. The calculations were badly astray. The Peronist gains—particularly Framini's successful candidacy for the governorship of Buenos Aires—were totally unacceptable to the military, who removed Frondizi a week later and installed the puppet regime of Guido.

7. As Perón put it, "I like to act a little like the Eternal Father, with the blessing 'urbi et orbi,' but letting Providence do its work, without appearing too much. I think that the force of the Eternal Father lies in the fact that he never appears. If we saw God every day, we would end up losing our respect for him and, moreover, we wouldn't be short of some fool who wanted to replace him" (Interview with Enrique Pavón Pereyra, end of 1968, appeared in *Siete Días,* no. 312, 1973).

8. It should be noted that this reluctance to overtly take sides in the Vandor-Framini rivalry was repeated in the 1968-1969 conflict between Vandor and Raimundo Ongaro, the leader of the CGT de los Argentinos, a combative rival organization to Vandor's more moderate CGT Azopardo. Despite initial encouraging remarks, Perón sent orders for reunification in late 1968. This was a crucial factor in the demise of the CGT de los Argentinos (Ongaro, 1970).

9. It is also worth pointing out that political activity had other dangers for union leaders. Defeat politically could have serious repercussions in terms of internal union government. Thus Torre notes (1974a: 66) that Framini's defeat by Vandor for the leadership of the trade union block of the movement in 1963-1964 crucially weakened his credibility among the leading group of the Textile Union and was a vital factor in the coup that removed him from the leadership of the union in 1968. A very similar process also led to the downfall of another leader of the most militant wing of the movement, Roberto García of the Rubber Workers' Union, in 1967.

10. In fact, the Mendoza election was the culmination of a dispute that had been going on since the middle of 1965. Perón had sent over his wife to enforce orders that would have effectively undercut the power of the union leadership around Vandor, and to rally the anti-Vandoristas in the movement. This led to the formation of a separate anti-Vandor Peronist union organization, the 62 Organisations de Pie Junto a Perón. It was one of the very few examples of Perón openly condemning a Peronist union figure. The weight of this condemnation can be gauged by Vandor's reaction to a *Primera Plana* headline asking "*Vandor o Perón*?" The next day he took out full-page notices in the press to respond: "Vandor answers: Perón."

11. Much of my analysis here and in the following pages relies heavily upon a series of interviews recorded in late 1973 and early 1974 with Alberto Belloni, Sebastián Borro, and Jorge di Pasquale, all active participants in the process being analyzed. It should be added, with reference to the specific argument being made at this point, that the increased democratic practice and rank and file participation in the unions was the chief feature emphasized by all the participants in the events of this period with whom I talked.

12. This is also from an interview with Alberto Belloni, January 23, 1974. Belloni was one of the two delegates who spoke against Cardoso.

13. The major recent government study on trade unions in Britain found for example, that the membership participation rate in the national elections of the British equivalent of the metal workers' union was 7 percent overall—with winning candidates usually getting no more than 3 percent of the votes of the electorate (Royal Commission, 1968: 171).

14. Most Argentine union statutes do, for example, enshrine the principle of the sovereignty of the supreme representative body within a union, the general assembly of delegates. In practice this is meaningless since at best, and ignoring leadership control of delegate selection, the general assembly usually meets no more often than biennially. Evidently, a body that meets once every two years can have no meaningful say in the daily decisions of the union.

15. Torre has touched on this point (1974b: 80). He sees the contracts signed in the post-1955 period as eroding the "workers' control institutions" of the Perón era. My own understanding would be that he is confusing this "workers' control" with what was in reality an ad hoc job control to be encountered in many situations where there is a high level of trade union organization and working class confidence. He also states that the contracts signed in 1956-1957 introduced the rationalization procedures and productivity measures which undermined this "workers" control. This is incorrect. There were, in fact, relatively few actual contracts signed in those years. Many disputes were dealt with by a government tribunal. This tribunal did have powers specifically to deal with productivity issues, but in practice, the government's attitude was ambiguous, and it frequently gave way in the face of strong union opposition on these issues. This was a government recognition of the militancy of the workers, particularly regarding these aspects of factory floor power. It was directly due to the downturn in militancy and confidence that Frondizi, from 1959 onward, was able to accomplish what Aramburu had not dared push through in a systematic way.

16. Vandor was arrested more than once in this period. *La Razón*, January 3, 1956, mentions his name as one of those arrested for intimidation of non-Peronists in the factories and for being implicated in sabotage. He spent several months in prison at this time. He was arrested again during the Lisandro de la Torre occupation in January 1959.

It is interesting to recall Cooke's description of him at this time to Perón. He was, said Cooke, "leading the most militant sector" of the Peronist unions during the general strike that followed the occupations, and, he added, "in addition to his personal merits, he can count on the complete backing of his union" (Perón-Cooke, 1972: 144).

## REFERENCES

ALEXANDER, R. J. (1962) "Industrial relations in Argentina, Brazil and Chile." Publ. Studies in Labor Management History. New York: Wertheim Committee.

ALLEN, V. L. (1971) The Sociology of Industrial Relations. London: Longman.

——— (1966) Militant Trade Unionism. London: Merlin Press.

ANDERSON, P. (1967) "Limits and possibilities of trade union action," in R. Blackburn and A. Cockburn (eds.). The Incompatibles. London: Penguin.

BELL, D. (1956) The End of Ideology. Glencoe, IL: Free Press.

CARRI, R. (1973) "Sindicalismo de participación, sindicalismo de liberación." Unpublished appendix to Carri (1967).

——— (1967) Sindicatos y Poder en la Argentina. Buenos Aires: Editorial Sudestada.

CORREA, J. (1972) Los Jerarcas Sindicales. Buenos Aires: Editorial Polémica.

DE IMAZ, J. L. (1970) Los Que Mandan. Albany: State Univ. Press of New York.

GAZZERA, M. (1970) "Nosotros los diregentes," in M. Gazzera and N. Ceresole (eds.) Peronismo: Autocritica y Perspectivas. Buenos Aires: Editorial Descartes.

GOODRICH, C. L. (1974) The Frontier of Control. London: Pluto Press.

HYMAN, R. (1971a) Marxism and the Sociology of Trade Unionism. London: Pluto Press.

——— (1971b) The Workers' Union. Oxford, England: Oxford Univ. Press.

JAMES, D. (1976) "The Peronist left, 1955-1975." J. of Latin American Studies 8 (November): 273-296.

LANDSBERGER, H. A. (1967) "The Labour Elite," pp. 256-301 in S. M. Lipset and A. Solari (eds.) Elites in Latin America. New York: Oxford Univ. Press.

LITTLE, W. (1973) "Party and state in Peronist Argentina, 1945-1955." Hispanic Amer. Historical Rev. 53 (November): 644-663.

MANN, M. (1973) Consciousness and Action among the Western Working Class. London: Macmillan.

MICHELS, R. (1958) Political Parties. Glencoe, IL: Free Press.

MILLS, C. W. (1948) The New Men of Power. New York: Harcourt Brace.

Ministerio del Trabajo (1972) Conflictos de Trabajo. Buenos Aires: División de Estadísticas Sociales, Dirección Nacional de Recursos Humanos.

O'DONNELL, G. A. (1976) Estado y Alianzas en la Argentina, 1956-1976. Buenos Aires: Documento de Trabajo No. 5, Centro de Estudios de Estado y Sociedad.

——— (1972) "Un juego imposible: Competición y coaliciones entre partidos políticos en Argentina, 1955-1966." Buenos Aires: Documento de Trabajo, Centro de Investigaciones en Administración Pública, Instituto Torcuato di Tella.

ONGARO, R. (1970) "Sólo el pueblo salvara al pueblo." Buenos Aires: Editorial de la Bases.

PERON-COOKE (1972) Perón-Cooke Correspondencia, Vol. II. Buenos Aires: Granica Editor.

PORTANTIERO, J. C. (1974) "Dominant classes and political crises." Latin Amer. Perspectives 1, 3: 93-120.

ROTUNDARO, R. (1972) Realidad y Cambio en el Sindicalismo. Buenos Aires: Pleamar.

Royal Commission (1968) Royal Commission on Trade Unions and Employers' Associations, 1965-1968. London: H.M.S.O.

SENEN GONZALEZ, S. (1971) El Sindicalismo después de Perón. Buenos Aires: Editorial Galerna.

TORRE, J. C. (1974a) El Proceso Político Interno de los Sindicatos en Argentina. Buenos Aires: Documento de Trabajo No. 89, Centro de Investigaciones Sociales, Instituto Torcuato di Tella.

——— (1974b) "The meaning of current workers' struggles." Latin Amer. Perspectives 1, 3: 74-81.

———(1972) La Tasa de Sindicalización en Argentina. Buenos Aires: Documento de Trabajo No. 77, Centro de Investigaciones Sociales, Instituto Torcuato di Tella.

TURNER, H. A. (1962) Trade Union Growth, Structure and Policy. London: George Allen & Unwin.

WALSH, R. (1969) Quién mato a Rosendo? Buenos Aires: Tiempo Contemporaneo.

ZORILLA, R. H. (1974) Estructura y Dinámica del Sindicalismo Argentino. Buenos Aires: La Pleyade.

*Daniel James is Research Officer at the Centre for Latin American Studies, University of Cambridge, England. He has contributed to the* Journal of Latin American Studies *and at present is writing a book on the Peronist trade union movement since 1955.*

**BENOIT OTIS BROOKENS**
*U.S. Department of State*
*Washington, D.C.*

# *DIPLOMATIC PROTECTION OF FOREIGN ECONOMIC INTERESTS*

## *The Changing Structure of International Law in the New International Economic Order*

December 12, 1974, the Twenty-ninth General Assembly of the United Nations (1974) passed the long-awaited Charter of Economic Rights and Duties of States by a vote of 120-6-10. This chapter, conceived by Mexican President Echeverría (UNCTAD, 1972) was drafted upon the supposition that definitive legal guidelines on international economic rights would suppress considerably world political-economic tension and protect the rights of all states, especially developing ones (Vanzant, 1974). Although a substantial proportion of the charter was adopted with relatively little controversy during the two years of negotiations, conflicts over key sections were insurmountable and the negotiating committee failed to attain unanimity on its final text. The inability of the working group to reach a consensus did not come as a complete surprise, since during the past decade important concepts embodied in the document had provoked considerable controversy (Haight, 1975). The primary agenda item over which there was considerable debate was the standard for the treatment of the property of foreign investors when it was expropriated by a host government. On that issue, prospects for a consensus were marginal. The result was a final document with sections vigorously opposed by several of the major industrialized nations, including the United States. This opposition by the major economic powers was viewed by the prestigious Section on International Law

Journal of Interamerican Studies and World Affairs, Vol. 20 No. 1, February 1978

of the American Bar Association (1974) as tempering future acceptability of the concept and rendering the charter ineffective as a legally binding document.

This essay seeks to analyze the significance of the new international standard as formulated in Chapter II, Article 2 (c) of the Charter of Economic Rights and Duties of States and to assess its legal effect on future rule changes regarding diplomatic protection of foreign investment interests.

## *Historical Evolution of Current Controversy*

The current conflict over standards for treatment of foreign investment has a history of a continuing century-long debate between the United States and its Latin American neighbors. For more than a century, United States diplomatic efforts to protect investment interests of its citizens in Latin America have been cloaked in controversy. Initially, the United States government intervened in expropriation disputes on behalf of U.S. foreign investors under generally accepted customary international law. During the first hundred years of the nation's application of international law, its position on expropriation of United States-owned investment was congruent to that of customary international law. However, during the last decade U.S. protection policy has become modified by domestic political and legal sanctions which dominate the fundamental international legal premises (Chadwick, 1971). Simultaneously, the Calvo Doctrine (Shea, 1955: 9-32; 107-120)—the major legal protagonist to the U.S. policy which seeks to limit the protective penumbra of foreign governmental intervention in Latin America on behalf of investors—has been gradually refined over the century and has subsequently received wider legal acceptance and recognition within the international legal community.[1]

### *FOUNDATION AND EXPANSION OF THE CALVO DOCTRINE*

Ironically, the Calvo Doctrine, which is directed primarily against the United States government, was derived from the

Drago Doctrine (1907), an argument against armed European governmental intervention in Latin America to enforce debt obligations of European citizens. The Calvo Doctrine, coupled with late-19th-century Latin America enforcement capacities, would have been rendered ineffective had there not been prospects for enforcement through operation of the Monroe Doctrine and the Root Corollary to the Monroe Doctrine (Hague Peace Conference, 1907). In effect, Drago theoretical parameters, as they developed into the more exclusive Calvo Doctrine, were coupled with the threat of United States Monroe Doctrine enforcement against European powers and eventually were aberrationally applied as the parrying instrument against U. S. governmental policy itself.

Despite the monumental developments taking place within the parameters of these competing systems of legal philosophies and values, the most significant development lies in the realm of mundial *realpolitik* induced by the post-World War II transformation of a substantial number of former British and French colonial territories into sovereign nations of the *Tiers Monde*. These states have influenced the structure of international diplomacy and diplomacy's mainstay, international law, by their dehomogenation of statal experiences. Their legal perspectives were analytical in a predominantly customary legal environment adhered to by the major powers of the world. In effect, they challenged the binding applicability of an international law that they had no role in creating.

A distinguished taskmaster of the problems of international law and diplomatic protection, Frederick S. Dunn (1932: 69), made this observation concerning the nature and objective of international law:

> If one looks into the matter carefully enough, one finds that international law, like every general concept, may have various different natures on different occasions, depending upon the frame of reference or realm of discourse in which the term is used, i.e., upon the particular purpose or set of problems one happens to be interested in at the moment. *In the present connection, we are concerned with international law, not from the standpoint of analytical jurisprudence, but as a going social*

> *instrument devised to serve a particular set of human needs. From this standpoint, it may be regarded as a process for adjusting the conflicting interests of the members of the international community* [emphasis supplied].

Another disciple of this controversy, Donald Shea (1955: 7), supports Dunn's conclusion and offers the following observation in his comprehensive study of the problem:

> The Calvo clause controversy is not solely one of law, however, but one of politics. It has played an important role in the political relations of the Americas. [An] understanding of the problem [for which the rules of law seek solutions] necessitates an examination of the political considerations involved. Political conditions have had an important bearing on the inception and development of this concept.

### *CONCERNS BEYOND THE PROTECTION OF PROPERTY: ACCESS TO STRATEGIC RESOURCES*

Since the October 1973 war in the Middle East, the problem of diplomatic protection of private investment interests has been complicated by the added dimension of governmental interest in guaranteeing its uninterrupted access to strategic economic resources (Shihata, 1975: 581; Kennedy and Gantz, 1974). These concerns of governmental access to limited economic resources have been intertwined into the expropriations debate, although without any noticeable intensity.

One American military strategist (Leider, 1973: 3) bluntly addresses the problem by pointing out the following fundamental problem:

> Much as we may dislike the idea, America has joined the ranks of have-not nations. The needs and expectations of the domestic sector—jobs and incomes—are growing dependent on expanding oversea investments, the relocation of power-hungry industries to nations where energy is cheap and the increasing import of bedrock commodities. In the course of this change, our way of life, once immune to foreign interference, is becoming as vulnerable to external disruption as survival itself. America, like so many of its business enterprises, has become multinational.

> *It cannot be defined by its borders.* The nation exists wherever capital, industrial process, technical skills, *raw materials and markets contribute to its well-being* [emphasis supplied].

The essence of Leider's concern is brought into focus by his poignant question: "How many wings must be kept operational to prevent a foreign supplier from unilaterally tearing up a contract for one with harsher terms?" The dynamics of these concerns have been reflected in the 1974 U. S. governmental campaign to lower petroleum prices and the sharp responses of defiance the campaign received from the Iranian and Venezuelan governments.

This problem, although having a parallelism intertwined with the subject of this essay, requires a substantial analytical differentation and will be precluded from any examination here. It, however, is a significant vector which should have bearing on future developments in U. S. foreign economic policy. In this regard, the challenge the developing countries have put to the industrialized nations has been rather persistent on a fundamental issue: the basic redistribution of wealth from the richer nations to the poorer ones (Walters, 1974: 527). This persistence has resulted in the expansion of the scope of the debate on this fundamental issue. It has now spilled over into specialized fora which generally have been free from blatant political issues and have dealt with more pressing concerns regarding human dignity, women's rights, food policy, and commodity trade (Gordon, 1975). The presumption behind the efforts of developing nations is that the less fortunate countries cannot develop unless dramatic changes occur in the structure and direction of the international economic order (U.S. Department of State, 1975).

## *Objectives of the Institution of Diplomatic Protection*

Although contemporary diplomatic intervention for the protection of foreign economic interests of nationals in foreign countries is derived from a theory of contractual liability, its historical roots are founded upon a tort liability theory. Under a tort liability theory, enforcement of a state's liability was limited to judicial comity and deference to other courts of record (Dunn, 1932: 54-55; Borchard, 1927: 836-838). The inflection point to transform liability from a tort to a contractual theory was derived by the extraction of elements placing liability for a statal denial of procedural and substantive justice (Lissitizyn, 1936: 632-635) and transplanting these elements into the concept of imposition. Only by invoking imposition could the presumption in favor of the validity of the act of a sovereign be overcome. Once an antagonistic legal theory could be established upon which a state could refuse to recognize the positive laws of another state, it was with little difficulty that an affirmative theory of diplomatic intervention could be invoked (Borchard, 1913).

Emmeric de Vattel (1758: 136), in one of the earliest formulations of the theory justifying one government's interventions into the domestic affairs of another, analyzed such acts with the following syllogism:

> Injury to an alien was actually an injury to a resource of another state [ergo the state itself]. If this major premise was accepted, the minor premise encounters slight scrutiny—injury to the state gives the state under color of its own right claimant status sanctioned under international law and thusly an appropriate subject for diplomatic discourse. We ought not then to say in general, that we have received any injury from a nation, because we have received it from one of its [citizen] members. But, if a nation, or its leaders, approves and sanctions the act committed by a citizen, it makes the act its own: the offense ought then to be attributed to the nation, as the author of the true injury, of which the citizen is, perhaps, only the instrument.

The element upon which Vattel hinges the enforcement of an international obligation is an international quasi-social contract theory:

> The law of nations is certainly a natural law, since the law of nations is not less obligatory with respect to states, or to men united in political society than to individuals. [p. ii].

Despite the assumed obligatory nature of international law which has resulted in statal acquiescence for centuries, the need exists and the search continues for a theoretical explanation of the basis for the enforcement of international law (Bros, 1972).

## *United States Diplomatic Protection Policy*

The traditional United States view of diplomatic protection has been congruent with that of customary international law (Brower and Tepe, 1975). This customary standard mandates a nondiscriminatory taking of property of foreign nationals; the exclusive utilization of such property taken for a public purpose; and the payment of prompt adequate, and effective compensation to the dispossessed. Developments in the U. S. government's position in recent years has provided *de novo* a policy more expansive than its traditionally stated views. Below is an examination of the elements of international law, municipal legislation, and administrative policy which constitutes the analytical jurisprudential posture of the U. S. government on expropriation.

### *UNITED STATES BASIS FOR U.S. GOVERNMENT INTERVENTION*

Outside of such categorizations as "routine" commercial disputes between private parties into which the U. S. government does not generally involve itself, rationale for intervention is predicated upon several distinct bases. This foundation upon which the United States exercises a valid interest is international law and those requirements stemming from its own municipal legislation.

By general categories these independent bases are segmented into the following:

—diplomatic protection under international law;

—espousal of rights of claimants;

—sanctions required by legislation;

—executive policy.

*Diplomatic Protection Under International Law*

A valid state-to-state concern for diplomatic discourse is predicated upon any act that is a denial of justice, or that is arbitrary or discriminatory according to the highest standard afforded by the contract laws of the forum, customary international law, or applicable treaty obligations. These acts, of course, must have resulted in some legal or economic detriment to the alien (Shon and Baxter, 1971).

*Contractual Problems*

Regarding breach or revision of contractual obligations, the U.S. government position is succinctly stated (Whiteman, 1967, 8: 906):

> It is not the practice of the Department [of State], save in exceptional circumstances, to intervene on behalf of American nationals in connection with claims or to pass on the merits of the controversy . . . and it considers that the matter is one which will be settled in accordance with the applicable principles between the contracting parties or by legal proceedings in the appropriate tribunals.

The Department of State has further stated regarding claims arising out of contractual relations and concessions agreements as a compendium of individual contracts (American Journal of International Law, 1961):

> [Contracts] between a national of this country and a foreign government do not, generally speaking, provide a proper subject for diplomatic intervention . . . in the absence of a clear showing that the American national has exhausted . . . local remedies as may be open . . . and has sustained a denial of justice as that term is understood in international law. [Whiteman, 1967, 8: 907]

Some writers, on the other hand, have recently suggested a view to the contrary. One author, Ingrid Delupis, in her work *International Law and Independence,* suggests that the striking similarity between some investment contracts of developing states and the coverage of some of their treaties will induce some future equitable quasi-treaty status for these agreements. Probably subscribing to this view is Dr. Mallison of the George Washington University National Law Center. His thesis breaks down the traditional dichotomy between public international law and private international law. His university lecture series continuously points out that the preponderance of public international law is concerning private rights. Examples within his analytical framework would include investment guarantee treaties, agreements on commercial rights of establishment and doing business in foreign jurisdictions, protocols concerning protection of social security and employment, and agreements regarding disability benefits of aliens taking permanent residence in jurisdictions of their prior or ancestral nationality. The author concedes some abridgement between public and private international law. However, the author must assert that prior to direct governmental intervention into a specific problem, the burden is upon the shoulders of the government to establish the basis for its concern. Absent some connective nexus or element of privity, the governmental authorities would lack standing and not have any "real" interest in the affair. This, to a considerable degree, would be analogous to the position of a private disinterested third party in a litigation action.

*Problems of Taxation*

In the matter of taxation or any other change of fiscal rates, the U.S. government has not found any explicit legal basis upon which to protect discriminatory acts (Whiteman, 1967, 8: 511), nor does any principle of international law forbid the territorial sovereign from imposing, in some instances, a heavier burden upon the interest of such individuals (notably aliens) than is placed on its own nationals (Hyde, 1945: 664). Especially in the absence of a treaty, foreigners may be more heavily taxed than nationals without any international consequences (Borchard, 1927: 95-96). The Department of State has, on occasion, instructed its representatives at posts abroad to protest on the ground of unfair discrimination all exactions on American property or citizens not equally applied to all inhabitants, whether natives or foreigners.

*Exercise of Rights by Subrogation*

U.S. subrogation rights can stem from either of two independent bases: subrogation from contractual privity (Mills, 1973) or subrogation under treaty relating to investment guarantees (U.S.-Venezuela Governmental Exchange, 1974).

Subrogation, in essence, is an equity concept providing relief for one under an obligation (Black's Law Dictionary, 1968) to compensate another for injury suffered at the hands of third parties. It puts one into the shoes of the wronged party, who then rises to the claimant's position. The subrogatee's attained position is congruent and identical with that of the subrogators, the exception being contracts with International Center for the Settlement of Investment Disputes (ICSID, 1975) clauses which deny ICSID jurisdiction for disputes that are between states.

*The Requirement of Privity*

The fundamental element of subrogation that must be noted is the obligatory nature of the reimbursement. Absent this element, the action ceases to be subrogation but rather one of assignment. The crucial nexus becomes the contractual thread of privity which provides the connective factor to distinguish subrogation from actions of assignment. Without an insurance arrangement or—in Overseas Private Investment Corporation (OPIC) language—"suitable legal arrangements" to yield some conceptualization of privity of contract, states could accept assignment of claims of its nationals to escalate tensions in the already tense international political arena. Without such a legal requirement a claim inadvertently becomes the subject of diplomatic discourse without the addition of factors as capriciousness or arbitrariness to bring the matter into the international forum. This move would also be without an infringement upon the rights of the exercising state and debasing the traditional conceptualization of international law as affecting the rights and obligations of the nation-states.[2]

*Treaty*

The device utilized by the U. S. government to provide the privity link is the Treaty of Investment Protection which allows

OPIC to attain the rights of the insured against the host government. The abrogation of a treaty which contains this provision without satisfactory compensation constitutes a proper subject of diplomatic disclosure within the bounds of traditional international law. In the absence of a formal treaty, however, subrogated OPIC claims would be mere commercial disputes lacking any international legal issues upon breach. It must be noted, however, that treaty termination provisions are so lax that even a contention of breach of treaty obligation could be easily circumvented.

*Espousal*

The espousal of claims by the U. S. government (Whiteman, 1967, 8: 1216) is rare and seldom undertaken: "Such a function is political in nature, within the province of the Executive and an effective bar to any actions of mandamus to compel the exercise of 'administrative discretion' (Adminstrative Procedures Act, 1970)."

The state, therefore, is conscientious and meticulous to ensure that the claims it does espouse are meritorious and claimworthy. In an espousal, the U. S. government not only presents an infringement under the rights of contract or other appropriate cause to action, but an espousal also merges the rights of governments under international law into an inseparable compound with the parties' claim. The application of this form of diplomatic protection, especially for smaller investors, is more likely to embroil the U.S. government into an investment dispute and closely tie U.S. diplomatic relations with a foreign government upon the plight of a single investor.[3]

*Legislative Requirements*

The enactment of the first Hickenlooper Amendment (U. S. Congress, 1961) was the major congressional initiative to make the United States expropriation policy legislative rather than one exclusively within the executive's prerogative. The remedy to be applied would be a direct economic sanction—foreign aid. Since this act, a series of measures for diplomatic protection of U. S. foreign investments have flourished and all have been directed at protecting the equity interest of U. S. shareholders in their controlled foreign affiliates. This in effect became the real interest of U. S. governmental protection: exported U. S. capital. The legislative sanctions escalated over the years from denying the benefit of U. S. bilateral economic resources (U. S. Congress, 1967) to denying sugar sales (U.S. Congress, 1948) in the United States and the vetoing of loans in the international financial institutions—the World Bank and Inter-American Development Bank—where the United States could exercise considerable power based on the weighing of its capital contribution. As students of international politics—Machiavelli to Morgenthau—have pointed out, frustration begets conflict. A country that has a negligible sugar quota, an economically insignificant U. S. foreign aid contribution, or substantial petroleum or commodities revenues, will be most likely to frustrate the application of U. S. economic sanctions. Absent the availability of U.S. economic leverage and the apparent self-confidence and self-esteem touching national pride involved in seeking redress for injury, it seems that U. S. protective measures will move from its legal and international forum to one more attuned to domestic politics.

Such a movement, however, would not taint legislative mandates of U.S. municipal laws that protect U.S. equity interests as political sanctions, although they are nonetheless internationally recognized only as secondary measures for the protection of the rights and property of nationals. As the International Court of Justice (1970) held in Barcelona Traction, the primary right of diplomatic protection to redress injury to economic interest of aliens lies with the government of which the company is a national. The "rights" of the country in which the shareholders are nationals are only residual rights and are limited to the protection of the shareholders' interests against the corporation and its management rather than to address the injury inflicted by the government upon the enterprise. The World Court in its famous opinion, however, does not touch the issue as to whether the right exists for the government of the shareholders to pierce the corporate veil and exercise direct diplomatic protection vis-à-vis the host government, nor does it address the issue as to when protective rights can be exercised by the government of the shareholders upon failure of the government of the company's incorporation/*siege sociale* to exercise any diplomatic protection activity.

### *Administrative Policy*

The United States policy on expropriation (U.S. President's Policy Statement, 1972) emerged in January 1972 on the heels of the Chilean nationalization program (U.S. Department of State, 1974a). This expropriation was the last in a series of irritants which could not be resolved through the facilitative good offices of the U.S. government. Although the talks between the companies and Peru were suspended, there was an indefinite deferral of the application of Hickenlooper sanctions against Peru. This waiver was followed by the Bolivian expropriation of Gulf Oil Company holdings and the controversial offsetting of past-due company debts against requirements of compensation (Einhorn, 1973). These two controversies were followed by the Chilean expropriation and that government's denial of compensation due to the companies because of outstanding company debts or, in the most controversial cases, the government claimed offsetting "excess profits" taxes against the companies. Behind these developments, the administration position hardened when Congress raised issues regarding these matters during hearings concerning the funding of the multilateral lending institutions.

### *Conflicting Views Within the U.S. Government*

In June 1971 the press reported rumors of a "tough" policy taken by the new secretary of the treasury with regard to lending by the international financial institutions to countries which failed to compensate expropriated companies (The Washington Post, 1971). On June 23, 1971, *National Journal* (1972) reported that the National Security Council issued a Study Memorandum —NSSM 131—calling for an "urgent study on U.S. policy toward expropriation without compensation." As reported by Einhorn (1973), then a student of interagency governmental politics, "the June NSSM touched off an interagency battle that was both substantive and organizational with the organizational lines drawn distinctly on the substantive issue." The Einhorn analysis continues:

> In bureaucratic terms, the NSSM raised a question as to which agency would have the determining voice in formulating policies regarding foreign economic decision-making in the U.S. government. In substantive terms, at stake was the choice between the conflicting views in State and Treasury on what the U.S. policy on foreign confiscation should be. Matters were even more complicated by the fact that within the State Department there was a difference in opinion between the regional bureau for Latin America [ARA] and the Economics Bureau [E]. As even in this debate, the regional bureau was most concerned with bilateral and the damaging effect on the whole spectrum of these relations—relations generated by a single-mindedly aggressive response to an expropriation of a U.S. enterprise in a foreign country. The Economics Bureau was more concerned with upholding the international legal principle governing U.S. policy in the area, but was still appreciative of the difficulties associated with hinging all of U.S. policy to a foreign country on only one area of interaction. In Treasury, especially under Connally, there was a desire to get tough and spell out an overt U.S. policy on expropriation which could act as a deterrent and put nations disregarding U.S. views on this matter on notice as to what they might expect as the U.S. response.

Since this analysis was written, the principal administration officials formulating the policy have been changed as well as the air of crisis surrounding the problem. However, the fundamental problem for the U.S. government remains: selection of a policy which provides optimal protection to U.S. foreign economic interests abroad with minimum disruption to the normal discourse of U.S. diplomatic relations with the involved countries.

*Effect on Policy Development*

The resulting presidential policy statement, in the administration's hurried effort to head off congressional protection legislation, became de facto an administrative regulation on the exercise of executive discretion in the conduct of foreign policy, although the general process and procedure for regulations was not applied, presumably due to operation of the Administrative Procedure Act's (1970) exemption for acts categorized as involving foreign affairs. Although the Department of State in recent years has moved toward a more limited utilization of its exemption, the policy statement, in all other respects, reflects the requirement of the acts. It specifies the procedure, sanctions, and the criteria upon which executive decisions will be made. The president's policy statement, in tandem with other legal and administrative sanctions, operates to provide a novel melange upon which the U.S. government exercises its diplomatic protection prerogatives—"significant U.S. interest." It appears from the policy announcement that implementive provisions were to be within the framework of current domestic law until Congress made statutory modifications along the lines which were to be proposed by the administration. In the interim, the Council on International Economic Policy (CIEP) established the Interagency Coordinating Group of Expropriation which was to administer the economic protection policy based upon the standard of "significant economic interest," a nebulous term composed primarily of size and general strategic market importance of the firm on industry and secondarily residual protection for property rights utilizing the "50 percentum beneficial U.S. ownership" legislative requirement in conjunction with customary diplomatic protection for "nationals" under international law.

The applications of this policy have been fairly rigorous in the international financial institutions and in the U. S. Agency for International Development (AID) programs. Between June 1971 and January 1973 the United States voted no, or failed to support World Bank and International Development Agency loans to Guyana, Bolivia, Iraq, and Peru. In each of these instances, the reason cited for the U.S. position was expropriation of property of U.S. nationals without compensation.

In regard to the extension of U.S. bilateral aid, the Hickenlooper Amendment was invoked once on February 8, 1963, against Sri Lanka (then Ceylon). From October 1968 to February 1974, U.S. assistance to Peru was carefully considered in light of the investment disputed during that period. Only earthquake relief loans were approved during that period. Similarly expropriated property during the early stages of the Allende period necessitated a review of U.S. aid policy toward Chile.

OPIC insurance also had to comply with provisions of the Hickenlooper Amendment and it ceased issuing contracts in Bolivia when a military junta seized power on September 26, 1969, but was reestablished with the government's settlement of the Mina Matilda claim on December 11, 1972. Also, OPIC's inconvertibility insurance program was terminated in Peru in mid-1969 and all operations in Chile were phased out by mid-1971 (U.S. Department of State, 1974b).

The presidential policy statement of 1972 was promulgated with the intent of crystallizing and providing greater coordination for the implementation of U.S. policy regarding expropriation. For the most part, this result was accomplished through operation of the watchdog Interagency Group on Expropriations. The group has a mission of keeping abreast of the status of all active or potential investment disputes which may involve international legal issues or which are of strategic economic importance. For each case under review, the Department of State's staff office provides an opinion on the application of appropriate international legal standards and on economic impact assessment of foreign governmental actions' effect on an entire economic sector or industry. This approach, however, would subject decisions made in cases where the legal issues were marginal—for example, as to the finding of a violation of international legal standards or the application of domestic sanctions—to tilt toward the maintenance of ongoing amicable relations in the absence of a definite finding of a legal violation. In the predicament where a difficult decision has to be made against the grain of current diplomatic relationships, it is conceivable that the easiest way out would be for the group to "further examine" the problem and hope for a change of circumstances to make the issues more lucid.

*Development of the New International Legal Norms*

The impetus for the current ongoing debate over the process of changing international duties and obligations of states toward foreign investors occurred in October 1972 at the Twelfth Session of the United Nations Conference on Trade and Development (UNCTAD) Board (1972a) when the Chilean government reported that U.S.-owned Kennecott Copper Company had requested a Paris court to temporarily enjoin the Chilean government's trading company's shipments destined for French buyers. The Chilean government claimed that Kennecott's petition to a foreign court and the court's grant of the provisional order was a flagrant violation of the principles of international law, especially the principles of nonintervention of a state in the affairs of another sovereign and that concept of the self-determination of people as set forth in the UN Charter.

Promptly, eight Latin American countries declared their solidarity with the Chilean government in a resolution to the Trade and Development Board urging that "expropriations and subsequent nationalization of natural resources are acts of undeniable sovereignty within the exclusive competence and subject to the sole decision of the State in which the resources are situated, in conformity with its National Constitution, laws and regulations" (UNCTAD, 1972). After considerable debate the Trade and Development Board passed a resolution including the gist of the Latin American Declaration "without prejudice" to the United Nations General Assembly Resolution 1803 (XVII) which, to the contrary, embodied an international legal standard for expropriation.

The objective of this qualifying statement was to prevent the group from being in the precarious position of going on record opposing the content of a UN resolution that it had previously adopted (Journal of World Trade Law, 1973: 382).

The Mexican representative to the session summarized the resolution saying that the draft resolution did not propose a new norm of international law, but rather enunciated a political, legal, and economic principle which could form the basis of such a norm. He noted, however, that the enunciation of the general norm was not a mere subterfuge to circumvent the procedure for international codification of such a norm (Journal of World Trade Law, 1973: 381). The Mexican ambassador to the United Nations, Garcia-Robles, who served as chairman of the working group on the charter, affirmed the loss of authority in the 1962 resolution as both a norm and as a legal standard. Before an American Society of International Law discussion on the charter, he summarized it succinctly (American Society of International Law, 1975): "[The Resolution of] 1962 is dead!" The same principles involved here, the development of international norms, were also enunciated in UNCTAD Resolution 45 (III) adopted during the spring of 1973. This resolution stressed the urgency "to establish generally accepted norms to govern international economic relations systematically." It importuned states to take prompt actions by advancing that "it is not feasible to establish a just order and a stable world as long as the Charter to protect the rights of all countries, and in particular the developing states, is not formulated." A reasoned interpretation of the language of the resolutions confirms the indication that states initially viewed the Charter on Economic Rights and Duties of States as the opportunity to formulate and codify the "new norms" for international economic behavior of governments. This conclusion is supported by the Programme of Action on the Establishment of the New International Economic Order adopted at the Sixth Special Session of the General Assembly. U.N. Resolution 3202 (SSVI) states in regard to the charter that it "shall constitute an effective instrument towards the establishment of a new system of international economic relations based on equity, sovereign equality, and interdependence of the interest of developed and developing countries" (United Nations Sixth Special Session, 1974).

### *Nonuniversal Application of New International Economic Norms*

One can propose, without hesitation, that the expectations of the developing international economic community were for the charter to embody the standards of states in their individual and collective capacities regarding states' economic obligations and rights within the international economic arena (White, 1975; Haight, 1975: 591).

Although a minority of industrialized states opposed a charter with binding applicability, the overwhelming preponderance of states sought a charter with some obligatory and legal significance. With the bulk of nations intending to give the charter a legal status and some binding effect, the nonassenting states should be treated vis-à-vis the charter in the same manner as one who registers a reservation to an international convention: binding applicability except for the provisions upon which the state registers a reservation (International Court of Justice, 1951). In its 1951 Advisory Opinion regarding "reservations to the Convention on Genocide," the World Court held that a provisional nonratifying state rendering a reservation to a convention can be regarded as being a party of the convention provided that the elements constituting the reservation are not fundamental to the objective of the agreement. The court states that in "treaty relations a State cannot be bound without its consent, and that consequently no reservation can be effective against any state without its agreement thereto." The court's rationale for the decision turned on two key elements of which applicability may be debatable regarding the present resolution: (1) the reservation must be compatible with the objectives of the convention; and (2) the convention itself has a purely humanizing and civilizing purpose for which states "do not have any interests of their own; they merely have, one and all, a common interest, namely, the accomplishment of those high purposes which are the *raison d'etre* of the Convention." Under these restrictive criteria, the compliance of the charter is debatable, and nonsupporting states may not be constructively deemed in support of those provisions it has not specifically disavowed assent to (Asomoah, 1966).

The question yet to be determined is whether the general practices of states themselves and their expressions embodied in resolutions of the General Assembly constitute a basis for a modified customary international law. Unanimity of 126 nations on basic legal principles would unquestionably constitute a new foundation of international law. Would the same principles, if acquiesced to by 99 percent of the states in the UN, with abstention or silence by the others in a meager minority, yield the same legal authority? It can be argued that silent acquiescence to such pronouncements by the General Assembly should yield the same legal operative effect as silence does in World Bank decisions—a tacit acquiescence.

In response to other structural legal strait-jackets of "Universal International Law" embodied in the United Nations' decisional procedures, the General Assembly in political acts has circumvented the confinements of their principles of legal reasoning. Political acts of the United Nations General Assembly have yielded results that are effective and decisive as solemn unanimous pronouncements of the Security Council itself.

In perspective, these acts as well as a host of others, it has conceded, are of paramount "international moral influence." Even states adhering to the customary school of international law which have balked on acquiescing to the General Assembly as a legislative authority concede to its moral influence. Former Justice of the International Court, Phillip C. Jessup, in inaugurating the Columbia Law School Wolfgang Friedmann Lecture Series (Jessup, 1973), reaffirmed his dissenting position taken in the 1966 Southwest Africa cases that General Assembly resolutions constitute mere proof of the international community standard, although UN resolutions do not have legislative character or "by themselves create new rules of law," but "the accumulation of expressions of condemnation of apartheid . . . especially as recorded in the Resolutions of the United Nations General Assembly, are proof of *the pertinent contemporary international* standard."

The late Columbia Law School professor, Wolfgang Friedmann, presents a more explicit formulation of the current state of international law in his work *The Changing Structure of International Law* by distinguishing the international law requirements of "coexistence" from those of "cooperation" and their correlation to the objectives to the pursuits of common human interests. From the unique development and different requirements of these bodies of law, Friedmann asserts that from this "follows the acknowledgement of the necessity of both universal and nonuniversal spheres of international law, depending on the degree of community of interests and purposes."

It is clear that although the constellations of universal and nonuniversal law have not been clearly identified or categorized, tacit acquiescence by states of the traditional international law school will go a long way toward making certain nonuniversal international law rules generally applicable.

*Legal Standards of Key Provisions of the Economic Charter of Rights and Duties of States*

The language of the charter adopted by the General Assembly regarding the treatment of expropriated foreign investment varies significantly with the language of the previous touchstone: the 1962 UN General Assembly Resolution on Permanent Sovereignty over National Resources. Article 2(c) of Charter II of the 1974 Charter provides the following:

> 2. Each State has the right: . . . (c) to nationalize, expropriate or transfer ownership of foreign property in which case *appropriate* compensation *should* be paid by the State adopting such measures, taking into account its relevant laws and regulations and all circumstances that *the State considers pertinent.* In any case where the question of compensation gives rise to a controversy, it shall be settled under the *domestic law of the nationalizing* State and by its tribunals, unless it is freely and mutually agreed by all states concerned that other peaceful means be sought on the basis of the sovereign equality of states and in accordance with the principle of free choice of means.

The above text, in comparison to the formulation made in 1962, lacks any reference to the following three key elements found in the previous document:

1. The public purpose or use requirement for expropriated foreign property;
2. Mandatory payment of prompt, adequate, and effective compensation;
3. Requirement of governmental action in conformity with international law.

*PUBLIC PURPOSE REQUIREMENT FOR GOVERNMENTAL ACTS OF EXPROPRIATION*

The charter's omission of public interest requirements for expropriation is consistent with the pattern set by previous General Assembly Resolutions on National Sovereignty over National Resources (1974a). The report of the secretary-general of the United Nations on permanent sovereignty (1973) has brief language suggesting that the public interest requirement for governmental actions against foreign interests has not been discarded. His formulation for expropriation is conditional: "It is inherent in the right that a State may undertake nationalization measures if and when these are considered to be *necessary* and *in the best national interest.*" In the implementation of this right, countries have utilized a variety of categories in which to classify these resources. Some have specified natural resources in general, while others have specified mineral assets, or the exploitation of these resources as within the exclusive domain of the state. This array includes land, subsoil, natural resources, and specific minerals including bauxite, copper, and natural gas as statutorily within the purview of the public domain. Other states utilizing similar formulations have designated specific activities as fishing or mining, the physical acts of exploitation or the marketing of the products of these resources as within the ambit of the national government. The United Nations secretary-general (1973: Appendix I, II), in examining the status of state's exercise of rights over permanent sovereignty, suggested in his 1973 report that states have not derogated from the previously established national interest standard, nor does he make inference to any other alternate criterion. Although states couch their legislation and decrees on expropriation in public interest terms, presumably in recognition of existing requirements, *Restatement Second of U.S. Foreign Relations Law* (Article 185) points out that there appears to be little authority in international law establishing any useful criteria by which a state's own determination of public purpose can be effectively challenged. The *Restatement* comments that the concept of a taking for public purpose or public use may have had a reasonably definite meaning in international law when the municipal state systems which led in the development in international law were based upon the free enterprise system and adhered to a system of private ownership of the means of production. However, the advent of socialist states to a prominent role in international law's development and the expansion of the area of governmental activity for market economy countries yields a concept of public purpose or use "that is increasingly vague and of doubtful usefulness."

During negotiations, several industrialized states, including the United States, offered draft language to reaffirm the "public purpose or use" concept. That draft provision, the text of which follows, however, was rejected by the working group: "Each State has the right (d) To nationalize, expropriate, or requisition foreign property for a *public purpose,* provided that just compensation in the light of all relevant circumstances shall be paid" (UNCTAD, 1974a).

Under this language the drafters from the developed states consciously sought to reaffirm the public purpose utilization standard. The official public record (UNCTAD, 1974b), however, does not indicate that the vote rejecting the amendment was an affirmative decision to eliminate the concept entirely. This view is supported by the absence of any indication by states of any intention to discontinue the requirement. Although the presumption is in favor of the standard, it is subject to rebuttal by governmental acts or statements to the contrary. Until that moment, the public purpose or use requirement apparently will be maintained in effect against states which expropriate alien interests in strategic sectors of their economies.

### *THE STANDARD OF COMPULSORY PAYMENT OF COMPENSATION*

The drafters of the Economic Charter appear to have recognized some rule requiring compensation and neutralized it with the following language: "Compensation *should be paid* taking into account its relevant laws and regulations and all circumstances that the State considers pertinent."

In comparison to the 1962 language, this formulation eliminates the obligatory element from the rule and goes one step further by allowing the state to weigh considerations other than those pertaining exclusively to valuation. The apparent immediate incentives for this language formulation were the charges and accusations levied against the United States firm, the International Telephone and Telegraph Company (ITT), arising from its activities in Chile in 1972 (U.S. Senate, 1972). The injection of political conduct considerations into valuation proceedings changes their basic nature from legal to quasi-equitable. Such a change opens a Pandora's box of equity considerations spanning the entire range of the discipline (Francioni, 1975). The following alternate language introduced by the developed states includes the term "just compensation," which connotes substantial and legal objectivity: "To nationalize, expropriate or requisition foreign property for a public purpose, provided that *just* compensation in the light of all relevant circumstances shall be *paid*" (UNGA, 1974).

In U.S. legal terminology, the "just" (New York Supreme Court) value of an asset as used synonymously with "fair" value is its current value on an open market, if a market exists, without exaggeration or depreciation. Apparently, the drafters of this proviso sought recognition of this standard. This view, however, was not accepted by the developing states and the amendment was rejected. *Restatement* (Article 187) specified the following elements of "just" compensation: (a) adequacy in amount; (b) reasonably prompt payment; and (c) effectively utilizable form. Regarding this point, the *Restatement* (Article 185, note 4) notes the significance of the 1962 UN Resolution on Permanent Sovereignty over Natural Resources as the persuasive authority on the previous existence and recognition of some international standard (Schwebel, 1973: American Bar Association, 1973). Today the question raised by the charter, on the other hand, is whether that standard has changed. The term "appropriate compensation," in the context of the concerns expressed in 1962, shows evidence of some passing interest in the ability rather than the willingness of some countries to pay. The 1974 concept of adequate compensation appears to be concerned not only with the legality of the conduct of enterprises but the political objectives of their activities as well. Whatever standards are considered in determining compensation, the charter's language is quite explicit: compensation should merely be paid without any admonitory language or compulsion for a state to actually do so.

### *EXPROPRIATION IN COMPLIANCE WITH INTERNATIONAL LEGAL STANDARDS OF JUSTICE*

The charter's language, unlike its predecessor 1962 Resolution on Sovereignty over National Resources, has omitted all references to any international standard for expropriation.[4] Mr. Justice Harlan observed in regard to this controversial standard in Banco Nacional de Cuba vs. Sabbatino (U.S. Supreme Court, 1964):

> There are few if any issues in international law today on which opinion seems to be so divided as the limitations on a State's power to expropriate the property of aliens. There is, of course, authority, in international judicial and arbitral decisions in the expressions of national governments, and among commentators for the view that a taking is improper under international law if it is not for a public purpose, is discriminatory, or is without provision for prompt, adequate, and effective compensation.
>
> However, communist countries, although they have in fact provided a degree of compensation after diplomatic efforts, commonly recognize no obligation on the part of the taking country. Certain representatives of the newly independent and

> underdeveloped countries have questioned whether rules of state responsibility toward aliens can bind nations that have not consented to them at all. It is argued that the traditionally articulated standards governing expropriation of property reflect "imperialistic" interests and are inappropriate to the circumstances of emergent states.

During the past decade, the debate over a general international legal standard has become intensified and has resulted in nation states choosing sides—the minority of industrialized states opposed to a charter with binding applicability and the overwhelming preponderance of developing states on record for a legally binding document (UN Center for Economic and Social Information, 1974). With the bulk of nations intending to give the charter a legal status and some binding effect, the nonassenting states should be treated vis-à-vis the charter in the same manner as one who registers a reservation to an international convention: binding applicability except for the provisions upon which the state registered a reservation. Therefore, states that voted affirmatively for the charter desire not to be bound to an international legal standard. This expectation, although controversial for states not supporting the charter, can be fulfilled by states that disavow the international standard itself. Future cases of expropriation involving nationals from countries supporting the charter can be examined to ascertain the consistency between the state's avowed standard and that which it actually practices. In any instance of divergence, the debate thus is one of significant legal effect. The distinction is that general political statements in the international forum have a little less legal significance than the actual practices of states, unless these statements are expressed as legal reservations (UNGA, 1974c).

In the charter, the substantive elements that constitute the general rule of international law on expropriation, namely the standard of public purpose and compulsory compensation, have been eliminated from the norms of the covenanting states. Absent these essential standards for ascertaining whether a breach of the general rule has occurred, and the effectiveness of the general rule has been negated. To be more explicit, one cannot violate a general rule of international law when the legal elements which constitute the offense have been eliminated. For the states voting affirmatively in support of the charter, the document itself embodies their new international norm and their proposed legal rules on the standards for expropriation and compensation. One reaches this conclusion from the fact that the document itself was derived from the expectations of the states to establish a new international economic regime and by virtue of the written documents as a reflection of the current views of the states supporting the charter on the international law regarding this subject matter. Even the most doubtful of skeptics must concede that even if the rule has not changed, the norms have. In effect, the charter has become a nonuniversal covenant of which its standards are applicable to supporters of the charter. Logically, this proposition is irrefutable. Although states can argue that other sovereign states cannot create a positive rule of law that is binding upon a nonassenting state, by the same token a rationale state cannot fail to recognize a covenant among a group of states to change the substance of the rules applicable among themselves. States while negotiating the charter merged their individual norms within their positions on the charter. Whether one accepts or not the charter as a document embodying new international law, it must be realized that the charter embodies a standard against which the world community can gauge its own conduct (UNGA, 1974d). The states that voted not to be bound by an "international" standard on expropriation, covenant that they will not hold another state to such international standard in addition to the fact that they themselves will not be bound. This view has been assented to by the overwhelming majority of states by virtue of their position on the charter. The norms and the rules derived from the charter are de facto nonuniversal (Jessup, 1973: 425) norms and rules with binding applicability on that assenting segment of the international subcommunity. With the acceptance of this hypothesis, the inquiry must only ascertain the extent to which states which have opposed these norms and have refused their acceptance are bound by them as members of the international economic community.[5]

## NOTES

1. Compare the 1962 UN General Assembly Resolution on the Permanent Sovereignty over National Resources and the 1974 Charter of Economic Rights and Duties of States, UN DOC A/Res 1803 XVII, 19 December 1962. Seventeenth Session, Agenda Item 39.

2. For rationale see "Lawless" case, European Court of Human Rights, Ser. A., July 1, 1961.

3. As an alternative, the U.S. government may negotiate lump sum settlements as is the practice for claims arising in Eastern European countries and in the 1974 claims settlement with Peru.

4. Compare Charter Chapter II, Article 2 (c) and 1962 Permanent Sovereignty Resolution, para 4.

5. For conflicting discussions on this issue see Lissitzyn (1963), "International Law in a Divided World," International Conciliation no. 542; Jessup (1964) "Diversity and Uniformity in the Laws of Nations," American Journal of International Law 58: 341; Anand (1962) "Role of the New Asian—African Countries in the Present International Legal Order," American Journal of International Law 56: 383; Castenada (1961) "The Law in International Order," International Organization 15: 38.

## REFERENCES

Administrative Procedures Act. United States Code (1970) Ed. Public Law 89: 80 U.S. Statutes at Large 378. Washington, DC: Government Printing Office.

American Bar Association, Section on International Law (1974) "United Nations adopts charter of economic rights and duties of states." International Law News 4: 2 (1975: 5); American Bar Association Resolution adopted August 1974, International Lawyer 9: 405.

——— (1963) The Protection of Private Property Invested Abroad. Chicago: American Bar Association.

American Journal of International Law (1961) 55: 566-567.

American Society of International Law (1975) Proceedings of the workshop on the UNCTAD Charter, April 27.

ASOMOAH (1966) The Legal Significance of the Declarations of the General Assembly of the United Nations. New York: Columbia Univ. Press.

Black's Law Dictionary (1968) Minneapolis, MN: West Publishing.

BORCHARD (1927) Diplomatic Protection of Citizens Abroad, or the Law of International Claims. New York: Banks Law Publishing.

——— (1913) "Contractual claims in international law." Columbia Law Rev. 12 (June): 460.

BROS, M. (1972) "Notices pours servis a une theorie de la force obligatoire de droit international" in Van Der Ven (ed.) Recueil de Melunges. Utrecht,Netherlands: Univ. of Utrecht.

BROWER and TEPE (1975) "The charter of economic rights and duties of states: a reflection or rejection of international law?" International Lawyer 9: 295.

CHADWICK, M. L. (1971) "Foreign policy report/Nixon administration debates new position paper on Latin America." National J. 46, 3: 2238.

DRAGO (1907) "State Loans in their relation to international policy." Amer. J. of International Law 1: 695; U.S. Foreign Relations (1903): 4.

DUNN, F. S. (1932) Diplomatic Protection. Baltimore, MD: Johns Hopkins Univ. Press.

EINHORN, J. (1973) "The Nixon administration's expropriation statement of January 19, 1972: A study of bureaucratic politics." Washington, DC: Johns Hopkins Univ., School of Advanced International Studies.

FRANCIONI (1975) "Compensation for nationalization of foreign property: borderland between law and equity." International and Comparative Law Q. 24: 255.

GORDON, L. (1975) "Resources and interdependence." Economic Import 4: 20.

Hague Peace Conference (1907) Second; Malloy, Treaties 2: 2248, Article I (1907), 36 U.S. Statutes 2251.

HAIGHT (1975) "The new international economic order and the charter of economic rights and duties of states." International Lawyer 9: 591.

HYDE, C. (1945) International Law Chiefly as Interpreted and Applied by the United States. New York: Little, Brown.

International Center for the Settlement of Investment Disputes (1975) Annual Report of the International Center for the Settlement of Investment Disputes. Washington, DC: International Center for the Settlement of Disputes.

International Court of Justice (1970) Barcelona Traction, Light and Power Co., Ltd., Decision cited International Legal Materials (1970) 9: 227.

——— (1951) Advisory Opinion: Reservation to the Convention on Genocide, International Court of Justice Report 1951: 15.

JESSUP, P. (1973) "Non-universal international law." Columbia J. of Transnational Law 12: 425.

Journal of World Trade Law (1973): 7.

KENNEDY, M. and D. GANTZ (1974) "Establishment of mechanisms of the settlement of economic disputes." Georgia J. of International Law 5: 145.

LEIDER, R. (1973) "An old strategist speaks to the young." Military Rev. 54: 3.

LISSITIZYN, O. J. (1936) "The meaning of the term denial of justice in international law." Amer. J. of International Law 4 (October): 632-635.

MILLS, B. (1973) Statement before U.S. Congress House Committee on Foreign Affairs, Subcommittee on Foreign Economic Policy, 93rd Congress, 1st Session, June 15.

National Journal (1972) January 22: 141-156.

New York Supreme Court. In re Board of Water Supply of City of New York, 277 NY 452; 14 NE 2nd 789.

Restatement Second of U.S. Foreign Relations Law (1965) American Law Institute. Philadelphia: American Law Institute.

SCHWEBEL (1973) "The story of the UN delegation of permanent sovereignty over natural resources." Amer. Bar Assoc. J. 49: 463.

SHEA, D. O. (1955) The Clavo Clause. Minneapolis: Univ. of Minnesota.

SHIHATA, I. (1975) "Distribution embargo of Arab oil: its legality under international law." Amer. J. of International Law 68: 581.

SHON and BAXTER (1971) "Second restatement of U.S. foreign relations law," Article 12. Amer. J. of International Law 55: 545; 566-567.

United Nations (1974) Center for Economic and Social Information, Information Note 296, 18 December, 1974, para I, II.

United Nations Conference on Trade and Development [UNCTAD] (1972) 19th Plenary Meeting of April 19, 1972. UNCTAD Proceedings Third Session, UNDOC TD/ 180, vol 1A, Part 1 at 184 (1972).

——— (1972a) UNDOC TD/B/SR. 317 Summary Record of 317-335 Meeting.

——— (1974a) Report of the UNCTAD Working Group A/C.2L 1404 cited at A/9949 p. 14, English.

——— (1974b) Fourth Session of the Working Group on the Charter of Economic Rights and Duties of States, Mexico City, June 10-28, 1974, p. 7-14.

United Nations General Assembly [UNGA] (1974) Charter of Economic Rights and Duties of States Draft Amendment A/C.2/L 1402 Chapter II, Article 2, Para 2(d).

——— (1974a) 29th Session 1974, Resolution A/3281 (XXIX), December 9.

——— (1974b) Resolution on National Sovereignty over National Resources A/Res/ 3171 (XXVIII 5 Feb. 1974), 28th Session Agenda Item 12.

——— (1974c) Reservations of Ethiopia (A/PV.2316 p. 26) and Turkey (A/PV.2316 p. 18-20).

——— (1974d) Delegates address on the Charter A/PV. 2315-2316, 12 December 1974.

United Nations (1974) Report of the Sixth Special Session of the UN General Assembly UNDOC A/9559 Res 3202.

United Nations Secretary General (1973) Report of the Secretary General of the United Nations, UNDOC E/5425, English edition.

U.S. Congress (1967) Fishermen's Protective Act of 1967, as amended 22 USC 1971-78, PL. 90-482 amended the act of August 27, 1954.

——— (1961) Foreign Assistance Act of 1961 Section 301(d); 78 stat. 1013 (1964) as amended 22 USCA 2370(3).

——— (1948) The Sugar Act of 1948, PL 80-338, 61 stat 933, sec 408, 7 USC 1158.

U.S. Department of State (1975) Selected Documents No. 1, "The challenge of the third world." Seventh Special Session of the U.N. General Assembly, September 1-12.

——— (1974a) Bureau of Intelligence and Research, "Disputes involving U.S. foreign direct investment July 1, 1971—July 31, 1973."

——— (1974b) Written response of Assistant Secretary of State T. O. Enders to question by Senator Lloyd Bentsen, Chairman, Economic Growth Subcommittee, Joint Economic Committee, July 25, 1974.

U.S. President's Policy Statement (1972) White House Policy Statement "Economic assistance and investment security in developing nations," January 19.

U.S. Senate (1972) Hearings, March, regarding International Activities of the International Telephone and Telegraph Company.

U.S. Supreme Court Reports (1964) United States Supreme Court Volume 376: 398; 428: 29; Supreme Court Reports 84: 923; 940-41; Lawyers Edition 2nd 11(1964): 804.

U.S.-Venezuela Governmental Exchange (1974) "Agreement relating to investment guarantees between the government of the United States and Venezuela." Exchange of notes at Caracas November 26 and 29, 1962; 14 U.S. Treaties 374; TIAS 5326; 474 UNTS 107. Washington, DC, U.S. Department of State, Bureau of Economic & Business Affairs.

VANZANT (1974) "Charter on economic rights and duties of states: a solution to the development aid problem?" Georgia J. of International Law 5: 441.

VATTEL (1758) The Law of Nations, Classics of International Law. (1920).

WALTERS, R. S. (1974) "UNCTAD: Intervenor between poor and rich states." J. of World Trade Law 7: 527.

The Washington Post, June 25, 1971.

WHITE (1975) "A new international economic order." International and Comparative Law Q. 24 (July): 544.

WHITEMAN, M. M. (1967) Digest of International Law 8: 906-907; 1216. Washington, DC: U.S. Government Printing Office.

*Benoit Otis Brookens II, Esq., is Staff Assistant to the Deputy Assistant Secretary of State for Oceans and Fisheries Affairs. He is a member of the American, Pennsylvania, and Wisconsin Bar Associations. Brookens previously served as a staff officer in the U.S. Department of State for the Inter-agency Coordinating Group on Expropriations.*

**Publisher's Note:** The following information is printed in accordance with U.S. postal regulations: Statement of Ownership, Management and Circulation (required by 39 U.S.C. 3685). 1. Title of Publication: JOURNAL OF INTERAMERICAN STUDIES AND WORLD AFFAIRS. 2. Date of Filing: September 26, 1977. 3. Frequency of Issue: Quarterly. 3A. No. of Issues Published Annually: 4 (four). 3B. Annual Subscription Price: institutions, $26.00; individuals, $15.00. 4. Location of Known Office of Publication: 275 South Beverly Drive, Beverly Hills (Los Angeles), California 90212. 5. Location of the Headquarters or General Business Offices of the Publishers: 275 South Beverly Drive, Beverly Hills, (Los Angeles), California 90212. 6. Names and Complete Addresses of Publisher, Editor, and Managing Editor: Publisher: Sara Miller McCune, 1102 South Oakhurst Drive, Los Angeles, California 90035; Editor: John P. Harrison, Box 248134, University of Miami, Coral Gables, Florida 33124; Managing Editor: None. 7. Owner (If owned by a corporation, its name and address must be stated and also immediately thereunder the names and addresses of stockholders owning or holding 1% or more of total amount of stock. If not owned by a corporation, the names and addresses of the individual owners must be given. If owned by a partnership or other unincorporated firm, its name and address, as well as that of each individual must be given.): Sage Publications, Inc., 275 South Beverly Drive, Beverly Hills, California 90212; Sara Miller McCune, 1102 South Oakhurst Drive, Los Angeles, California 90035; Marvin Sirot, Mohawk Lane, Greenwich, Connecticut 06830; Gustave Sirot, Wingate Road, Guilford, Connecticut 06340; John B. Hurford, 220 East 63rd Street, New York, New York 10021; Albert L. Zesiger, 1125 Fifth Avenue, New York, New York 10028; Judith C. Zesiger, 1125 Fifth Avenue, New York, New York 10028. 8. Known Bondholders, Mortgagees, and Other Security Holders Owning or Holding 1% or More of Total Amount of Bonds, Mortgages or Other Securities: None. 9. For Completion by Nonprofit Organizations Authorized to Mail at Special Rates (Section 132.122, PSM): Not Applicable.

| | Av. No. Copies Each Issue During Preceding 12 Months | Actual No. of Copies of Single Issue Published Nearest to Filing Date |
|---|---|---|
| 10. Extent and Nature of Circulation | | |
| A. Total no. copies printed (net press run) . . . | 1679 | 1615 |
| B. Paid circulation: | | |
| 1. Sales through dealers and carriers, street vendors and counter sales . . . . . . . . . | 19 | 21 |
| 2. Mail subscriptions . . . . . . . . . . . . . . | 1239 | 1242 |
| C. Total paid circulation (sum of 10B1 and 10B2) . . . . . . . . . . . | 1258 | 1263 |
| D. Free distribution by mail, carrier or other means: samples, complimentary, and other free copies . . . . . . . . . . . . . . . . . . . | 43 | 63 |
| E. Total distribution (sum of C & D) . . . . . . | 1301 | 1326 |
| F. Copies not distributed: | | |
| 1. Office use, left-over, unaccounted, spoiled after printing . . . . . . . . . . . . | 378 | 289 |
| 2. Returns from news agents . . . . . . . . . | — | — |
| G. Total (sum of E, F1 and 2)—should equal net press run shown in A) . . . . . . . . . . . | 1679 | 1615 |

11. I certify that the statements made by me above are correct and complete, (Signed) Sara Miller McCune, Publisher. 12. 39 U.S.C. 3626 provides in pertinent part: "No person who would have been entitled to mail matter under former section 4359 of this title shall mail such matter at the rates provided under this subsection unless he files annually with the Postal Service a written request for permission to mail matter at such rates." In accordance with the provisions of this statute, I hereby request permission to mail the publication named in Item 1 at the reduced postage rates presently authorized by 39 U.S.C. 3626. (Signed) Sara Miller McCune, Publisher.

**RONALD H. BERG**
*Department of Anthropology*
*University of Michigan*
*Ann Arbor, Michigan 48014*

**FREDERICK STIRTON WEAVER**
*School of Social Sciences*
*Hampshire College*
*Amherst, Massachusetts 01002*

# TOWARD A REINTERPRETATION OF POLITICAL CHANGE IN PERU DURING THE FIRST CENTURY OF INDEPENDENCE

The central purpose of this paper is to show that the character of Peruvian national politics changed substantially during the century after independence from Spain and that a focus on the shifting relations between the central government and social and economic power in the private sector is crucial for appreciating the significance of these political developments and for comprehending their sources. Clearly a wide variety of forces conditioned the organization and exercise of political power in nineteenth-century Peru, but historical interpretations that stress the roles of economic elites (e.g., Bourricaud, 1970), foreign interests (Yepes del Castillo, 1972) or leaders' personalities (Pike, 1967) obscure the magnitude of these political changes and do not adequately explain them.

In the first section, we divide the post-independence century into three periods: Independence to the early 1840s; the Guano Age, reaching its zenith in the 1850s and early 1860s; and the period following the 1884 withdrawal of Chilean troops that occupied Lima in the aftermath of the War of the Pacific. Such a periodization of Peruvian history certainly is not novel, but in the following pages we argue that the nature of Peruvian politics

Journal of Interamerican Studies and World Affairs, Vol. 20 No. 1, February 1978

was qualitatively different in each of the three periods and that these differences are integral to historical understanding of Peruvian society and state. As we hope will be apparent from our presentation, the distinguishing features of each period are but strong tendencies and not stable equilibria. We are not, moreover, proposing a progressive, teleological movement from lower to higher stages of political development. Rather, out intent is to outline the effects of changing sets of economic and social circumstances upon the political structure. A summary of the argument and a discussion of some of its broader implications for comparative history comprise the last section of the paper.

## *I*

Peru was, with Mexico, a center of the Spanish colonial mining economy. A large rural population was tapped for working in the mines and for producing an agricultural surplus to feed the miners and urban dwellers. This population was controlled by a highly centralized, bureaucratic state which was careful to eliminate political competition. A major source of potential competition came from local haciendas, appropriating peasant land and labor after the Indian communities were decimated and scattered by epidemics and other dislocations of the conquest. The state responded by moving the peasants onto proscribed areas of land *(reducciones),* limiting the growth of the haciendas, and retaining the ability to levy the head tax and the mine draft (mita).[1]

With independence from Spain in 1824, the colonial political apparatus was destroyed. The subsequent political disintegration was the result of a number of factors: the colonial state had effectively suppressed any internal political organization not directly dependent on the central authority; the wars of independence had destroyed a large portion of the existing economic infrastructure and organization; and the post-Waterloo depression in Europe severely contracted export markets for Peruvian goods. As a consequence, production of minerals, cotton, and wool fell off sharply, and with the decline of national and international markets and of economic interdependence, political power came to reside primarily in the haciendas and local bosses. The new central government had virtually no authority over the isolated valleys of the coast and of the sierra, and the national government in Lima was dependent on the local economies for revenues, principally from the Indian head tax.[2]

These conditions were not necessarily to the advantage of the regional caudillos, however, for even local control was uncertain and an essentially Hobbsian condition of constant war against internal and external enemies prevailed throughout the period, even in areas that were well-organized export production centers in colonial times. For instance, bands of escaped slaves regularly extorted protection money from cotton growers between 1836 and 1840 (Piel, 1970: 122). But this chaos should not obscure the central fact that political power, in the first two decades of political independence, flowed from the local bosses to the central government to such an extent that difficulties at the local level only further eroded centralized political power. The political record of the national government during this period is one of consistent failure. The external debt of 1.5 million pounds sterling was defaulted because of the inability of the central government to levy and collect taxes (Pike, 1967: 97); Bolívar's early land reform legislation had no chance of implementation (Romero, 1967: 32-35); and abolitionist legislation passed in 1823, 1828, 1829, and 1839 to insure the freedom of all those born in the republic and to end the traffic in slaves was totally ineffective (Basadre, 1963b: 553-557).

This distribution of political power in Peru began to change rapidly in the early 1840s with the emergence of a strong central state. In part these changes were due to the new fiscal revenue the national government received from the guano export boom from the 1840s through the late 1860s. Total Peruvian government revenues in 1846-1847 were slightly in excess of 4 million pesos, of which about 250,000 pesos were derived directly from guano exports, but proceeds from guano exports comprised about one half of the 10 million peso fiscal total in the mid-1850s and 18.5 million out of a 23 million peso total in the early 1860s. Moreover, customs revenues, on imports largely made possible by guano exports, supplied over 3 million pesos of the last total (Levin, 1960: 93-96).[3] But fiscal affluence alone is insufficient to explain the character of the Peruvian state in the Guano Age, and a fuller understanding requires a closer look at the organization of guano extraction and export.

This rich fertilizer, consisting of the excretion of a certain type of bird eating a certain type of fish, had for centuries been deposited on an uninhabited collection of rocks called the Chincha Islands, off the arid Peruvian coast some 70 miles south of Lima where no rain fell to leach out the high nitrogen content of the droppings. While private Peruvian entrepreneurs, allied with a Liverpool banking house, organized the first large-scale guano export in 1841, the Peruvian government asserted its ownership over the deposits as soon as the first boatload demonstrated the potential value of the new export. In the next four decades, the various Peruvian governments acted consciously and aggressively to secure maximum revenue from guano exports, experimenting with different selling arrangements to exploit its world monopoly of guano to the greatest advantage, to a considerable degree independent from the interests of even its most powerful European customers (Levin, 1960: 48-76; Mathew, 1968; Mathew, 1972). The means employed to extract and load the guano were extremely rudimentary, and, in its essentials, remained unchanged throughout the Guano Age: the mountains of guano were cut and broken up with light tools and wheelbarrowed over to chutes through which it was dropped into holds of waiting ships. The modest capital needs, principally workers' housing and simple tools, were largely met from foreign sources, and most of the guano labor force consisted of indentured Chinese workers "recruited" by labor contractors and supplemented by convicts and army deserters (Levin, 1960: 31-47, 77-90).

The conditions of guano extraction and exportation contained two elements whose appreciation is crucial to an understanding of the development of the Peruvian state. First, through its direct ownership of the guano deposits, fiscal revenues from guano export did not require the consent of any domestic constituency. Second, the guano industry's location was physically isolated from the center of Peruvian life, its labor force and capital were supplied from external sources, its extraction and loading were extremely simple operations, and no processing was required. All of this meant that the guano trade was virtually the prototype of an enclave industry, and all the activity that produced over 11 million tons of guano that sold for the equivalent of over U.S. $600 million between 1840 and the War of the Pacific in 1879 did not directly stimulate other national economic activity, even internal transport.[4] Thus, guano export was not the source of any new local interest group—owners or workers—who might have been expected to have political influence, nor did it strengthen the bases of existing economic elites.

The Peruvian state, as a consequence, possessed a source of immense revenues whose collection and expenditure were independent of the action and influence of even the most powerful domestic groups and which was based on an economic activity that did not strengthen domestic economic elites. These were the conditions which enabled the establishment of decisive state hegemony over national affairs reminiscent of Spanish viceregal authority of colonial times in the ability to administer from above. And it was the executive branch of government in which this political authority was vested. Congress, dominated by rural elites, opposed presidential actions on several occasions and found that it could bring little effective power to bear on the executive and on the shape of national governmental policy. The waning influence of congress was made formal in the successively diminishing role allotted to it in rewritten constitutions between 1839 and 1860, but even the powers it appeared to retain in the constitutions overstated the position of congress in the actual exercise of political power (McCoy, 1971: 330-331).

The centralization of political power into the institution of the national executive can be seen most clearly in the regime of Ramón Castilla, president from 1845 to 1851 and from 1854 to 1862. The first national budget was prepared in 1848, a strong army was built up and used to crush the slave rebellions on the coast and the church was made fiscally dependent on the state. Then, in 1854, Castilla unequivocally demonstrated the power of the executive vis-à-vis the most powerful domestic classes by the abolition of slavery and the abolition of the Indian head tax.

The end of slavery was a serious blow to coastal landowners. Although they were partially compensated for the loss of the slaves, the scarcity of wage labor in mid nineteenth-century Peru meant that the money they received could not be used to replace the slaves with hired workers. Moreover, Castilla refused, in spite of the landowners' protests, to relieve their difficulty by allowing the importation of indentured Chinese laborers (Piel, 1970: 125; Pike, 1967: 112; Romero, 1967: 48; Stewart, 1951: 23-24).[5]

The abolition of the Indian head tax did nothing to help the coastal landowners, but it was the large landowners in the sierra who felt its major impact. The head tax had been an important coercive device for making labor available to the haciendas in the interior, and it had been the principal source of revenue for local governments which thereafter were forced to rely on Lima (Kubler, 1952: 6; Pike, 1967: 112-113).

Castilla's actions of 1854 have been attributed to both his moral sensibilities and his personal ambitions as president (Basadre, 1963a: 1078, 1089; Stewart, 1951: 27; Pike, 1967: 103), but for the purposes of our argument his intentions are not important. The central point is that he could implement sweeping policies which were recognized by the most powerful domestic classes as being seriously inimical to their interests. Castilla's ability to do this, including putting down the intermittent rebellions in opposition to these policies, depended upon his control of the single most powerful institution in Peruvian society, the central state (Basadre, 1963a: 1084-1088). This stands in sharp contrast to the preceding period in which the central state was so weak that it was not even an effective tool of private interests.

The Peruvian state in the Guano Age was, of course, not omnipotent; foreign and domestic pressures did constrain and qualify the executive's freedom of action. The foreign debt was a constant source of concern for those managing the state's affairs, and coastal landowners, strengthened by the world-wide shortage of cotton during the U.S. Civil War, finally succeeded in readmitting Chinese workers in spite of presidential resistance (Levin, 1960: 61-64, 80-81, 94; Stewart, 1951: 27).

Nevertheless, at its height, the state possessed a policy-making capability remarkably independent of even the most powerful domestic institutions and groups. An important example of how slightly the Peruvian government was beholden to private interests is the treatment of the stratum of urban Peruvians who had become rich by the export and sale of guano. From 1849, the Peruvian government's policy was to let guano sales franchises for individual countries, preferentially to Peruvians. Although these sales contractors generally subcontracted the transportation and marketing functions to foreign concerns, they quickly accumulated fortunes and became prominent civic and cultural leaders. But it is an error to deduce from their wealth and visibility that these domestic contractors possessed decisive political power. The income of this group was derived directly from governmental policy, and in 1869, President Balta and his finance minister, Nicolás de Piérola, decided that discrimination in favor of local contractors was too inefficient and expensive in governmental revenues foregone, cancelled the contracts held by Peruvians, and granted exclusive selling rights to Dreyfus Bros. and Co. of Paris. The Dreyfus Contract sparked immediate and impassioned political activity among the domestic contractors, but it took three years for them to install a president of their choice, and then another three years went by before there was even a minor change in the Dreyfus Contract favoring domestic contractors (Levin, 1960: 96-98, 104-107). This clearly is not an impressive record of political influence.

Still, the late 1860s and the decade of the 1870s was a period of decline in state authority, due not to challenges from competing sources of private domestic groups but to the weakening of the major pillar supporting the state's position—guano revenues. Because of the exhaustion of the highest quality guano, price and management mistakes by the Peruvian government, and the increasing competition by natural nitrates, guano production began to decline and its European price weakened (Greenhill and Miller, 1973; Mathew, 1970). In an effort to augment diminishing fiscal revenues, the Indian head tax was reinstated in 1866, precipitating Indian rebellions and a civil war in 1867 (Basadre, 1964: 1699-1702). These revolts were finally contained, but dissatisfaction with the Dreyfus Contract sparked urban riots and a change in government in 1872; revolts spread among Chinese workers on the coastal plantations beginning in 1870, and foreign bond holders pressed for repayment. Responding to these problems severely strained the government's shrinking resources, which were further reduced by the world depression of 1873, and by the mid-1870s the government had defaulted the foreign debt (Basadre, 1964: 1973; Levin, 1960: 106-108) and virtually lost control over the nation as widespread rebellions broke out (Basadre, 1964: 1966-1968). While there were some obvious dialectical elements in the situation, (e.g., the urban elites that had been nurtured by state policy helped to destroy the state), the central source of state weakness was the decline in the guano revenues that had supported it. In the 1870s, central authority has been so eroded that it strongly resembled the nominal state of 1825-1840. Attempts by the Peruvian government to interfere with natural nitrate extraction and export led to Chile's declaration of war against Peru and Bolivia in 1879 (Greenhill and Miller, 1973; Levin, 1960: 109), and Peru's defeat in the War of the Pacific brought the Guano Age to a disastrous and final close.

In the decades following the withdrawal of Chilean troops from Peru, new political configurations emerged. As in the guano era, domestic social and political power was still closely linked to successful export activity, but the character of the exports was very different from that of the guano industry, and the resulting patterns of political development were distinct from those of the mid-nineteenth century. Beginning in the 1880s, sugar and cotton exports from coastal plantations became increasingly important, later followed by copper in the sierra, rubber from the Amazon basin, and oil. Expanding export production on the coast and in the interior stimulated the development of internal transportation facilities and commercial activities, and the workers in these and related sectors created markets for foodstuffs, the basis of expanded production by haciendas in the sierra (Romero, 1967: 171-197).

Wealthy and influential regional elites formed around the coastal plantations, the mines and haciendas of the sierra, rubber gathering in the eastern lowlands, and commerce, transportation, and finance centered in urban areas. Foreign investment contributed importantly to export expansion by investing directly in sugar, copper, and oil production and in supporting facilities and services. Unlike the portfolio investment in government bonds which had typified foreign investment during the Guano Age, this pattern of external financing directly operated (and enlarged) productive resources and meant that foreigners had an immediate stake in the particulars of Peruvian governmental policy (Klarén, 1973; Pinelo, 1973: 14-34; Goodsell, 1974 88).

At the same time, heightened economic activity required the formation of a domestic wage labor force, and in this period various working class groups entered the national political arena. Increased communication, concentration of workers, and geographical mobility enabled these groups to organize and exert political pressure on the national level, and miserable work conditions and remuneration together with the food shortages brought about by the wearing down of the subsistence economy gave these people an urgent need to engage in politics. In the countryside, unrest by workers on the coastal plantations and concerted resistance to the haciendas in the central sierra (Cotler, 1970: 534-535; Mishkin, 1963: 437-438), and in the cities, strikes by dock workers and political agitation by white collar workers became important facts of life that had to be explicitly dealt with by the central government (Klarén, 1973).

The emergence of these regional elites and working classes on the national political scene fundamentally altered the nature of Peruvian politics and the position of national government. The conflict between President Billingshurst and congress between 1912 and 1914 indicates the changing character of the new arrangements. Billingshurst was elected on a reform platform, appealing to the growing numbers of urban workers. Congress, representing domestic propertied classes, was able to block the president's attempts to pass a minimum wage law and other labor legislation, and when he made threats to limit the power of congress, its leaders instigated a military coup (Pike, 1967: 200-201).

Clearly the coup was a setback to working class aspirations and political activity, but it vividly illustrates how different the new configurations of political forces were from those of the Guano Age. No longer did the government stand apart from and above society; instead, it was compelled to respond to potent demands from important class and regional interests. The changed character of Peruvian politics did not preclude a powerful, centralized state, but such a state was possible only so long as it could successfully mediate the interests of frequently conflicting groups. The *oncenio* of Augusto Leguía's dictatorship (1919-1930) is a prime example of this process. While a close associate of some of the major domestic and foreign economic interests (sugar, banking, commerce), he supported labor and student movements and entered the presidency by the route of the new politics (Klarén, 1973: 43-44; Pike, 1967: 193-196). Once in office, he capitulated to some labor demands and adopted *indigenismo*—the doctrine popular with the middle class of uplifting the peasants by opposing the sierra hacendados. In all of his concessions to the lower classes, however, he made sure that the power of the most influential elites was not shaken by labor agitation or by effective land reform (Klarén, 1973: 45-58; Pike, 1967: 221-222; Payne, 1965: 38-41). As the balance between different groups became more difficult to sustain, Leguía increasingly relied on overt repression, and the depression of the 1930s destroyed what was left of his support.

Leguía's administration marked the beginning of coalition politics in Peru, a condition that would become more apparent in the twentieth century with the formation of national parties attempting to balance the interests of different groups. Political rule in the twentieth century would be based on coalitions, and coalitions whose components would change over times as their socioeconomic bases changed.

*II*

In our interpretive sketch of nineteenth century Peruvian political development, we have stressed the importance of socio-economic structural changes, principally those emanating from the organization of export production. In the early postindependence period, a confluence of factors impeded the development of a viable export sector in Peru and thereby the emergence of a coherent elite capable of taking charge of national political affairs. The consequence was the decentralization of political power, and regional caudillos became the principal political force in the new nation.

The rise of guano exports radically changed this pattern, and between the 1840s and early 1860s a powerful, highly centralized national state exercised effective hegemony over the local bosses. Guano extraction and export was an enclave industry with few linkages to other sectors, and it was precisely this character of the guano industry which fostered the rise of the central state in Peru and the primacy of politics in the Guano Age. The nature of these processes become clearer when one looks at the export economics of Argentina and the Brazilian state of São Paulo in the decades around the turn of the twentieth century. In both of these areas, export production was an integral part of national economic activity directly and indirectly involving large proportions of the working populations. Exports of meat and wheat and of coffee formed the bases of coherent elites who wielded decisive hegemony over the politics in these two areas as expressions of their social and economic power (Ferrer, 1967: 91-132; Romero, 1963: 1965-1204; Furtado, 1965: 119-192; Dean, 1969: 3-48). Guano Age Peru represented the other extreme; there the state was the principal *source* of social and economic power, and the position of groups in the private sector in large part depended on their favorable treatment by a virtually autonomous polity. In this respect, Peruvian politics more resembled the conditions of Diaz's Mexico with its mineral exports and of Venezuela in the 1920s and 1930s with its oil exports than the more firmly class-based politics of Argentina and Brazil.

After the decline of the guano industry and the Peruvian state, culminating in the War of the Pacific, the political rise of several competing groups linked to expanding export industries brought a new complexity to Peruvian politics. The need to balance and mediate a considerable range of different interests moved the content of Peruvian politics closer to that of, say, Colombia in the early twentieth century where the large coffee planters in the east, the small coffee growers of the west, foreigners operating banana plantations on the northern coast, and the workers in commerce, transport, and rural and urban production placed conflicting demands on the Colombian governments. These were the types of pressures which ushered an era of coalition politics into Peru.

As we mentioned in our introductory paragraph, this paper presents a dual argument. First, Peruvian politics underwent two watershed changes during the first century of independence. Although recognizing the magnitude of the changes is crucial for understanding this period of Peruvian history and interpreting subsequent political changes, these fundamental political shifts are obscured by historiographical approaches which emphasize the political roles of the propertied classes, foreign investors, or key individuals. All these factors are important to a full interpretation of the era, but our second methodological argument is that they must be properly placed within a broader conceptual framework which encompasses the social and political structure in which they operated. The major determinant of this structure in nineteenth-century Peru was the organization of export production, and as this was true for most other Latin American nations, such a focus is a sound beginning for comparative studies of nineteenth-century Latin American politics.

In our stress on the influence of the export sector, it is important to keep in mind that the major political consequences of a nation's integration into international commodity and capital markets works through the existing social processes. Studying these effects thereby requires an investigation of the export sector and its relation to other dimensions of social life that goes considerably beyond the scope of questions that most models of foreign trade and economic development are designed to handle. The economic resources gained by "the nation" through international trade and investment is only one, perhaps relatively minor, aspect of a study of political change that requires knowledge of who received those resources, how they were used, and the manner in which the organization and distribution of political power was affected.[6]

As our discussion of Peru demonstrates, an enclave export sector can have far-reaching effects on national life with little occurring in the purely economic realm. But, again, these effects emanating from the export sector were felt on the organization and distribution of national political power only as mediated by the extant structure of that society.[7] In the early nineteenth century, Peruvian social and political organization was in disarray, and export activity was so important quantitatively that it could deeply influence the direction of qualitative changes. To the degree that other Latin American nations were in a similar position during the nineteenth century, the character of export production is a good vehicle for studying political changes in individual nations and a useful organizing device for comparing them. But these are specific and unusual historical conditions; as the societies became more complex, their mediating effect became stronger, and the ability of the export sector to exert decisive influence on the shape and direction of national affairs declined.

## NOTES

1. Wilson (1967) has written an excellent survey of European mercantilism which brings out the peculiar narrowness of Spanish colonial aims, and Piel (1970: 112-114), Mörner (1970: 92-93), Pike (1967: 24-29), and Service (1955: 415-418) discuss the manner in which Spanish colonial policy and the pre-conquest organization of indigenous societies were reflected in the character of the colonial state in Peru.

2. Griffin (1949) surveys the destructiveness of the Spanish American wars of independence; Furtado (1970: 19-34) describes the early-nineteenth-century market conditions for Latin American exports; and Wolf and Hanson (1967) present a suggestive model for the rise and operation of caudillo politics in early-nineteenth-century Latin

America. For the good fit between these general, comparative portrayals and the specific conditions within early-nineteenth-century Peru, see Basadre (1963b: 552-555), Piel (1970: 116-120), Romero (1967: 9-10, 43), and Kubler (1952: 2, 6-7).

3. Contemporary Peruvians recognized the full political and social importance of the guano revenues; in 1858, the Peruvian Finance Minister stated, "So great is the value of this branch of natural riches that without exaggeration it may be affirmed that on its estimation and good handling depend the subsistence of the State, the maintenance of its credit, the future of its income, and the preservation of public order." Cited by Mathew (1970: 12).

4. For the particular mechanisms by which a growing export sector can transmit growth impulses to domestic economic activity, see Baldwin (1956), Caves (1971), and Roemer (1970: 3-38).

5. Marx (1973: 502-515) makes a penetrating distinction between money and capital, the latter requiring the presence of a wage labor market. This pertains directly to the plight of the compensated Peruvian slaveholders who had money but were unable to hire workers for their plantations.

6. Meier (1968), Singer (1950), and Frank (1969: 1-120) demonstrate how widely diverging conclusions are possible from a narrow focus on economic resources.

7. Thus our approach must be sharply distinguished from those which impute some peculiar potency to international economic relations. Frank (1972) is a good example of this ahistorical formulation.

## REFERENCES

BALDWIN, R. E. (1956) "Patterns of trade and development in newly settled regions." Manchester School of Economic and Social Studies 24: 161-179.

BASADRE, J. (1964) Historia de la República del Perú, Vol. 4. Lima: Ediciones Historia.

———(1963a) Historia de la República del Perú, Vol. 3. Lima: Ediciones Historia.

———(1963b) Historia de la República del Perú, Vol. 2. Lima: Ediciones Historia.

BOURRICAUD, G. (1970) Power and Society in Contemporary Peru. New York: Praeger.

CAVES, R. E. (1971) "The export-led growth model as a research tool in economic history," pp. 403-422 in J. Bhagwati (ed.) Trade, Balance of Payments and Growth. Amsterdam: North Holland Publishing Co.

COTLER, J. (1970) "Traditional haciendas and communities in a context of political mobilization in Peru," in R. Stavenhagen (ed.) Agrarian Problems and Peasant Movements in Latin America. New York: Anchor.

DEAN, W. (1969) The Industrialization of São Paulo, 1880-1945. Austin: Univ. of Texas Press.

FERRER, A. (1967) The Argentine Economy. Berkeley and Los Angeles: Univ. of California Press.

FRANK, A. G. (1972) Lumpenbourgeoisie: Lumpendevelopment. Dependence, Class, and Politics in Latin America. New York: Monthly Review Press.

———(1969) Capitalism and Underdevelopment in Latin America. New York: Monthly Review Press.

FURTADO, C. (1970) Economic Development of Latin America. Cambridge, Eng.: Cambridge Univ. Press.
———(1965) The Economic Growth of Brazil. Berkeley and Los Angeles: Univ. of California Press.
GOODSELL, C. (1974) American Corporations and Peruvian Politics. Cambridge, MA: Harvard Univ. Press.
GREENHILL, R. G. and R. M. MILLER (1973) "The Peruvian government and the nitrate trade, 1873-1879." J. of Latin Amer. Studies 5: 107-131.
GRIFFIN, C. C. (1949) "Economic and social aspects of the era of Spanish American independence." Hispanic Amer. Historical Rev. 29: 170-187.
KLAREN, P. (1973) Modernization, Dislocation and Aprismo. Austin: Univ. of Texas Press.
KUBLER, G. (1952) The Indian Caste of Peru, 1795-1940. Washington, DC: Smithsonian Institution.
LEVIN, J. V. (1960) The Export Economic. Cambridge, MA: Harvard Univ. Press.
McCOY, T. L. (1971) "Congress, the president and political instability in Peru," in W. H. Agor (ed.) Latin American Legislatures: Their Role and Influence. New York: Praeger.
MARX, K. (1973) Grundrisse. New York: Vintage.
MATHEW, W. M. (1972) "Foreign contractors and the Peruvian government at the outset of the guano trade." Hispanic Amer. Historical Rev. 52: 598-620.
———(1970) "Peru and the British guano market, 1840-1870." Economic History Rev. 23: 113-128.
———(1968) "The imperialism of free trade: Peru, 1820-1870." Economic History Rev. 21: 562-579.
MEIER, G. M. (1968) The International Economics of Development. New York: Harper & Row.
MISHKIN, B. (1963) "The contemporary Quechua," in H. Steward (ed.) The Handbook of South American Indians, Vol. 2. New York: Cooper Square Publishers.
MORNER, M. (1970) Race Mixture in the History of Latin America. Boston: Little, Brown.
PAYNE, J. (1965) Labor and Politics in Peru. New Haven, CT: Yale Univ. Press.
PIEL, J. (1970) "The place of the peasantry in the national life of Peru in the nineteenth century." Past and Present 46: 108-133.
PIKE, F. (1967) The Modern History of Peru. New York: Praeger.
PINELO, A. (1973) The Multinational Corporation as a Force in Latin American Politics: A Case Study of the IPC in Peru. New York: Praeger.
ROEMER, M. (1970) Fishing for Growth: Export-Led Development in Peru, 1950-1967. Cambridge, MA: Harvard Univ. Press.
ROMERO, E. (1967) Historia Económica del Perú, Vol. 2. Lima: Editorial Universo.
ROMERO, J. L. (1963) A History of Argentine Political Thought. Stanford, CA: Stanford Univ. Press.
SERVICE, E. R. (1955) "Indo-European relations in colonial Latin America." Amer. Anthropologist 57: 411-425.
SINGER, H. W. (1950) "The distribution of gains between investing and borrowing nations." Amer. Economic Rev.—Papers and Proceedings 40: 473-485.
STEWART, W. (1951) Chinese Bondage in Peru. Durham, NC: Duke Univ. Press.

WILSON, C. H. (1967) "Trade, society and the state," pp. 487-575 in E. E. Rich and C. H. Wilson (eds.) Cambridge Economic History of Europe, Vol. 4. Cambridge, Eng.: Cambridge Univ. Press.

WOLF, E. R. and E. C. HANSON (1967) "Caudillo politics: a structural analysis." Comparative Studies in Society and History 9: 168-179.

YEPES DEL CASTILLO, E. (1972) Perú 1920-1920: Un Siglo de Desarrollo Capitalista. Lima: Instituto de Estudios Peruanos.

*Ronald H. Berg is currently a graduate student in the Department of Anthropology, University of Michigan, and was a paralegal worker for VISTA in New Jersey prior to going to Michigan.*

*Frederick Stirton Weaver has taught economics and history at Cornell, the University of California at Santa Cruz, and Hampshire College, where he is Dean of the School of Social Sciences.*

# REVIEW ESSAY

## *MEXICO'S FOREIGN POLICY—INDEED A FOREIGN POLICY?*

*Pellicer de Brody, Olga. MEXICO Y LA REVOLUCION CUBANA. México: El Colegio de México, 1972.*

*Centro de Estudios Internacionales, ed. LA POLITICA EXTERIOR DE MEXICO: REALIDAD Y PERSPECTIVAS. México: El Colegio de México, 1972.*

*Centro de Estudios Internacionales, ed. MEXICO Y AMERICA LATINA: LA NUEVA POLITICA EXTERIOR. México: El Colegio de México, 1974.*

*Ojeda Gómez, Mario. ALCANCES Y LIMITES DE LA POLITICA EXTERIOR DE MEXICO. México: El Colegio de México, 1976.*

All four titles reviewed in this essay were published during the administration of President Echeverría. This is hardly accidental, since that was exactly the time when, for the first time, Mexican foreign policy had some weight in the international system. At the same time, the members of El Colegio de México who wrote the contributions to the reviewed books became influential in the formulation of Mexico's foreign policy, some in their capacity as advisers and others as critics.

Both the monographs and the collection of essays reflect the problems of Mexico's new role in the international system, as well as the scepticism of the authors with regard to the form in which the Echeverría administration tried to achieve its foreign policy goals. An important aspect that can be traced through all of the studies is the new preoccupation with Latin America and the Third World in general. Contrary to the traditional preoccupation with the "Colossus of the North," since approximately 1970 Mexico has taken an increasing interest in the development of the other Latin American nations and the new nations of the Caribbean. The parallel development of a new consciousness as a member—and an important one as it is—of the Third World, has given Mexican foreign policy a new kind of drive. This is not quite as strange as it appeared at first to some observers inside and outside of Mexico, as it can easily be argued that Mexico, in its relationship with the United States, has given an exemplary demonstration of handling problems between nations of the First and the Third World.

The common denominator of the studies under review can be found in the manner in which foreign policy problems have been integrated into or at least related to the domestic problem of the political crisis within the Mexican system. Almost all authors measure the impact of Mexican foreign policy behavior against its domestic function. The use of foreign policy as a means for internal change should not be seen in a short-term context, but rather as a possibility for gradual change within a rigid domestic political structure.

It seems to be significant to question not only the specific content of Mexican foreign policy during the Echeverría administration but also the analysis derived from this policy by the researchers of the Colegio de México. Contrary to countries like Brazil, the Mexican concept of its place within the international system or its project of a regional hegemonic role is not as important as its efforts to condition the internal political development by employment of external factors.

This fact cannot be applied solely to the unusual expansion of foreign activity during the Echeverría administration, but must also be traced back to the origins of the Mexican revolution. The important role external factors have played during and after the revolution and the critical situation which derived from the cooperation of external and internal linkage groups (for a general analysis, see Chalmers, 1969) with regard to the gains of the revolution have contributed enormously to the Mexican understanding of foreign policy. This is equally true with regard to the traditionally moralistic and legalistic policy of defending national sovereignty as well as to the almost hectic or at least activistic Third World policy which Mexico pursued during the Echeverría administration. The principles and experiences of its own revolution have indeed been projected into Mexico's foreign policy behavior. James F. Engel has aptly said: "Mexican foreign policy, it may be simply stated, is an extension into international affairs of principles and practices developed and tested in the Mexican revolution" (1969: 532). Examples for this way of acting in the realm of foreign policy can be found especially in Mexico's campaign in favor of the "Charter of the Economic Rights and Duties of States." The impact of the Mexican revolution on foreign policy behavior also explains why Mexico has always been attracted to other revolutionary regimes. This applies to the Soviet Union, to Republican Spain, to revolutionary Cuba, and to the Chile of Allende.

This type of foreign policy can hardly be regarded as untypical; the Soviet Union or—to choose a Latin American example—Cuba have over certain periods of time employed a very similar foreign policy strategy. The problem which arises in this context is twofold: Does such a concept of foreign policy lead to the desired results? Does such an understanding of foreign policy behavior—and this is especially true of the studies reviewed here—restrain the analysis of true foreign policy activities?

The first of the studies under review, *México y la Revolución Cubana*, is an outstanding example for the very specific interpretation of Mexican foreign policy by a Mexican social scientist. By far the largest part of the book is concerned with the impact of the Cuban revolution on Mexican domestic policy; the impact on Mexican foreign policy is treated by the author as being of secondary importance. There is no doubt that the Cuban revolution has, in many respects, been of considerable importance to Mexico. Its impact on Mexico's foreign policy can be judged by the interest Mexico began to show for Latin America in general during the administration of López Mateos. Due to the specific Mexican concept of its own revolution, the Cuban revolution has been looked upon with considerable sympathy. It has been viewed, in many respects as the second Latin American revolution, since the Bolivian revolution of 1952 was not generally accepted as having been a true revolution. On the other hand, the radical development of the Cuban revolution constituted an example of what could happen to the Mexican revolution if it were finally completed, as has been promised for decades. The discussion of the Cuban revolution in Mexico, therefore, was not a discussion of a foreign policy phenomenon; rather, it ought to be considered as having been a kind of "shadow-boxing" in which the term "Cuba" at that time was a synonym for the Mexican left, as the term "USA" was for the right. The same arguments were repeated in Mexican politics while discussing Allende's Chile between 1970 and 1973. But that time, the Mexican government, having learned its lesson from the discussion of the Cuban revolution, tried to avoid a similar domestic conflict (see Arriola, 1974).

The excellent study by Olga Pellicer de Brody stresses the domestic implications of Mexico's relations with Cuba in such a way as to integrate nearly all the foreign policy factors into a general analysis of the role of the Cuban revolution for the Mexican political system.

The official policy that Mexico could not break relations with Cuba because of its general adherence to a policy of nonintervention has to be seen in this context. Olga Pellicer de Brody proves very convincingly how unimportant the foreign policy context has been in shaping the relations between Mexico and Cuba. To understand this behavior it is important to know that the progressive image of Mexico abroad has always been used to counterbalance a rather conservative domestic policy vis-à-vis its left-oriented critics. Within the Mexican system, foreign policy very often serves as an escape in case a compromise on domestic policy issues cannot be reached. Because the Mexican system is constantly forced to satisfy: (1) the middle class, which is oriented toward private enterprise and the United States; (2) the "government class," oriented toward state planning and the Third World; (3) the well-organized working class, with slightly leftist leanings; and (4) the influential entrepreneurs, foreign policy is frequently used for political compensation (see Grabendorff, 1976).

The study by Olga Pellicer de Brody has conceptualized this issue in a much better way than the other three books under review. They suggest, though not quite as distinctly, the strong interdependence between Mexico's self-assessment of its revolution, its domestic politics, and its foreign policy behavior. In a later essay, Pellicer de Brody (1975) offers a similarly lucid analysis of the role of Third-Worldism during the Echeverría administration. It would be most useful if the author would develop this analysis into a more general study of Echeverría's foreign policy.

The two books edited by the Centro de Estudios Internacionales are actually reprints of nos. 50 (1972) and 56 (1974) respectively of the prestigious journal *Foro Internacional*, published by El Colegio de México. The articles by Meyer, Pellicer de Brody, Green, Torres, Medina Peña, Sepúlveda Amor, Segovia, Valero (1972) and those by Ojeda Gómez, Medina Luna, Arriola, König, Flores Caballero (1974) offer a good view of the increasing importance of Mexican foreign policy as well as the problems which result from this very fact for Mexican domestic politics. Unfortunately, none of the authors, with the exception of Meyer (1972) gives a general analysis of Mexican foreign policy. The different case studies serve as elements for an understanding of the variety of problems Mexico faces by diversifying its foreign policy. By far the most stimulating article was written by Valero (1972). He does not fail to indicate the possibilities and limitations that Echeverría's new foreign policy was exposed to. In retrospect, his warnings seem to be very much justified.

The second volume concentrates upon the problems of Mexico's foreign policy vis-à-vis Latin America. The essays are marked by considerable more pessimism about Mexico's possibilities than those of the first volume. This can be partly attributed to the fall of Allende in Chile, since there can hardly be any doubt that Echeverría had mainly based his Latin American strategy on strong cooperation with Allende. Echeverría had hoped that the reforms in Chile would to a certain extent positively affect internal politics in Mexico. Arriola's article presents a very thoughtful insight into the development of Mexican-Chilean relations in that period and argues very clearly that "las perspectivas sobre el futuro de la nueva política exterior de México son menos favorables" (1974: 125).

The recently published book by Ojeda Gómez is the first attempt in the last few years to present an overall view of Mexican foreign policy. He is especially perceptive with regard to the limitations with which Mexican foreign policy has to deal. The entire study concentrates mainly on Mexican-U.S. relations, which is hardly surprising taking into consideration Mexico's tremendous dependence on the United States. The wealth of political and economic data offered in his analysis gives evidence of Mexico's restricted leverage in international affairs because of United States hegemony. The obvious irritation of the United States with regard to the foreign policy activities of the Echeverría administration has clearly been demonstrated by a very critical attitude toward its southern neighbor. This low in United States-Mexican relations was much more affected by Mexico's position in the North-South conflict than by direct bilateral problems. The idea that

Mexico could possibly become a leading member of the Third World in fighting U.S. political and economic interests has shocked many U.S. policy makers. The new Mexican president, López Portillo, therefore, has withheld from demonstrating a similarly "radical" foreign policy position as his predecessor Echeverría. In spite of his obvious intentions not to change the general Third World orientation of his country, he has adopted a more low-key strategy in identifying with Third World objectives.

It would be most interesting to speculate about the often-discussed pendulum theory in regard to Mexican foreign policy. Such a pendulum could easily be detected in the foreign policy behavior of López Mateos as compared to Díaz Ordaz. There are at least some indications that the same holds true of Echeverría and López Portillo. But the question has to be raised whether the foreign policy behavior can be isolated from the general political profile of a Mexican president and/or his administration. It appears to be more likely that the foreign policy differences between two presidents are more obvious than the domestic differences, since it is much easier to stress a different profile in a foreign policy context than in domestic politics where the rigid system of the PRI permits only a limited presidential leverage.

The penetrating analysis by Ojeda Gómez leaves one important question open: why does not Mexico pursue a "truly" independent foreign policy? When asking this question, the three most important factors restraining such a project have to be taken into account: the continuous preoccupation with its own uncompleted revolution; the overwhelming neighborhood with the United States; and the necessity to guarantee by all means the internal political consensus. If Mexican foreign policy has to be regarded—as during the Echeverría administration—as an extension of revolutionary principles and practices, as an instrument of defense against the United States, and as a factor of stabilization for the internal political system, it can hardly qualify as a *real* foreign policy.

There can be little doubt that because of its problems with the political, social, and economic model, Mexico must continue to use its foreign policy as a factor of internal stabilization. It is especially relevant in this context that all four publications under review carry this message home, some in an explicit manner, others implicitly.

Unfortunately, most scholarly works about Mexican foreign policy concentrate on Mexico's relationship with the United States. Again, most of them are written from a U.S. perspective. Ojeda Gómez's excellent study demonstrates that the same can be done from the Mexican point of view. What is missing in Ojeda's as well as the other studies is a concept of Mexico's role as a middle power in the global system (Vela, 1975). This is all the more incomprehensible since Mexico has been viewed as a very responsible actor within the international system for several decades. But obviously the United States has become or continues to be of such overriding importance for Mexico that very little thought is given to its regional position in Central America (except Medina Luna, 1974) and in the Caribbean.

The future position of Mexico as an important oil-exporting country will make studies on its regional impact as necessary as on its position within the North-South conflict. The studies by El Colegio de México reveal that Mexico is still much more preoccupied with its domestic political scene and the problems of its very own political system. Therefore, it still does not seem to have a coherent conception or even a general vision of its international role.

—*Wolf Grabendorff*

## REFERENCES

ARRIOLA, C. (1974) "El acercamiento mexicano-chileno," pp. 83-125 in Centro de Estudios Internacionales (ed.) México y América Latina: La Nueva Política Exterior. México: El Colegio de México.

CHALMERS, D. A. (1969) "Developing on the periphery: external factors in Latin American politics," pp. 67-93 in J. N. Rosenau (ed.) Linkage Politics. New York: Free Press.

ENGEL, J. F. (1969) "The Revolution and Mexican Foreign Policy." J. of Inter-American Studies 11, 4: 518-532.

FLORES CABALLERO, R. (1974) "México y el pacto Andino," pp. 161-201 in Centro de Estudios Internacionales (ed.) México y América Latina: La Nueva Política Exterior. México: El Colegio de México.

GRABENDORFF, W. (1976) "Die Aussenpolitik Mexicos und ihre innenpolitischen Ziele." Berichte zur Entwicklung in Spanien, Portugal und Lateinamerika (Munich) 2, 8: 40-48.

GREEN, M. del Rosario (1972) "Deuda pública externa y dependencia: el caso de México," pp. 55-77 in Centro de Estudios Internacionales (ed.) La Política Exterior de México: Realidad y Perspectivas. México: El Colegio de México.

KONIG, W. (1974) "México frente a la ALALC y los otros mecanismos latinoamericanos de integración económica," pp. 127-159 in Centro de Estudios Internacionales (ed.) México y América Latina: La Neuva Política Exterior. México: El Colegio de México.

MEDINA LUNA, R. (1974) "Proyección de México sobre Centroamérica," pp. 9-46 in Centro de Estudios Internacionales (ed.) México y América Latina: La Nueva Política Exterior. México: El Colegio de México.

MEDINA PENA, L. (1972) "Mexico y la politica exterior japonesa: limites y posibilidades," pp. 111-131 in Centro de Estudios Internacionales (ed.) La Política Exterior de México: Realidad y Perspectivas. México: El Colegio de México.

MEYER, L. (1972) "Cambio político y dependencia. México en el siglo XX," pp. 1-38 in Centro de Estudios Internacionales (ed.) La Política Exterior de México: Realidad y Perspectivas. México: El Colegio de México.

OJEDA GOMEZ, M. (1974a) "Presentación: la nueva política de México hacia América Latina," pp. 3-7 in Centro de Estudios Internacionales (ed.) México y América Latina: La Nueva Política Exterior. México: El Colegio de México.

——— (1974b) "Las relaciones de México con el régimen revolucionario cubano," pp. 47-81 in Centro des Estudios Internacionales (ed.) México y América Latina: La Nueva Política Exterior. México: El Colegio de México.

PELLICER DE BRODY, O. (1975) "Tercermundismo del capitalismo mexicano: ideología y realidad." Cuadernos Políticos (México) 3: 52-59.

——— (1972) "Cambios recientes en la política exterior mexicana," pp. 39-54 in Centro de Estudios Internacionales (ed.) La Política Exterior de México: Realidad y Perspectivas. México: El Colegio de México.

SEGOVIA, R. (1972) "Nacionalismo e imagen del mundo exterior en los niños mexicanos," pp. 172-191 in Centro de Estudios Internacionales (ed.) La Política Exterior de México: Realidad y Perspectivas. México: El Colegio de México.

SEPULVEDA AMOR, B. (1972) "Derecho del mar: apuntes sobre el sistema legal mexicano," pp. 132-171 in Centro de Estudios Internacionales (ed.) La Política Exterior de México: Realidad y Perspectivas. México: El Colegio de México.

TORRES, B. (1972) "México en la estructura del comercio y la cooperación internacional de los países socialistas," pp. 78-110 in Centro de Estudios Internacionales (ed.) La Política Exterior de México: Realidad y Perspectivas. México: El Colegio de México.

VALERO, R. (1972) "La política exterior en la coyuntura actual de México," pp. 192-210. in Centro de Estudios Internacionales (ed.) La Política Exterior de México: Realidad y Perspectivas. México: El Colegio de México.

VELA S., E. H. (1975) "Cual debe ser la política internacional de México?" Relaciones Internacionales (México) 3, 11: 25-38.

*Wolf Grabendorff is a Research Associate for Latin American Affairs at Stiftung Wissenschaft und Politik (Research Institute for International Affairs) at Ebenhausen. He has recently acted as policy advisor for Latin America to the West German government and at present is completing a study on Mexican foreign policy. He is editor of the recent* Latin America and the Third World, *and author of numerous articles on contemporary foreign policy of Latin American nations.*

# REVIEW ESSAY

## *ON THE VIRTUES OF TOTAL SUBMERSION*
### *An Essay on the Trials and Tribulations of Development Literature Through the Bright Light of a New Product*

*Wiarda, Howard J. DICTATORSHIP, DEVELOPMENT AND DISINTEGRATION: POLITICS AND SOCIAL CHANGE IN THE DOMINICAN REPUBLIC. 3 Volumes. Ann Arbor, MI: Xerox University Microfilms, Monograph Series, 1975.*

All nations, rich and poor, have a tendency to remind themselves that history is a playground in which the rules of the game often have nothing to do with either conduct or outcome. Being at play in the fields of the Lord means harshness mixed with expectation, brutality with societal charm, and collective hope vicariously traded for individualized despair and a sense of futility. A journey to the Dominican Republic—to Santo Domingo—is a journey through the endless accounts of the agonies of existence.

History's assignment and perjorative verdict have not been kind. As in most human affairs, evaluation and value judgment come first, followed by knowledge, facts, and exposure later, if at all. Therefore, perhaps we do know that the Dominican Republic is part of the Caribbean islands where Columbus lies buried and where the Arawaks lived only for some twenty years after initial exposure to Spanish rule. It is a land that has been lumped conveniently into the collective dustbin of "banana republics," featuring brutal tin-horn dictators and the vulgarization of life randomly shared by all in a society of despair. The outer layer and inner-core hid nothing, betrayed nothing, and pleased no one except those few who managed to stay above the quagmire of societal malaise—usually at the expense of those treading the dreary mill of life below. As this author observed in the mid-sixties, while working in the countryside of the Dominican Republic, "In Villarpando there was no church, no priest and no God . . . just poverty, despair, and the agony of existence."

But how does a country become a "banana republic"? How does one unify, explain, and rationalize a history of poverty, social degradation, and political brutality of unprecedented magnitude? Who sells the tickets to the cruelest show in town, and who are the ticket-takers at the gates of economic dependency, political subservience, and international buffoonery? What are the possible departures, where are the development strategy openings, the policy options, and the faint rays of hope for a people to effect a "take-off" toward a minimal measure of self-determination, toward minimal improvement in the conditions of life and social dignity?

Professor Howard Wiarda chose one of the most difficult of all when he took on the case of the Dominican Republic. This massive (1,921 pages) and monumental masterpiece is, in my opinion, the finest diary of the "agonies of existence"—one of measured composure and brilliant workmanship. Of the few who have worked in this beautiful and unfortunate land, Wiarda above all knows his history, facts, and universe as it was, is, and perhaps as it likely will be in the future. But that is not all. Wiarda knows his heart, his sentiments, and his gut feelings. He is no "salon revolutionary" or *kaffeklatsch* leftist expounding on a never-never world in which the McLuhanesque dictate glorifies the manipulator while the manipulated—in this case the poor masses of society—continue to eke out the barest existence at the lowest price to those nominally representing their interest.

Wiarda has done his homework admirably. He knows what is important conceptually, and in specifics. His sense of evaluative criticism lends a great deal of dignity to the value judgments he forms and expresses in this volume. Doing so, he also puts the reader at ease in terms of linking history, contemporary events, conflict, and conversion with that of his own judgment, feelings, and sentiments.

It is, therefore, quite clear that I have a high esteem for the writer personally and professionally. Obviously I like and value this work, what it represents, and the way it presents itself. So let me set aside the praise and joy of a pleasant intellectual surprise and continue with some thoughts that emerge from reading the volume regarding the intellectual, scholarly and, alas, market values of such publishing ventures, and also comment on the possible adjustments that future authors and publishers of this type and size of study might consider. To do so, I will inevitably sail into the dangerous labyrinth of evaluating the "state of the art" in terms of the development literature, especially as it pertains to the world of Latin America and the Caribbean. Without doing so, any and all criticism of such ventures remains an empty intellectual nit-picking exercise, one, alas, in which the academic community rejoices. But on with the clearing of the underbrush!

"Is statistics lovelier than a poem?" queried the poet with some inner sense of despair. Of course, I suppose the answer depends on one's perspective and objectives. In drawing on the past to explain the present and to project this into the future, the "development community" has not been effective in integrating the microphenomenon with the macro, the economic with the political, the societal with the interpersonal, and the individual.

Where do we fail? Why is it so difficult to integrate the economic with the social and the political? Why is it that one—the economic—is considered in terms of its scientific value and orientation, while the other two diddle along with some bashful sense of reverence bordering on self-pity? It seems to me that the problems the development community faces are those of the human use of information and data about human activity and its consequences, the difficulty arising from sorting out and identifying what is economic, political, or social—or for that matter, merely explaining and justifying why these phenomena should be considered as distinct from the way we conceive of public policy, its formulation, meaning, and implementation—and finally, the manner with which we tend to sweep under the rug of intellectual arrogance the changes that appear on the micro level of society.

Let me take up these points one by one. To state that the basic preoccupation of writers on development has been characterized by an excessive sense of ethnocentrism is merely to elaborate on the obvious. The way we organize our research work on issues ranging from agriculture to urbanization tends to reflect on value judgments we make regarding what is important, what should be studied, how, and what research methods should be used. Naturally, times have changed from the days when the foreign researcher trooped about "observing and researching" the natives, leaving behind nothing but a trail of bewildering self-importance shrouded in the mist of scientism, teaching no one and understanding even less. Now we are more attuned to the niceties of "collaborative ventures" and "institutional exchanges of research technologies," the like of which provide for some learning, some true transfer of educational-research technologies, and certainly for mutual exposure to worlds far apart in structure and composition, but often amazingly close in problems. Still, the data, the information, the "photo-flashes of life" we are searching for, often are not those that might hold the most direct answer in exploring the problems of underdevelopment.

Wiarda's three-volume work is a reasonably well-balanced storehouse of data collection on which his narrative, conclusions, and analysis are based. It seems unfair to draw comparisons with other works that reflect different objectives, work experiences, and levels of exposure to economic, social, and political life. Clearly the "horror story" of misused and, at times, useless data-mania is the one which clutters the archives of the World Bank. Probably what represents the world's greatest collection of project and program experience is growing daily, if for no other reason than to satisfy the system-needs of an institution where attention to social change is called "integrated rural development focus," and where the "bottom line" always justifies the end. Thus, just as World Bank loans do not default, neither does this exceptional collection of human information contribute to social change. It might not be terribly significant, but I find that rather than resembling the international bureaucratic model-builders, the language, concerns, and above all the use of Wiarda's data and information, more closely resemble the approach of an Oscar Lewis or Albert Hirschman—or that of the Inter-American Foundation in its preoccupation to "hear-out" what people in less developed countries think about themselves, described in the foundation's recent description of its activities in . . . *they know how*. . . . It is this *humane use of human information* that qualitatively sets these works apart from the large majority, which represent facts without life and observations without substance.

On the matter of what is of importance in societies in development and change, I would suggest that research leading toward the examination and explanation of the linkages between economic and social developmental processes might be of the greatest practical and pedagogical utility. In terms of my own present value preferences and priorities, talking about the politics of nutrition, energy use, agricultural productivity, and modes of production, as well as alternate medical and educational systems and intermediary technology, is vastly more important for today's student of politics than one more study on political parties, elites, or voting behavior. The need is clearly there to link these problem areas with the manipulative processes of public policy. This, in turn, necessitates the development of criteria by which the "product"—for example, a line of public policy decisions as implemented over time—is evaluated. Therefore, it seems to me that interlinks between the factors of production, resource allocation, skills, and bureaucratic implementative capacities could possibly be forged into a coherent set of observations linking societal preferences with government action. My plea would be to strengthen future volumes, if any are envisaged, in this way: place more focus on public policy, require greater accountability for the impact of resource policy, and provide more commentary on the biopolitical impact of public decisions. Of course, this is easier said than done. To submerge one's self in the totality of the ecology of a country is a lifetime occupation, but perhaps the Wiarda volume is one that might suggest a solution.

Clearly my preference is *not* for a multiauthor volume of an all-inclusive nature. Nor is it for country case studies that emphasize a specific focus or set of methodological predispositions that limit both the universe of data and the range of phenomenon observed and reported. While the Wiarda volume, due to its incredible comprehensiveness, is simply a bit too weighty and burdensome to manage for the reader, its relative weaknesses lie not in the simple magnitude of the things reported about, but rather to *what extent* certain aspects assume an overly copious character in their treatment. If anything, I would argue to shorten the historical narrative and excessive political detail that meander through whole sections, and instead solidify the institutional and political structural part. I would also add more economics in terms of public policy focus and, above all, reach for the available explanations regarding the problems of human existence on a highly personal level. But is this bill of lading an impossible one to process? I do not think so. Excellent and thorough writers, like Wiarda, have been "there," and this volume is almost "there"—at perfection. Somehow if the publishers could only convince the authors to stop chasing the elusive dream of trying to catch up with the intricacies and travesties of daily politics and leave behind the compulsion to report on one more event—idiosyncratic as it may be—we would have a tighter treatment of country cases, a more lucid analysis on a conceptual level, and clearly, to the joy of publisher and reader alike, a speedier appearance on the market.

The Wiarda study is clearly the "baseline" study for all work that students of the Dominican Republic might wish to undertake in the future. Despite the limitations I alluded to, this volume has now become an important source of memory, organization, and reflection on an almost unprecedented scale. I can only hope—and I trust that some of my colleagues share this sentiment—that several more "baseline" studies will be published. One hopes that others might not be country case studies, but rather focus on problem areas such as nutrition, health delivery systems, and so on. By all means, however, the focus should be on the economics, politics, and societal implications without omitting the public policy emphasis. Obviously the Wiarda-type country case study volume does not lend itself easily to classroom use. Its inherent value lies in the way it can blend into the resource and data bank of a class or seminar that seriously intends to attack the analysis of a society's change process in toto. I envisage technical volumes of a similar scope, extent, and depth becoming a veritable resource base for research seminars and advanced courses in the future.

Many institutions of the so-called development community have an extensive "history" but no "memory"; others have "memory" but no recall capability. Is it possible that through publishing ventures such as this, some of those histories and memories can be tapped and made readily available for the student of development and societal change? There is no doubt in my mind that the mechanism for such a proposition is a costly one, but the product at this stage of the art is one that cannot wait any longer for the nodding approval of a marketplace-oriented editorial decision.

The problem remains as to how the product can be subsidized, barring foundation or government assistance. Still, this publication points the way for utilizing vast storehouses of knowledge that are presently neglected. Xerox's effort in launching this trial balloon is most commendable. The real question now is how publishing firms can identify and seek out what is needed in terms of opportunities and market demands, and how to develop criteria for evaluating future volumes.

Howard Wiarda deserves our thanks and recognition because as the result of his travels, observations, and listening, he wrote with imagination, care, and solid objectivity. I am grateful for the good reading and learning—but above all, for having had the opportunity to ramble on at the margins of a fine opus.

*—Arpad von Lazar*

*Arpad von Lazar is Professor of International Development Studies at the Fletcher School of Law and Diplomacy, Tufts University. His major works include* Latin American Politics: A Primer, Reform and Revolution *and "Oil and Development Planning: Implications for Nigeria,"* Energy Policy, *December 1976.*

# BOOKS RECEIVED

## *GENERAL AND REGIONAL LATIN AMERICA*

Dibbaco, Thomas V., ed. PRESIDENTIAL POWERS IN LATIN AMERICAN POLITICS. New York: Praeger, 1977. Index. ix, 124 pp.

Diniz, Artur José Almeida. SUBDESENVOLVIMENTO E DIREITO DAS GENTES. Belo Horizonte, Brasil: Estudos Sociais e Politicos 34, UFMG, 1977. 148 pp. (paper).

Espinosa, J. Manuel. INTERAMERICAN BEGINNINGS OF U.S. CULTURAL DIPLOMACY, 1936-1948. Washington, DC: Bureau of Educational and Cultural Affairs, U.S. Department of State, 1976. Historical Studies No. 2. Map, appendices, index. xvi, 365 pp.

ESTUDIOS LATINOAMERICANOS 3. Warsaw, Poland: Academica de Ciencias de Polonia, Instituto de Historia, 1976. 322 pp. (paper).

Fishlow, Albert. THE MATURE NEIGHBOR POLICY: A NEW UNITED STATES ECONOMIC POLICY FOR LATIN AMERICA. Policy Papers in International Affairs No. 3. Berkeley: Institute of International Studies, University of California, 1977. References (paper).

Gilderhus, Mark T. DIPLOMACY AND REVOLUTION: U.S.-MEXICAN RELATIONS UNDER WILSON AND CARRANZA. Tucson: University of Arizona Press, 1977. Bibliographic essay, chapter notes, index. xiv, 159 pp. $10.50 (cloth), $4.25 (paper).

Inter-American Development Bank. ECONOMIC AND SOCIAL PROGRESS IN LATIN AMERICA. 1976 Report. Washington, DC: 1977. Statistical appendix. 446 pp. (paper).

Naciones Unidas. ESTUDIO ECONOMICODE AMERICA LATINA 1975. Santiago, Chile: Comisión Económica para América Latina, 1976. 430 pp. (paper).

Peterson, Harold F. DIPLOMAT OF THE AMERICAS: A BIOGRAPHY OF WILLIAM I. BUCHANAN (1852-1909). Albany: State University of New York Press, 1977. List of illustrations, notes, bibliography, index. xvi, 458 pp. $40.00.

Thebaud, Schiller.STATISTICS ON SCIENCE AND TECHNOLOGY IN LATIN AMERICA: EXPERIENCE WITH UNESCO PILOT PROJECTS 1972-1974. Paris: Unesco Press, 1976. List of tables, annex. 76 pp. $3.30 (paper).

Truitt, Nancy S. and David H. Blake, with others. OPINION LEADERS AND PRIVATE INVESTMENT: AN ATTITUDE SURVEY IN CHILE AND VENEZUELA. New York: Fund for Multinational Management Education, 1976. Appendices. vi, 125 pp. $5.50 (paper).

Van Der Karr, Jane and Juan Carlos Basile. JOSE INGENIEROS: THE STORY OF A SCIENTIST-HUMANIST. New York: Vantage Press, 1977. 64 pp.

Walton, John. ELITES AND ECONOMIC DEVELOPMENT: COMPARATIVE STUDIES ON THE POLITICAL ECONOMY OF LATIN AMERICAN CITIES. Austin: Latin American Monographs No. 41, Institute of Latin American Studies, University of Texas, 1977. Notes, bibliography, index. 257 pp. $14.95 (cloth), $5.95 (paper).

*ARGENTINA*

Falcoff, Mark and Ronald H. Dolkart, eds. PROLOGUE TO PERON: ARGENTINA IN DEPRESSION AND WAR, 1930-1943. Berkeley: University of California Press, 1976. Notes, bibliographical note, index. 254 pp. $12.00.

Hodges, Donald C. ARGENTINA, 1943-1976: THE NATIONAL REVOLUTION AND RESISTANCE. Albuquerque: University of New Mexico Press, 1976. Appendix, selected bibliography, index. xviii, 207 pp. $9.95 (cloth), $4.95 (paper).

Rock, David, ed. ARGENTINA IN THE TWENTIETH CENTURY. Pittsburgh, PA: University of Pittsburgh Press, 1975. Index. 230 pp. $14.50.

*BOLIVIA*

Taborga, Huascar. MITO Y REALIDAD DE LA UNIVERSIDAD BOLIVIANA. La Paz and Cochabamba, Bolivia: Editorial Los Amigos del Libro, 1970. Tables. 101 pp. (paper).

*BRAZIL*

Graham, Ann Hartness. SUBJECT GUIDE TO STATISTICS IN THE PRESIDENTIAL REPORTS OF THE BRAZILIAN PROVINCES, 1830-1839. Austin: Institute of Latin American Studies, University of Texas, 1977. Abbreviations. 454 pp. $8.95 (paper).

INDICE DO BRAZIL. Brazilian Index Yearbook 1977-1978. Brasilia: Secretaria de Planejamento, 1977. In Portuguese and English. Includes 20 years of Brazilian economy in data. 346 pp.

Lobo, Pelagio A. VELHAS FIGURAS DE SAO PAULO. Sao Paulo: Biblioteca Academia Paulista de Letras, Vol. 5, 1977. 268 pp. (paper).

Nuñes Leal, Victor. CORONELISMO: THE MUNICIPALITY AND REPRESENTATIVE GOVERNMENT IN BRAZIL. New York: Cambridge University Press, Cambridge Latin American Studies No. 28, 1977. Notes, bibliography. 237 pp. $16.95.

Raffard, Henrique. ALGUNS DIAS NA PAULICEIA. São Paulo: Biblioteca Academia Paulista de Letras, Vol. 4, 1977. 109 pp. (paper).

Schneider, Ronald M. BRAZIL: FOREIGN POLICY OF A FUTURE WORLD POWER. Boulder, CO: Westview Press, 1977. Bibliographic essay, index. xix, 236 pp. $16.50.

Universidade Federal de Minas Gerais. IV SEMINARIO DE ESTUDOS MINEIROS. Ediçoes do Cinquentenario da UFMG 1. Belo Horizonte, Brasil: Universidade Federal de Minas Gerais, 1977. 260 pp. (paper).

Wagley, Charles. WELCOME OF TEARS: THE TAPIRAPE INDIANS OF CENTRAL BRAZIL. New York: Oxford University Press, 1977. Glossary, kinship charts, references, index. xx, 328 pp. $12.95.

Wigder, Roberta C. BRAZIL REDISCOVERED. Philadelphia and Ardmore, PA: Dorrance and Co., 1977. 486 pp. $10.00.

*CARIBBEAN REGION*

Brunner, Henrich. CUBAN SUGAR POLICY FROM 1963 TO 1970. Pittsburgh, PA: University of Pittsburgh Press, 1977. Tables, notes, bibliography, index. ix, 163 pp. $9.95.

Carter, Purvis M. CONGRESSIONAL AND PUBLIC REACTION TO WILSON'S CARIBBEAN POLICY, 1913-1917. New York: Vantage Press, 1977. Notes, bibliography, index. 164 pp. $7.95.

García-Zamor, Jean-Claude. THE ECOLOGY OF DEVELOPMENT ADMINISTRATION IN JAMAICA, TRINIDAD AND TOBAGO, AND BARBADOS. OAS: Program of Development Financing, General Secretariat, 1977. Bibliography, index. 122 pp. (paper).

*CENTRAL AMERICA*

Asturias, Miguel Angel. GUATEMALAN SOCIOLOGY. English and Spanish. Tempe: Arizona State University, Center for Latin American Studies, 1977. 106 pp. (paper).

Bray, Wayne D. THE COMMON LAW ZONE IN PANAMA: A CASE STUDY IN RECEPTION. Some observations on the relevancy to the Panama Canal Treaty controversy. Bibliography, cases cited, index, illustrations. 150 pp. $20.00.

Creedman, Theodore S. HISTORICAL DICTIONARY OF COSTA RICA. Metuchen, NJ: Scarecrow Press, 1977. Latin American Historical Dictionaries No. 16. Bibliography. 262 pp.

DeWitt, Jr., R. Peter. THE INTERAMERICAN DEVELOPMENT BANK AND POLITICAL INFLUENCE: WITH SPECIAL REFERENCE TO COSTA RICA. New York and London: Praeger, 1977. List of tables, figures, acronyms, selected bibliography, index, appendix. 197 pp.

GUATEMALA INDIGENA. Guatemala: Instituto Indigenista Nacional, Vol. X, 1975, 187 pp. Vol. XI, 1976, 210 pp. (paper).

Markman, Sidney David. COLONIAL CENTRAL AMERICA: A BIBLIOGRAPHY. Tempe: Center for Latin American Studies, Arizona State University, 1977. Index of authors. 345 pp.

Millett, Richard. GUARDIANS OF THE DYNASTY: A HISTORY OF THE U.S. CREATED GUARDIA NACIONAL DE NICARAGUA AND THE SOMOZA FAMILY. Maryknoll, NY: Orbis Books, 1977. Appendix, bibliographical note, index. 284 pp. $6.95.

Sanchíz Ochoa, Pilar. LOS HIDALGOS DE GUATEMALA: REALIDAD Y APARIENCIA EN UN SISTEMA DE VALORES. Sevilla, Spain: Publicaciones de la Universidad de Sevilla, serie del Seminario de Antropología Americana, Vol. 13, 1976. Bibliografía, fuentes documentales, índice. 193 pp. (paper).

*CHILE*

Behrman, Jere R. FOREIGN TRADE REGIMES AND ECONOMIC DEVELOPMENT: CHILE. A Special Conference Series on Foreign Trade Regimes and

Economic Development Vol. VIII. New York: National Bureau of Economic Research, Inc., 1976. Appendix, bibliography, index. xxv, 408 pp.

de Vylder, Stefan. ALLENDE'S CHILE: THE POLITICAL ECONOMY OF THE RISE AND FALL OF THE UNIDAD POPULAR. New York: Cambridge University Press, Cambridge Latin American Studies No. 25, 1976. $13.95.

Donoso Loero, Teresa. LOS CRISTIANOS POR EL SOCIALISMO EN CHILE. Santiago, Chile: Editorial Vaitea, 1976, tercera edicion aumentada y complementada con abundante material grafico y documentacion. Indice, perfiles, bibliograficos, bibiografia. 314 pp. (paper).

Frei, Eduardo. THE MANDATE OF HISTORY AND CHILE'S FUTURE. Papers in International Studies, Latin America Series No. 1. Athens: Ohio University Center for International Studies, Latin American Program, 1977. Lists other major publications by Eduardo Frei Montalva. vi, 79 pp. $4.00 (paper).

Gil, Federico G., Ricardo Lagos E., Henry A. Landberger et al. CHILE 1970-1973: LECCIONES DE UNA EXPERIENCIA. Madrid: Editorial Tecnos, 1977. 470 pp. (paper).

Gelcich, Sergio, with text by Ahyd Custodo Gonzalez. CHILE. This selective and professional photographic portrait of Chile from the northern altiplano to the antarctic, prepared for distribution to the general public, is the best short presentation of one nation's landscape known to the author. The Hague, The Netherlands: Pacific Ores and Trading B.V., Nassaulaan 23, 1975. $9.00 FOB Holland.

Moran, Theodore H. MULTINATIONAL CORPORATIONS AND THE POLITICS OF DEPENDENCE: COPPER IN CHILE. Princeton, NJ: Princeton University Press, 1974. List of tables, statistical appendix, bibliography, index. xiv, 286 pp. $4.25 (paper).

Roxborough, Ian, Phil O'Brien, and Jackie Roddick. CHILE: THE STATE AND REVOLUTION. New York: Holmes & Meier Publishers, 1976. Postscript, chronology, notes, select bibliography, index. x, 304 pp. $20.00.

*ECUADOR*

Bromley, R. J. DEVELOPMENT PLANNING IN ECUADOR. London: Grant and Cutler Ltd., 1977. Latin American Publications Fund. Tables, figures, bibliography. ix, 116 pp. $2.80 (paper).

*MEXICO*

Alonso, Jorge. LA DIALECTICA CLASES-ELITES IN MEXICO. México, D.F.: Centro de Investigaciones Superiores, Ediciones de La Casa Chata, 1976. Apendices, bibliografía. 255 pp. (paper).

Bazant, Jan. A CONCISE HISTORY OF MEXICO FROM HIDALGO TO CARDENAS 1805-1940. New York: Cambridge University Press, 1977. Statistical tables, chronology, notes, index. x, 222 pp. $14.95 (cloth), $4.95 (paper).

Fernández, Raúl A. THE UNITED STATES-MEXICO BORDER: A POLITICO-ECONOMIC PROFILE. Notre Dame, IN: University of Notre Dame Press, 1977. Notes, index. 174 pp. $10.95.

Grindle, Merilee S. BUREAUCRATS, POLITICIANS, AND PEASANTS IN MEXICO: A CASE STUDY IN PUBLIC POLICY. Berkeley: University of California Press, 1977. Glossary of acronyms, appendices, bibliography, index. xix, 239 pp. $12.50.

Meyer, Lorenzo. MEXICO AND THE UNITED STATES IN THE OIL CONTROVERSY, 1917-1942. Austin: University of Texas Press, 1977. Appendix, notes, sources cited, index. 367 pp. $19.95.

*PARAGUAY*

Ferraro, Oscar. DATOS Y ESTUDIOS SOBRE EDUCACION EN EL PARAGUAY. Asunción: Centro Paraguayo de Estudios Sociológicos, Serie bibliográfica 1976. 71 pp. (paper).

Rivarola, Domingo M. et al. LA POBLACION DEL PARAGUAY. Asunción: Centro Paraguayo de Estudios Sociológicos, 1974. Indice. 194 pp. (paper).

*PERU*

Burneo, Jose, Adolfo Ciudad, and Luis Pasara. EMPLEO Y ESTABILIDAD LABORAL. Lima: DESCO, Serie Praxis, 1976. Anexo, decreto ley No. 18471. 204 pp.

Kuczynski, Pedro-Pablo. PERUVIAN DEMOCRACY UNDER ECONOMIC STRESS: AN ACCOUNT OF THE BELAUNDE ADMINISTRATION, 1963-1968. Princeton, NJ: Princeton University Press, 1977. List of tables, statistical appendix, bibliography, index, map. xiv, 308 pp. $16.50.

Losada, Alejandro. CREACION Y PRAXIS: LA PRODUCCION LITERARIA COMO PRAXIS SOCIAL EN HISPANOAMERICA Y EL PERU. Lima: Universidad Nacional Mayor de San Marcos, 1976. 289 pp. (paper).

Otero, Carlos, Luis Jiménez, and Alicia Reyes. ECONOMIA POLITICA: ELEMENTOS BASICOS. Lima: DESCO, 1977. 228 pp. (paper).

Pease García, Henry, Diego García-Sayán, Fernando Eguren López, y Marcial Rubio Correa. ESTADO Y POLITICA AGRARIA. Lima: DESCO, 1977. 351 pp. (paper).

Pease García, Henry and Alfredo Filomeno. PERU 1975: CRONOLOGIA POLITICA, Tomo IV. This fourth volume of the exceptional series published by DESCO is even more detailed than its predecessors. The series is paginated continuously from Volume I and each entry is numbered consecutively starting with Volume I. There is an imaginatively organized and complete index to facilitate the use of this source book, unique, in the experience of the editor, for any Latin American nation. Lima: DESCO, 1977. Indice, xviii, 516 pp. (paper).

van den Berghe, Pierre L. and George P. Primov. INEQUALITY IN THE PERUVIAN ANDES: CLASS AND ETHNICITY IN CUZCO. Columbia: University of Missouri Press, 1977. Methodology, note on Quechua orthography, statistics, glossary, bibliography, index. 324 pp. $17.50.

*VENEZUELA*

Dessau, Ralph. LOS TUCUSITOS DE CARACAS. Caracas: Concejo Municipal del Distrito Federal, 1977. 159 pp.

Fulgencio López, Casto, Américo Briceño Valero, and Elías Pérez Sosa. LA GUAYRA: PRESENTE Y PASADO. Caracas: Concejo Municipal del Distrito Federal, 1976. Indice. 218 pp.

Montenegro, Juan Ernesto. LA CAPILLA DE SANTA ROSA DE LIMA. Caracas: Concejo Municipal del Distrito Federal, 1977. 333 pp.

Nazoa, Aquiles. CARACAS FISICA Y ESPIRITUAL. Caracas: Concejo Municipal del Distrito Federal, 1977. 271 pp.

*MISCELLANEOUS*

Aveni, Anthony F., ed. NATIVE AMERICAN ASTRONOMY. Austin and London University of Texas Press, 1977. References, index. xvii, 286 pp. $15.95.

Aviel, JoAnn Fagot. RESOURCE SHORTAGES AND WORLD POLITICS. Washington, DC: University Press of America, 1977. ii, 157 pp. $7.75 (paper).

Barzel, Yoram and Christopher D. Hall. THE POLITICAL ECONOMY OF THE OIL IMPORT QUOTA. Stanford, CA: Hoover Institution Press, 1977. Illustrations, tables, bibliography, index. xiii, 96 pp. $8.95.

Crozier, Brian, ed. ANNUAL OF POWER AND CONFLICT 1976-77: A SURVEY OF POLITICAL VIOLENCE AND INTERNATIONAL INFLUENCE. London: Institute for the Study of Conflict, 1977. 356 pp.

Heizer, Robert F. and Alan J. Almquist. THE OTHER CALIFORNIANS: PREJUDICE AND DISCRIMINATION UNDER SPAIN, MEXICO, AND THE UNITED STATES TO 1920. Berkeley: University of California Press, 1977. 289 pp. $3.95 (paper).

Kim, Choong Soon. AN ASIAN ANTHROPOLOGIST IN THE SOUTH: FIELD EXPERIENCES WITH BLACKS, INDIANS, AND WHITES. Knoxville: University of Tennessee Press, 1977. Prologue, notes, bibliography, index. 155 pp. $8.95.

STRATEGIC STUDIES REFERENCE GUIDE. Vol. 1, 1975. First annual edition of significant reference work to social science disciplines related to strategic and conflict studies. Indexes and document descriptions. Pittsburgh, PA: University of Pittsburgh, Center for International Studies, 1977. ix, 232 pp. (paper).

Viqueira, Carmen. PERCEPCION Y CULTURA: UN ENFOQUE ECOLOGICO. México, D.F.: Centro de Investigaciones Superiores del INAH, Ediciones de la Casa Chata 4, 1977. Bibliografía. 319 pp. (paper).

Weisberg, Herbert F. and Bruce D. Bowen. AN INTRODUCTION TO SURVEY RESEARCH AND DATA ANALYSIS. San Francisco: W. H. Freemen and Co., 1977. 19 illustrations, index, x. 243 pp. $10.00 (cloth), $3.95 (paper).

# METROPOLITAN LATIN AMERICA:
# The Challenge and the Response

**Latin American Urban Research, Volume 6**

edited by **WAYNE A. CORNELIUS,** *Massachusetts Institute of Technology*
**ROBERT V. KEMPER,** Southern Methodist University



This volume focuses on the most critical problems confronting nine major Latin American and Caribbean cities, and the actual responses of local and national governments to these problems. Each chapter provides a comprehensive overview of urban development problems and government performance in dealing with them in a single metropolitan area. Contributors also discuss the role of the metropolitan area in regional and national development, and the tensions between government policies aimed at the problems of the metropolitan area and policies for national and regional development. The volume provides indispensible source material for scholars doing research on specific cities as well as an empirical base for comparative urban studies. It also includes a 1,600-item bibliography of studies on urban Latin America published during the 1974-1976 period.

**CONTENTS**

Introduction, WAYNE A. CORNELIUS

**Case Studies**

1. Guadalajara: Creating the Divided City, JOHN WALTON, *Northwestern University*
2. Mexico City: The Emerging Megalopolis, GUSTAVO GARZA, *El Colegio de México* and MARTHA SCHTEINGART, *El Colegio de México*
3. Bogotá: Politics, Planning and the Crisis of Lost Opportunities, ALAN GILBERT, *University College, London*
4. Urban Development and Governmental Response: The Case of Medellin, DAVID W. DENT, *Towson State College*
5. Port-au-Prince: Awakening to the Urban Crisis, SIMON M. FASS
6. Urban Problems and Policy Responses for Metropolitan Guayaquil, RICHARD J. MOORE, *University of Texas, Austin*
7. Metropolitan Lima: Urban Problem-Solving under Military Rule, HENRY A. DIETZ, *University of Texas, Austin*
8. Caracas: The Politics of Intensifying Primacy, DAVID J. MYERS, *Pennsylvania State University*
9. Towards a Development Strategy for Grande Rio de Janeiro, DAVID M. VETTER, *Universidade Federal do Rio de Janeiro* and ANA MARIA BRASILEIRO, *Instituto Brasileiro de Administração*

BIBLIOGRAPHY: RECENT URBAN STUDIES ON LATIN AMERICA (1974-1976)

**February 1978** **352 pages** **ISBN 0-8039-0661-7** **hardcover** **$18.50**

SAGE Publications, Inc.
275 South Beverly Drive
Beverly Hills, California 90212

SAGE Publications Ltd
28 Banner Street
London EC1Y 8QE

Vol. 20 No. 2
May 1978

# OURNAL OF NTERAMERICAN STUDIES

# nd ORLD AFFAIRS

A Publication of the Center for Advanced International Studies,

The University of Miami

SAGE PUBLICATIONS

*Journal of INTERAMERICAN STUDIES and WORLD AFFAIRS*



The editors and publisher wish to acknowledge with gratitude the assistance and encouragement of the Center for Advanced International Studies, University of Miami, in providing ancillary services and support for this journal.

*Journal of*
INTERAMERICAN
STUDIES
*and* WORLD AFFAIRS

Vol. 20
No. 2
May
1978

# CONTENTS

*La Campaña Permanente: Mexico's Antidrug Campaign*
RICHARD B. CRAIG 107

*Guyana: Socialist Reconstruction or Political Opportunism?*
RALPH R. PREMDAS 133

*Diaz' Executive Agents and United States Foreign Policy*
WILLIAM E. GIBBS 165

*The Peasants as a Revolutionary Class: An Early Latin American View*
HARRY E. VANDEN 191

---

**REVIEW ESSAY**

*Argentina at the Crossroads*
ALBERTO CIRIA 211

**BOOKS RECEIVED** 221

SAGE PUBLICATIONS / *Beverly Hills* *London*

**POLICY: THE JOURNAL OF INTERAMERICAN STUDIES AND WORLD AFFAIRS** reflects the interests of the scholarly community and interested public concerned with the social, economic, political, and cultural aspects of life in Latin America (including the Caribbean); particularly in those instances where the subject is of concern to more than one of the traditional disciplines. As these concerns change, so will the content of the journal.

**ARTICLES** which have special relevance for interrelationships between American nations and of those nations with the rest of the world will be given special consideration. An effort will be made to include occasional articles that state an unusual or even discordant position on a subject of broad interest to be supplemented by critical comments of authorities representing differing positions on the topic. The editors continue to welcome articles by scholars from all parts of the world.

**MANUSCRIPTS** should be submitted in duplicate to: Editor, JOURNAL OF INTER-AMERICAN STUDIES AND WORLD AFFAIRS, Box 24-8134, University of Miami, Coral Gables, Florida 33124. Manuscripts should be typewritten, double-spaced, with footnotes, references, tables, and charts on separate pages, and should follow the current journal style. A brief biographical paragraph describing each author's current affiliation, research interests, and recent publications should accompany the manuscript.

**CORRESPONDENCE** regarding book reviews should be sent directly to: Book Review Editor, JOURNAL OF INTERAMERICAN STUDIES AND WORLD AFFAIRS, Box 24-8134, University of Miami, Coral Gables, Florida 33124.

---

**JOURNAL OF INTERAMERICAN STUDIES AND WORLD AFFAIRS** is published four times annually—in February, May, August, and November. 

**Subscriptions:** Regular institutional rate $26.00. Individuals may subscribe at a one-year rate of $15.00. Add $1.00 per year for subscriptions outside the United States. Orders from U.K., Europe, the Middle East, and Africa should be sent to the London office (address below). Noninstitutional orders **must** be paid by personal check.

Second-class postage paid at Beverly Hills, California.

**Inquiries:** Address all correspondence and permissions requests to SAGE PUBLICATIONS, INC., 275 South Beverly Drive, Beverly Hills, California 90212. Inquiries and subscriptions from U.K., Europe, the Middle East, and Africa should be sent to SAGE PUBLICATIONS LTD, 28 Banner Street, London EC1Y 8QE, England. Other orders should be sent to the Beverly Hills office.

**Advertising:** Current rates and specifications may be obtained by writing to the Advertising Manager at the Beverly Hills office (address above).

This journal is abstracted or indexed in **Historical Abstracts, Human Resources Abstracts, Sage Urban Studies Abstracts, International Political Science Abstracts, Public Affairs Information Service, Current Contents, Social Sciences Citation Index, Social Sciences Index, ABC POL SCI** and **United States Political Science Documents.**

**Back Issues:** Information about availability and prices of back issues may be obtained from the publisher's order department (address above). Write to London office for sterling prices.

**Claims for undelivered copies** must be made no later than three months following month of publication. The publisher will supply missing copies when losses have been sustained in transit and where the reserve stock will permit.

---

**Change of Address:** Six weeks' advance notice must be given when notifying of change of address. Please send old address label along with the new address to insure proper identification. Please specify name of journal.

RICHARD B. CRAIG
*Department of Political Science*
*Kent State University*
*Kent, Ohio 44242*

# *LA CAMPAÑA PERMANENTE*
## *Mexico's Antidrug Campaign*

The problems associated with drug abuse in the United States have received considerable attention in recent years. By the mid-1970s, approximately 500,000 Americans were addicted to heroin, while at least 15 million were regular or casual users of marijuana. None of this heroin originates domestically, and only a small percentage of the marijuana, and this of low potency, is home-grown. Consequently, the question of source has become cardinal to most analyses of drug use and abuse in the United States.

Mexico has long been the primary source of high potency marijuana for the American market. Despite the recent influx from Jamaica and Colombia, Mexico still supplies an estimated 70% of the annual American consumption, or some 10 million pounds. More importantly, Mexico is currently the source of 70% to 80% of the heroin on the U.S. market, an alarming 6-8 ton annual figure. Furthermore, Mexico is both a primary transshipment route for cocaine, an increasingly popular drug originating in South America, and the source of vast quantities of psychotropic substances.

As a result, narcotics traffic has become a crucial aspect of contemporary Mexico-United States relations, ranking on a par with such perennial questions as trade and illegal migrants. The U.S. government has brought increasing pressure to bear on its Mexican counterpart, especially since the fall of 1969, to take more effective action against the cultivation, manufacture, and traffic of narcotic drugs. Concomitant with these

Journal of Interamerican Studies and World Affairs, Vol. 20 No. 2, May 1978

pressures, vast amounts of money and equipment have been allotted Mexico to aid its antidrug campaign. The Mexican response has been impressive, particularly since the fall of 1975. Yet despite this effort, American public and congressional criticism of Mexico's *campaña* has continued during the 1970s. "Just what," question such critics, "is Mexico doing about these drugs?" The query is commonplace and constitutes the subject matter of this paper.

## *La Campaña: A Brief History*

According to Barona Lobato (1976), a nationwide antidrug campaign to halt the illicit cultivation, manufacture, and shipment of narcotic drugs dates from 1948. Unofficially, however, Mexican efforts began early in the century when Chinese immigrants, whose use of opium was suppressed in Mexico City, migrated to the states of Sinaloa and Sonora and became the nation's first opium growers. Whereas their product was grown only for personal consumption prior to World War I, it clandestinely entered the United States market during the war when the traditional world opium trade was interrupted. Traffic in Mexican opium abated during the interwar years, only to be revived again in 1939.

With the official launching of the 1948 *gran campaña* in Mexico Northwest, the government's approach consisted primarily of occasional raids against opium or marijuana cultivation throughout the nation and search and destroy forays into the states of Sinaloa, Sonora, Chihuahua, and Guerrero during the growing seasons. In these initial years three facts emerged which were to crucially affect the Mexican initiative to this day. First, the remote and often inaccessible areas where marijuana and opium poppies are grown make the utilization of aircraft a requisite to any degree of success. Second, without the extensive use of herbicides or defoliants, a truly successful campaign against the cultivation of opium and marijuana would prove impossible. Third, any effort to eliminate drug cultivation and traffic would be forcefully resisted.

Aircraft spotter planes have been an integral part of *La Campaña* since its inception. However, during its early years the campaign's success was sharply curtailed by a lack of aircraft, spare parts, and skilled pilots. Not until the period 1961-1962, following Mexican acquisition of $500,000 in aircraft, helicopters, jeeps, weapons, and spare parts from the United States was the impact of such equipment realized. Its employment had two apparently contradictory effects. The newly acquired technology resulted in a dramatic increase in the amount of opium poppies destroyed in the field: 3,890,316 square meters in the period 1961-1962, as compared to 139,765 square meters during 1960-1961. Yet it also made future campaigns more difficult as opium and marijuana cultivators, aware of the increased probability of aerial detection, began concealing their crops amidst legitimate ones and planting smaller plots in even more remote regions.

Despite the accelerated Mexican effort, increasing amounts of Mexican marijuana and a consistent supply of heroin entered the United States during the 1960s, as an alienated youth culture literally became the "turned on" generation. Responding to mounting drug problems, the Nixon Administration launched new diplomatic initiatives designed to ease America's drug dilemma by attacking the problem at its foreign source. While Turkey became the primary target of Washington's heroin diplomacy, Mexico came under increasing diplomatic pressure as the principal supplier of marijuana.

Such pressure was epitomized by the launching on September 21, 1969, of Operation Intercept, "the nation's largest peacetime search and seizure operation by civil authorities." The unilateral offensive was ostensibly designed to halt the flow of marijuana into this country in one massive maneuver. However, according to Craig (1977), it constituted a classic example of economic blackmail designed "to get the Mexicans to come around and really start doing something about dope." Perhaps, in the long run, Intercept did succeed in "bringing the Mexicans around." However, in the short run, it became a major diplomatic incident and was replaced on October 11 by Operation Cooperation, a face-saving binational arrangement still in effect with this writing.[1]

The relative merits and demerits of Operation Intercept will long be debated. There is no doubt, however, that it constitutes a benchmark in United States-Mexico narcotics diplomacy and a turning point in Mexico's antidrug campaign. Despite its negative impact, Intercept spawned several positive developments: under Operation Cooperation, the binational antidrug effort has continued to improve. Furthermore, the unilateral American action was in part responsible for a revived, expanded, and far more thorough Mexican campaign. And, as an indirect result of Intercept, Mexico came to publicly admit the existence of a growing domestic drug problem and to address the question as an integral part of its national campaign.

## *Mexico's Drug Problem*

Accurate statistics on the number of Mexican drug addicts and users are hard to come by. Publicly, Mexican officials acknowledge the existence of some 10,000 heroin/opium addicts. Privately, they admit the number may be much higher. "Like your own country," observed a high-ranking Mexican narcotics official (Interview: 1976a), "we know how many hard drug addicts we are treating. What we don't know is how many others there are out there that we are not treating."

The use of marijuana by young people is considered a serious problem by Mexican authorities. Although no official figures have been published regarding the extent of marijuana smoking, "a hell'ova lot of Mexican high school and college kids are turning on with grass nowadays" (Interview: 1975). As regards the use of most drugs, Mexican officials and laymen generally consider the current trend in marijuana usage to be the result of a "cultural transplant" from the United States. Yet while there is a large grain of truth in such reasoning, marijuana usage in Mexico has been an acknowledged fact for centuries. However, it was one thing for *indios,* soldiers, *campesinos,* and urban *pelados* to smoke *la yerba*; it is quite another for the children of middle- and upper-class families to "do some *mota.*"

Refusing to accept the reasoning that no direct connection exists between marijuana smoking and eventual hard drug usage, most federal narcotics officials and the great majority of Mexican parents deem such activity a serious first step to ultimate addiction. Accordingly, and despite 1977 revisions, the penalties for marijuana possession and trafficking may be particularly harsh, with fines ranging from 1,000 to 10,000 pesos and prison terms from two to nine years.

Their growth potential notwithstanding, the problems of opium/heroin addiction and marijuana usage are relatively minor considering Mexico's population. However, such is not the case with the use of inhalants. Again, accurate figures are unavailable, but literally thousands of poor urban youth are "turning on" with several types of inhalants, the most damaging of which is *tiner*. Numerically speaking, the number of inhalant abusers surpasses the combined totals of opium, heroin, and marijuana users. Very conservative government estimates list 25,000 inhalant addicts in the capital alone.

The use of solvents is particularly disconcerting to narcotics and medical officials, who list a number of impressive reasons for their concern. First, the problem is growing in direct proportion to Mexico's massive urbanization. Second, the inhalant user is very young compared to other addicts, with the typical age ranging between 14 and 17 and numerous cases of 7 and 8 year old users being documented (*Excelsior,* June 24, 1976). Third, there appears to be no means of curing or rehabilitating the solvent addict, such is the extent of physical and mental deterioration. Fourth, inhalants, unlike other drugs, may be purchased very cheaply, and there currently exist no laws regulating the manufacture or sale of glues and solvents.[2]

Mexican officials are also well aware of the growing popularity of psychotropic drugs, and they have responded in recent years by expanding and tightening drug and prescription laws. The impact of such "pill" legislation on the transshipment of stimulants and depressants, when coupled with accelerated confiscation efforts, has been impressive. However, despite the extension of prescription laws to include many heretofore nonprescription items, the internal black market in such pills continues to flourish. Furthermore, many druggists persist in selling some listed drugs without a prescription, while others such as Librium and Darvon may still be legally purchased over the counter.

Of less concern to law enforcement and medical officials is the domestic use of native hallucinogens. Long before the Spaniard arrived, the Indian consumed such substances as *peyote, ololiuhqui* (a seed from the plant commonly called *Manto de la Virgen*), and *Teonanacatl* (the hallucinogenic mushroom, or *hongo*) for religious and medical purposes. Although currently outlawed, the use of such mind-expanding drugs by the Indian population is not deemed a serious problem and is generally ignored by law enforcement officials. However, consumption by non-Indians and trafficking in these hallucinogens are considered serious offenses punishable on a par with hard drugs under Article 195 of the *Código Penal.*

Mexico views its own drug problem from a broad perspective. Since the inception of La Campaña, Mexican officials have approached domestic drug abuse as a medical, educational, social, and law enforcement question. As is the case with international trafficking, the major role in Mexico's domestic campaign is assigned to the Attorney General's Office (Procuraduría) and its enforcement arm, the Mexican Federal Judicial Police. In addition to directing the permanent campaign against cultivation and shipment of narcotic drugs, the Procuraduría acts as a primary resource agency in the nationwide effort to preserve the collective health of the Mexican community. In this capacity it assists in the organization of civic events, social and cultural gatherings, sporting events, and recreational activities. Secondly,

Procuraduría officials prepare and orient groups involved in drug education activities by working with parents, teachers, doctors, youth groups, and the media, and by serving as key resource personnel for the press, radio and television stations, schools, family organizations, and youth conferences.

Research, information, and publication on the question of drug abuse constitute a second aspect of the domestic campaña. Although various departments and individuals are involved in this function, the primary organization is Mexico's Center for the Study of Drug Dependence (CEMEF). Created in 1972, CEMEF is one of 12 international centers functioning under co-auspices of the United Nations. It conducts research, acquires data, and disseminates scientific information on the broad question of drug abuse in Mexico and abroad. The Center is currently conducting extensive investigations in three areas: the negative effects resulting from the use of solvents and inhalants, the physical properties and effects of marijuana grown in various geographic regions, and the possible therapeutic effects of marijuana in treatment of rheumatism, visual hypertension, and cancer. In addition to its role as a bona fide research and information center, CEMEF works in close cooperation with the Procuraduría, the Ministry of the Interior, the Department of Health and Welfare, individual states, and universities in a coordinated program against drug dependence.

Treatment and rehabilitation comprise the third part of Mexico's domestic antidrug effort. These functions are reserved exclusively for the Department of Health and Welfare, which in turn coordinates its efforts with hospitals and youth rehabilitation centers throughout the nation. In addition to its primary activity in treating known drug addicts, the Department has, along with CEMEF, devoted considerable money, personnel, and energy to the establishment of youth treatment and rehabilitation centers throughout the nation. Rehabilitation efforts in hospitals and youth centers have combined both medical and psychiatric techniques, with the latter being emphasized.

Accurately assessing the performance of Mexico's domestic antidrug program is rendered difficult by its inseparability from the international campaign and by a lack of reliable comparative data. The author has encountered opposing schools of thought regarding the basic question: is Mexico succeeding in its internal antidrug efforts? Representative of the positive view is Dr. Antonio Gamiochipi Carbajal, director of Mexico City's Doctor Samuel Ramirez Morales Hospital, who contends that the number of patients now being treated for drug addiction is actually less than in the past few years. However, he does not mention the number of current addicts not seeking treatment. Furthermore, while noting a reduced number of officially treated addicts, Dr. Gamiochipi Carbajal admits the possibility of an increased number of casual drug users and experimenters (*El Universal,* January 25, 1976).

Reflecting the negative side of the question is the remark of a State Department narcotics official in Mexico City (Interview: 1976b): "I'd like to say that they're succeeding, but quite honestly the domestic drug problem is getting worse." Such reasoning is buttressed by a reading of the Mexican press which, although often sensationalist, does not generally relish publishing articles and editorials that place government programs in a negative light. At least once a week, each of the Mexico City dailies reports on or editorializes some aspect of the growing national drug problem. In July 1976, CEMEF director Guido Belsasso reported (*Excelsior,* July 12, 1976) that a staggering 80% of the population of the state of Morelos between the ages of 13 and 15 engages in some type of drug abuse. Equally alarming are the estimates of Dr. Miguel Cacho Villa, the director of a Mexico City children's home, who contends there may be as many as 800,000 juvenile drug addicts nationwide (*Los Angeles Times,* June 6, 1976). The truth probably lies somewhere between the two extremes and will not be known until more accurate statistics are available.

## *Two Sides of La Campaña*

The jury is, indeed, still out in its judgment of the campaign's domestic impact. Such is not the case, however, regarding

Mexico's commitment to cooperate in multilateral and bilateral efforts to control illicit traffic in narcotic drugs. Having become a signatory to every major international drug treaty now in effect, Mexico's attitude toward its role in international efforts to control the flow of illicit drugs is one of pride and commitment. Even more indicative of this attitude has been the government's cooperation with the United States in seeking to control the cultivation and shipment of marijuana and heroin.

Primary law enforcement responsibility for Mexico's permanent antidrug campaign is lodged in the Procuraduría, which coordinates the activities of the Mexican Army and other state and municipal law enforcement officials. In addition, the attorney general's office supervises the activities of and works in close liaison with U.S. agents of the Drug Enforcement Administration (DEA) stationed in Mexico. Although often inseparable in practice, we may, for analytical purposes, divide the antidrug efforts of the Procuraduría and its approximately 600 Federal Judicial Police agents into parts: halting the cultivation and manufacture of opium poppies, marijuana, and psychotropics; and preventing domestic and international traffic in these and other drugs.

### *HALTING CULTIVATION AND PROCESSING*

One of the most logical means of eliminating or reducing the consumption and shipment of illegal drugs is to attack the problem at its source by eradicating cultivation and production. In theory, the location and destruction of opium poppy fields and marijuana plots appears a simple task. One need only locate the plots through informants or aerial surveys, send in the troops, destroy the fields, and arrest the violators. In practice, however, the task is *far* more difficult and, until just recently, an impossibility given the methods employed.

The enormous extent of opium and marijuana cultivation in Mexico poses a particularly difficult problem for the Procuraduría and the Mexican army. Early in 1976, 20,000 plots of opium poppies were said to exist throughout Mexico, and the figure may have been more accurately listed at 40,000. Opium poppies, which are usually planted in the fall and harvested in the spring, are grown primarily in remote areas of the Northwest, with Sinaloa forming an epicenter for the states of Durango, Sonora, Chihuahua, and Nayarit. And while their cultivation is extensive, it in no way compares to that of marijuana which, according to the sweeping gesture of a high-ranking official in the Procuraduría, *"se encuentra por todas partes."* The eradication of a weed which grows "everywhere" is no mean task.

The eradication program has traditionally been conducted by the Mexican army, working under the direct supervision of the Procuraduría. Some 5,000 Mexican soliders and airmen are "permanently" involved in La Campaña. In fact, one of the army's primary tasks lies in the eradication of opium/marijuana cultivation and the interdiction of drug traffickers. Militarily, Mexico is divided into 35 zones, the great majority of which correspond roughly to state boundaries. In most instances the deployment of army troops is compatible with the aims of La Campaña. Throughout the year and particularly during the intensive campaign months of September through May, army units in the areas of heavy cultivation are perpetually involved in the eradication campaign in one of two ways. Under direction of the Procuraduría, soldiers are either sent on foot or dropped by helicopters into areas under cultivation with the assignment of destroying the crops and apprehending the growers. In addition, military units initiate periodic ground sweeps aimed at discovering and eradicating especially well-hidden plots. In both instances, the army has registered impressive statistical successes under difficult circumstances. However, cultivation continues, and particular problems have marred an otherwise laudable military effort.

The first involves an unfavorable ratio of available men to area of responsibility. In many cases no more than 500-1,000 men are responsible for up to 100 square miles of *very* rough and often all-but-inaccessible terrain. The lack of resources and equipment constitutes a second impediment to a more effective army role in the campaign. Until very recently, a shortage of helicopters proved especially detrimental. Not only are they indispensable in reconnaissance and location of opium and marijuana fields, but in most instances helicopters constitute the only effective means of transporting troops into the areas of cultivation.

The lack of modern light weaponry has proved a second important resource problem for the army, federal agents, and local police. In some cases it is simply a question of being outgunned by growers and traffickers, some of whom are equipped with the most recent types of automatic weapons acquired under a barter system of guns-for-dope.[3] This lack of sophisticated arms has posed an especially troublesome problem in the states of Sinaloa and Guerrero which respectively form the hub of Mexico's opium and marijuana zones.

Corruption is a third problem area for the military in its eradication role. Illicit activities invariably include graft, and in the case of drugs the Mexican military enjoys no special immunity. Rumors of army officers being involved in drug-related corruption are commonplace, but perhaps as a result of accelerated anticorruption efforts by the Secretary of Defense and the constant rotation of zonal commanders and lesser officers, the author has been unable to document specific recent instances. It appears that "resident" noncommissioned officers and enlisted men are more prone to involvement with growers and traffickers than are their superior officers. In either case, such corruption should come as no surprise to realistic analysts of either Mexican society or the American drug scene.

The lack of a true commitment to their antidrug role on the part of some zonal commanders and officers when coupled with interagency friction constitutes a fourth problem. "Some Mexican officers simply do not relish the nonmilitary nature of their antidrug role," observed one American official. "They feel they're supposed to be soldiers, not commanders charged with chopping down and burning marijuana plants."[4] Some officers also resent being at the "beck-and-call" of federal police agents who are the ultimate source of control in the army's drug-related activities. Although this friction is more pronounced as regards the army's role in interdicting drug traffic, its very existence, even at a minimal level, impedes the campaign's overall results.

### *INTERDICTING DRUG TRAFFIC*

Despite such problems, most knowledgeable observers are impressed by the military's efforts. Nevertheless, the flow of Mexican drugs into the United States continues, and if Mexico City has until recently found it difficult to eliminate drug production at the source, it is in an equal quandary regarding the interdiction facet of La Campaña. This is the case despite a sincere commitment on the part of the Procuraduría and its agents to "do something about stopping the flow of dope."

Mexico's Attorney General and his cadre of some 600 federal judicial police (MFJP) are irrevocably committed to fighting the flow of narcotic drugs into, within, and out of the country. This dedication is evidenced in many ways, but perhaps it is epitomized by the large number of federal police who have lost their lives in the line of duty and the esteem which they are held by Mexicans and foreigners alike.

While numerous Mexican soldiers have been killed in drug-related activities, the proportion of MFJP to lose their lives in the campaign has been far greater. Attorney General Ojeda Paullada (Drug Enforcement, 1974: 12) perhaps best expressed the ultimate dedication of his agents when he remarked that "the physical risk is far greater than in the investigation of any other type of crime. We have had many violent encounters with traffickers. . . . I regret to say that several heroic Mexican agents have lost their lives in the performance of their duties."

A second indicator of the sincere dedication of the MFJP to the antidrug campaign is the respect and esteem accorded them by an otherwise highly cynical Mexican public and by Americans who work with them. Anyone acquainted with the extent of public cynicism regarding Mexican officials in general and the police in particular must be impressed with the respect accorded the MFJP. "They've got *huevos,* and most of them are honest by Mexican standards," remarked a veteran Texas narcotics agent (Interview: 1971). "Give them a few more years of American training and they're going to shock hell out of a lot of *traficantes.*"

Indeed, these federal agents have "shocked hell out of a lot of traficantes" in recent years. Approximately one-half of Mexico's 600 MFJP are involved "exclusively" in the antidrug efforts.[5] Not only has their number doubled during the last four years, but all MFJP now receive three months of intensive training in the area of narcotic drugs. Today's federal agent is more carefully selected, much better trained, and far better equipped than his predecessor. He must be, for his task is a formidable one.

Although often inseparable, the interdiction efforts of the MFJP may be divided into two categories: actions directed against the flow of drugs manufactured in Mexico and those aimed at halting narcotics originating outside the country. The MFJP's most demanding and dangerous task involves the interdiction and arrest of individuals attempting to transport drugs from the interior into the United States. Arrests and seizures are made in every conceivable environ: in homes, offices, cars, trains, busses, and airplanes; in the field, in the city; at sea; at specially erected roadblocks; and at customs inspection points. In the great majority of cases such actions are met with violence, for perhaps more than any other narcotics smugglers the Mexican trafficker "shoots now and talks later.

A second and less violent facet of the interdiction aspect of La Campaña involves actions taken to halt the shipment of drugs through Mexico. Mexico has long been an important conduit for drugs originating in other countries and bound for the American market. In the past it was heroin being transshipped through Mexico. Today it is primarily cocaine being sent through Mexico into the United States. Concentrating their efforts on southern ports and border crossings, major metropolitan airports, and the

Mexico City terminal in particular, Mexican federal agents have consistently made cocaine seizures and arrested a large number of international traffickers. Particularly vulnerable have been smugglers aboard the "cocaine express," which originates in Buenos Aires with stops in several Andean countries. Here, perhaps more than in other facets of the campaign, the key to drug seizures has been the highly effective exchange of information on traffickers between Mexican, American, and officials of other countries. "Many times we know who will be carrying drugs even before they board the plane in La Paz," observed a Mexican official (Interview: 1974b). "To get cocaine through the Mexico City Airport, one must be either a very smart trafficker, an innocent 'mule,' or just plain lucky."

Analyzed from a statistical perspective, recent results of Mexico's *Campaña Permanente* are impressive. Comparative figures combining the search and destroy aspects of the campaign with those of interdiction for the campaign years 1973-1974 through 1975-1976 are shown in Table 1.

## *The United States and La Campaña: Point and Counterpoint*

Despite such impressive statistics, Mexico continues to produce literally tons of marijuana and heroin annually, the great bulk of which is destined for the American market. As a result, the Mexican government has been under continuous pressure from Washington to accelerate its antidrug effort. These pressures have been particularly intense since 1974, when it became clear that Mexico had become the primary source of heroin for American addicts. In response to these demands and because of an increased awareness of its own burgeoning drug problem, Mexico responded in late 1975 with a truly intensified effort that has since been acclaimed by even its harshest American critics. Yet particular charges remain, and it is within the context of these criticisms that the United States role in Mexico's campaña can best be understood.

**TABLE 1**
**Selected Results of Mexico's Antidrug Campaign (1973-1976)[a]**

| Action | 1973-1974 | 1974-1975 | 1975-1976 |
|---|---|---|---|
| Marijuana | | | |
| Plots Destroyed | 8,112 | 6,762 | 16,686 |
| Area in Sq. Meters | 19,922,675 | 20,801,448 | 56,184,977 |
| Opium Poppies | | | |
| Plots Destroyed | 6,540 | 13,580 | 21,405 |
| Area in Sq. Meters | 17,759,403 | 44,951,140 | 58,120,088 |
| Opium Seized | 193K., 699G. | 880K.,146G. | 676K.,608G. |
| Morphine Seized | 620G. | 6K.,900G. | 4K.,370G. |
| Heroin Seized | 129K., 47G. | 452K.,222G. | 292K.,581G. |
| Cocaine Seized | 146K., 974G. | 255K.,317G. | 214K.,581G. |
| Vehicles Seized | | | |
| Automobiles/Trucks | 880 | 758 | 828 |
| Airplanes | 27 | 41 | 77 |
| Persons Detained | | | |
| Nationals | 2751 | 2524 | 4021 |
| Foreigners | 415 | 228 | 378 |
| Total | 3166 | 2752 | 4399 |
| Labs Dismantled | --- | --- | 24 |
| Drug Trafficking Rings Disrupted | --- | --- | 16 |

SOURCE: Procuraduría General de la República Mexicana. Mimeographed
a. Between September 1 of one year and August 31 of the following.

By the early 1970s narcotics traffic had become one of the most important aspects of Mexico-United States-relations. How, it may reasonably be asked, did drug traffic between the two countries achieve such a prominent position in so short a time? Or perhaps more to the point: why Mexico as the source of so much marijuana and heroin?

In seeking a straightforward answer to the why of Mexican drug production one is faced, first, with the tradition chicken-or-the-egg dilemma. In recent years the United States has sought to ease its drug dilemma by attacking the problem at its foreign source. Until the mid 1970s this meant pressuring and rewarding Turkey, the primary source of heroin for the American market, and Mexico, the principal supplier of high-potency marijuana.

Today Mexico receives the lion's share of American attention in both instances. In response, the Mexicans reluctantly admit their productive capacity. Yet they counter by contending that if it were not for the American demand there would be no reason for Mexican farmers to cultivate marijuana and opium poppies. Obviously, the Mexicans are correct. However, the demand is a given, and this poses a second fundamental problem, one exclusively Mexican.

Despite remarkable economic advances in recent years, Mexico is still a poor country in many respects. This is particularly true of the rural sector which, despite rhetoric to the contrary, has largely been neglected by Mexico City. It is no mere accident that principal marijuana and opium producing states are also centers of grinding rural poverty and have long been the scenes of guerrilla movements, land seizures, *caciquismo,* and rural unrest. They lie outside the mainstream of Mexican life and are populated by contemporary *olvidados,* the great majority of whom are economically desperate. And desperate men seek desperate solutions to their problems. They turn to alcohol, leave their villages and families, become *mojados,* migrate to the teeming metropolitan slums, seize haciendas, become guerrillas or opium/marijuana farmers, or both. Such is the plight of these *campesinos* that they have little to lose and much to gain by cultivating or trafficking in illicit drugs.[6] They number in the thousands and ultimately supply "Mexican brown" to American addicts.

Within this context of poverty, demand, and profit, several points of controversy have marred otherwise improving Mexican-United States relations in the area of drug control. Generally, Mexicans point to recent campaña results to counter American charges. In some instances their rebuttals are quite effective; in others, they are less so.

Critics of the Mexican campaign have long cited a lack of funding to support their charge that Mexico City is not truly committed to eliminating the cultivation and trafficking of narcotic drugs. The Mexicans reply to this charge by indicating that theirs is a comparatively poor country, with many developmental problems to finance on a limited budget. And they couple this with the firm reminder that Mexico is actually devoting more of its public funds to the antidrug campaign than Americans believe. According to José Juan de Olloqui, Mexico's Ambassador to the United States in 1976, "Mexico is dedicating a much greater proportion of its budget to combatting drug traffic than the United States" (*Excelsior,* January 23, 1976).

Critics of La Campaña contend, secondly, that Mexican officials refuse to commit their forces in certain key areas of Sonora, Sinaloa, and Guerrero for fear of literally being outgunned by growers and traffickers. Until recently such charges were largely true. There were, and perhaps still are, regions into which troops are not sent and in which many would not serve if ordered to do so. The Mexicans chide such critics who too often have no knowledge of these terrains and the dangers they pose. And they flatly contend that there is currently no area of Mexico immune from the MFJP and the army, no matter how wild the terrain or how well armed the traffickers.

The refusal of Mexican officials to extradite their nationals accused of drug-related offenses in the United States constitutes a third area of criticism. In this regard the critics are correct, but so are Mexican officials. Mexico, like most countries, often refuses to extradite its own citizens for trial in foreign countries. But during the last three years, under the so-called JANUS program, Mexican federal attorneys have come to this country, secured depositions against their nationals, returned, and used this evidence to gain numerous convictions.[7] "By using this method," remarked an American diplomat (Interview: 1976b), "the Mexicans have made some good cases against some big traffickers. The days when a Mexican could commit a drug offense in the States and then flee to the haven of home are gone."

It is contended, fourthly, that relations between Mexico City and particular state and local officials are so fragile as to preclude an effectively coordinated campaign at the grass-roots level.

Despite official Mexican denials, this charge is valid in particular regions, some of which are important cultivation and trafficking zones. And it is a problem not only in the area of drugs. The *frontera al norte,* for example, has long maintained a somewhat separate identity from the rest of Mexico. When this regionalism is coupled with the power of local *caciques,* any nationally directed campaign, including that against drugs, is bound to suffer.

Critics charge that corruption is so endemic to Mexico that it thwarts the efforts of even the most dedicated narcotics officials. Mexicans reply to such charges in several ways. Some flatly deny it and ask: "what about Nixon and Watergate?" Most officials involved in the campaign, however, make no effort to refute the charge. They admit that some of their countrymen are "on the drug take." Yet these same individuals deny that corruption of officials is as widespread as many contend. More importantly, they emphasize the recent campaign to oust federal, state, and local officials suspected of collaborating with drug smugglers and point with pride to the indictments of federal judges in Tijuana and Hermosillo during 1976 for having accepted *mordidas* in the form of bail from known traffickers.

A sixth American criticism of the Mexican campaign concerns the Army's role. In addition to the previously discussed question of drug-related corruption, it is charged that the military is not well equipped to perform its antinarcotics role. In many respects the charge is well founded, particularly as it involves the Army's role in the interdiction phase of the campaign. Although it is not seen as a primary force in intercepting smugglers, the army could do a much better job were it not wholly at the command of the Procuraduría when it comes to drug trafficking. Unlike their eradication role, soldiers cannot move against smugglers without specific orders. This is particularly true of high-ranking officers outside the important marijuana and opium zones, many of whom harbor a pronounced dislike for drug-related activities and the MFJP. Furthermore, the Army cannot realistically be expected to move effectively against the shipment of drugs if it is primarily equipped and prepared to perform an eradication role.

Until quite recently Mexican officials were accused of not fully cooperating with their American counterparts. In particular, it was charged, they refused to fully share drug-related information. Undoubtedly, cooperation could be better, but one hears few complaints from American personnel in this respect. On the contrary, based on the experience of previous years, Mexican officials appear to be sharing information and working with Americans as never before.

The eighth charge leveled against Mexico concerns who is being arrested and which drug rings are being disrupted. It is held that the Mexicans are arresting only small operators while not touching the big dealers. Again, there was, and still is, some validity to this accusation. In the past Mexican officials seldom disrupted major drug rings. However, this situation has improved markedly in the past three years. During the 1975-1976 campaign, for example, 16 large operations were disrupted and their leaders indicted. Among those subsequently imprisoned were three of the region's most sought-after traffickers: Jorge Favela Escobosa, Cesar Nungaray Garibaldi, and Alberto Sicilia Falcón. Granted, major dealers are still operating, but this condition was best explained by an official in the Procuraduría: "You surely realize that these are not 'easy fish to catch.' They are very powerful, very rich, and very intelligent men. . . . Look at your own campaign. How many Mafiosos has your DEA busted?" (Interview: 1976a.).

Particular American sources have been highly critical of the treatment accorded United States citizens accused of drug offenses. By mid-1977, some 600 Americans were imprisoned in Mexico. Of that number, approximately 85% were charged with violations of Mexican drug laws. In summary form, Mexican police, prison officials, or lawyers have been accused of committing or sanctioning the following: physical and psychological torture, coerced confessions, failure to notify American officials promptly of the arrest of their nationals, prolonged pretrial detentions, unscrupulous conduct by attorneys, failure to return confiscated property, poor medical care, extortion, denial of commissioned or "good time" work, rape, homosexual assaults, and failure to grant bail on an equal basis.

Mexican officials generally deny such charges and counter by reminding their critics that foreign nationals are treated no differently than Mexican citizens similarly accused and by pointedly observing that one cannot expect Mexico to conduct a concerted antidrug campaign and simultaneously coddle the traffickers, many of whom are United States citizens. "American authorities and citizens alike should decide what they want," remarked Ambassador Juan de Olloqui in January 1976, "that we cooperate with them as we are doing . . . or that we are indulgent with the delinquents. It is not possible to reconcile these two exigencies" (*Excelsior,* January 23, 1976).

Mistreatment charges place State Department officials in a very awkward position. They obviously do not like to see their countrymen tortured or denied humane treatment in any way. On the other hand, they have been reluctant to criticize their Mexican hosts overtly for pressing the intensified interdiction aspect of the antidrug campaign, something the United States government and in particular the DEA have long demanded. This reluctance has, in turn, drawn the ire of particular congressmen and riled even their own diplomatic colleagues directly involved with imprisoned Americans.

Such interagency friction as well as American criticism has been eased somewhat by recent developments, one of which has an important bearing on Mexico-United States narcotics diplomacy. The condition of imprisoned Americans is receiving far more attention than in the past. The number of embassy and consular personnel involved with accused and incarcerated Americans has been considerably augmented. Visits to prisons occur more frequently, more individualized conferences are being held with inmates, and responding to official American pressure, the treatment of prisoners and the response of Mexican officers in matters relating to arrests of U.S. citizens have shown improvement.

Of even greater importance to imprisoned Americans is the prisoner exchange agreement between the two countries.

Although it was never admitted publicly, the Mexican government was embarrassed by publicity surrounding the mistreatment of both foreign and national prisoners. On the heels of the announced closing of the infamous Lecumberri prison, the opening of three new facilities in the Federal District, and the granting of a partial amnesty to selected political prisoners, President Luis Echeverría Alvarez boldly suggested to Secretary of State Kissinger in June 1976, an unprecedented formal exchange of Mexican and American prisoners. Three months after the exchange idea was broached, negotiating teams held their first session in Mexico City. Two months later, on November 25, the treaty was signed by the U.S. Ambassador and Mexico's Foreign Minister. A necessary amendment to the Mexican constitution was soon effected, and on December 30, 1976 the Mexican Senate approved the treaty. Having sanctioned the agreement, Mexican official assumed a deservedly smug attitude. During his February 1977 visit to Washington for talks with President Carter, President López Portillo touched on the subject at a news conference. Asked how long it would be before American prisoners return, he replied: "When you want to have them, you will have them returned home. We are ready" (*Excessior,* February 16, 1977).

A final criticism of the antidrug effort concerned the reluctance of Mexican officials to use herbicides or defoliants in the eradication program. American authorities had long sought to convince their Mexican counterparts that such chemicals constituted the key to an effective eradication effort. For years the Mexicans listened, studied, and experimented on a very limited basis. Yet it was not until the fall of 1975 that they decided to employ herbicides on a massive scale. There were two primary reasons for the delay. Mexican officials and laymen feared the possibly harmful side effects of such chemicals on individuals and legitimate crops. Negative publicity given the results of herbicide usage in American agriculture and Viet Nam did little to ease their fears. In fact, herbicides and Viet Nam are still inseparable in the minds of many Mexicans. More importantly, Mexicans in both public and private life simply could not, or would not, acknowledge the massive extent of drug cultivation and production taking place in their country. It was as if it were out there but not really out there, at least not to the extent the Americans claimed. But by the summer of 1975, in the wake of continued publicity from international and domestic sources, even the skeptics came to admit, at least in private, that their country had become one of the world's largest heroin producers. Furthermore, despite their sincere eradication efforts, the problem was getting worse. Something simply had to be done, something drastic. On November 7, 1975, a secret meeting was held in Mexico City between Attorney General Ojeda Paullada and Sheldon Vance, senior adviser to the Secretary of State and coordinator for international narcotics matters. The following day Ojeda advised Vance and American Ambassador Joseph John Jova that beginning immediately the campaña would include the all-out use of defoliants.

## *Concluding Observations*

With the launching of the 1975-1976 campaign Mexico entered a new phase in its war on narcotic drugs. And under the new López Portillo administration Mexico has updated, expanded, and intensified the program to unprecedented levels. Modern technology has replaced the antiquated methods of the 1960s and early 1970s. Infrared photography, fixed wing aircraft, helicopters, and the massive application of herbicides now constitute the core of the most extensive national drug eradication program on record. Yet despite this prodigious effort the international flow of heroin and marijuana continues, and Mexico's internal drug abuse problem worsens. Within such extant realities several factors will determine the relative success of La Campaña.

The use of defoliant chemicals must be continued and expanded for both poppies and marijuana as growers seek new cultivation zones. The army must receive more and improved equipment for its eradication role and greater leeway in the performance of its interdiction function. Zonal commanders who refuse to cooperate fully in both phases of the program must be replaced with more dedicated men. The number of MFJP assigned exclusively to drugs should be expanded. Even the doubling of this force in recent years leaves too few agents for the demanding and dangerous task at hand. A more thorough coordination of the overall antidrug effort must be undertaken. Neither phase of the campaign can truly succeed as long as regional and local independence stands in the way.

Bold steps must be taken to reduce corruption and graft currently associated with drug production and trafficking. Realistically, one cannot expect miracles in this regard. Instead, he must hope that drug corruption among Mexican officials at all levels is attacked with sincerity. A necessary step in this direction would be the creation of a thorough and impartial internal investigation system. Hopefully, the new government's drive against corruption will soon include such a system.

Cooperation between United States and Mexican drug officials must continue to expand and improve. In reality, they need one another's help. The same holds true for American aid and technology: not only do our helicopters, airplanes, and technicians help stem the flow of drugs into the United States, they also reduce the supply of narcotics available for domestic consumption.

Viewed from a long range perspective, Mexico must do more to relieve the plight of its rural sector. As long as the campesino lacks land, water, fertilizer, and credit—all of which add up to dignity—he will be forced to seek desperate remedies, including poppy and marijuana cultivation. The time for rural rhetoric is rapidly drawing to a close. And one of the best means of preventing today's campesino from becoming tomorrow's Lucio Cabañas is to offer him a chance to earn a decent legitimate living.

Finally, United States officials and laymen have an important role to play in La Campaña. While Americans should continue to criticize shortcomings in the Mexican program, we must be equally vocal in recognition of its accomplishments. As the primary recipient of Mexican drugs, this country must seek enlightened means of reducing the demand side of the scale. The Mexicans are correct in asserting that the root problem is ours, not theirs. There are approximately the same number of American heroin addicts today as there were in the mid-1960s when Turkey was the primary source country. When illegal Turkish production was checked, Mexico filled the gap. Should Mexico's campaign prove successful, another country will take its place. For as long as the demand exists, and with it the enormous profit incentive, a source will surely be forthcoming.

## NOTES

1. An insightful analysis of Intercept's domestic impact is contained in Gooberman (1974).

2. With this writing, Mexican authorities are seriously considering: (1) legal reforms involving severe penalties for the sale of inhalants to minors; (2) means of controlling the production, distribution, and sale of raw materials used in manufacturing solvents; and (3) the elimination or substitution of particular toxics in solvents and glues.

3. Undoubtedly, traffickers occasionally barter weapons for drugs. However, it is the author's opinion that no more than 10%-15% of the total is acquired in this manner. But even this amount leaves the grower/trafficker very well armed and Mexican officials very concerned.

4. However, such officers appear to be in a distinct minority; as one American military officer put it in early 1974: "Mexico's five hottest drug zones are now being commanded by men who are, in my honest opinion, truly dedicated to the campaign" (Interview: 1974a).

5. The word "exclusively" is relative. Obviously, not all of these men work drugs all of the time. It must be remembered that the entire corps of MFJP numbers only some 600 men whose duties encompass a wide variety of activities, including those related to the antidrug campaign.

6. This is not meant to imply the absence of a risk factor, because Mexico is perhaps the only country to apply agrarian and penal sanctions for drug cultivation. *Campesinos,* however, have countered the risk of losing their acreage by often tilling their opium plots on government owned land.

7. Under Article VI of the *Código Penal* a Mexican citizen who commits a crime in another country that is also a crime under Mexican law can be tried in Mexico so long as he has not been finally tried in the foreign country.

# REFERENCES

BARONA LOBATO, J. (1976) México ante el reto de las drogas. México, D.F.: Impresiones Modernas.

CRAIG, R. B. (1977) "Operation Intercept: the international politics of pressure." Presented to the Organization of American Historians (April).

Drug Enforcement (1974) "Interview with Attorney General Paullada." 1 (Fall): 9-13.

GOOBERMAN, L. A. (1974) Operation Intercept: The Multiple Consequences of Public Policy. New York: Pergamon.

Interview (1976a) México, D.F.: Procuraduría General de la Republica Mexicana (February 13).

——— (1976b) México, D.F.: United States Embassy (Jaunary 16).

——— (1975) México, D.F.: United States Embassy (February 18).

——— (1974a) México, D.F.: United States Embassy (March 9).

——— (1974b) México, D.F.: Procuraduría General de la República Mexicana (February 28).

——— (1971) Laredo, TX: United States Bureau of Customs (July 12).

*Richard B. Craig is Associate Professor of Political Science at Kent State University with a Ph.D. from the University of Missouri. He is currently involved in the whole question of international narcotics traffic in the Americas and has written several articles on narcotics in general. He is author of* The Bracero Program: Interest Groups in Foreign Policy, *published by the University of Texas Press, 1969.*

**RALPH R. PREMDAS**
*Department of Political & Administrative Studies*
*The University of Papua, New Guinea*
*Box 4820—University P.O.*
*Papua, New Guinea*

# *GUYANA*

## *Socialist Reconstruction or Political Opportunism?*

Guyana has become the second "socialist" republic in the Western Hemisphere after Cuba. The history of how this occurred is an almost classic example of the futility of inept intervention by outside great powers. Prime Minister Forbes Burnham, brought to office in 1965 by Anglo-American intervention that ousted Marxist Cheddi Jagan from power, has turned Guyana from a safe U.S. client committed to a capitalistic economic model into a strident anti-American bastion on the South American mainland, with a politicoeconomic system in theory and increasingly in practice inspired by Marxism-Leninism. The Burnham regime has nationalized all significant foreign firms, declared itself a cooperative socialist republic, and has forged close collaborative links with Cuba, the People's Republic of China, and such left-oriented African countries as Tanzania, Guinea, Angola, and Mozambique.

Jagan, who was twice evicted from office—in 1953 by British troops and in 1964 by an arbitrary rearrangement of the colony's electoral system—has pledged "critical support" to the Burnham regime. From 1965 to 1971, Jagan's forces were ruthlessly suppressed. His People's Progressive Party (PPP) was reduced from a vibrant vehicle that operated in all parts of Guyana to a bare skeleton organization with little open popular support. To the outside world Jagan was finished, and it was widely thought that

Journal of Interamerican Studies and World Affairs, Vol. 20 No. 2, May 1978

with his demise all socialist and communist influences in Guyana were destroyed permanently.

The purpose of this article is to identify the factors and analyze the processes that have led Guyana to adopt a socialist program to solve its problems of poverty and political power. Hopefully this exercise sheds some light on one significant variant of radical political change increasingly resorted to by many Third World countries. We have tried to show that the initial acts of nationalization by the Burnham government were not consonant with socialist practices. Our contention is that socialist principles were invoked ex post facto to justify a desperate need for revenue to keep the regime in power. The socialist rhetoric so opportunistically seized upon to rationalize the first nationalization, however, did assume a subsequent determinative role in economic policy. Repeatedly invoked and recited, socialist slogans would be sincerely adopted by its symbol swayers and become the ideological map inspiring the direction of the government.

Equal in importance to the nationalizations are the problems which any government will encounter in engrafting an unfamiliar politicoeconomic system on a political culture of a conflict-ridden communal society. In part, the article analyzes the constraints on socialist reconstruction emanating from (1) the political culture of the conflicting ethnic communities, and (2) the political interests of the two communal leaders as they move toward political reconciliation. Like the communal struggles between Africans and Indians which intensified over a twenty-year period of nationalist party politics and periodically spilled over into open violence and demands for partition, the new socialist experiment in Guyana is sponsored by changing interelite relationships. The political elites of the major parties are westernized and educated and have much in common. The masses whose loyalties were manipulated for political ends in the past are the *object* of the new experiment. The evidence suggests that the separate communities have been driven so far apart that talk of socialist reconstruction involving intercommunal cooperation and fellowship at the grassroots is viewed with great skepticism.

Finally, on top of the layers of difficulties that must be overcome in transforming Guyanese political culture and partisan interests to fit the requirements of a socialist framework, is the formidable geopolitical obstacle of executing this experiment in the Western Hemisphere in defiance of U.S. hegemonic security interests. In a curious twist of events, Burnham, who was brought to power by Anglo-American intervention, alleges that his government is the target of an externally inspired destabilization campaign from the same source. The article also deals in part with this aspect of the problem.

The materials are set forth in three parts. Part I provides a brief background to the Burnham government, identifies the factors that have led to the socialist conversion, and examines the nationalization process for its socialist content. Part II analyzes the constraints derived from political culture and partisan interests to socialist reconstruction and political reconciliation. Part III examines some other problems involved in implementing socialism, particularly the constraint imposed by Guyana's location in the Western Hemisphere.

## *Part I*

### *BACKGROUND TO THE BURNHAM GOVERNMENT*

Initially Burnham assumed power in 1965 in coalition with Peter D'aguiar, the leader of the most vocal pro-American free enterprise party in the country. Together they participated in a series of externally financed strikes and demonstrations in 1962 and 1963 that disrupted the Jagan government, requiring the insertion of British troops to maintain law and order (Newman, 1964; Report of a Commission of Inquiry, 1962; Sheehan, 1967; Pearson, 1964; Lens, 1965; Chase, 1964; Schlesinger, 1965). Subsequently, the British government reneged on its promise to let Jagan lead the country into independence (Report on British Guyana, 1962; New Nation, 1971), using the strikes and demonstrations as the pretext to alter the colony's electoral laws to permit the removal of Jagan from office. Independence under a D'aguiar-Burnham coalition was then granted in May 1966. At the time, a state of emergency was in effect, and many of Jagan's supporters languished in the Mazaruni prisons without trial.

During the first years, the new Burnham-led government received abundant financial support from Washington, which was determined to eliminate Jagan and the potential threat of another Cuba in the hemisphere. When he was premier, Jagan profusely praised Fidel Castro as one of the world's greatest liberators. At the same time, while nearly all of the Western Hemisphere countries yielded to American pressure to sever diplomatic and trade links with Cuba, Jagan established cultural and economic ties. Guyana's abundant timber and rice products found a lucrative market in Cuba; additionally, many government and party personnel made frequent visits to witness the radical transformations initiated by the Castro regime. When the Burnham-D'aguiar coalition acceded to power, all Guyana-Cuba links were forthwith terminated. Similarly, in support of their overseas sponsors, Guyana voted consistently until 1969 against the seating of the People's Republic of China in the United Nations.

The coalition ruled by a slim parliamentary majority. In the 53-seat unicameral legislature, the PPP had 24 seats, but Burnham's People's National Congress (PNC) had 22 seats, and D'aguiar's United Force (UF) had 7 seats, a total of 29 for the coalition. Although its margin seemed tenuous, the government was stable because party discipline was strong. However, at the grass roots, the coalition was weak. Political parties in Guyana are built around the country's ethnic cleavages. Race is the determinant of party affiliation (Premdas, 1972a; Premdas, 1973b). Jagan's PPP is supported by East Indians who constitute 51% of the population, while Burnham's PNC is supported by Africans and some mixed race persons—about 40% of the population—and D'aguiar's UF by Portuguese, Europeans, Amerindians, Chinese, and an assortment of middle-class mixed race, African, and East Indians—about 8-9% of the population (Smith, 1962).

Because of the manner in which Jagan was ousted from power and the racially based party politics, the coalition government lacked cross-sectional majority support. The fact that over half of Guyana's population consisted of persons of Indian descent who steadfastly supported Jagan weakened the legitimacy of the government. During the bloody 1964 PPP-sponsored sugar strike, Jagan had demonstrated that he could bring the country's economy to a virtual halt (Jagan, 1966; Sims, 1966). In order to enable the government a minimum of security to implement its programs, the Jagan party machinery had to be crushed. This was done by coercion, but at the cost of perpetuating the impaired legitimacy of the coalition.

The partnership between Burnham and D'aguiar was never a comfortable arrangement, especially for Burnham who saw D'aguiar's party as the representation of the old colonial privilege and racism. Jagan never permitted Burnham to forget that in terms of what the latter professed to believe, the United Force was anathema. A few months prior to the 1968 general elections Burnham, with the aid of certain PPP defectors in parliament, wrested control of the government from D'aguiar. The PNC then proceeded to reconstitute the Electoral Commission with party sympathizers and to tamper with the electoral machinery. Consequently, the PNC won sole control of the government in the 1968 elections (Sunday Times, 1968; Mitchell, 1968). Like the Indians before, now D'aguiar's ethnic supporters were alienated from the government. After 1968, in this racially plural society Burnham had the support of less than 40% of the population. He moved to consolidate his power to prevent possible disruption by purging the army and police of practically all non-African elements, for the coercive apparatus of state became critical in preserving the regime's power.

By 1969, with undisputed control over the government, the PNC charted a course consonant with overall U.S. wishes and the free enterprise system. The government's power was enhanced as the PPP suffered disaffection and defections stemming from interminable internal party ideological battles. The

Indian and other non-African groups, excluded from power, were despondent. Those who had the means and cultivated the right connections emigrated to Canada, the United States, and the United Kingdom, further enfeebling the anti-Burnham forces. Washington continued to support the PNC regime despite the fact that the most fervent anticommunist elements, the United Force, had been eliminated from participation in the government. Active collaboration between Burnham and Washington continued without any tangible sign that a change was in sight. How and why then did the PNC regime in less than three years after decisively "winning" the 1968 elections adopt a radical ideological change of position?

*FACTORS THAT LED TO THE CONVERSION*

Burnham is known as an ambitious man who craves the recognition of the Third World's "progressive" leaders. While practically muted at home, the Jagan forces were effective in disseminating information abroad that linked Burnham to the CIA. Burnham's collaboration with Washington became an embarassment; the stigma of CIA intervention in 1964 and rigged elections in 1968 severely tarnished his international image. Perhaps no other single factor explains the ideological about change in Burnham after 1970 better than this obsession with his international reputation as shall be suggested throughout the paper. Note, for example, how every act of nationalization was widely publicized by the regime, as was the steady stream of dignitaries visiting Guyana including Fidel Castro, Julius Nyerere, and Madam Bandaranaike. Burnham himself was hosted by the court of Mao Tse-tung, while Guyana sponsored several international conferences and festivals at great cost to herself. The upshot was that Guyana's image as a backward client state of western imperialism governed by a supine and submissive government gradually shifted so that Burnham acquired a reputation himself as a progressive Third World leader. However, his close identification with the left-leaning Third

World leaders did not come until after this group had gained significant attention at international forums calling for a restructuring of trade agreements and for the formation of commodity cartels to control raw material prices.

Objective factors that led to the radical changes in Guyana were also at play. Indians who dominated the rice and sugar industries boycotted government policy. Rice production fell from the 1964-1965 level of 101,424 tons to 48,651 tons in 1973-1974. The contribution of rice to Gross Domestic Product plummeted from 5.7% in 1966 to 2.9% in 1971, to 2.1% in 1973 (Economic Bulletin, 1974). For the first time, Guyana faced food shortages and the threat of a famine. Chronic strikes on the sugar belt led to unpredictable sugar exports. Skilled non-African government employees migrated from Guyana as racial discriminatory practices intended to consolidate PNC control over the civil service became open and widespread. Adding to the economic depression was an inflationary rate that averaged between 20% to 30% annually. Private foreign investment fell dramatically, from $17-$18 million (U.S.) in the late 1960s to about $7 million (U.S.) in 1972 (Mandle, 1977). Unemployment especially in the urban areas average about 20% while underemployment was about 36%. The main sources of revenue from rice, sugar, and bauxite exports were not enough to meet the needs of an increasingly expectant African population. Simultaneously, other industries such as livestock, fishing, forestry, food, and tobacco contributed about the same 15% to 16% of the Gross Domestic Product in 1971 as they did in 1966, although the rate of population growth was about 3% annually. Foreign aid and loans were not only difficult to obtain because of a weakening domestic economic base, but interest rates on Guyana's previous aid program led Burnham to describe aid as a form of "raid." With Jagan ostensibly reduced to an insignificant force, the so-called communist menace in Guyana no longer provided Washington with an incentive to continue its lavish support of the Burnham government. Burnham's relations with Washington gradually cooled.

The PNC's internal popular base, the African sector, was kept in line by the reminder that "it is either we or the coolies (pejorative for Indians) who will run Guyana." Uninhibited racial jingoism in quest of political power nurtured and maintained intact the strength of both the PPP and PNC. But the very prejudices invoked to maintain party solidarity inevitably must reappear to haunt whichever party finally controls the government. Victory at the polls in Guyana's ethnically segmented system is viewed as conquest of one race over the over. The party in power discovers that it is held captive to its pre-election racist appeals. Followers demand that patronage be granted to them alone at the expense of the "outsector." Consequently, formulating programs to restore a minimal amount of multiethnic legitimacy is thwarted.

The Burnham regime fell victim to this pattern of racial politics. The civil service alone consumed nearly 50% of the annual budget and it was already overstaffed with political appointees. But the more the government neglected agriculture, the more urgent became not only the revenue and unemployment situation, but also the food supply problem. The implications were clear. The coercive state machinery employed frequently to suppress the non-African population would have to be applied increasingly against frustrated African sympathizers. African trade unionists who went on strike were already the first victims. Strike frequency increased from 126 in 1969 to 190 in 1971.

In summary, Burnham's craving for international approbation, the increasing unavailability and high cost of foreign aid, and a deteriorating economy constitute the forces that sparked the radical changes that began in 1971. The country's economy, based on sugar, rice, and bauxite production, export-oriented at the mercy of fluctuating world market prices, had to be altered. Further, economic reconstruction, regardless of strategy, could not be achieved when more than half of the population did not cooperate with or boycotted government policies. Burnham was presiding over an increasingly impoverished society whose political and economic image was being compared to Papa Doc's Haiti.

For a number of years, the PNC's *New Nation* carried articles in praise of socialism. But no one believed them because the government continued its dependency on the United States and United Kingdom for its markets and aid. Further, no attempt was made to challenge or restructure the capitalist economy inherited from the days of colonialism. But by 1971, the government was beset by grave economic difficulties and needed revenues to stay in power. It needed revenues to service its overstaffed bureaucracy which could not be retrenched; to pay interests on overseas loans from public and private creditors to preserve the country's credit worthiness; to pay for food imports to avert large scale food shortages; and to pay the police and military whose loyalty ensured the regime's survival. The image of a poor, dependent Guyana, run by a dictatorship that pitted one nonwhite group against another, was inconsistent with Burnham's ambition for international recognition as a progressive leader.

*THE NATIONALIZATION AND SOCIALISM*

Between 1971 and the present, the government nationalized all the major foreign firms in Guyana; these ranged from the bauxite industry to the foreign banks. It would, however, be misleading to regard nationalization of the bauxite industry as an act consonant with socialist practice. There was no explicit plan or policy on nationalization. The first occurred almost by accident, and the others followed on an erratic and uneven scheduled. But once the first was nationalized and yielded revenues, the others soon became victims as the domestic economic situation worsened because of the Arab oil boycott and the accompanying skyrocketing price of fuel. In effect, the nationalizations proceeded in Guyana not by long-term design inspired by a socialist philosophy, but by financial necessity.

Take, for example, the first nationalization of the Demerara Bauxite Company (DEMBA) which was a subsidiary of Alcan Aluminum Ltd. of Canada. DEMBA was the larger of two foreign-owned bauxite companies in Guyana. Together they accounted for 8% of the world's supply of metal grade bauxite and 90% of the calcined bauxite (Litvak and Maule, 1975). In addition, they made Guyana the world's fourth largest producer of bauxite and producer about 45% of the country's foreign exchange. DEMBA's capital investment was $130 million (U.S.), with the company owning all 100% of its assets. However, it employed only 4% of the country's work force. Because "its operations were vertically integrated into Alcan's corporate system," it offered little stimulus to the development of other sectors of the economy (Litvak and Maule, 1975). Although the company paid very attractive wages to its employees, it was slow in involving locals in decision-making which irked Guyanese nationalists as did its de facto segregated housing and recreational facilities.

Over the period 1966-1970, the government had expended much of the funds derived from foreign loans to establish an infrastructure of roads and other facilities to attract private enterprise. But the foreign investment never materialized. Consequently, the seven-year development plan the government adopted in 1966 calling for three times as much expenditure as the previous plan had to be abandoned by 1970 for lack of revenues. Then with thc growing financial crisis compounded by high inflation and unemployment rates, the government moved in on DEMBA.

The first indication of government intentions occurred on February 23, 1970, when Guyana declared itself the first "Co-operative Republic" in the world. Burnham said:

> In the Exploitation of these (forest and mineral resources), we are prepared to enter in consortia with foreign investors, but only on certain conditions, and one such condition henceforth will be that government alone or government and cooperatives, hold in each case no less than 51% of the equity [Burnham, 1974].

It is clear from this statement that complete nationalizations were not contemplated. Explained the Minister of Mines, "Our position was always one of participation, not nationalization" (Severo, 1972).

When the government finally acted to implement its new policy, it turned retrospectively to DEMBA first. It argued that its revenue from the company was too small and "attributed this fact to the company's intra-corporate sales, based on Alcan-established transfer prices" (Litvak and Maule, 1975). In seeking a 51% ownership, the government had hoped to control management and have access to the financial transactions of the company. This strategy would have fulfilled the need for revenue and created input linkages into the local economy while retaining DEMBA's management expertise to continue its profitable operations. In the negotiations with the government, however, DEMBA's team was unwilling to grant this concession.

It is critical to note the popular scenario unfolding at the time of the negotiations. The government had mobilized its followers and held rallies to display its determination at the negotiating table. Further, Burnham openly sought Jagan's support. In an agreement called the "Peace Plan," Jagan supported not merely the 51% equity participation, but outright nationalization; Burnham reciprocated by promising to concede certain rights to Jagan's party. When DEMBA refused to relinquish the 51% ownership, the government was left with one of two choices: first, back down and abandon its plan, which would entail an enormous loss of face and credibility; second, to respond to Jagan's demand (which was shared by a number of other small left-wing groups) to "tek al" (pidgin for "take all"). With a highly mobilized and excited population practically looking on, DEMBA's intransigence forced the government to opt for the second choice—complete nationalization.

The manner in which this first acquisition occurred had little to do with the socialist demand to "control the commanding heights of the economy." However, after the nationalization decision was reached, Burnham and his party paper, *New Nation,* dug up old speeches and selectively extracted quotations to show that their act was part of a socialist design planned in advance and that tactics alone dictated their initial overture aimed at the 51% "meaningful participation" formula.

But even this accidental act of nationalization, taken under great pressure, could not convince the government's more perceptive critics that socialism was its objective. The nationalization of DEMBA was not followed up by any structural alterations of the economy. Apart from the fact that the government continued to invite foreign firms to invest in Guyana (Severo, 1972), other more decisive evidence made suspect the loudly proclaimed socialist intentions of the Burnham regime. First, the Chase Manhattan Bank (Guyana branch) loaned the government funds to make an initial payment on the $53.5 million (U.S.) compensation price for DEMBA to be paid over a 20-year period. Second, once DEMBA was acquired, it became a state corporation called Guybau which continued the old employer-employee organizational practices. Most noteworthy, the racially discriminatory employment practices favoring PNC supporters prevailed. Further, the new "mastas" simply moved into the executive houses of the departing expatriate staff who had lived in de facto segregation. Third, whereas socialist nationalization is likely to be accompanied by the loss of western, particularly U.S. markets, this did not occur in the case of Guyana. To be sure, the government had to find new markets for some of its bauxite and alumina, but these were obtained in the West. In this regard the most astounding act was the appointment of Phillip Brothers, the U.S. subsidiary of the giant Ango-American corporation of South Africa, as Guybau's marketing sales manager. This act was astounding because the Burnham government has made an annual grant of $50,000 (G) now increased to $80,000 (G) to the organization of African Unity's fund established to support the freedom fighters against Rhodesian and South African apartheid practices in Africa. Finally, the profits from Guybau were not distributed as a surplus to diversify the economy and render the country less dependent on foreign sources for food and other materials, but rather were diverted in part to pay the burgeoning state bureaucracy to help maintain the government in power.

Another substantial part of Guybau's profits was allocated to pay for interest and capital costs owed to the Chase Manhattan

Bank. However, the government's popularity among its followers soared. The acquisition process was an adeptly played out drama that distracted attention from the domestic economic crisis. Significantly, the international support previously denied Burnham was forthcoming. The nationalization, although lacking in socialist content, symbolized for certain Third World leaders Burnham's break with the "reactionary forces" that brought him to power. For them, the nationalization represented a bold act by a small black Third World country to wrest control over its resources from the hands of exploiting multinational corporations.

The applause was encouraging and from it expectations were entertained that Burnham would extend his action to other areas. The PNC felt that its tarnished image was being erased, and above all, that it would preempt the socialist reputation of the PPP. The *New Nation* continued to publish socialist articles and international visitors journeyed to Guyana to witness the "transformations" taking place. However, the PPP, an assortment of left-wing groups, and the *Guyana Graphic* (Guyana's most popular paper) did not accept the PNC's self portrait. They pointed to the inconsistencies between the claims of the government and the practices of racial discrimination and political victimization. The "Peace Plan" between Burnham and Jagan was terminated. Open political conflict became widespread, expressed mainly through government harassment of its opponents and, in turn, strident criticism of PNC policies by opposition elements. This set the stage for the 1973 elections. Again the results were rigged, but this time the PNC used the army to assist in administering the elections and handling the ballot boxes, many of which disappeared for days (Third World, 1973). The PNC, with only a minority popular base, received an astounding two-thirds (37) of the 53 seats, enough to alter the constitution. The PPP, which received only 14 seats, boycotted the Parliament. The United Force won 2 seats and became the government opposition.

The national and particularly international criticisms and exposures mounted mainly by the opposition groups in Guyana following the 1973 elections led finally to the government acquisition of the *Daily Graphic* and the "voluntary" departure of its editors to reside in other Caribbean countries. Apart from Jagan's own newspaper, *The Mirror*, which was denied newsprint and was consequently very illegible, press freedom in Guyana was practically muffled. Small irregular pamphlets such as *Ratoon, Creole,* and *Liberator,* distributed by the other left- and right-wing groups came under state harassment. Their editors and supporters were either shot (as in the case of *Ratoon's* editor) or faced libel suits and unusual tax claims issued by the government against them. They had to face a judiciary which like the press and parliament was being purged of all independent and critical personnel.

The jubilation that followed DEMBA's nationalization died. After the 1973 elections, the government sought to control the means by which its international image was exported through a state monopoly of information. But the continuing economic crisis, now exacerbated by the massive increase in oil prices, could not be erased through a two-thirds legislative majority or by repressive fiat. The African sector remained loyal to Burnham, but migration to Canada and the United States continued steadily, although intending migrants found it difficult to get their savings out of the country. Substantially constituted of Indian middle-class elements, the migrants numbered between 5,000 and 7,000 annually in a total population of approximately 750,000.

### *THE REYNOLDS NATIONALIZATION*

The next nationalization was carried out almost three years after the first. Although it involved a smaller firm, it was of immensely more importance than DEMBA. The firm was Reynolds Bauxite Company, a wholly owned subsidiary of Reynolds Metals Company of the United States. Unlike DEMBA, which was Canadian, Reynolds was symbolic of the hovering omnipresence of Burnham's metropolitan sponsor, the United

States, to which an understanding was given that private investment in Guyana would be protected and promoted. The same economic reasons that led to the demand for 51% equity participation in DEMBA's case would impel the government to move in on Reynolds.

Reynolds, which commenced production in 1954, declared a loss in its operations until 1963 and hence paid no income tax during this entire period. When Burnham came to power, he entered into an agreement with Reynolds under which the company would increase production to 1 million tons by 1976. In return for this the government would freeze the company's taxes at less than $1/4 million (U.S.) annually for 25 years (Sunday Times, 1968; Sunday Mirror, 1974). But by 1973, Burnham's receipt of aid from the United States had been reduced to a trickle and he needed revenues desperately. Just as importantly, the price of aluminum had doubled on the world market from 20 cents per pound in 1972 to 40 cents in 1973, and while Reynolds Metals of the United States declared a $19.2 million (U.S.) profit on the first quarter of 1974, Guyana received barely .05% of the selling price of aluminum from the local Reynolds operations (New Nation, 1974).

The government opened talks with Reynolds on July 10, 1974 for majority participation. The company's reply was that it was willing to pay back taxes of nearly $3.5 million (U.S.) but demanded that future taxes were not to be related to increased prices for bauxite, and the government must abandon nationalization intentions and other forms of participation for five years (Osman, 1974). The talks broke down. On September 25, 1974, the government legislatively imposed a bauxite levy on Reynolds under which the company was required to pay nearly $6 million (U.S.), half of which was due within 15 days. Reynolds refused to pay, took the government to court for breach of contract, lost, retrenched workers, repatriated overseas staff, and so on, and eventually the government nationalized the company.

Burnham described the economic pressures that forced his government to impose the levy as follows:

> It was at the end of 1973 that the Guyanese economy was struck by a devastating blow by the escalating fuel costs and associated rising prices for fertilizers, machinery, raw materials, consumer goods, and food supplies. The increased cost of wheat alone will result in doubling in the price of flour to the Guyanese consumer. A number of vital development projects had to be rescheduled and so far the main burden has had to be bourne by the people of Guyana. It is evident that if a disaster of major proportions were to be avoided, substantial injections of revenue into the economy would be required [New Nation, 1974].

He further claimed that opportunities for long-term borrowing were all but dried up (New Nation, 1974). Consequently, Reynolds had to pay more, but instead of increasing production to the promised one million ton mark, Reynolds decreased production by 1970 and paid less taxes than in previous years to the government (New Nation, 1974).

At a rally held after the nationalization, Burnham warned: "There is reason to believe that all American aid to Guyana will be cut off" (Graphic, 1974). That did take place. But from that point onward Burnham increasingly turned to Cuba and the People's Republic of China for help. Burnham's international image skyrocketed among many Third World leaders. Cuba granted him its highest award, the José Martí award, and Mao Tse-tung hosted him. Guyana, however, could not be a model to other left-leaning Third World countries until it had eliminated: (1) all vestiges of foreign control of its economy, and (2) the racial conflict among Africans and Indians. Further, Burnham now had to cope with the possible consequences of defying U.S. interests in the Western Hemisphere. In turn, all of this meant only one thing—reconciliation with Jagan to promote national unity.

## *Part II*

### *RECONCILIATION WITH JAGAN AND THE NATIONALIZATION OF BOOKERS*

Any development of the Guyanese economy that seeks to eliminate dependency on food imports and maximize domestic self-sufficiency must entail the support of rural dwellers. Significantly, even though Burnham controlled the government, Jagan remained the most powerful rural figure. In essence, if Burnham's antiimperialist rhetoric against dependency was to be realized, Indian support was indispensable. Throughout the previous ten years, the PNC tried unsuccessfully to wean away segments of the Indian population from Jagan. Those who crossed the ethnic line were well rewarded, but had to live socially ostracized from their community. Those who did not cooperate, that is, practically the entire Indian community, suffered from undisguised discrimination. Among the punitive measures used were the loss of fertilizer and fuel subsidies for rice production, the bypassing of the farmer-controlled Rice Producers' Association in decision-making affecting the grading and pricing of rice over which the government had sole monopoly rights to purchase, and the refusal of the government to recognize the Guyana Agricultural Workers' Union (GAWU) which represented sugar workers.

The PPP initiated a boycott against the government's self-sufficiency program charging that surplus profits were extracted to finance the civil service.

Rice production fell to unprecedented levels and the sugar industry was plagued by chronic strikes. During early 1975 alone, the government admitted that it lost about $100 million (G) in foreign exchange (New Nation, 1975c). Administrative services related to agricultural production were almost inaccessible to Indian farmers as the government embarked on a program to launch Africans into farming. Added to this was the fact that Indians were routinely intimidated and harassed by an African-dominated constabulary and a picture emerged in which racial repression of Indians, partly intended to destroy the PPP's base of support, was pervasive and undisputed.

Indian alientation and animosity, then, was the primary obstacle that frustrated Burnham's plan to mobilize the entire population to fulfill socialist principles - which had begun to play not merely an ex post facto justifying function, but had assumed a guiding, determinative role in the PNC government. Consequently, Jagan became indispensable to Burnham's designs. However, it would be inaccurate to assert that Jagan had nothing to gain from Burnham's new socialist image. Indeed, Jagan had many incentives to discontinue or modify his total opposition to the PNC regime. Burnham's socialism may be fraudulent when measured for consistency against his domestic policies and past performance, but his international reputation now rivaled Jagan's as a Marxist. Visits by Castro, Nyerere, Bandaranaike, and the like challenged Jagan's exclusive claims to the socialist antiimperialist ideology in Guyana. Further, he could not continue his unqualified criticism of Burnham when the latter was implementing the very policies advocated for 25 years by the PPP. In effect, while Burnham needed Jagan's cooperation, Jagan in turn had sufficient selfish reasons of his own to reciprocate.

Jagan announced his change of attitude on the 25th anniversary of the PPP in August 1975. Addressing the PPP's annual convention, Jagan said:

> The fact is that the changes, though compromised, have the effect of weakening imperialism. If we are to arrive at our goal of socialism, imperialism must first be destroyed. And whoever helps must be praised. We must continue to apply pressure on the PNC government and also take our own initiatives in this direction. The situation now therefore demands a more flexible approach on the part of the PPP. The party had previously declared that it does not have a monopoly on socialism, that it is prepared regardless of ideological and tactical differences to work with others if they are interested in building socialism in Guyana. And this includes the PNC. Our political line should be changed from non-cooperation and civil resistance to critical support" [Sunday Mirror, 1975a].

Clearly, Jagan was not giving unequivocal support to the PNC. What then was the extent of his support? Said Jagan:

> Critical support does not mean unconditional support. It means just what it says—giving support for any progressive measure, opposing any reactionary moves and criticizing all shortcomings [Sunday Mirror, 1975a].

Elaboration of the terms of the agreement was worked out in private sessions between the two leaders. The main concessions by Burnham related to the sugar industry.

Since 1949, Jagan had insisted on the nationalization of the foreign-owned sugar plantations. The sugar industry in Guyana is the mainstay of the economy. Two companies controlled the 11 huge sugar estates. Jessel Securities Ltd. of Britain controlled two estates occupying 21,000 acres and employing 2,500 workers. The company also locally owned 63% of the shares in a liquor factory, 20% in a sugar terminal, 2,000 acres of land partly under oil palm, and a major retail-wholesale outlet. Extensive retrenchment of workers at the last named facility led the government in February 1975 to nationalize the entire Jessel-owned enterprises in Guyana paying $15 million (G) in compensation (New Nation, 1975b). The Jessel nationalization was viewed as a necessary act against a socially irresponsible company that was oblivious to workers' interests and had allowed its equipment in the sugar plantations to run down without replacement. But the Jessel plantations were a small part of the sugar industry. Jagan's demand was to nationalize the remainder.

Most of Guyana's sugar was produced by the other foreign firm, Booker McConnell of Britain. So overwhelming was the role of this company in Guyana's emergence as a state that the country is often referred to as "Bookers Guyana." The company's operations predated British acquisition of the colony. Bookers owned six sugar estates, had an interest in three others, and branched out into other activities ranging from rum and molasses to rubber, retailing, and shipbuilding. Altogether, Bookers was represented by 23,000 persons who provided a livelihood for about 150,000 persons. Thousands of others indirectly depended on the company. Approximately 85% of Guyana's sugar was produced by Bookers, which occupied the best irrigated lands on the five to ten mile strip of coast on which 90% of the Guyanese live. In addition, it provided 40% of Guyana's exports, 30% of the G.N.P., 35% of the foreign exchange, and employed 13% of the work force, but was 90% owned by

Booker McConnell (Litvak and Maule, 1975; Burnham, 1976; Caribbean Contact, 1976).

Sugar, it was remarked, flows like blood through the entire body of the nation. Guyana's immigrant population came to the British colony as slaves and indentured laborers to provide a cheap and abundant source of manpower for the plantations. When slavery was abolished in 1831, the ex-slaves left the plantations and gradually moved to urban centers. East Indians who replaced the African workers became the new rural residents. It is among this rural proletariat in the sugar belt that Cheddi Jagan launched his anticolonial agitation for Guyana's independence after World War II. To be sure, his movement embraced and benefited both African and Indian workers, but the leadership schism with Burnham in 1955 left the rural areas as his most loyal and reliable base. When Jagan sought the nationalization of Bookers, he was not only tending to the needs of his own popular stronghold, but because of the sweep of Bookers' presence in Guyana, unlike DEMBA and Reynolds which were isolated enclaves, the act could imprint profound and radical changes in the property and production structure in the entire economy and society.

On the tenth anniversary of Guyana's independence in May 1976, Booker McConnell was nationalized and placed under the management of several state corporations run by Guyanese personnel. The government agreed to a compensation price of $102.5 million (G) payable over 20 years; Jagan had insisted on no compensation arguing that the original capital invested by Bookers had been recovered many times over and that the assets had been increased over the years without any new injection of capital from the owners (Sunday Mirror, 1975b). Nevertheless, the acquisition was a concession to Jagan. The government had imposed a special tax levy two years earlier to extract a portion of the huge profits that accrued to Bookers as a result of the unusually high prices of sugar on the world market. In 1975, this levy yielded over $200 million (G). But what Burnham wanted after he nationalized Reynolds was national unity. He feared possible U.S. intervention of the same sort that brought him to power. The Angolan incident best illustrates the point.

During early 1976, when Cuban troops were inserted into Angola to aid the MPLA, the Guyana government was charged with allowing its airport to be used by Cuban troops on the way to Conakry, Africa. Rumors were also spread by a newspaper, *O Estado De Sao Paulo* of Brazil, and a news-magazine, *Resumen* of Venezuela, that several thousand Cuban and Chinese troops were training paramilitary forces in Guyana (Omag, 1976). The government responded that it was a victim of a destabilization campaign. Burnham attributed the false rumors to "some elements that see our relationship with Cuba as too close . . . who don't want to see a little country on the road to socialism succeed" (Omag, 1976). The government warned of the possibility of an invasion from Brazil and together Burnham and Jagan openly pledged solidarity against any external threat (Latin America, 1976). Jagan was paying the full price for this real or imagined threat. He later said:

> Critical support was and remains the correct line because any country which takes an anti-imperialist course is likely to be attacked. The PPP has a patriotic duty to defend Guyana's sovereignty, independence, and integrity [Hamaludin, 1976].

The relationship between Burnham and Jagan has not extended to the formation of a coalition government. Jagan has agreed instead to return with his party (13 seats) to the government-dominated 52-seat Parliament. But he defines the role of his party in the following terms:

> The PPP, as the vanguard of the working class, must maintain its identity so as to propagate the ideology of the working class—Marxism—Leninism—and fight against revisionism and deviationism; elaborate correct strategy and tactics; and set up the necessary organization for mass action for the improvement of living conditions and the attainment of working class power [Hamaludin, 1976].

Hence, although the PNC claims to be Marxist-Leninist, the PPP sees its role as the enforcement of the faith. Jagan said that Cabinet positions were not as important as correct programs (Hamaludin, 1976). Specifically, the PPP will continue to pressure the PNC government to start the process of making socialism a reality in the domestic context. Next we turn to the kinds of constraints which limit the implementation of socialist principles in Guyana.

### *BURNHAM'S POWER BASE AND DOMESTIC SOCIALISM*

The internalization of socialism remains the main task of the Burnham regime in order to establish unequivocally its bona fide socialist credentials. It is here Burnham will be tested, for his very power base must be abandoned in the process. Specifically, the pillars of PNC power, namely the civil service, police, and military and Trades' Union Council, will have to be reorganized. When Burnham acceded to power, he refused to implement the recommendations of the International Commission of Jurists that investigated the problem of racial imbalance in the civil service (Report on Racial Problems, 1965). Instead, especially after the 1968 elections, it was purged of nearly all high-ranking Indian personnel. This pattern was repeated more decisively in the Police Force and especially in the Guyana Defense Force. The PPP complained bitterly that "the PNC is establishing a military-bureaucratic one-party state" (Jagan, 1975) which it called "neo-fascist" and compared to the "Hitlerite and Ian Smith parties" (Jagan, 1975).

The government's socialist philosophy challenges its racial recruitment procedure. The nationalization of DEMBA, Reynolds, Jessels, Bookers, and most recently, all foreign banks and private schools requires a racially balanced civil service not only to increase legitimacy but to mobilize all available talents to successfully run public corporations which now have the responsibility for over 80% of the economy. Jagan has continued to pressure the PNC. Returning from Moscow in September 1976, he demanded that the government draw up and implement socialist programs "before talking about having a socialist state" (Weekly Gleaner, 1976). He noted that despite the nationalizations "the same basic structures remain in these industries" (Weekly Gleaner, 1976). Turning to the procedures by which the PNC acquired power, he said "it is impossible to build socialism until the whole social life of the country is democratized" (Weekly Gleaner, 1976).

But he got to the crux of the racial recruitment policy when he observed that the PNC had "a rightist base" which does "not want to take positive steps that will result in socialism" (Weekly Gleaner, 1976). Specifically, he pointed to the "corrupt bureaucratic system that had developed in Guyana and that some people who were enmeshed in this corruption were opposed to any further changes" (Weekly Gleaner, 1976). The problem could be stated more objectively. The national pie must be so divided that Jagan's supporters become full beneficiaries. In stark power terms, the problem concerns the sharing of strategic positions with the previously excluded group. Should socialist principles be implemented, Burnham may witness not only a dilution of his power base, but may encounter acts of sabotage and rebellion from those party people who rose to prominence by skillfully manipulating racial symbols in the past. The PNC well remembers the days when it accused the PPP of precisely the same sorts of flagrant discriminatory practices of which it is now charged. The PPP government (1957-1964) was called "coolie or rice government" (Premdas, 1973a) that allegedly titled its annual budgets and development plans in favor of rural residents (Hope and David, 1974). Should the PNC risk the loss of power by inviting Indians to share command of the strategic levels of government? Should the African sector in the name of elusive socialist principles jeopardize its security and welfare by sharing power with Indians whose superior numbers could one day catapult them into the government? These are the most crucial constraints which Burnham faced as he sought to fulfill his promise of socialism in Guyana.

*JAGAN'S BASE AND SOCIALISM*

Jagan is not immune from antisocialist pressures emanating from his own community of support. Since their arrival as indentured laborers, Indians have maintained living patterns different from the African and other communities. Indian-African conflict can be traced to the beginning of Indian settlement in Guyana. The Indian presence triggered off two immediate reactions. First, it diluted the bargaining power of those ex-slaves who continued to work on the plantations. Second, Indians willingly performed degrading plantation tasks that Africans refused to do thereby incurring the contempt of the emancipated slaves. Over the next hundred years, separate job categories were occupied by Africans and Indians with their rural-urban residential pattern reinforcing the prejudices that separated them. In addition, they formed their own exclusive voluntary associations around which they organized community life (Premdas, 1972b).

The suspicion that separated the two communities was exacerbated during the period of nationalist politics, particularly from 1955 when Jagan and Burnham parted company and formed their own parties. Electoral rivalry in 1957, 1961, and 1964 intensified racial animosity between Africans and Indians as each party covertly, but systematically, appealed to racial sentiments for votes. Since then, at all levels of interaction Indian-African contact was characterized by competition and conflict (Despres, 1967).

It is upon this structure of intercommunal fear, distrust, and hostility that socialism must be erected. But for the Indian community one must add another dimension. A majority are small property holders who have accumulated more physical property than Africans, and many own small businesses. They consider themselves economically more industrious than Africans. It will be the unenviable task for Jagan to mobilize this peasant and property-based Indian population that is very contemptous of their economic performance, to join an experiment in intercommunal cooperation and solidarity.

Burnham's own position on private property is not reassuring to Indians: "We socialists hold that property is for the use and benefit of the society and nation, and not for hoarding, profiteering and manipulation by private individuals for their own ends and benefits" (Graphic, 1975). In an attempt to assuage fears, Burnham sought to distinguish between private property which will be nationalized and personal property which will be retained by individuals (Bliss, 1976). Burnham elaborated that "(P)ersonal property is that which a family or individuals use for its own needs, while private property is defined as that which is used to create excess wealth" (Bliss, 1976).

The implications are that the private infrastructure of businesses and factories owned by Indians, plus the large land holdings of others, would be in jeopardy. Already Jagan has come under pressure from these persons who may be regarded as his "rightist" base. They consider Jagan's "critical support" as a "sellout" to which he replied:

> We reply by exposing the positions of those who make the false "sellout" charge. The rightists, particularly some Indian professionals, businessmen, and landlords who fear socialism, say that the PPP is aware that the government is discriminating against the Indians, reducing them to second-class citizens, and propose to use compulsory national service to destroy "Indian race and culture," yet we are supporting it. We say that this is a distortion of our position. "Critical support" does not mean unconditional support. It means national unity and struggle—unity in defence of the nation and struggle against wrong-doings and shortcomings and for the well-being, rights, and liberties of the working people. In this respect, we are calling for the observance of the Fundamental Rights laid down in the constitution, and equal opportunity law, and an independent commission to administer the Act [Chronicle, 1976].

Fortunately for Jagan, a substantial number of the more wealthy and militant Indian middle class has emigrated. But, nevertheless, forging a socialist system into existence would still entail such a monumental task of inducing the Indian community to work with the African that it may well require coercion. It is not inconceivable that the future of socialism in Guyana may have to be implemented by a dictatorship jointly headed by Jagan and Burnham.

## *Part III*

### *THE FUTURE: CONSTRAINTS, DESTABILIZATION AND SOCIALISM*

Guyana's multiethnic structure will militate most strongly against the implementation of socialism. Each ethnic community is not merely different in living patterns, but hostile to and scornful of each other. Coexistence within the same community would require, fundamentally, the sharing of a minimal amount of common understandings and expectations among Indians and Africans. The socialist framework that is now proposed for Guyana, like the racial antagonisms that were provoked over the last two decades, is sponsored by changing interelite relationships. The political elites, westernized and educated, have much in common. The masses, whose loyalties were manipulated for political ends in the past, are the *object* of the new experiment. The evidence suggests that the separate communities have been driven so far apart that talk of socialist reconstruction involving intercommunity cooperation and fellowship must appear as a very cruel hoax.

The elites may be sincere in seeking to alleviate poverty and destroy dependency. However, these tasks would require more than the standard flourishes of socialist rhetoric. Constraints inherent in the social structure render socialist reconstruction, personalistically propelled by Jagan and Burnham, more than a short-term expedient intended to fulfill the ego needs of the leaders for international recognition. Even if an atmosphere of interracial trust can be restored, the objective needs of each community still have to be reconciled. As pointed out earlier, these refer to cultural dissimilarities and different economic occupations and structures. The Indian economic and demographic threat in particular constitutes a powerful force that inhibits the African community from wanting to share political control of the government.

The immediate constraints in constructing socialism, however, are rooted in two crucial factors. First is the sharing of the limited resource and patronage pie between the PPP and PNC. We have discussed the implications of this item earlier. Second is the question of hemisphere politics. The presence of another Cuba challenges U.S. hegemony in the Americas. Events in Chile that witnessed the bloody overthrow of Salvador Allende serve as a stern reminder that socialist governments in the Western Hemisphere are likely to face formidable obstacles to their viability. Burnham has already made explicit charges that attempts have been made to destabilize his government (Omag, 1976). Guyana's Foreign Minister, Fred Wills, elaborated at the nonaligned conference in Algiers:

> There is a concerted attempt to destabilize the governments of non-aligned countries in Latin America. More particularly, in the Caribbean—Guyana, Jamaica, and Barbados—have been subjected to the full fury of insidious techniques aimed at procuring their alignment, deliberate and well orchestrated attacks in the media, the selective sale of arms and so-called defence services, the promotion of inter-regional conflicts, the formenting of internal unrest, and the manipulation of pliant surrogates—all these and more have threatened the uneasy peace in our hemisphere and retarded the economic development of its peoples [Chronicle, 1976].

Destabilization from within Guyana is not too probable. Unlike Chile where a large middle class existed and where foreign firms continued to operate, Guyana has eliminated or controlled these forces. Jagan, however, is fearful of the PNC's "rightist base" which allegedly is vulnerable to foreign influence.

> Under the umbrella of nationalized and public sector enterprises, there can develop a whole new mediatory bourgeouise—neo-

> comprador, reactionary, bureaucratic, cooperative-capitalist contractors who will try to turn the anti-imperialist process to their own advantage [Hamaludin, 1976].

But many middle-class persons have emigrated which, while entailing a loss of managerial-administrative personnel, has drained away a substantial body of discontent from the society.

Finally, the trade unions and the military because of their predominantly uniethnic composition are firmly aligned to either the PNC or PPP. The Trades Union Council, which during the 1960s was affiliated with AIFLD and ORIT, which in turn were linked to the American AFL-CIO through which CIA funds were channeled to finance the strikes that destabilized the Jagan government (Lens, 1965; Pearson, 1964), has now practically severed all connections with these organizations. Regarding the Guyana Defense Force, objections were raised by Jagan when, as recently as 1975, the government sent military personnel to be trained in Brazil and Britain. That point apart, the African-dominated military, now called the People's Army in which Burnham is Commander-General, is very politicized and committed to the PNC government. The loyalty of the military is difficult to assess. They are deployed for border patrols, grow their own food, engage in civic projects such as road- and bridge-building, and are well paid. Fears that Brazilian forces may invade Guyana have led Jagan to call for the establishment of a people's militia, multiracial in composition, to deter aggression. A National Service has been established to provide compulsory quasi-military training and discipline to Guyanese youth. It is, however, a source of current PNC-PPP controversy. The PNC views it not only as a means of military training, but as a vehicle to inculcate socialist norms (New Nation, 1975a). The PPP regards it as a means to extract cheap labor and to impart the PNC's view of socialism history (Mirror, 1975).

Finally, note must be taken of the finer ideological differences that separate the PNC and PPP leadership. Both groups are presently engaged in a vigorous discourse over their relative Marxist-Leninist purity. They each invoke familiar Marxist slogans to make claim to the mantle of socialist legitimacy. Burnham refers to his brand of socialism as "cooperative socialism" indicating that the cooperative will be the foundation of economic organization in Guyana. Jagan refers to cooperativism as a "false ideology." Said Jagan:

> Socialism means public ownership of the means of production, distribution, and exchange. While supporting the cooperative movement, we must continue to expose and oppose the false ideology that cooperatives will be the means by which socialism will come to Guyana, that the cooperative sector will become the dominant sector. Turning over nationalized enterprises into cooperatives is not the way to build socialism. Rather, it is the way to construct a new form of capitalism [Sunday Mirror, 1975a].

Similar ideological differences over strategy and tactics contributed to the fateful split of the independence movement in 1955 between Jaganite and Burnhamite factions (Premdas, 1975). Today, significant doctrinal differences exist, with Jagan a staunch Moscow adherent and Burnham a Maoist supporter. Both the PNC and PPP maintain links with their respective sponsor's communist parties, although the Cuban Communist Party serves both the PPP and PNC equally. Presently, the ideological differences and affiliations are not difficult to manage partly because of the concerted efforts by Jagan and Burnham to prevent externally inspired destablization efforts from succeeding. Jagan has described the PNC regime as antiimperialist, but withholds the socialist label until domestic socialist practices are initiated. Doctrinal differences are not likely to become significant until such time that objective economic difficulties arise. Then, from frustration, ideological positions would be invoked in arguments to attribute blame.

## *Conclusion*

The nationalization of foreign firms in Guyana originated from economic necessity. Socialist principles invoked post facto to justify the nationalizations later became the determinative guide in government decision-making. Burnham and Jagan have entered into a limited agreement under which national unity and socialist practices are preeminent priorities. However, racial animosity between the two communal groups continues as the main internal impediment to socialist reconstruction (Premdas, 1977). Externally, the Guyanese leadership has closed ranks to forestall attempts at destabilizing the government. The internalization of socialist practices may require a dictatorship jointly sponsored by Jagan and Burnham.

## REFERENCES

BLISS, S. (1976) "Guyana's Jagan re-emerges." Guardian [Canadian] (April 7): 17.

BURNHAM, L.F.S. (1976) "One destiny." New Nation (May 30): 1.

——— (1974) "We'll control our resources." New Nation (July 13): 8.

Caribbean Contact (1976) "Farewell to Booker's empire." (March): 10.

CHASE, A. (1964) A History of Trade Unionism in Guyana. Georgetown, Guyana: New Guyana Company.

Chronicle (1976) "Stand firm—evil forces at work." (June 2): 20.

DESPRES, L. (1967) Cultural Pluralism and Nationalist Politics in British Guiana. Chicago: Rand McNally.

Economic Bulletin No. 8 (1974) (October): Table VIII, 6.

Graphic (1975) "Basic differences between capitalism and socialism." (August 10): 10.

——— (1974) "Burnham warns U.S. aid may be cut off." (October 28): 1.

HAMALUDIN, M. (1976) "PPP's attitudes today." Sunday Chronicle (September 12): 11.

HOPE, R. and W. C. DAVID (1974) "Planning for development in Guyana: the experience from 1945 to 1973." Inter-American Economic Affairs (Spring): 34.

JAGAN, C. (1975) "We must exert relentless pressure on the PNC." Sunday Mirror (January 5): 7.

——— (1966) The West on Trial. London: Michael Joseph.

Latin America (1976) "United we stand." (June 4): 1.

LENS, S. (1965) "American labor abroad." The Nation (July 5): 10.

LITVAK, I. and C. MAULE (1975) "Foreign firms: social costs and benefits in developing countries." Public Policy (Spring): 172.

MANDLE, J. (1977) "Continuity and change in Guyanese underdevelopment." Revista/Interamericana (Spring): 4.

Mirror (1975) "PPP calls on Guyanese to oppose compulsory national service." (August 31): 1.

MITCHELL, A. (1968) "Jagan and Burnham: it's polling day tomorrow. Has Guyana's election already been decided in Britain?" Sunday Times [London] (December 15): 5.
New Nation (1974a) "National Service." (April 13): 5.
——— (1975b) "The Jessel takeover." (June 1): 3.
——— (1975c) "GAWU gets desperate." (November 16): 1.
——— (1974) "Reynolds must pay more taxes." (July 13): 1.
——— (1971) "Independence plan." (April): 1.
NEWMAN, P. (1964) British Guiana: Problems of Cohesion in an Immigrant Society. London: Oxford Univ. Press.
OMAG, J. (1976) "U.S. blamed for campaign to 'destabilize' Guyana." Guardian [London] (March 21): 17.
OSMAN, R. (1974) "Reynolds bauxite tax levy for parliament on Wednesday." Sunday Graphic (September 22): 1.
PEARSON, D. (1964) "U.S. faces line holding decision." Washington Post (May 31): 24.
PREMDAS, R. R. (1977) "Guyana: communal conflict, socialism, and political reconciliation." Inter-American Economic Affairs (Spring): 75-77.
——— (1975) "The rise of the first mass-based multi-racial party in Guyana." Caribbean Q. (January): 17.
——— (1973a) "Competitive party organizations and political integration in a racially fragmented state: the case of Guyana." Caribbean Studies (January): 33.
——— (1973b) Party Politics and Racial Division in Guyana. Denver: Univ. of Denver Press.
——— (1972a) "Elections and political campaigns in a racially bifurcated state: the case of Guyana." J. of Interamerican Studies and World Affairs (August): 271-296.
——— (1972b) Voluntary Associations and Political Parties: The Case of Guyana. Guyana: Univ. of Guyana Printery.
Report of a Commission of Inquiry into Disturbances in British Guiana (1962) London: Her Majesty's Stationery Office, No. 354.
Report on British Guyana's Independence Conference (1962) London: Her Majesty's Stationery Office, cmd 1870.
Report on Racial Problems in the Public Service (1965) Geneva: International Commission of Jurists.
SCHLESINGER, A. Jr. (1965) A Thousand Days. New York: Houghton Mifflin.
SEVERO, R. (1972) "Guiana building a 'cooperative socialism' wants foreign capital." New York Times (October 31): 12.
SHEEHAN, N. (1972) "C.I.A. men aided strikes in Guiana against Dr. Jagan." New York Times (February 22): 3.
SIMS, P. (1966) Trouble in Guiana. London: George Allen & Unwin.
SMITH, R. (1962) British Guiana. London: Oxford University Press.
Sunday Mirror [Guyana] (1975a) "Dr. Jagan's address." (August 17): 9.
——— (1975b) "PPP calls for nationalization of Bookers." (March 2): 1.
——— (1974) "The Reynolds debate." (November 17): 6.
Sunday Times [London] (1968) November 5: 4.
Third World (1973) "Guyana faces new struggle against the ruling elite." (October): 11-12.
Weekly Gleaner [Jamaica] (1976) "Jagan: Guyana not yet a socialist state." (September 19): 27.

*Ralph R. Premdas is chairman of the Department of Political and Administrative Studies at the University of Papua, New Guinea, and has taught at the University of Guyana and the University of California (Berkeley). His Ph.D. is from the University of Illinois. He is the author of* Racial Politics in Guyana *(Denver, 1972) and several periodical articles on Guyanese politics. He is preparing a book comparing politics in Guyana and Fiji.*

**WILLIAM E. GIBBS**
*Department of History*
*New Mexico Military Institute*
*Roswell, New Mexico 88201*

# *DIAZ' EXECUTIVE AGENTS AND UNITED STATES FOREIGN POLICY*

Seldom can one turn to the news without encountering disclosures exposing the magnitude and nature of United States covert operations designed to influence the disposition of political affairs in a number of countries. As usual, Latin America has come in for its share of clandestine attention, with Chile being the most publicized recent example. This certainly should not surprise anyone with even a superficial knowledge of Latin American history. Latin American countries, however, have themselves not been free of responsibility for domestic manipulation in the United States. Although their endeavors have not dramatically altered the course of hemispheric history, they on occasion have produced significant diplomatic gains. One such occasion took place in 1877 and 1878 when Mexico, under Porfirio Díaz, sponsored covert activities in the United States designed to evoke public support and thus to secure the much needed formal recognition.

Historians in both the United States and Mexico have not perceived the importance of these operations. While some of the former have demonstrated a familiarity with the agents' activities, they have not tried to closely monitor their actions nor to measure their effectiveness. Instead, they have generally credited the United States Minister, John W. Foster, with convincing the State Department to establish formal relations. This is not

Journal of Interamerican Studies and World Affairs, Vol. 20 No. 2, May 1978

surprising since Foster (1909: 95), in his memoirs, claims responsibility.[1] The foremost Mexican historian, Cosío Villegas (1956; 1963: 219) does correctly argue that public opinion produced recognition. But he, too, fails to acknowledge the significance of the Mexican agents in awakening from its semidormant condition in the United States an expression of commercial interest in Mexico. This paper aims to examine the activities of these agents and to indicate their influence upon United States foreign policy.

An understanding of Díaz' special desire for recognition and an explanation of President Rutherford Hayes' decision to withhold it requires some familiarity with the domestic problems confronting both men in the spring of 1877. Mexico had again been plagued by its nemisis—revolution, and as the beneficiary, Porfirio Díaz inherited its negative by-product: political instability. Supporters of his strongest opponents, Sebastián Lerdo de Tejada and José María Iglesias, kept things stirred up throughout the country. The continuation of a free press enabled followers of the former to use the Lerdista newspaper, *El Federalista,* to disseminate their dissent.[2] In addition, Lerdista military units under General Mariano Escobedo continued to operate across the Rio Grande from Texas fomenting discontent in the volatile northern states. Such conditions made Díaz especially solicitous of foreign recognition to reinforce the hold on the office of the presidency. The power and proximity of the United States made its establishment of formal relations especially important to the general from Oaxaca.

The failure of the government of Ulysses S. Grant to immediately establish normal relations prompted the Porfiristas to take overt action to secure recognition. Although in desperate financial straits, the government, through voluntary and forced loans, accumulated $300,000 to make the installment payment awarded to the United States by the Claims Convention of 1868. Furthermore, Díaz attempted to meet the demands for more security on the Rio Grande by acting to end the petty political bickering responsible for that situation. He also sent traditional troops led by the distinguished general, Cerónimo Treviño, to the area. The Mexican government even attempted to comply with other State Department requests by providing greater protection to United States citizens in Mexico (Gibbs, 1973: 55-57).

About three months after Díaz victoriously entered Mexico City, Rutherford B. Hayes took office. Like Díaz, Hayes' claim to the presidency was subject to some question, and the circumstances of his election caused him to act cautiously. In addition, the barrage of criticisms leveled at the Chief Executive and his administration produced a self-consciousness in that office which made it sensitive to every political inference. As a result, even diplomatic issues which under normal circumstances would have been treated routinely were given special attention. One such issue involved the question of extending recognition to the new government in Mexico.

In April the United States Minister, John W. Foster, took up the matter of recognition and other problems with the Mexican Secretary of Foreign Relations, Ignacio Vallarta. In his account of the meeting, Foster reported that his efforts to secure Mexican action on United States grievances were countered by Vallarta's demand for recognition. In a confidential letter written shortly thereafter, Foster indicated his respect for Vallarta and his belief that General Díaz was the "only hope of the country." Consequently, he recommended that he be given the authority to extend recognition (Foster to Evarts, April 24, 1877, DSD File no. 528; confidential letter; Foster to Evarts, April 28, 1877, DSD filed between 530-531).

Numerous forces, however, pressured the administration to use recognition as a diplomatic "carrot," withholding it in exchange for Mexican concessions on matters of special interest to them. The Texas congressional delegation composed the most active such group. They sought to gain greater Mexican efforts toward controlling the marauding Indians which they alleged were responsible for the theft of large numbers of cattle and numerous deaths in their state (U.S. House, 1876: i-xviii; U.S. House, 1877: 43).[3] The Army especially in the persons of General Phillip Sheridan, Commander of the Military Division of Missouri, and General E.O.C. Ord, Commander of the Division of

Texas, supported the claims of the Texans and added their support for withholding recognition (Correspondence of March 19, April 3, 1877, U.S. War Department, File no. 1653). The former minister to Mexico, E. L. Plumb, also voiced opposition to establishing formal relations. As a railroad investor-agent, Plumb had negotiated contracts for construction of lines to the Rio Grande with Díaz' predecessor, Sebastian Lerdo. Díaz' annulment of these contracts moved Plumb to actively lobby for the continued recognition of Lerdo (Plumb Papers, vol. 13; Ord to Sherman, April 2, 1877, Sherman Papers, Letterbook; Pletcher, 1958: 97).

The limited experience of the Hayes official in dealing with Mexican matters in conjunction with the administration's sensitivity to political attack and need for congressional support made it increasingly responsive to the anti-Mexican pressures. This was especially the case when military reports from the Rio Grande continued to substantiate Texas claims of border raiding (Colonel William Shafter to the Adjutant General, April 28, 1877; endorsed by Philip Sheridan, May 5, 1877; Secretary of War George McCrary to William Evarts, May 16, 1877, U.S. War Dept., File no. 1653). Under these conditions, the State Department decided to disregard Foster's suggestion and to continue to withold recognition. On May 16, 1877, Assistant Secretary of State Frederick W. Seward informed Foster that recognition by the United States was more than a "mere formal assent" but was "an important moral influence" which could serve to "strengthen the power and lengthen the tenure of an incumbent." Seward added that his government would continue to defer recognizing Díaz until Mexico had approved of him and "until his administration is possessed of the stability to endure" (Seward to Foster, May 16, 1877, DSI File no. 390).

Ignacio Vallarta's decision to make recognition a condition precedent to formal action on American grievances and the State Department's determination to make such action a prerequisite to recognition created a virtual diplomatic deadlock. Within two weeks, however, the Hayes government decided to get things moving by unilaterally authorizing troops to cross the Rio

Grande in pursuit of marauding Indians (Sec. of War George McCrary to Gen. W. T. Sherman, June 1, 1877, U.S. War Dept. File no. 1653). This approval of the doctrine of "hot pursuit" functioned as a diplomatic "stick" to prod Díaz to act and thus to break the stalemate. With few exceptions, the administration had public support for this hard-line position. Newspapers lauded the government for abandoning the "shilly-shally forbearance on the subject" and for actions to "end the disorders which have so long disgraced the border" *(New York Herald* 1877a). Rumor of war even circulated, and the President received a number of letters advising him to use this opportunity for war to unite the country torn by Civil War and by Reconstruction (Correspondence from W. C. Stout, April 23, J. J. Gillow, May 28, W. H. Estill, Aug. 7, 1877, Hayes Papers; Foster, 1909: 92).

Efforts on the part of both governments to resolve their differences proved futile and relations continued to deteriorate over the summer of 1877. Two incidents were particularly exasperating. The first involved Evarts' peremptory treatment of Díaz' special envoy, José María Mata. This proved especially insulting to the highly nationalistic and sensitive Mexicans (Foster, 1909: 93-94). The second related to renewed border difficulties, notably the raid on the Rio Grande City jail which left several Texans dead. This especially fed the flames of the jingostic United States press and several papers called for war. One such paper, the *New York Herald,* even printed a map indicating that portion of Mexico which should be annexed (New York Herald, 1878). The failure of the extensive Foster-Vallarta talks in the late summer and Mexico's increasingly more intractable stand on troop crossings prompted Foster to conclude in November that any accord with the Díaz government was highly unlikely (Foster to Evarts, Nov. 28, 1877, DSD File nos. 635, 636).

In the fall of 1877, both governments expressed concern with the existing state of affairs. State Department leaders lamented the failure of the carrot/stick policies to produce results, and President Hayes referred to the Mexican situation as "perplexing" (Hayes Diary, Oct. 4, 1877, Hayes Papers). Díaz officials experienced considerable anxiety over the failure of their efforts to secure recognition. The jingoistic cries of the United States press which revived memories of 1846 and the subsequent humiliation of Guadalupe Hidalgo did little to calm their fears. Mexican leaders, consequently, perceived they would have to take action to break this potentially dangerous diplomatic stalemate. The presence of a hypernationalistic sentiment throughout the country complicated matters considerably, limiting their options and precluding any real concessions to the United States.

In order to remove its country and itself from the horns of this dilemma, the Díaz government undertook a rather sophisticated three-dimensional offensive designed to appease local xenophobia, to meet international obligations on the border, and to secure recognition through the creation of popular and political support in the United States. Two aspects of this effort provided basically for an escalation of existing policies. The first, primarily concerned with appeasing Mexican nationalism consisted of taking an uncompromising stand on most United States demands (Foster to Evarts, Oct. 12, Nov. 12, 1877, DSD File nos. 613, 629; Vallarta to Zamacona, Jan 13, 1878, AHDM, 1961: 262). In conjunction with this policy of diplomatic obduracy, the Secretary of Foreign Relations initiated a practice of "Yankee-baiting" (publicizing each rebuff) to bolster domestic support. The Mexican leaders realized, nevertheless, that while this intransigence helped consolidate internal strength, it aroused further criticism in the United States. Hoping to reduce this hostility, Díaz implemented the second part of his program. He sent an additional 2,000 troops to help stabilize conditions on the Rio Grande border (Foster to Evarts, Nov. 10, 14, 28, 29, 1877, DSD File nos. 628, 631, 635, 636, 637; The National Republican, 1877).

Although these measures did temporarily prevent a further deterioration of relations, they did not produce significant changes in the Hayes/Evarts position. In order to accomplish this, the Porfiristas became convinced they would have to neutralize the influence of the most powerful opposition groups. These included the speculator-annexationist interests, the Texas Congressional lobby, and the United States Army command. The third dimension of the Díaz offensive attempted to counter the adverse publicity and to create a favorable impression of Mexico. In the early months of the administration, Díaz used the promise of commercial concessions to convert hungry American capitalists such as Simon Stevens into propagandists.[4] But with the tense state of affairs in late 1877, the Mexican leaders concluded that something more would have to be done. Consequently, they undertook a concentrated propaganda campaign directed toward the American public—a strategy which played a significant role in producing a change in the Evarts policy and in securing the recognition of Porfirio Díaz.

This propaganda offensive primarily attempted to win support by exploiting political divisions and by exporting, especially in the commercial stronghold of New York, economic opportunity in Mexico. They hoped to carry this out through the use of executive agents exercising influence upon private and public figures and particularly upon the news media.

Díaz' representative in Washington, José María Mata, had, for some time, encouraged his government to undertake such an operation. In fact, he even took it upon himself to find a confidential agent who would pressure Congress and the Cabinet on Mexico's behalf. On September 13, 1877, Mata informed his government that the Honorable Caleb Cushing, "an intelligent and respected citizen of the United States," was willing to sell his influence (ASRE, classificación decimal, herafter, class. dec., H/300). The Secretary of Foreign Relations approved Mata's suggestion to employ Cushing (Vallarta to Mata, Sept, 29, 1877, ASRE, class. dec. H/300), and shortly thereafter, Mata negotiated an arrangement in which the Mexican government agreed to pay Caleb Cushing $2,000 to use his influence in a fashion favorable to Mexico among members of Congress and the Hayes cabinet (Mata to Vallarta, Oct. 3, 1877, ASRE, class. dec. H/300). Although this action did not prove especially productive to Mexican interests,[6] it did launch the project to manipulate the United States opinion as well as indicate how far the Porfiristas were willing to go in their efforts.

Shortly after finalizing the agreement with Cushing, an alarmed Mata wrote Vallarta of the seriousness of the situation in Washington. He pointed out that only congressional opposition, which he argued could only be aroused through the activities of confidential agents, could prevent the Hayes government from initiating a war with Mexico. As a result, Mata again called for immediate action upon his recommendations (Mata to Vallarta, Oct. 4, 1877 as reported in Zamacona to Vallarta, April 8, 1878, AHDM, 1961: 277).

Soon after receiving Mata's confidential despatch, the Díaz government acted upon his suggestions. The first and most importance step it took was to appoint Manuel M. Zamacona as confidential agent to the United States. Both as special agent and later as minister, this man exercised far-reaching influence upon the course of United States-Mexican relations. His background and individual capacities especially qualified him for this role. Earlier he spent three years in the United States representing his country on the Joint Claims Commission of 1868. This, along with his experience as Benito Juárez' Secretary of Foreign Relations, familiarized him with the Washington diplomatic atmosphere. Personal qualities also suited him for the job for as the late Mexican historian, Cosío Villegas, (1956; 1963: 143) pointed out, Zamacona spoke English well enough to use his highly cultivated persuasive skills, but not sufficiently well to give vent to his Latin temperament.

The Porfirista's decision to secretly employ additional propagandists indicated the degree of importance attached to the project. Some of these included William Pritchard, a British resident of Oaxaca as well as friend and former business partner of Díaz, who played a leading role in these efforts to win over the American public (Cosío Villegas 1956; 1963: 147). A United States citizen, C. Edwards Lester, also acted in support of Mexico's interests. José Mata secured this noted author's services in late October (Carreño, 1960a: 7-8). George D. del Bryon, another British citizen, worked closely with Lester in the New York area (Carreño, 1960a: 31-34). Finally, General John Frisbie, a resident of California, circulated throughout the country speaking on behalf of Díaz (Carreño, 1960a: 73-74).

While there were not the only other agents operating in the United States, they were the most active. This is particularly true of Pritchard and Lester.

The government secured these agents' services through direct monetary payments and promises of other types of economic gain. Díaz pledged to pay William Pritchard $350 each month. By later December he confirmed that his government had paid this agent at least $800 and promised another hundred shortly thereafter (Díaz reply to Pritchard letter of Dec. 8, 1877, Carreño, 1960a: 81). Although the terms of Lester's agreement were less clear, Mata most likely guaranteed him a similar amount (Foster to Evarts, Sept. 5, 1878, DSD File no. 775).[6] Díaz, moreover, did pay Lester at least an additional $2,000 to write a highly favorable history of Mexico to "educate" the American public (Lester to Pritchard, June 1, 10, 1878, enclosed in Foster to Evarts, Sept. 5, 1878, DSD File no. 775). Mexican officials did not make direct payments to Bryon or Frisbie. The former's correspondence with Díaz indicated that he, instead, sought commercial gain in England in exchange for his services (Bryon to Díaz, Nov. 16, 1877, Carreño, 1960a: 34). The latter, too, sought economic concessions but probably in Mexico (Callahan, 1931: 379-381).

The Díaz government, therefore, committed at least $6,000 to this effort. Initially, this may not appear to be a significant sum, but it takes on more importance when it is recalled that this government was experiencing severe financial difficulties. In fact, it had to borrow (by force) to make the earlier claims payment, and it could not always even meet its payroll. Yet, under these fiscal conditions, Díaz officials felt the propaganda campaign sufficiently important to commit substantial amounts of its meager resources.

In his instructions to both Zamacona and Pritchard, Ignacio Vallarta spelled out the objectives of the operations. He directed Zamacona to search generally for the most satisfactory solution to the problems between the two countries and to rectify the public opinion with respect to Mexico (AHDM, 1961: 261; Cosío Villegas, 1956; 1963: 145).[7] Vallarta's instructions to Pritchard were more explicit. On October 31, 1877, the Secretary of Foreign Relations charged Pritchard with defending Mexico as well as the acts of the Mexican government from the "daily slanders" in the United States newspapers. In addition, he instructed the agent to use the news and literary media to correct erroneous images of Mexican culture, most notably those relating to its alleged political instability. Finally, Vallarta ordered Pritchard to frequently point out the commercial and industrial opportunities which might accrue to those who took advantage of them (New York Herald, 1878).

Zamacona, influenced by Mata's earlier suggestions, clarified and expanded the propaganda approach. He reasoned that Mexico could overcome its enemies in the United States only by appealing to the "good sense" of the general public and to the "capitalist sense" of the business community. According to Zamacona, there were masses of laboring peoples and various religious groups in the United States who might be appealed to on the basis of their repugnance to war. He pointed out, furthermore, the specific need to use the commercial and financial media to make a special appeal to those who might have an economic interest in Mexico. In order to make a forceful impression, Zamacona called for the use of "simultaneous and extraordinary methods" capable of "electrifying" public opinion in the United States (Cosío Villegas, 1956; 1963: 143-144).

A few inquisitive newspapermen, both Mexican and American almost foiled the mission at the very start. Their questions prompted John W. Foster to take the matter up with Díaz officials. The Mexican government, however, succeeded in covering up. The official newspaper, *El Diario Oficial,* replied to the press and Foster stating that the government had not employed any such persons—especially one William Pritchard. It added that it assumed he (Pritchard) had gone to the United States "on mining business." According to Foster, the Secretary of Foreign Relations assured him that Díaz would not "resort to such objectionable methods to influence his action of the government of the United States or the public sentiment." As a result, Foster dropped his inquiry (Foster to Evarts, Sept. 5, Oct. 26, 1878, DSD File nos. 775, 818).

Conditions to the North, nevertheless, proved especially propitious for the Mexican agents. Texas representatives, Gustav Schleicher in the House and William Maxey in the Senate, used a debate on a military appropriations bill to subject the administration's Mexican policy to closer scrutiny. Their accounts of border conditions produced a resolution calling for the House Military Committee to investigate the strength and deployment of the Army. This inquiry, particularly in the testimony of General of the Army William T. Sherman and Secretary of War George McCrary, exposed considerable administrative indecision on the Mexican question (Congressional Record, 1877a; U.S. House 1878b: 3-4, 38). These congressional activities and the publicity given them raised both public and private consciousness of the Mexican affairs. This recently acquired "newsworthiness" of Mexico and closely related matters such as the border significantly facilitated the efforts of the agents. As a result, both public and private sectors of society now appeared somewhat receptive to their overtures.

Although Lester, Bryon, and Frisbie had begun their activities, the campaign did not really begin to develop until Zamacona and Pritchard arrived in late November 1877. Upon arriving, Zamacona held a press conference—a practice he continued along the route from New Orleans to Washington. Before going to the capital, however, he continued on to New York where he met privately and publicly with representatives of leading newspapers and important commercial concerns (AHDM, 1961: 278-279; Carreño, 1960a: 77; New York Herald , 1877e). Leaving Pritchard there to continue the efforts, Zamacona then proceeded on to Washington. There, as he later stated, he sought to influence congressional proceedings and to create an atmosphere incompatible with the opinions of those he considered most antagonistic to Mexico-Secretary of State William Evarts and Assistant Secretary Frederick W. Seward (Zamacona to Vallarta, April 8, 1978, AHDM, 1961: 279-280).

While some of Zamacona's activities were public in nature, William Pritchard worked almost exclusively behind the scenes. He spent most of his time seeing newspaper editors, promoting commercial interests, and arranging speaking engagements. Soon after arriving, he made an agreement with Charles A. Dana, editor of the *New York Sun,* to secretly write some editorials dealing with the Mexican situation and to advise the paper on related matters. In a letter to Díaz on December 8 (Carreño, 1960a: 79-80), Pritchard indicated that he tried to make it appear that his editorials attacking the Hayes policy and starting an interest in greater commerce with Mexico were expressions of the sentiment of the American people.[8] After having made a similar arrangement with the *New York Herald,* Pritchard boasted that the two papers with the greatest circulation, the *Herald* and the *Sun,* were Díaz supporters. He also noted that he spent almost every night at their offices preparing replies to the anti-Díaz *New York World.* Furthermore, he even predicted that within the near future the *New York Tribune, New York Times,* and the *New York Journal of Commerce* would join the Porfirista ranks (Pritchard to Díaz, December 8, 12, 1877, Carreño, 1960a: 124).

While Pritchard successfully infiltrated the ranks of important newspapers, his fellow agent and friend, C. Edwards Lester, used another approach to carry out his own "campaign of facts and truths" (Carreño, 1960a: 7-8). Starting in late October, Lester sought to focus international as well as national attention on the United States "aggression" on the Rio Grande. In order to accomplish this, Lester first attempted to enlist the support of England by recounting in a letter to the Prime Minister, William E. Gladstone, the fine qualities of President Díaz and the belligerent nature of the Hayes administration. He then sent copies of the "Open Letter" to the heads of state and to influential newspapers in various European countries. The energetic Lester did not stop there for he also distributed 500 copies to members of the Senate, House, Supreme Court, and other important Washingtonians including the President. In addition, he mailed copies to 45 daily newspapers throughout the country as well as to influential members of the nation's business community (Carreño, 1960a: 31-34). Lester's efforts, most likely, contributed significantly to the "newsworthiness" of Mexican matters.

The other agents, Bryon and Frisbie, merely played supporting roles in the propaganda production. Bryon remained in the United States only until the middle of December. During that time he worked with Lester and reported to Díaz on the activities of his cohort. Frisbie, also functioning on the periphery, made a few speeches and secured a number of interviews in order to "rectify" opinion. He, furthermore, generally kept the Porfiristas informed on the nature of affairs in the North. Their activities, while informative and, in Frisbie's case, gratifying, appear to have had little real influence (Carreño, 1960a: 31-34, 73-74, 77-78; José T. Cuéllar to Vallarta, Nov. 24, 1877, ASRE class. dec. H/910).

Although their contacts with the news media were effective, the agents did not limit their operations to this approach. They also made numerous personal appeals to the administration's political opponents and to the nation's commercial opportunists. Their advances were always essentially the same: seek out those who had a political and/or economic interest in listening and appeal to them on the basis of the gain, both political and commerical, that would accrue to them or to their constituents if the Hayes government would alter its policy and extend recognition. These measures were especially important for they not only complemented the press manipulation, but they also enabled the agents to cultivate congressional allies.

Zamacona was particularly adept at establishing congressional contacts. For example, upon learning that the Chairman of the House Military Committee which was reviewing the border policy was an old political foe of Hayes, he arranged a meeting with him to explain the Mexican position. In a letter to Secretary Vallarta (AHDM, 1961: 248-249), Zamacona recalled that Congressman Henry Banning was especially cordial and responsive to their interests and had even invited him to speak before the committee. Although Zamacona later claimd to have significantly influenced the committee (Zamacona to Vallarta, April 8, 1878, AHDM, 1961: 279), there is no record of his testimony. This does not rule out, however, the possibility that he conferred informally with the members.

Zamacona along with Pritchard and Lester made the New York delegation their primary congressional target. From the outset, they were especially successful in enlisting, in the House, the powerful Samuel S. Cox (Davison, 1972: 123) and, in the Senate, the ignoble Roscoe Conkling. Partisan politics as well as matters of business most likely moved Cox to consider the agents' solicitations. As a New York Democrat, Cox actively supported that state's governor, Samuel J. Tilden, for the presidency in 1876. The outcome of the election controversy particularly angered Cox motivating him to seek opportunities to subvert the Hayes government. As the representative of the New York financial interests, Cox also demonstrated a special interest in the propangandists economic appeals. In their correspondence with Díaz officials, the agents, on a number of occasions, referred to their conversations with Cox (Zamacona to Vallarta, March 1, 1878, AHDM, 1961: 266; Lester to Pritchard, June 10, 1878, enclosed in Foster to Evarts, Sept. 5, 1878, DSD File no. 775). John W. Foster in a letter written after the disclosure of the agents' activities even identified Cox as the source responsible for leaking restricted information to Pritchard (Foster to Evarts, Sept. 5, 1878, DSD File no. 775).

Party politics and commercial interests also influenced Roscoe Conkling. The former, however, probably played a more significant role, for Hayes and Conkling represented different factions of the Republican party. The President and most of his cabinet belonged to the more liberal group known as the "Half-Breeds," and Conkling represented the Old Guard, then referred to as the "Stalwarts." Their political differences surfaced immediately with Hayes' appointment of Conkling's foremost New York opponent, William M. Evarts as Secretary of State. The President's efforts to oust Conkling's cronies from the New York Customs House created an even more embittered relationship (Hutton, 19866: 173).[9]

Conkling, as a result, sought every opportunity to embarrass the Hayes government. The Mexican situation proved ideal for this, as it enabled him to attack the administration generally and Evarts' handling in foreign affairs specifically. In addition, it proved an occasion for Conkling, who was up for reelection in 1878, to ingratiate himself with the New York capitalists who had expressed their special interest in expanding commerce with Mexico. Conkling, therefore, exhibited a keen interest in what Díaz' executive agents had to say. While Zamacona and Lester reported talking with Conkling (Zamacona to Vallarta, January 17, 1878, ASRE class. dec. H/210; Lester to Pritchard, June 10, 1878 enclosed in Foster to Evarts, Sept. 5, 1878, DSD File no. 775), Pritchard probably exercised more influence on him. After several confidential discussions, Pritchard went so far as to confidently proclaim to Díaz that this New York Senator was definitely a supporter of the Mexican cause (Dec. 8, 12, 1877, Carreño, 1960a: 79, 87).

Congressional inquiries along with the unfavorable publicity associated with his Mexican diplomacy prompted the President to respond in his annual message of 1877. On December 3, Hayes stated that the customary extension of recognition to de facto governments had been "deferred by the occurrences on the Rio Grande border." He added, nevertheless, that the new government had given assurances of its disposition to "prevent any unlawful invasions and depredations," and that it had faithfully met its obligations under the claims treaty of July 4, 1868. He, nonetheless, stated:

> While I do not anticipate an interruption of friendly relations with Mexico, yet I cannot but look with some solicitude upon a continuance of border disorders as exposing the two countries to initiations of popular feeling and mischances of action which are naturally unfavorable to complete amity. Firmly determined that nothing shall be wanting on my part to promote a good understanding between the two nations, I yet must ask the attention of Congress to the actual occurrences on the border, that the lives and property of citizens may be adequately protected and peace preserved [Richardson, 1907: 4419-4420].

The irresolute and ambiguous nature of these remarks triggered a congressional attack which coincided with a volley of press criticism to significantly pressure the administration to reconsider its Mexican position. Sam Cox along with another

New York Democrat, Abram Hewitt, led the House incursion. Cox, not surprisingly, stated on the House floor that he was "utterly at a loss" to understand why the Hayes government had not recognized Díaz. He contended the administration should conform to the customary practice and establish formal relations in the "interest of commerce and peace." (Congressional Record, 1877b). Hewitt called for "trade with Mexico not war" warning that if Congress did not find a peaceful solution, war would follow. Hewitt then offered an amendment to an earlier House resolution calling for an investigation of State Department handling of Mexican matters. Upon its passage, the House Foreign Affairs Committee, with Samuel Cox as a ranking member, proceeded to subject the Hayes-Evarts policy to additional scrutiny (Congressional Record, 1877c; U.S. House, 1878a, H. Rept. 701).

Just one day after the House endorsed Hewitt's amended resolution, the Senate approved a similar measure introduced by none other than Roscoe Conkling. This resolution called for a special committee chaired by Conkling and composed of six others senators to inquire into what "can be devised to promote commercial intercourse with and to establish a just and peaceful condition of affairs on the borders of this county and Mexico" (Congressional Record, 1877b). Consequently, within two weeks of the President's address, two additional congressional committees were convened to review executive handling of the Mexican situation.

It is more than just coincidence that the primary individuals responsible for these actions happened to be Mexican contacts in Congress. Díaz agents functioned to influence the direction of the inquiries. The agents' correspondence confirmed this. In a letter to Díaz written just three days before Conkling introduced his resolution, Pritchard reported having presented the senator with letters and other references from New York commerical interests which supported the establishment of closer ties with Mexico (Dec. 8, 1877, Carreño, 1960a: 79). In their efforts to influence the conclusions of the hearings, Zamacona spoke before the House Foreign Affairs Committee (Zamacona to Valarta, Dec. 7,

1877, AHDM, 1961: 247), and Lester even, confidentially, promised both Cox and Conkling to write their committee reports (Lester to Pritchard, June 10, 1878, enclosed in Foster to Evarts, Sept. 5, 1878, DSD File no. 775). This matter, however, did not remain confined only to the halls of Congress.

During the same December period, the newspaper assault, also orchestrated by the Díaz agents, reached its peak. With Pritchard circulating behind the presses, the *New York Sun* and the *New York Herald* leveled their guns upon administration handling of Mexican affairs. The *Sun,* always critical of Hayes, now became more biting in its attacks. Charles A. Dana interpreted the congressional reservations about the executive's Mexican policy as confirmation of the *Sun's* persistent position on the matter. Having added a Mexican propagandist to his arsenal, Dana escalated his strikes, condemning Hayes for "fomenting border disorders" and "committing military outrages on Mexico." The paper additionally characterized Hayes as a "raider" and "leader of filibusters." It lauded the House's decision to investigate the matter, stating that by doing so it "rebuked" Hayes and his efforts to start a war. The *Sun* even called upon Congress to remove Mexican affairs from the administration's incompetent hands (New York Sun, 1877a, 1877b, 1877c, 1877d).

The *New York Herald* must have amused or bemused its readers by its abrupt change in position after Pritchard began to write the editorials. The *Herald's* December comments on the Mexican matter hardly resembled the "ripe pear" theory espoused in June, when it insisted the northern states of Mexico should and would drip into United States hands (New York Herald, 1877b, 1877c). On December 8, the paper called for the United States "to repose a generous confidence in Mexico." It also stated, "It is sheer folly for our government to maintain troops on the border to do what Mexico herself is bound to do, and what her present government offers and engages to do" (New York Herald, 1877f, 1877g). The *Herald* (1877h), additionally, criticized the State Department for yielding to the Texas interests by enacting the doctrine of "hot pursuit" which it considered a violation of international law and an attempt to "breed trouble with Mexico."

Although most historians attribute little significance to it, the period of the last two weeks of December 1877, was, nevertheless, an important one in United States-Mexican relations, for in this span the Hayes government began to review and reconsider its Mexican policy. The timing of these actions are, again, notable for they came amidst the clamor of a hostile press and an increasingly critical Congress—both, at least indirectly, the product of the Díaz propaganda offensive.

In mid-December, the Hayes cabinet made recognition of Díaz the first order of business. The *Providence Morning Star* reported on page one of its December 18, 1877 edition that only Secretary of State Evarts opposed extending recognition. Shortly, thereafter, even he hinted (Carreño, 1960s: 123) there would be some changes made.

During the last week of December, Secretary Evarts held a secret meeting with the most outspoken opponent of the Mexican interests, Congressman Gustav Schliecher of Texas. The line of Evarts' questioning during this important discussion suggested that the cabinet had probably already decided to extend recognition, and he was simply trying to ascertain the feelings of the influential Schliecher who was chairman of the House Foreign Affairs Committee. The secretary opened the questioning by asking Schleicher if he did not think Mexico had done as much as could be expected of her in relation to the border trouble. Schleicher agreed except on the matter of extradition. He then stated that he still favored further delay in extending recognition so that he might be able to complete his report to Congress on the "Mexican Troubles." In order to complete that project, the Texas congressman requested John Foster be summoned from Mexico City for consultation. Evarts agreed and indicated he would bring the matter before the cabinet (Journal, Dec. 28, 1977, Evarts Papers).[10]

On December 31, 1877, the Secretary of State instructed Foster to return to Washington to testify before the House Foreign Affairs Committee (DSI File no. 437). His instructions provide interesting evidence of the administration's sensitivity to press criticism and significant testimony to the efforts of the

Mexican agents. The secretary took precautions to avoid any leaks, ordering Foster "strictly" to limit his "communications whether oral or written upon relations of this country with Mexico to the Department and the Committee." Rather than have Foster give his testimony in the committee room at the Capital, Evarts even suggested that Foster confer with committee members in a confidential manner at the Department of State (Journal, Jan. 12, 1878, Evarts Papers).

During the first three months of 1878, the Hayes government continued to mark time on the matter of recognition while Foster discussed Mexican matters with Evarts, State Department officials, and the House Foreign Affairs Committee. Although some of his testimony tended to substantiate cabinet predispositions which Evarts communicated to Schleicher in their December meeting, Foster remained somewhat critical of the ability and/or willingness of the Díaz government to maintain order, particularly on the Rio Grande border (DSD filed between nos. 672-673).

During the same period the confidential agents continued to be active. President Díaz himself even took a hand in coordinating their efforts, ordering Pritchard on December 25, 1877, to work *"en consonancia con otras personas animadas igualemente de las mismas loables intenciones"* (Carreño, 1960a: 81). On January 4, 1878, he again instructed Pritchard to communicate with Zamacona "in order to systematize and organize" their actions (Carreño, 1960a: 89). Meanwhile, Zamacona kept in touch with his best contact, Samuel Cox. According to Zamacona, Cox, on two occasions, responded to his suggestions and introduced resolutions in the House calling for Hayes to establish official relations with Mexico (Zamacona to Vallarta, March 1, 1878, AHDM, 1961: 266; Congressional Record, 1878). This agent also continued to speak before Chambers of Commerce which he considered especially receptive to the commercial appeals. He frequently addressed the New York City Chamber, and over the following year he lectured to similar audiences in Baltimore, Pittsburgh, and Chicago (Carreño, 1960a: 77, 88; 1960b: 221, 274, 307-308).

Pritchard liked to appeal to more scholarly groups, and he informed Díaz that he had secured permission to speak before the prominent Cooper Institute of New York as well as the American Society of Geography (Carreño, 1960a: 122). Prior to his return to Mexico in April, he published a critical account of the Evarts policy in the March edition of the prestigious journal, *International Review* (Pritchard, 1878). His article, "The Mexico of the Mexicans," charged Evarts with "defiantly disregarding treaty obligations," being "trifling, evasive and fantastic," and "merely taking advantage of a weaker country." Writing as Will T. Pritchard, member of the Geographical Society of Mexico, this agent informed the readers that this country could "retrieve the palpable errors of the fantastic Mexican policy of Mr. Evarts" only by manifesting "loyalty, frankness, and sincerity rather than evasion, duplicity, and defiance in its diplomacy."

After hearing Foster's testimony and submitting the matter of recognition to the scrutiny of the Diplomatic Bureau, the Hayes government in late March instructed Foster (Evarts to Foster, March 23, 1878, DSI File no. 457) to establish formal relations with Díaz. The official explanation reasoned that since Díaz managed to maintain peace and respect, take vigorous measures on the border, and make the claims payments, the United States government could "waive its own preferences as the fullest manner and time of adjusting the difficulties . . . which have prevented a good understanding " (DSI File no. 457). This statement, however, is hardly convincing in light of two things. First, the Mexican government had demonstrated these same characteristics for at least four months.[11] Yet four months earlier in late November 1877, the United States Minister could only lament the fact that conditions precedent to extending recognition would not or could not be satisfied by the Díaz government (Foster to Evarts, November 28, 1877, DSD File nos. 635, 636). Second, the Schleicher report which was published shortly thereafter actually supported the Hayes-Evarts policy and called for its continuation (U.S. House, 1878a, H. Rept. 701, appendix G). Why then the change in position at this time?

Secretary of State Evarts provided the answer to this question. While State Department officials publicly continued to argue that Mexican cooperation had produced the policy change, privately Evarts acknowledged the pressure of public opinion. This pressure continued to mount as new forces joined the opposition. As early as January 12, 1878, the *New York Times* emphatically stated, "we see no reason why the recognition [of Díaz] should not now be accorded." Shortly after formal relations were established, this same paper explained that the "tardy action of the State Department at Washington was hastened by an expression of public opinion" (New York Times, 1878). The West Coast also revealed a special interest in establishing relations with Mexico, and the California State Assembly passed a resolution calling for recognition of Díaz (Pennanen, 1969: 158-160). In a meeting with Zamacona in mid-February, Evarts admitted being approached by a number of businessmen interested in establishing closer times with Mexico. As a result, the Secretary of State even conceded that "the national interest appeared to favor establishing general relations between the two countries" (Zamacona to Vallarta, February 17, 1878, ASRE class. dec. H/310).

While the *New York Times* recognized the function of public pressure in securing the establishment of normal relations, it showed no awareness of the covert operations. In fact, the *Times* (1878) stated that recognition of Díaz "is no more due to Mexican diplomacy then it is to the changes of the moon."

Mexican officials, however, did not agree for they considered themselves victorious in the matter and attributed their success to the operations of the agents. In his compliments to the Secretary of Foreign Relations, the Charge d'Affaires in Washington, José T. de Cuéllar, credited success to the pro-Mexican, anti-Evarts climate of opinion which greeted Foster upon his return to testify (April 14, 1878, AHDM, 1961: 285). Ignacio Vallarta indicated his belief in the propaganda approach in a letter to the Mexican Minister to Spain, General Ramón D. Corona (April, 22, 1878, AHDM, 1961: 287-288). In defense of his diplomacy, Vallarta argued that the methods employed did the country great good eventually securing recognition through the influence they exercised in political and commercial circles. On another occasion, he again demonstrated his confidence in the tactics exhorting Zamacona to continue their use (May 28, 1878, AHDM, 1961: 298-299).

Manuel M. Zamacona provided the most complete explanation of the entire episode in a letter to Vallarta (April 8, 1878, AHDM, 1961: 271-282). In this correspondence marked *reservadisma,* this agent recalled the failures of traditional diplomacy to resolve the difficulties and the serious deterioration of relations by the time of his arrival in the United States. He blamed this condition on the influence of hostile groups upon the Secretary of State. Like Cuéllar and Vallarta, Zamacona credited the propaganda offensive with neutralizing the adverse publicity and with eliciting a "popular spirit" in favor of Mexico. As a result, he noted, both press and political groups began to observe the "evils" of the administration's policy and "light began to penetrate the halls of Evarts and Seward." To avoid a recurrence of a similar situation, Zamacona advised his government to keep a permanent representative in the United States who believed in the "circulation of personal relations" and who understood the politics and economics of the country. In another communication (May 31, 1879, AHDM, 1961: 300), he again indicated his belief in this approach proudly informing Vallarta of United States press references to the "Mexicanization of American Politics."

Although these statements are somewhat self-serving, they do reflect the judgment of important Porfiristas as to which aspect of their foreign policy was responsible for their diplomatic victory. Their comments would have been no less self-serving if they had chosen to emphasize some other dimension of their diplomatic program. But the fact that they did not lends support to the significance of the covert operations.

Certainly, it would be easy to exaggerate the importance of these propagandists and their operations. They were not responsible for the industrial transformation which created such interest in foreign markets nor did they engineer the political controversy which grew out of the election of 1876. They did, however, function to accelerate and to give direction to both economic and political discontent producing a reaction (recognition) favorable to the Mexican President. In this sense, they might be best referred to as "catalytic agents."

Their presence in the United States also indicated a shift in the Díaz position—one which would long affect United States-Mexican relations. As a rebel, Díaz had been a determined anti-imperialist, and upon becoming President, he immediately cancelled the contracts to build railroads to the Rio Grande negotiated by his predecessor. But his failure to receive recognition and the continued deterioration of relations produced a change. In exchange for certain political concessions Díaz, by late 1877, was willing to open the door to United States economic penetration. Thus, the agents also acted as salesmen marketing a new product—Mexico.

## NOTES

1. For some of the historical accounts that accepted this position, see (Barrows, 1941: 358; Callahan, 1931: 392; Dyer, 1933: 200; Rippy, 1926: 303; Hackett, 1924: 53). For a more recent statement, see (Davison, 1972: 201).

2. Keep in mind that this was Díaz' first term, and he did not yet have the power to censor that he later exercised so extensively.

3. The chairman of the House Committee on Foreign Relations, Gustav Schleicher, was a Texan who continued his efforts to produce a tough Mexican policy. For Schleicher's effort to influence Hayes in this direction, see U.S. House, 1877: 42.

4. Upon his return to the United States, Stevens requested permission to sent a portrait of Díaz to the President. He informed Hayes that when Porfirio Díaz was recognized he would prove to be a "great reformer of Mexico giving it perpetual peace and prosperity " (Stevens to Hayes, Oct. 10, 1877, Hayes Papers).

5. For an additional account of this, see (Zamacona to Vallarta, April 13, 1878, AHDM, 1961: 277). The Mexican experience with Caleb Cushing proved unproductive. On February 5, 1878, Mexican confidential agent, Manual Zamacona, reported that Cushing had been in Massachusetts during most of the period he was supposed to have been in Washington. As a result, Zamacona decided not to enter into another contract for the "services" of Mr. Cushing (Zamacona to Vallarta, February 5, March 25, 1878, ASRE, class. dec. H/300).

6. This source of information (Foster to Evarts, Sept. 5, 1878, DSD, File no. 775), which is invaluable to this paper, came into the possession of the American minister in a

rather bizarre fashion. William Pritchard, while in Mexico City to confer with Díaz, appears to have lost a packet of papers including his correspondence with Díaz, other Mexican agents, and American political and business officials. Although Pritchard offered a reward for the papers, they found their way into the hands of a news correspondent of the *New York Herald* (1877d) who turned them over to Foster.

7. Upon Zamacona's departure Foster wrote Evarts that Zamacona was competent but probably no more "tractable" than either Mata or Vallarta (Personal letter, Nov. 13, 1877, DSD, filed between nos. 630-631).

8. Charles A. Dana's contempt for Hayes and the administration grew out of the election controversy. Dana constantly attacked Hayes in the *Sun's* editorials as a fraud, and he sought out any aspect of the administration's program which he considered vulnerable. For an excellent account of the *Sun* and its editor, see (Stone, 1938).

9. George Frisbie Hoar, a Hayes supporter, wrote to his wife that "Conkling's anger with the President is unabated" (Hoar to Ruth A. Hoar, November 10, 1877, as cited in a footnote in Welsh, 1971: 92).

10. Forrest (1967: 244) also argues that the administration was ready to extend recognition in December, but at Schleicher's request it postponed recognition until after completion of the House Foreign Affairs Committee hearings.

11. The Mexican Congress showed its "respect" for Díaz as early as May 5, 1877 (Foster to Evarts, May 7, 1877, DSD, File no. 532) confirming him as constitutional President. Díaz made his first claims payment in January of 1877, even before the Hayes government took office (Foster to Evarts, March 3, 1877, DSD, File no. 503). The Mexican Presidnet initiated a more vigorous military campaign on the border in November, 1877 (Foster to Evarts, Nov. 10, 14, 1877, DSD, File nos. 629, 631). For additional information on the degree to which Díaz conformed to United States expectations, see (Hamilton Fish to Foster, Feb. 12, 1877, DSI, File no. 370).

## REFERENCES

AHDM [México, Archivo Historico Diplomatico Mexicano] (1961) "La labor diplomatica de Ignacio Luis Vallarta." Numero 12. Segunda Series de Archivo historico diplomático mexicano. México: Publicación de la Secretaría de Relaciones Exteriores.

ASRE [México, Archivo de la Secretaría de Relaciones Exteriores] Clasificación decimal H/300 (72: 73) 16, Topográfica 1-12-1322. Asunto: "Informes, datos, gestiones, y todo los relaciones con la reanudación de relaciones diplomáticas entre México y Los Estados Unidos." México.

——— Clasificación decimal H/910 (73 72) "877," Topografica 1-15-1689. Asunto: "Corresponsales de la prensa de la Estados Unidos en México, 1877-78." México.

———Clasificación decimal H/210 (73: 72) 16, Topográfica Z-1-1780. Asunto: "Datos e informes de la legación sobre comisión del senado de aquel país en relaciones de los Estados Unidos con México y la América Central, 1878-1889." México.

——— Clasificación decimal H/310 (72: 73) 4, Topográfica 1-14-1640. Asunto: "Conferencias del Ministerio de México con el secretaría y subsecretaría del departmento de los Estados Unidos." México.

BARROWS, C. L. (1941) William M. Evarts: Lawyer, Diplomat, Statesman. Chapel Hill: Univ. of North Carolina Press.
CALLAHAN, J. M. (1931) American Foreign Policy in Mexican Relations. New York: Macmillan.
CARREÑO, A. M. [ed.] (1960a) Archivos del general Porfirio Díaz: memorias y documentos. Vol. 28. Mexico City: Instituto de Historia de la Universidad Nacional.
——— (1960b) Archivos del general Porfirio Diaz: memorias y documentos. Vol. 29. Mexico City: Instituto de Historia de la Universidad Nacional.
Congressional Record (1878) 45 Cong. 2 sess. Vol. 7: 290, 1664.
——— (1977a) 45 Cong. 1 sess. Vol. 6: 182, 246, 288-289, 295-301, 322-326.
——— (1877b) 45 Cong. 2 sess. Vol. 7: 120.
——— (1877c) 45 Cong. 2 sess. Vol. 7: 290, 1664.
COSIO VILLEGAS, D. (1956) The United States versus Porfirio Díaz. [Trans. by Nettie Lee Benson (1963)] Lincoln: Univ. of Nebraska Press.
DAVISON, K. E. (1972) The Presidency of Rutherford B. Hayes. Westport, CT: Greenwood.
DSD [U.S. Department of State] Despatches from United States Ministers to Mexico, 1823-1906. Record Group 59, Microcopy No. 97, Rolls 55-61. Washington, DC: National Archives.
DSI [U.S. Department of State] Instructions to United States Ministers to Mexico, 1833-1906. Record Group 59, Microcopy No. 77, Roll 115. Washington, DC: National Archives.
DYER, B. (1933) The Public Career of William M. Evarts. Berkeley: Univ. of California Press.
EVARTS, W. E. (n. d. ) Papers. Washington, DC: Library of Congress.
FORREST, J. L. (1967) "United States recognition of the Porfirio Diaz government, 1876-1878." Ph.D. dissertation, Oklahoma University, Norman.
FOSTER, J. W. (1909) Diplomatic Memoirs, Vol I. New York: Houghton Mifflin.
GIBBS, W. E. (1973) "Spadework diplomacy: United States-Mexican relations during the Hayes Administration, 1877-1881." Ph.D. dissertation, Kent State University, Kent, Ohio.
HACKETT, C. W. (1924) "The recognition of the Diaz government by the United States." Southwest Historical Q. 38 (July): 35-56.
HAYES, R. B. (n. d.) Papers. Fremont, Ohio: Hayes Memorial Library.
HUTTON, M. (1966) "William M. Evarts: Secretary of State, 1877-1881." Ph.D. dissertation, Catholic University, Washington, DC.
The National Republican (1877) December 8.
New York Herald (1878) September 25: 4, doc. 1.
——— (1877a) June 2: 4.
——— (1877b) June 19: 5.
——— (1877c) July 6: 4.
——— (1877d) September 25: 4, 6.
——— (1877e) November 27: 7.
——— (1877f) December 8: 4.
——— (1877g) December 14: 4.
——— (1877h) December 16: 4.
New York Sun (1877a) December 5: 2.
——— (1877b) December 12: 2.

——— (1877c) December 23: 1.
——— (1877d) December 11: 1.
New York Times (1878) April 24: 4.
PENNANEN, G. (1969) "The foreign policy of William M. Evarts." Ph.D. dissertation, University of Wisconsin, Madison.
PLETCHER, D. M. (1958) Rails, Mines, and Progress in Mexico, 1967-1911. Ithaca, NY: Cornell Univ. Press.
PLUMB, E. L. (n. d.) Papers. Washington, DC: Library of Congress.
PRITCHARD, W. T. (1878) "The Mexico of the Mexicans." International Rev. 5 (March-April): 170-184.
RICHARDSON, J. D. [ed.] (1907) Compilation of the Messages of the Presidents, Vol. VII. Washington, DC: Government Printing Office.
RIPPY, J. F. (1926) The United States and Mexico. New York: Alfred A. Knopf.
SHERMAN, W. T. (n. d.) Papers. Washington, DC: Library of Congress.
STONE, C. (1938) Dana and the Sun. New York: Dodd Mead.
U.S. House (1878a) Relations With Mexico. H. Rept. 701. 45 Cong. 2 sess. Washington, DC: Government Printing Office.
——— (1878b) Texas Border Troubles, N. Misc. Doc. 64. 45 Cong. 2 sess. Washington, DC: Government Printing Office.
——— (1877) Mexican Border Troubles. H. Exec. Doc. XIII. 45 Cong. 1 sess. Washington, DC: Government Printing Office.
——— (1876) Texas Frontier Troubles. H. Rept. 343. 44 Cong. 1 sess. Washington, DC: Government Printing Office.
U.S. War Department. Records of the Adjutant General's Office. Affairs on the Rio Grande and Texas Frontier, 1875-1881. File no. 1653. Washington, DC: National Archives.
WELCH, R. E. (1971) George Frisbie Hoar and the Half-Breed Republicans. Cambridge, MA: Harvard Univ. Press.

*William E. Gibbs, Assistant Professor of History at New Mexico Military Institute in Roswell, received his Ph.D. from Kent State University in Latin American history, with a special emphasis on United States-Mexican relations. His research continues in the late-nineteenth-century relationship between the two countries.*

**HARRY E. VANDEN**
*Department of Political Science*
*University of South Florida*
*Tampa, Florida 33620*

# *THE PEASANTS AS A REVOLUTIONARY CLASS:*
## *An Early Latin American View*

*We do not regard Marx's theory as something completed and inviolable; on the contrary, we are convinced that it has only laid the foundation stone of the science which socialists* must *develop in all directions if they wish to keep pace with life.*

V. I. Lenin (Our Program)

The peasant is one of the least understood and most abused actors on the modern political stage. He is maligned for his political passivity and distrust of national political movements. Yet, most of the great twentieth-century revolutions in the Third World have, according to most scholars, been peasant based (Landsberger, 1973: ix; Wolf, 1969). In Latin America the peasant was once pictured as the archetypical parochial who was more suited for siestas under his sombrero than serious political activity. Stereotypes aside, the region has been no exception to the growing tendency of peasants to become involved in major revolutionary processes. Indeed, beginning with the Mexican Revolution, Latin America has experienced an ever increasing number of revolutionary movments which count on the peasants as a key force in their bid for power. The land occupations which

---

AUTHOR'S NOTE: An earlier version of this article was presented at the Sixth National Meeting of the Latin American Studies Association, Atlanta, March 1976. I wish to acknowledge my special indebtedness to the Mariátegui family, Julio Portocarrero, Antonio Navarro Madrid, and Jorge Basadre for many courtesies extended while in Peru, and to Edgar Nesman, George Ginsburgs, and Harvey Nelson for critical reaction to the manuscript in various stages of completion. Field research for this paper was made possible by a Fulbright-Hays grant for Peru in 1973-1974.

Journal of Interamerican Studies and World Affairs, Vol. 20 No. 2, May 1978

occurred in Northern Mexico and El Salvador in 1976 and 1977 readily attest to the continued restiveness among the masses of the Latin American peasantry. Indeed, even in Latin America, it now seems rather trite to suggest the largely untapped potential for revolutionary action which resides among the rural masses.

Marxism—as the most widespread ideology of revolution—has had a somewhat curious record on incorporating the revolutionary potential of the peasantry (Mitrany, 1951). While enjoying growing popularity in Latin America, it did not, in the opinion of most scholars, produce an original theorist of peasant revolution until Che Guevara's writings began to appear in the early 1960s. Many would, of course, explain this seeming deficiency on the basis of Marx's belief that it was the urban proletariat which, because of its position in capitalist society, would first achieve revolutionary consciousness and thus lead the socialist revolution. Indeed, in the *Communist Manifesto,* he and Engles suggested that "the proletariat alone is a really revolutionary class" and that the peasantry is conservative and even reactionary (Marx, 1959: 17-18). The unreconstructed interpretation of Marx which was dominant in the Soviet Union under Stalin thus led the Communist International (during the 1930s and 1940s) to advise the Latin American Communist Parties to wait until a more advanced historical stage had engendered a revolutionary proletariat before they fomented revolutionary action (Program of the Communist International, cited in Miroschevsky, 1942: 56).

There has, nonetheless, been increasing interest in the revolutionary potential of the peasantry among Marxist thinkers.

### *Leninist View*

Lenin, who creatively applied most of Marx's essential thought to the special conditions he encountered in Russia, did not believe that the Russian peasants, who had been heavily influenced by Russian populism, would form the vanguard of the revolution. This position was reserved for Marx's urban proletariat. He did, however, believe that the historic conditions were such that the Russian peasantry could enter into *alliance* with the workers and their vanguard party to overthrow the Czarist regime. Indeed, he broke the peasant population down into four groups (rich peasants, middle peasants, poor peasants and agricultural workers), suggesting that the poorer peasants and rural laborers would be most susceptible to propaganda and organization by the Bolshevik Party ("Preliminary Draft Theses on the Agrarian Question," in Lenin, 1971: 592ff.).

Lenin was, however, aware of the importance of special conditions in developing nations in Africa, Asia, and Latin America. In his opening address to the Second Congress of the Communist International (1920) he called for the creation of a revolutionary spirit among the peasantry, and for the formation of peasant soviets in developing areas (Lenin, 1971: 602-606).

Although the document that contains this last aspect of Lenin's thought does not seem to have been widely circulated in Latin America, it seems certain that José Carlos Mariátegui had access to this or similar documents which were circulated by the Third (Communist) International (Vanden, 1975: 78). New directions within the International seem, however, to have focused on the Soviet model, to the exclusion of revolutionary Marxist-Leninist thought which was more adapted to the specific conditions encountered in the Third World.[1]

## *Mao*

Unlike many orthodox European communists, Third World Marxists have, however, interpreted Marx and Lenin (who was himself a master of adapting theory to concrete reality) in the light of the specific conditions in which they had to develop their thought. Confronted with the increasingly restive peasant masses in rural China and the abysmal failure of the urban workers uprisings, Mao began, in 1927, to evolve a theory of Marxist revolution which was to place the peasants—and not the workers—in the forefront of the socialist struggle (Mao, 1965,

Vol. 1: 23-59). His belief that the peasants were the most important revolutionary class in agricultural China developed when he and the other party cadres were forced into the countryside and found that the long-suffering Chinese peasant was ready and willing to revolt against the forces that oppressed him (as indeed he had done sporadically throughout Chinese history). By carefully educating the peasant masses with Mao's interpretation of Marxist-Leninist thought, the communists were able to mobilize them and incorporate them into their revolutionary ranks (Vanden, 1977: 4-5). Thus, Mao concluded that

> It was the class struggles of peasants, the peasant uprising and peasant wars that constituted the real motive force of historical development in Chinese feudal society [Mao, 1965, Vol. I: 18].

This view of the peasantry did not, however, emerge full blown from the 1927 "Hunan Report." Rather, it evolved over a period of years as the dynamics of revolutionary praxis forced Mao to revise and refine his original constructs. In fact, as late as 1929, Mao (in a report to the Central Committee of the party) suggested that:

> The laying of the Party's proletarian base and the establishment of Party cells in industrial enterprises in key centers are the greatest organizational tasks of the Party at present [Mao, in Schram, 1969: 259-260].

Nonetheless, the non-Western, rural peasant perspective which Mao eventually acquired allowed him to adapt revolutionary Marxism to a Third World reality situation in which the peasantry, and not the urban proletariat, was the most exploited and most numerous class (Vanden, 1977: 6).

*Guevara*

Che Guevara also forged his Marxist revolutionary theory in the process of struggle. He, like Mao in China, developed his

Marxist thought in light of the concrete historical conditions which were encountered in Cuba, and thus came to emphasize the rural nature of the struggle. The peasants, and not the urban workers, were to staff the ranks of the rural foco. The revolutionary movement was from the peasant-dominated countryside to the cities. The peasantry would provide the revolutionary force necessary to overthrow the existing regime.

Before Guevara Latin American was not, however, generally believed to have produced any important Marxist-Leninist thinkers. Regis Debray further deplored the general unrevolutionary nature of Latin American Marxist-Leninists and the parties they staffed. The picture he painted of bureaucratized party leaders and intellectuals suggests they were more interested in their jobs as party functionaries than original thought or revolutionary action (Debray, 1967). One is thus led to believe that Latin American revolutionaries had, before Guevara and Castro, been incapable of developing a Marxism which was both revolutionary and suited to the peasant-oriented societies which have characterized most of Latin American up to the present.

## *Mariátegui*

Such a view would, however, leave out the first major Marxist-Leninist thinker in Latin American history—José Carlos Mariátegui. Mariátegui (1894-1930) was a Peruvian intellectual who is best known for his book, *7 ensayos en interpretación de la realidad peruana* (Lima, 1928)[2] and his magazine, *Amauta* (Lima, 1926-1930). He was also a Marxist *pensador* of considerable acumen.

Although the *7 Ensayos* and some of Mariátegui's literary work have been widely disseminated throughout Latin America and indeed much of the Western world,[3] his political writings have not been widely read. This is due not only to the Euro-centered nature of the intellectual world, but to the loss of a collection of his writings on the political and ideological evolution of Peru which he mentions in the preface to the *7 Ensayos.*

Lamentably, the manuscript of this work was lost when it was sent to Spain for publication. Nor was the *7 Ensayos* ever intended to be a work in political theory (Mariátegui, 1969: 15-16). Up to 1969, Mariátegui's ideological theses and labor writings were either unpublished or buried in obscure publications which never reached a wide audience (Martínez de la Torre, 1947). With the publication of Mariátegui's collected works, a collection of his ideological and political writing was, however, brought to light (Mariátegui, 1969). *Ideología y política* helps to clarify Mariátegui's ideological orientation and, when supplemented by letters and other documents from the Mariátegui family archive,[4] gives a solid indication of the innovative nature of Mariátegui's political thought and closely related practical political activity (praxis).

The *7 Ensayos* does, however, give some indication of Mariátegui's agrarian-rural focus (see chs. 2 and 3) and of the spontaneous way in which his thought and written work often developed (see the preface and epigram). As to this latter point, it should further be noted that Mariátegui was a journalist by profession and despised the pedestrian, overly organized writing which characterized many academics. Thus, one must often look to several sources to ascertain Mariátegui's thought on a particular matter. Because, then, of this creative style, the loss of the above mentioned manuscript, and the secretive nature of much of Mariátegui's organizational work, this approach becomes particularly important if one is to understand Mariátegui's thoughts on the peasant question.

When Mariátegui returned to Peru from Europe, he was strongly influenced by his contact with classical Marxist writings and the revolutionary socialist forces in France and Italy. Beside reading Marx, Engels, and Lenin, he was exposed to many other European socialists including H. Barbusse, G. Sorel, B. Croce, and A. Gramsci (Vanden, 1975: 25-83). Responding to such European interpretations of Marxism, he initially viewed the industrial workers as the principal revolutionary force in a socialist revolution in Peru and thus dedicated much of his time to preparing a workers' vanguard for its class role (Mariátegui, 1971a: 77ff.). Mariátegui never, however, thought Marxism should be dogmatically applied and even in this early period (1923-1924) was expanding the classical Marxist conception of the workers as *the* revolutionary class to include large numbers of class-conscious intellectuals.[5] Indeed, he was evolving a flexible revolutionary praxis which, although similar to currents in Italy, was to later occasion severe criticism from orthodox communist sectors.

As Mariátegui synthesized the fruits of his ongoing study of Peruvian reality and his voluntaristic reading of Marx, Lenin, and Antonio Gramsci (Vanden, 1975), he began to construct an "American" socialism which, although remaining within the parameters of revolutionary Marxist-Leninist thought, would not be a copy or imitation of another system. "We must," he stated, "give life to Indo-American socialism with our own reality, our own language." It should be "creación heroica" (Mariátegui, 1969: 249). His brilliant study of Peruvian reality (the *7 Ensayos*) and nondogmatic approach to Marxism thus enabled him to interpret Marxist thought in light of the rural, agrarian conditions which predominated in Peru and indeed most of Latin America at that time. As such, his thought was very similar to that which we find being applied in much of the Third World today.

The great mass of exploited human beings in Peru was not found among the urban proletariat, which was small, unorganized and (in the mid-1920s) lacking in revolutionary consciousness. There were only a few thousand industrial workers in the entire nation and these were concentrated in Lima. There were, however, millions of peasants who were engaged in agriculture.[6] This group comprised the vast majority of the total population. Most of this rural population was Indian and tended to work on their own and/or the *hacendado's* land. Although dissimilar to a classical proletariat, the peasants—Indian and mestizo—were an oppressed and exploited class. Classical Marxist theory would not, however, have viewed this group as a revolutionary class.

Mariátegui, on the other hand, began to view them differently. He was aware of the many peasant uprisings which had occurred throughout Peruvian history, and of the deep-seated feelings of hostility which the *campesino,* especially when he was Indian, harbored toward the *gamonal* and other members of the ruling classes. Huizer and Stavenhagen have, along the same lines, observed that:

> Over the years and long before land reform had become a political catchword, the peasants of Latin America had resisted and protested (often violently) the process whereby the expanding haciendas robbed them of their lands and turned them into oppressed peons [Landsberger, 1973: 379].

Indeed, many modern observers have strenuously attacked the "myth of the passive peasant" (Whyte, 1976: 247).

By the late 1920s Mariátegui, like Mao, became convinced that the peasants had the potential for revolutionary action in agrarian society. Indeed, he believed that the only way to improve the living conditions for the (peasant) masses was through a complete structural change of Peruvian economic and social conditions, beginning with a change in the land tenure system which would eliminate the feudal conditions which so oppressed the peasants. Such change was, however, to be accomplished not by an urban vanguard, but by the Indian peasants themselves (Mariátegui, 1928: 6). Thus, the mostly Indian peasants emerge as the strong revolutionary class in Peru.[7]

The Indian peasants would, according to Mariátegui, have a strong disposition toward socialism because of their communal heritage from the Incan Empire (which Mariátegui mistakenly believed was a type of primitive communism) and from their experiences in their "communidades." Their conversion to socialism might be a slow process, but once they had adopted the doctrine, they would hold on to it like few other proletarians:

> the socialist idea will serve them with a discipline, a tenacity and a force that few other proletarians from other places could surpass them [Mariátegui, 1969: 46].

The history of rebellions and peasant uprisings indicated that the Indian peasants were not docile, as many people thought. Recent history had shown that—as in the case of the rebellion led by Major Gutierrez[8]—the Indian peasants were capable of rising up against the forces which oppressed them (Mariátegui, 1969: 40). Such uprisings had been brutally repressed because they lacked national leadership or any unifying ideology. Socialism, Mariátegui argued, was the doctrine which could give constructive meaning to this struggle (Mariátegui, 1969: 187-188). He further observed that:

> The Indians themselves are beginning to show signs of a new consciousness. . . . The new generation knows that Peru's progress will be a fiction or at least will not be Peruvian so long as it is not the work of—and thus benefits—the Peruvian masses who are four-fifths Indians and peasants [Mariátegui, 1928: 6].

Thus it was to be the peasants themselves (most of whom were Indian) who would throw off the yoke of the *gamonal* and thus initiate the revolutionary process which would result in the implantation of Peruvian Socialism. Indeed, Mariátegui's focus on the rural, agrarian nature of Peruvian society (as in the *7 Ensayos*) suggested such a conclusion.

The peasant uprisings which broke out throughout Peru in the 1960s suggest not only the correctness of Mariátegui's Marxist theory, but the accuracy of his empirical observation. In a recent work, Handelman (1975: 126) cites a pamphlet put out by the League of Hacendados in the 1920s which notes 33 peasant revolts in a (typical) 13-month period. Likewise, he suggests that there "is ample evidence that mobilizations of highland communities in the early 1960s were actually the latest of a continual series of peasant revolts against external exploitation" (Handelman, 1975: 126). Indeed, Mariátegui foresaw the organizational potential of Peru's peasants some 35 years before Hugo Blanco and other Marxist organizers aided in the mobilizations in the Valley of La Convención and elsewhere. One must wonder, then, what the exact potential of Peruvian Marxism would have been if it had followed Mariátegui's rural focus, rather than subordinating its national praxis to the Soviet model.

As was the case with Mao, the original nature of Mariátegui's Marxism-Leninism in this and other areas caused considerable conflict with the less flexible Moscow-based Communist International and its followers in and outside Peru. Indeed, the Stalin-dominated post-Zinoviev period witnessed increasing criticism of Mariátegui's ideas. The most spectacular instance of this occurred at the first meeting of Latin American Communist Parties held in Buenos Aires in 1929, where the Peruvian's ideas were crudely attacked by the Latin American Bureau Chief (V. Codovilla of Argentina) and by the Latin Secretary of the International, Jules Humbert-Dorz ("Camaradu Luis"; *El movimiento revolucionario,* and Portocarrero interview, 1974). Subsequent pressure from the International, the arrival of Eudocio Ravines from Europe, and Mariátegui's untimely death in 1930 allowed a more orthodox Moscow-oriented position (which was championed by Ravines) to triumph within Peru.

Mariátegui's thought was further attacked as national populism in the early 1940s by a well-known Soviet historian who specifically cited Mariátegui's focus on the peasantry as evidence of the unscientific nature of his Marxism (Miroschevsky; 1942). Subsequently (and in large part due to the efforts of now Secretary General of the Peruvian Communist Party, Jorge del Prado), Mariátegui emerged as not only the founding hero of the Peruvian Communist Party (see note 13), but a revolutionary Marxist-Leninist who is frequently lauded by Soviet writers (see note 14; Seminov and Shulgovsky, 1960).

Nor did the Apristas view Mariátegui's formulations with great enthusiasm. After an initial period in which Mariátegui worked with Haya de la Torre in the Universidad Popular González Prada, Haya was exiled from Peru and was eventually to change APRA from a loose alliance which might *temporarily* accommodate a socialist group into a nationalist, multiclass party. Although the Apristas and Mariátegui and his followers were both very much interested in the rural, mostly Indian, peasantry, they were quite far apart on other issues. The Peruvian APRA was to be a multiclass party which was to include the bourgeoisie, while Mariátegui's Socialist Party was to be solely a working class party. First Luís Alberto Sánchez and then Haya de la Torre accused Mariátegui of being a "Europeanizer" because of his ties to international Socialist thought (Martínez de la Torre, 1947, Vol. 2: 271-286). Mariátegui, in turn, dubbed the APRA the Kuo-Min-Tang of Latin America (Mariátegui, 1969: 87-95). The dispute between the Apristas and Peruvian Marxists was never resolved, and continues into the present day.

Mariátegui's thought was, however, very heavily framed in the context of Peruvian reality and thus it did not, as did Maoist thought, follow the classification scheme which Lenin used (rich peasants, middle peasants, poor peasants, and agricultural workers). He was aware of the special conditions which confronted the sharecroppers (*yanacón*)[9] and of the differences among peasant groups in Peru's varied regions. The main focus in most of Mariátegui's writing was on the Sierra peasants whom he usually equated with the Indian population. He did not, however, fail to mention the coastal peasant population, which included a substantial percentage of mestizos as well as Indians.

Indeed, he argued that the coastal peasants had demonstrated their combativeness on several occasions. For instance, in the countryside around Huacho (central coast) "advanced tendencies" had been displayed.

> Classist theory and spirit have found a favorable environment there. The first manifestations of proletarian ideology quickly found propagandists among the peasants in Huacho. Their struggles in the epoch of agitation for the 8-hour working day and against the increased prices for basic foodstuffs put the Huacho peasant in the vanguard of our social movement [Mariátegui, 1929a: 7].

Mariátegui realized that it might be difficult to organize the coastal haciendas but felt that past struggles (such as that of Chicama) indicated the peasants' receptiveness to class propaganda and organization which could penetrate the most secure hacienda through the going and coming of workers and the new possibilities offered by the motor car (Mariátegui, 1973: 7).[10]

Nor was the Peruvian thinker unaware of the special conditions which the foreign-dominated agribusiness sector in the North was creating. He believed that the conflict between the modern capitalist enterprises and remnants of the traditional agricultural workers were experiencing (because of their exploitation) could be utilized to hasten the arrival of the socialist revolution. He further suggested that his local contacts set up Marxist study groups to focus the local conflicts in Marxist terms (Mariátegui, 1929b).

The industrial proletariat was not to be the only revolutionary class in agrarian Peru, even though its more conscious elements might contribute more heavily to an initial vanguard which would be responsible for some of the early organizational tasks. A socialist revolution was impossible until the peasant masses became aware of their class role and began a unified socialist movement. These two classes, along with the intellectuals, miners, and even artisans were to form the revolutionary force in Peru. The vanguard which was to lead these groups was not simply a workers party but a party based on the organized work and *peasant* masses (Martínez de la Torre, 1947, Vol. 2: 397-398). Indeed, Mariátegui seems to have been redefining Marx's concept of the proletariat to fit new historical conditions and thus including class conscious peasants as well as urban workers (Mariátegui, 1973: 17). Unlike Lenin's view of the peasantry, it was not to form an alliance with the urban proletariat to overthrow the bourgeois state, but was to be the most powerful revolutionary class in the struggle to establish a socialist regime. This seems completely consistent with Mariátegui's desire to implant socialism directly in Peru (Mariátegui, 1973: 17). In Peru, as in most of what later became known as the Third World, any popular revolutionary movement which was not based principally in the peasantry would have little chance of success in the foreseeable future. But how, then, was Mariátegui to organize this class?

*Organization*

He realized that the peasantry might be slow to respond to classist propaganda. Thus only some peasants would participate in the initial organizational tasks which were to be carried out largely by class conscious urban workers and intellectuals. Mariátegui's voluntaristic conception of Marxism (which was influenced by Lenin, Henri Barbusse, Georges Sorel, and Antonio Gramsci) would not allow him to wait for the economic conditions to force the peasants to act. He planned to use the vanguardist party, newly created in 1928, and General Confederation of Peruvian Workers, organized in 1929, to educate and organize the rural as well as urban masses. Likewise, he planned to utilize his magazine *Amauta* and working class newspaper *Labor* to spread his message. The flexibility of his tactical considerations and the fact that he wanted to create a "worker-peasant" party was later criticized as national populism by the above mentioned Soviet writer who further accused Mariátegui of considering the urban proletariat as nothing more than an "appendage" of the peasant masses (Miroschevsky, 1942: 46-47). Although this would seem to overstate Mariátegui's view, it does indicate how this innovative aspect of his thought was viewed in most orthodox Marxist circles for quite a few years after his death in 1930.

As an indicator of how Mariátegui integrated peasant and worker organization, we would note that the "Manifesto" of the General Confederation of Peruvian Workers (which Mariátegui organized) was "directed to the workers *and peasants* of the nation so that they would respond to their historic class call and proceed to create union organizations in factories, companies, mines, ports, *and* in the haciendas, valleys, and Indian communities" (Maríatequi, with A. Navarro and J. Portocarrero, 1969: 139). One of the founding organizations was, in fact, the Federación de Yanaconas (see note 9). Mention was made of the numerous peasant organizations which exist throughout the country and how important it was to have an organization which could educate the peasants in their class role and work for their unification. Indeed, he envisioned a peasantry organized

> in peasant leagues, in peasant communities which tend toward the creation of a "National Federation of Peasant Leagues" [Mariátegui with A. Navarro and J. Portocarrero, 1969: 147-148].

Peasant leagues, we would further note, were among the most effective vehicles used by the Chinese communists and Hugo Blanco to organize the peasantry.

To stimulate rural organizing, Mariátegui devoted entire sections of his literary magazine *Amauta* ("El Gamonalismo") and his working class newspaper *Labor* ("El Ayllu") to agrarian problems and peasant organizing. He was even planning to found a separate paper (*El Ayllu*) to heighten class consciousness in rural areas (Mariátegui, 1929c), but was prevented from doing so first by a government crackdown and then by his premature death. He felt that the literacy and linguistic barriers could be overcome by more conscious elements who would translate the main themes of the articles and commentary to their fellow peasants. Likewise, the party cells which were forming throughout Peru were to be used for this purpose. As of 1929, Mariátegui had already begun to send "prepared" workers, peasants, and intellectuals to selected locations on the coast and in the Sierra. These organizers were to bolster classist organization in these areas (Portocarrero Interview, 1974).[11] Another important way of reaching the countryside was to send peasants who had already been exposed to socialist thought back to their villages so that they could disseminate the doctrine.[12] This program does not seem to have been implemented on a large scale, although Mariátegui seems to have sent back some peasants whom he knew personally. Unlike some later revolutionaries, he realized that a white or mestizo would be viewed as an outsider in many of the Sierra villages and that it was extremely important to send someone from the same area who could speak the indigenous language.[13] The importance of this type of contact is stressed in Mariátegui's "Thesis" on the "Racial Problem in Latin America," which was presented at the First Meeting of Latin American Communist Parties in 1929 (Mariátegui, 1969: 83). He also foresaw the possibility of transforming the agrarian committees which were forming in the North into instruments of class struggle (Mariátegui, 1929b). Nor should one overlook the fact that Mariátegui never relented in his call for total land reform in order to return the land to those who worked it. In so doing he could not but attract wide peasant support of his programs.

## *Conclusion*

By 1929, Mariátegui had thus grasped the importance of the peasants as a revolutionary class in less developed societies such as Peru. Likewise, he had even begun to organize this group. The concrete historical conditions had forced him to creatively apply Marx's thought and certain aspects of Lenin's doctrine. In the process, he had evolved an Indo-American socialism which anticipated one of the most controversial, yet original, interpretations of Marxist-Leninist doctrine—that of viewing the peasants, as well as the workers, as a class in society which had a great revolutionary potential because of its relation to the means of production. This was accomplished at about the same time that Mao Tse-tung was evolving a similar doctrine in China. Indeed, the strong emphasis placed on the peasants and land reform by Mariátegui may have actually predated some of the formulations by the Chinese communists. At the very least, the Peruvian's ideas were remarkably advanced for the time in which he was working. He, like Mao, was responding to a Third World reality situation which was vastly different from that which Marx originally envisioned as the locus for socialist revolutions. In so doing, he made an interpretation of Marxism which—while maintaining the revolutionary nature of the doctrine—liberated it from its European birthplace, and indeed made it surprisingly relevant to the rural mobilizations which have come to characterize twentieth-century revolutions in the Third World (see Wolf, 1969).

Although Mariátegui emphasized political education and organization building rather than simply armed struggle, his rural focus anticipated that of Guevara and Castro by almost 30 years. Similarly, his flexible interpretation of Marxist-Leninist thought occurred better than two decades before most Latin American Marxists could divest themselves of the shackles imposed by a Stalinist-oriented international movement. Nor did he underestimate the importance of violent revolution (see Mariátegui's letter in Espinoza, 1932) or the domination of foreign imperialism (Mariátegui, 1969: 87-95).

Mariátegui's premature death at the age of 35 abruptly terminated the development of his political thought just as he was coming to a mature—if unique—understanding of Marxism-Leninism. Much of his political thought was never known outside of a small group of Peruvians. Few of his political writings were, until recently, widely circulated. When Hugo Pesce and Julio Portocarrero presented several of his theses to the First Meeting of Latin American Communist Parties held in Buenos Aires in 1929, his ideas were pointedly attacked by representatives of the Communist International (La Correspondencia Sudamericana, 1929). Nor did Mariátegui's formulations meet with a sympathetic audience among most orthodox communists outside of Peru[14] until the 1960s, when even the formerly critical Russians reexamined their position on Mariátegui (Seminov and Shulgovsky, 1960).

The unavailability of most of Mariátegui's political writings until very recently, has also made the task of evaluating his thought and praxis a difficult one. As aspects of his political thought become better known, he will almost certainly emerge as the first major Latin American Marxist-Leninist thinker and, indeed, one of the first theorists of Marxist peasant revolution. His, then, was a remarkably current interpretation of Marxist-Leninist thought in the Latin American-Third World context. As such, it deserves much more attention and a much wider reading.[15]

## NOTES

1. See Humbert-Dorz (1968), Gruber (1974), and M. N. Roy, "Subtleties in the Anti-Imperialist Struggle" in Gruber (1974: 299-307).

2. First translated into English by Marjory Urquidi as *Seven Interpretive Essays on Peruvian Reality* (Mariátegui: 1971b).

3. The *7 Ensayos* will soon be in its thirtieth edition, and has been translated into five other languages, including Russian (1963).

4. I am particularly indebted to Dr. Javier Mariátegui and Mr. Sandro Mariátegui for bringing many of the more important documents to my attention. Editora "Amauta" (Lima) will publish Mariátegui's letters in the near future.

5. Letter from Jorge Falcón to a group of Peruvian Socialists, dated Madrid, September 15, 1923. (This letter is found in the Mariátegui family archive.)

6. Mariátegui's definition of "peasant" would seem to be very similar to one of those developed by Landsberger in *Rural Protest*— "all rural cultivators of low economic and political status" (Landsberger, 1973: 17). Since virtually all the peasants in the highland and most of those on the coast were Indian, he often, however, uses peasant and Indian interchangeably.

7. This aspect of Mariátegui's thought is briefly mentioned in Chang-Rodríguez (1957: 164) and Jorrín and Martz (1970: 280). Neither, however, dwell on the point.

8. This was a rebellion in the 1920s which involved some 70,000 peasants from Southern Peru.

9. In Peru, Yanacón came to mean a type of Indian sharecropper/laborer who would be allowed to farm part of a (usually coastal) hacienda in return for his labor on the owner's land and/or some other form of payment. Their unique status made them especially susceptible to exploitation by the landowner.

10. This pamphlet is mainly composed of an interview with Mariátegui which was published in La Sierra (Lima) in 1929 and has not yet been included in the Obras Completas.

11. Julio Portocarrero was, at this time, the Socialist group's labor organizer.

12. Interestingly, Handelman (1975: 188ff.) finds that traditional village leaders who had been exposed to modern ideas in the city were key figures in mobilizing traditional communal villages in the Sierra.

13. This was, of course, precisely one of the reasons for Hugo Blanco's initial success in the Valley of la Convención (Blanco: 1972), and conversely, for Che Guevara's failure in Bolivia.

14. After Mariátegui's formulations had been discouraged during the Ravines-dominated 1930s, M. Arroyo Posadas and Jorge del Prado began to defend many of his ideas in the early 1940s in *Dialéctica* (Havana) and elsewhere. By 1960, Mariátegui had become the hero of the Peruvian communist movement. See especially del Prado's excellent work, *Mariátegui y su obra* (1946).

15. Mariátegui's thought and praxis are now being reexamined by many scholars in Eastern and Western Europe and in Latin America. See B. G. Kononof et al., *José Carlos Mariátegui: Glorious Fighter for Triumph of Marxist-Leninist Ideas in Latin America* (in Russian; Moscow: Editorial "Science," 1963); Antonio Melis; Adalbert Dessau, and Manfred Kossok, *Mariátegui: tres estudios* (Lima: Biblioteca Amauta, 1971); and Diego Meseguer Illan, *José Carlos Mariátegui y su pensamiento revolucionario* (Lima: Instituto de Estudios Peruanos, 1974).

North American works on Latin American thought have accorded Mariátegui a prominent place among Leftist thinkers and have acknowledged the original nature of his Marxism. See W. Rex Crawford, *A Century of Latin-American Thought* (Cambridge, 1967); Martin Stabb, *In Quest of Identity* (Chapel Hill, 1967); Miguel Jorrín and John D.

Martz, *Latin American Political Thought and Ideology* (Chapel Hill, 1970); and Harold Eugene Davis, *Latin American Thought* (Baton Rouge, 1972).

Considering the importance of Mariátegui, his political thought would seem to merit more extensive treatments in English. Lamentably, the only full-length English work, John M. Baines, *Revolution in Peru: Mariátegui and the Myth* (University, Alabama, 1972) does not make any significant contribution to an understanding of Mariátegui's views on the peasantry, or in most other areas.

See also the forthcoming work by Jesús Chavarría, *José Carlos Mariátegui, 1894-1930: And the Rise of Modern Peru* (University of New Mexico) and Harry E. Vanden, "José Carlos Mariátegui: Revolutionary Political Thought and Praxis in a Developing Nation" (New School, 1975).

## REFERENCES

BLANCO, R. (1972) Land or Death: The Peasant Struggle in Peru. New York: Pathfinder.

CHANG-RODRIGUEZ, E. (1957) La literatura política de González Prada, Mariátegui y Haya de la Torre. México: Colección Studium-18.

La Correspondencia Sudamericana (1929) El movimiento revolucionario Latinoamericano. Buenos Aires: La Correspondencia Sudamericana.

DEBRAY, R. (1967) Revolution in the Revolution. New York: Grove.

ESPINOZA, E. [Samuel Glusberg] (1932) Trincera. Buenos Aires: BABEL.

FALCON, J. (1923) Letter to a group of Peruvian Socialists (September 15).

GRUBER, H. [ed.] (1974) Soviet Russia Masters the Comintern. New York: Anchor Books, Doubleday.

HANDELMAN, H. (1975) Struggle in the Andes. Latin American Monograph Series No. 35. Austin: Univ. of Texas Press.

HUMBERT-DORZ, J. (1968) L'origine de l'Internationele Communiste. Boundry, France: Baconniere.

JORRIN, M. and J. D. MARTZ (1970) Latin American Political Thought and Ideology. Chapel Hill: Univ. of North Carolina Press.

LANDSBERGER, H. A. [ed.] (1973) Rural Protest: Peasant Movements and Social Change. New York: Barnes & Noble.

LENIN, V. I. (1971) Selected Works (one vol.). New York: International Publishers.

MAO TSE-TUNG (1965) Selected Works (four vols.). Peking: Foreign Language Press.

MARIATEGUI, J. C. (1973) Acerca del carácter de la sociedad peruana. Lima: No Publishers.

——— (1971a) Historia de la crisis mundial. Vol. 8, Obras Completas. Lima: Biblioteca Amauta.

——— (1971b) [Translation of 1928 edition, 7 ensayos en interpretación de la realidad peruana] Seven Interpretive Essays on Peruvian Reality. [M. Urquidi tr.] Austin: Univ. of Texas Press.

——— (1969) Ideología y política. Vol. 13, Obras Completas. Lima: Biblioteca Amauta.

——— (1929a) "El Ayllu." Labor (Lima) 10 (September 7): 7

——— (1929b) Letter to Nicanor A. de la Fuente (June 20).
——— (1929c) Letter to M. Arroyo Posadas (June 5).
——— (1928) "Sobre el problema indigena." Labor (Lima) 1 (Novemer 10): 6.
——— [ed.] (1926-1930) Amauta. Lima.
MARTINEZ DE LA TORRE, R. (1947) Apuntes para una interpretación Marxista de la historia social del Peru (four vols.). Lima: Empresa Editora Peruana.
MARX, K. (1959) The Communist Manifesto in Lewis S. Feuer, Marx and Engels, Basic Writings. Garden City: Anchor Books, Doubleday.
MIROSCHEVSKY, V. (1942) El populismo en el Perú. Dialéctica (Havana) I (May-June): 41-59.
MITRANY, D. (1951) Marx Against the Peasant. Chapel Hill: Univ. of North Carolina Press.
PORTOCARRERO, J. (1974) Interview with Julio Portocarrero (August 25).
PRADO, J. del (1946) Mariátegui y su obra. Lima: Ediciones Nuevo Horizonte.
SCHRAM, S. R. (1969) The Political Thought of Mao Tse-Tung. New York: Praeger.
SEMINOV, S. and A. SCHULGOVSKY (1960) "El papel de José Carlos Mariátegui en la formación del partido comunista del Perú." Hora del Hombre (Lima) 1 (January): 65-82.
VANDEN, H. E. (1977) "Marx and the peasantry in Latin America: marginalization or mobilization." Presented at 1977 SECOLAS meeting. (mimeo)
——— (1975) Mariátegui: influencias en su formación ideológica. Lima: Biblioteca Amauta.
WHYTE, W. F. (1976) "Rural Peru: peasants and activists," pp. 241-251 in David Chaplin (ed.) Peruvian Nationalism, a Corporatist Revolution. New Brunswick: Transaction Books.
WOLF, E. R. (1969) Peasant Wars of the Twentieth Century. New York: Harper & Row.

*Harry E. Vanden is presently Assistant Professor of Political Science at the University of South Florida. From late 1973 to early 1975 he lived in Peru, first doing research as a Fulbright Scholar, and then working with the Peruvian government. His publications include* Mariátegui: influencias en su formación ideológica. *An executive council member of the Society for Iberian and Latin American Thought, he is particularly interested in political thought in Latin America and the Third World.*

# REVIEW ESSAY

## *ARGENTINA AT THE CROSSROADS*

*Rock, David. POLITICS IN ARGENTINA 1890-1930: THE RISE AND FALL OF RADICALISM. London: Cambridge University Press, 1975.*

*Falcoff, Mark and Ronald H. Dolkart, eds. PROLOGUE TO PERON: ARGENTINA IN DEPRESSION AND WAR, 1930-1943. Berkeley and Los Angeles: University of California Press, 1975.*

*Hodges, Donald C. ARGENTINA, 1943-1976: THE NATIONAL REVOLUTION AND RESISTANCE. Albuquerque: University of New Mexico Press, 1976.*

*Kirkpatrick, Jeane. LEADER AND VANGUARD IN MASS SOCIETY: A STUDY OF PERONIST ARGENTINA. Cambridge, MA, and London: M.I.T. Press, 1971.*

*Rock, David, ed. ARGENTINA IN THE TWENTIETH CENTURY. Pittsburgh: University of Pittsburgh Press, 1975.*

Argentina has been, for many decades, the "odd man out" of Latin American politics. A marginal area of the Spanish colonial empire, at least up to the eighteenth century, it progressed in the nineteenth century from a backwoods region to central importance in South America. This, of course, was due mainly to its early specialization in meat and cereals production, which consolidated the country's

Journal of Interamerican Studies and World Affairs, Vol. 20 No. 2, May 1978

comparative advantages in the "international division of labor" then labor" then present on a world scale. By 1900 massive injections of present on a world scale. By 1900 massive injections of capital and manpower (mostly from Italy and Spain) had already patterned Argentina's outward-oriented development of its economy vis-à-vis the leading power of the day, Great Britain. Furthermore, the early development of an indigenous landowning-commercial elite with managed to survive internecine struggles by local or national caudillos (Juan Manuel de Rosas) and ended up by strengthening the economic, political, and social hegemony of a city over a nation.

In close association with British interests—the railroads that linked the interior's producing areas to the capital being one of the well-known major examples—the "landed oligarchy" was able to crush the last vestiges of provincial autonomies, and in the process it acquired an almost absolute control over the state through its spokesmen and politicians. At the same time, however, discontent was also spreading among displaced members of the elite, together with the beginnings of labor and social agitation in Buenos Aires, which was already at play by the 1900s. Most of this turbulence in an apparently stable milieu was soon going to channel itself into the political arena via frustrated armed revolts or eventually through increased electoral participation.

My purpose here is not to sketch a history of Argentina in the nineteenth and early twentieth centuries, but merely to suggest that without a clear understanding of that period, it will be almost impossible to fully comprehend later events. This is, in essence, the starting point for any meaningful interpretation of contemporary Argentina. Fortunately, most of the books under review help to substantiate this approach, which puts phenomena such as Radicalism, the 1930s, Peronism, and post-Peronism in a more realistic perspective. It is high time to abandon ad hoc, comfortable explanations that tend to underline certain specific features—Hipólito Yrigoyen's real or alleged senility, Juan Domingo Perón's personalistic and demagogic attributes—to account for the complexities of the once-called "Argentine paradox."

The five books address themselves, each in its own particular way, to key issues related to a better appraisal of present-day Argentina and can be considered indicative of recent trends of research on the River Plate country. With the exception of a few articles in the collections of readings edited by Rock, and Falcoff and Dolkart, most of the material belongs to English-speaking authors. The general tone is historical, with partial emphasis at times on economic matters. There is also a representative sample of the political science variety of survey-oriented techniques as shown in Kirkpatrick's volume.

The books under examination, quite appropriately, lend themselves to a chronological-thematic order and progression. Rock's discussion of the rise and fall of the *Unión Cívica Radical* bridges the period from the dominance of the landed-commercial elite to the military coup that overthrew Yrigoyen in 1930. By pinpointing the basic characteristics of the Radical administrations in power, Falcoff and Dolkart deal with economic crisis and conservative restoration as they developed in the 1930s, and close the narrative with another military coup in 1943, when Argentina was experiencing the consequences of World War II. Peronism, from its inception in those crucial years up to the present, permeates most of Hodges' analysis from a self-styled revoutionary perspective, and of Kirkpatrick's attempts to provide a picture of the movement's composition and attitudes by the mid-sixties. Rock's *Argentina in the Twentieth Century* offers a handful of interpretations on relevant topics of recent and not-so-recent Argentine history, as a synthetic panorama of the last 100 years or so.

I will try to show how some of the major problems dealt with in each individual work relate to a cumulative understanding of today's Argentina. Hopefully, in the final part of the essay the author's views on very basic issues will be briefly considered, together with suggestions for urgently needed research.

Rock's *Politics in Argentina 1890-1930* squarely places the rhetoric and practice of Radicalism in a more illuminating perspective than generally has been the case in Argentine historiography. With few recent exceptions, the tendency has been to confuse the party with the nation, as Gabriel del Mazo did in his day, or, conversely, to disregard it as the sole expression of Yrigoyen's strong leadership, and even to treat it as an *avant la lettre* prefiguration of Peronism.

This documented study makes intelligent use of secondary literature and clarifies certain key points that throw additional light on the structural causes of processes and events in contemporary Argentina. Such is its discussion of changes in the UCR from a "mass movement managed by upper status groups" (p. 58) in the 1890s into a party that represented the interests of a dependent middle class—both through electoral support and access to its own leadership—by the 1920s. The important role played by state patronage and "political machines"—the legendary UCR *comités*—in building up Radical majorities at election time are vividly described by the author. So are the relationships of Radicalism with labor groups, an aspect of the period that had not received adequate treatment in previous works. Rock's discussion of "syndicalist" currents is also extremely useful for a better understanding of the links between Perón and organized labor in the more sophisticated context of the forties.

The essential continuity between the oligarchy's economic policies and those of the Radical administrations between 1916 and 1930 is further explained by the author's analysis of the UCR as basically a "coaliton of landowners and nonindustrial middle class groups" (pp. 98-99). The weight of local industrialists and, for that matter, of workers in the Radical coalition of forces was in general a less decisive factor than in Peronism. Without disregarding leadership's discrepancies concerning economic policies, most of the significant conflicts of the period took place in the political arena, such as the infighting between the executive and conservative provincial governments with their over-representation in the senate. The penetration of foreign capital *other than British* in industrial activities during the 1920s also contributed to the relative weakness of native entrepreneurs.

Yrigoyen's demise in 1930 is realistically shown to have taken place by a combination of the 1929 crisis and ensuing world depression as they began to affect the Argentine economy (structurally dependent on a continuous flow of primary exports), and their repercussions on a corresponding decline in the state's patronage that particularly alientated middle-class support for the administration. The army takeover allowed the landholding-commercial elite to regain control of the state and deal directly with the pressing question of economic survival in the 1930s. Rock's requiem on the UCT is worth quoting:

> The contribution made by Radicalism to the development of Argentine society was more in the nature of anticipation and precedent than performance. While it reflected the emergence of a plural social structure, it also portrayed for the first time the difficulties of applying a system of power-sharing in a society markedly biased towards elitism and entrenched privilege. If it served temporarily to defer conflict, it could not fully overcome it [p. 274].

Another step in the right direction of searching for explanations of the present in the recent past without indulging in mechanistic parallels is provided by *Prologue to Peron*, edited by Falcoff and Dolkart. The pieces do not always possess even quality, and range from Arthur P. Whitaker's traditional overview of the period to Gustavo Sosa-Pujato's preliminary thoughts on popular culture.

The legacy of the thirties—once called, in a polemical vein, "the infamous decade" by the nationalist writer José Luis Torres—still hangs over the Argentine present as the immediate prologue to the ongoing crisis. Those years witnessed political fraud at the polls, massive rural-urban migrations, acceleration of industrialization, state intervention in the economy to cope with the internal consequences of the depression, marginalization from meaningful political and social participation of important sectors of the population (Radicals, workers' organizations), direct military intervention in governmental affairs, and even small-scale revolts against the authorities. (For a critical and complementary analysis of the period, see this reviewer's Parties and Power in Modern Argentina, 1930-1946. Albany: State Univ. of New York Press, 1974.)

It becomes more and more apparent that Peronism finds many of its objective preconditions in the 1930-1943 years, and that it can be fruitfully investigated as (partially at least) a reaction against the state of affairs prevailing in that era (see Falcoff's "Epilogue," pp. 196-203). Two important articles that deal with the continuities and tactical changes in the 1930s, and that can be read as synthetic introductions to Peronist practical policies, are Javier Villanueva's "Economic Development" (pp. 57-82) and Joseph S. Tulchin's "Foreign Policy" (pp. 83-109).

Villanueva shows that the problems of import-substitution industrialization were much more complex than previously assumed. Its dependent character and the documented fact of Argentina's industrialization without an industrial revolution," i. e., a local bourgeoisie that carried the process forward, constitute fundamental points of departure for any examination of today's issues. Tulchin's contribution underlines the continuities and tactical changes in foreign policy of the 1920s, 1930s and early 1940s, which prepare the reader to assess the real scope and built-in limits of Perón's "Third Position" in international affairs.

*Prologue to Perón* also explores, albeit briefly, certain areas of interest for the student of Argentine society and politics as they materialized in the thirties but have carried over into the seventies. Two examples are the historical polemics between "liberals" and "revisionists" and the recurring manifestations of antisemitism, reflected at the time in Hugo Wast's best-selling novels (pp. 116-117).

Hodges' *Argentina, 1943-1976*, stands in a quite different position vis-à-vis the rest of the volumes covered in this review. It is one of the latest in a long series of works published in the past decade to suggest the viability of a revolutionary guerrilla warfare strategy for Argentina and eventually for Latin America. It is also a partisan defense of the alleged revolutionary potentialities of the Peronist movement, tracing its roots to the "Resistance" period in 1955-1958.

If, on the one hand, the author makes extensive use of hitherto inaccessible publications and internal documents of the militant groups themselves (the different currents within the Peronist "Left"), his optimistic and at times uncritical presentation of events partially mars the obvious documentary value of his book.

After going over Hodges' analysis, I still find that the reasons for Peronism's appeal to sectors of the radicalized youth in the late 1960s and early 1970s are not sufficiently explored in his text. Let me suggest a few possible areas in which further research is needed to balance the picture: first, the cumulative impact of civilian administrations and military governments alternating in power from 1955 to 1973 and their common incapacity to deal with the "Peronist problem"; second, the "revolutionary" transformation of the exiled Perón as opposed to his conciliatory, reformist policies when he was voted back into the presidency in 1973; third, the objective contradictions between the nebulous concept of *socialismo nacional* (socialism as adapted to national peculiarities) held by the political-military organization of the *Montoneros,* and Peróns's more conventional ideas about an "organized community," which became quite evident during his comparatively brief term in office from October 1973 to his death on July 1, 1974. Finally, the elitist and voluntaristic nature of self-proclaimed "hegemonic vanguards" in the Argentine context requires further analytical refinements as can be provided, say, by social psychology and related disciplines to account for the complexities of the "reperonization" of Argentina in recent years. This applies not only to the armed guerrillas, both of Peronist and non-Peronist origins, but also to wide masses of voters and sympathizers that supported Peronist tickets in the 1973 elections in reaction to a military regime and with expectations of social justice, economic redistribution, and civil peace.

For different reasons, Jeane Kirkpatrick's study of Peronist Argentina, *Leader and Vanguard in Mass Society*, remains only a preliminary and not very satisfactory answer to the question about the real nature and self-perceptions'among other related issues—of the Peronist movement as it appeared in late 1965. The core of the volume is the analysis of data gathered through 2,014 "personal interviews conducted among a representative sample of adult Argentines," the fieldwork having been carried out "by International Research Associates" (p. 234). Brief references in a preface and epilogue (especially pp. 228-233) to later years up until 1970-1971 do not substantially alter the author's predominantly static perspective.

Even within the chosen parameters of this type of inquiry that draws heavily from Gabriel A. Almond and Sidney Verba's *The Civic Culture: Political Attitudes and Democracy in Five Nations* as acknowledged by Kirkpatrick in pp. 10-11, the findings arrived at are not particularly meaningful for the understanding of such an important topic. The questionnaire itself reads like a superficial adaptation of North American "political culture" values with obvious concessions to Argentine idiosyncratic features. The issue of the strong emotional relationships between Perón and his followers is hardly touched upon, and the references to "foreigners"—for instance, questions, 24, 24a, and 25m, pp. 242-243—are obviously too general to encompass foreign penetration of the economy, pressure group activities, and so on, and therefore evaluate the nationalist components of Peronists' perceptions and attitudes. The Cold War rhetoric excessively permeates some of the questions on foreign policy (18c, 22, 22a, 22b), and this reviewer misses the *Spanish text* of the questinnarie as it was administered to Argentine respondents (only the English version is provided by the author, pp. 239-248).

Deeply concerned as she seems to be with institutional-formal matters in the context of democratic-authoritarian politics, Kirkpatrick dismisses or treats lightly some fundamental issues of recent Argentine history when she endeavors to provide a background to her survey data analysis. Reliance on United States sources, plus an insufficient selection of Argentine studies, allows her to consider as "free elections" those of 1958 and 1963, but not Perón's 1946 victory (p. 15), to omit serious references to the 1930s and 1940s, and to the role of foreign investment in the national economy—to mention just a few instances of her superficial handling of events.

*Argentina in the Twentieth Century*, the volume edited by David Rock, is a welcome departure from more traditional writings on this South American country. The process that in the past had been summarily dismissed as a transfer of economic—and to some degree political—leverage from the orbit of British "free trade imperialism" to United States' economic penetration, acquires renewed relevance through the contributions by A. G. Ford (on British investment and Argentine economic development, 1880-1914), Roger Gravil (Anglo-U.S. trade rivalries in the 1920s), and Colin Lewis (Anglo-Argentine trade, 1945-1965). It is precisely the dimension of United States imperialism's presence in the Argentine economy—and the so-called "internalization" of that powerful influence through its links with local industry, banking, finance, and political lobbying—that still requires more deep-searching scrutiny and historical interpretation. Let me suggest, in passing, that some preliminary but significant manifestations of the trend can be found in the last few years of Peron's administration (1952-1955), as a reaction against the economic crises then looming: Kaiser automobile plant, law on foreign investments, negotiations with U.S. oil corporations, and so on.

Other major articles in this timely reader address themselves to a detailed analysis of the interior provinces, such as Ian Rutledge's "Plantations and Peasants in Northern Argentina: The Sugar Cane Industry of Salta and Jujuy, 1930-1943" (pp. 88-113), and to specific aspects of Peronist economics as Jorge Fodor's "Perón's Policies for Agricultural Exports, 1946-1948: Dogmatism or Commonsense?" (pp. 135-161). Again, both pieces can be useful for a realistic appraisal of what kind of reforms Peronism did in fact introduce in traditional strongholds of provincial oligarchies, such as the sugar cane barons; or the structural constraints imposed by post-1945 world economic conditions on Argentina's primary commodities, a process still at play, in a quite different setting in the late 1970s.

Rock underlines a basic point in his introduction when he states: "The more [Argentina's] links with advanced society are established, the more chronically unstable she becomes. All the signs are at present [c. 1974] that these internal conflicts will increase rather than diminish with the passing of time" (p. 1). Events up to and since the military coup of March 24, 1976, have validated his assertion even further.

It is this writer's opinion that the root causes of Argentine "instability" have to be looked for in structural processes rather than in random activities of sectorial, power-hungry groups or towering personalities such as Perón. The "tip of the iceberg" simile still applies in this context.

Argentina, therefore, can be considered as a living museum of classes and factions within classes, together with decisive institutionalized groups such as the military establishment (with its well-known inter-service rivalries) that constantly bid for economic-social supremacy, and the corresponding translation of that preeminence into political power, namely, the control of the state. As Argentine history has shown in the twentieth century, none of the competing groups has been able, on its own or leading specific class coalitions, to exercise long-range political hegemony over the nation at large. In deadlock situations, usually connected with socioeconomic or international crisis, the military has acted to break the social "draw" among classes, but their attempts have been only partially successful (to say the least) as witnessed by the outcome of the 1966-1973 "Argentine Revolution," which ended by paving the way to the electoral triumph of Peronism. Wholesale repression and authoritarianism may produce short-term law-and-order results, but do not replace consensus and shared goals as prerequisites for civilized, legitimate rule.

The story of the landholding-commercial elite's resilience to changed environments and circumstances could become a most illuminating area of investigation. Its "defensive" adaptability in the 1930s, its survival under Peronism in the 1946-1955 period at the cost of being stripped of political and social supremacy (but maintaining its solid economic foundations), and the more complicated arrangements it had to enter into with new constellations of forces (Frondizi's "developmentalism,"

U.S. investors and their local representatives), are only instances of a fascinating play that is still being performed under today's military stage management. If, at present, the oligarchy does not reign supreme in Argentina, its veto-power capabilities cannot be easily dismissed, as Generals Juan Carlos Onganía and Juan Domingo Perón discovered when, in different contexts, they attempted a mild modernization through taxing the landholders' estates.

The interrelationships between economic cycles (stop-go policies, years of inflation and deficit financing, followed in circular fashion by short-lived austerity programs) and political developments can be employed as a guiding principle in the analysis of Argentina's alternation of civilian and military administrations, and of the corresponding class alliances and conflicts. The cases of Peronism in power from 1946 to 1955 and from 1973 to 1976 can be more appropriately examined in this light. Peronism—and the issue could perhaps be extended to include other populist coalitions in Latin America—benefited from a (relative) economic bonanza in its first few years in power that allowed it to preside over a fleeting "economic miracle" of increased benefits for workers and employers alike. Later on, more conventional austerity measures plus growing authoritarianism contributed to the regime's survival until the 1955 demise, without losing—be it said in passing—working class support, which cannot be measured exclusively in bread-and-butter terms. The first months of the Peronist restoration in the seventies were only a pale copy of the golden forties, but still managed to keep alive a moderate mix of nostalgia and hope, to be followed by another, more pronounced, economic and social crisis which inexorably led to Isabel Peron's political defeat.

The physical absence of Peron remains one of the most important elements in any evaluation of the present military regime's short-term prospects. The presence of the "Peronist masses" and the question of their permanent incorporation into the country's body politic, is bound to appear sooner or later high on the agenda, in spite of the temporary state of disarray in a movement without recognizable, unanimously accepted leadership, such as at one time was provided by Peron. The picture is made even more complex by the potential challenge to absolute military rule, represented by the action-prone *Montoneros,* who claim to have inherited Peronism's "revolutionary" mantle. In the meantime, the junta's economic and social policies will have to face the test of eventual popular reactions, predominantly, but not only, from labor groups facing the consequences of their relative deprivation vis-à-vis more privileged sectors profiting from the "free enterprise" model put in practice by the government: landholders, foreign entrepreneurs, speculators, and so on.

Indiscriminate repression as carried on in today's Argentina cannot become a permanent feature of policy-making. Its scope and intensity do not match the more isolated instances of violence and counterviolence in the not-too-distant past, as is indicated by some of the books in this review essay. An exploration of the mutually reinforcing dialectics of "revolutionary violence" and official (or officially tolerated and/or encouraged) repression in the immediate past is a more pressing, if dangerous, task for social scientists.

*—Alberto Ciria*

*Argentine-born Alberto Ciria is Professor of Political Science at Simon Fraser University, Burnaby, Canada. He has published* Parties and Power in Modern Argentina, 1930-1946 *(1974), and at present is researching populism in Mexico, Peru, and Argentina.*

# BOOKS RECEIVED

## *GENERAL AND LATIN AMERICA*

Alvaro Moisés, José, Liisa North, and David Raby. CONFLICTS WITHIN POPULIST REGIMES, BRAZIL AND MEXICO. Toronto, Canada: LARU (Latin American Research Unit) Studies, 1977. Notes, references, glossary. 56 pp. Paper.

Caldera, Rafael. ANDRES BELLO: PHILOSOPHER, POET, PHILOLOGIST, EDUCATOR, LEGISLATOR, STATESMAN. Reading, MA: Allen & Unwin, Inc., 1977. Index of personal names, bibliography. 165 pp. $18.75.

Keith, Robert G., ed. HACIENDAS AND PLANTATIONS IN LATIN AMERICAN HISTORY. New York: Holmes & Meier Publishers, Inc., 1977. Notes, bibliographical note. vi, 200 pp. $18.00.

Mendes de Almeida, Candido. BEYOND POPULISM. New York: State University of New York Press, 1977. Notes. xii, 112 pp. $10.00.

Spalding, Hobart A., Jr. ORGANIZED LABOR IN LATIN AMERICA: HISTORICAL CASE STUDIES OF URBAN WORKERS IN DEPENDENT SOCIETIES. New York: Harper & Row, 1977. Postscript, index. xv, 297 pp. Paper.

Wilgus, A. Curtis. LATIN AMERICA, SPAIN AND PORTUGAL: A SELECTED AND ANNOTATED BIBLIOGRAPHICAL GUIDE. Metuchen, NJ: Scarecrow Press, Inc., 1977. Index of names. xv, 910 pp.

Wilkie, James W., ed. MONEY AND POLITICS IN LATIN AMERICA: STATISTICAL ABSTRACT OF LATIN AMERICA SUPPLEMENT 7. Los Angeles: UCLA Latin American Center Publications, 1977. Tables, charts, symbols. 92 pp. Paper.

Wilkie, James W. and Kenneth Ruddle, eds. QUANTITATIVE LATIN AMERICAN STUDIES: METHODS AND FINDINGS. STATISTICAL ABSTRACT OF LATIN AMERICA SUPPLEMENT 6. Los Angeles: UCLA Latin American Center Publications, 1977. Tables, figures, symbols. 92 pp. Paper.

## *ARGENTINA*

Newton, Ronald C. GERMAN BUENOS AIRES, 1900-1933: SOCIAL CHANGE AND CULTURAL CRISIS. Austin: University of Texas Press, 1977. Notes, bibliography, index. xvii, 225 pp. $15.00

## *BOLIVIA*

Lora, Guillermo. A HISTORY OF THE BOLIVIAN LABOUR MOVEMENT: 1894-1971. Edited and abridged by Laurence Whitehead. New York: Cambridge University Press, Cambridge Latin American Studies 27, 1977. Editor's introduction, notes, editor's suggested reading, index. x, 497 pp. $24.95.

## *BRAZIL*

Arruda, Marcos, Herbet de Souza and Carlos Alfonso. MULTINATIONALS AND BRAZIL: THE IMPACT OF MULTINATIONAL CORPORATIONS IN CONTEMPORARY BRAZIL. Toronto: LARU/Brazilian Studies, 1975. Tables and additional notes. 219 pp. Paper.

Wirth, John. MINAS GERAIS IN THE BRAZILIAN FEDERATION, 1889-1937. Stanford: Stanford University Press, 1977. Appendices, notes, bibliography, index. xx, 322 pp. $17.50.

## *CARIBBEAN REGION*

LA INVESTIGACION DEMOGRAFICA EN LA REPUBLICA DOMINICANA: UNA EVALUACION. Santo Domingo: Asociación para el Desarrollo, 1977. 80 pp. Paper.

Lewis, Vaughan, A., ed. SIZE SELF-DETERMINATION AND INTERNATIONAL RELATIONS: THE CARIBBEAN. Mona, Kingston, Jamaica: Institute of Social and Economic Research, University of the West Indies, 1976. Index. 358 pp. Paper.

## *CENTRAL AMERICA*

Schwartz, Norman B. A MILPERO OF PETEN, GUATEMALA: AUTOBIOGRAPHY AND CULTURAL ANALYSIS. Newark: Latin American Studies Program, University of Delaware, 1977. Occasional Papers and Monographs No. 2. Bibliography. 141 pp. Paper.

## *CHILE'*

Kirsch, Henry W. INDUSTRIAL DEVELOPMENT IN A TRADITIONAL SOCIETY: THE CONFLICT OF ENTREPRENEURSHIP AND MODERNIZATION IN CHILE. Gainesville: University Presses of Florida, a University of Florida book, 1977. Latin American Monographs, Second Series. Appendices, bibliography. xiv, 210 pp. $10.00.

OAS. THIRD REPORT ON THE SITUATION OF HUMAN RIGHTS IN CHILE. Washington, DC: Inter-American Commission on Human Rights, OAS, 1977. 92 pp. Paper.

## *COLOMBIA*

Buitrago Salazar, Evelio. ZARPAZO THE BANDIT: MEMOIRS OF AN UNDERCOVER AGENT OF THE COLOMBIAN ARMY. University: University of Alabama Press, 1977. xiv, 168 pp. $8.95.

Safford, Frank. ASPECTOS DEL SIGLO XIX EN COLOMBIA. Medallín, Colombia: Ediciones Hombre Neuvo, Serie Historia/2, 2977. 284 pp. Paper.

## *MEXICO*

Centro de Estudios Internacionales. LAS CRISIS EN EL SISTEMA POLITICO MEXICANO (1928-1977). Mexico: El Colegio de México, 1977. Colección Centro de El Colegio de México, 1977. 376 pp. Paper.

Centro de Estudios Internacionales. LECTURAS DE POLITICA MEXICANA. México: El Colegio de México, 1977. 376 pp. Paper.

Falcon, Romana. EL AGRARISMO EN VERACRUZ: LA ETAPA RADICAL (1928-1935). Mexico: El Colegio de Mexico, 1977. Collección Centro de Estudios Internacionales XVIII. Conclusiones, bibliografía. 180 pp. Paper.

González Navarro, Moisés. ANATOMIA DEL PODER EN MEXICO (1848-1853). México: El Colegio de México, Centro de Estudos Históricos, Nueva Serie 23, 1977. Epílogo, fuentes, indice analítico. 498 pp. Paper.

Green, Rosario. EL ENDEUDAMIENTO PUBLICO EXTERNO DE MEXICO, 1940-1973. México: El Colegio de México, 1977. Colección Centro de Estudios Internacionalies XV. Conclusiones, anexos. 231 pp. Paper.

Krauze, Enrique, con la colaboración de Jean Meyer y Cayetano Reyes. HISTORIA DE LA REVOLUCION MEXICANA: PERIODO 1924-1928. LA RECONSTRUCCION ECONOMICA. México: El Colegio de México, 1977. Anexos, índice de nombres. 323 pp. Paper.

Russell, Philip. MEXICO IN TRANSITION. Austin, TX: Colorado River Press, 1977. References and bibliography. 176 pp. Paper.

## *PANAMA*

Valdés, Eduardo. THE ROOTS OF THE PROBLEM: A POSITIVE APPROACH TO THE PANAMA CANAL ISSUE. New York: Vantage Press, 1977. Appendix. xviii, 65 pp.

## *VENEZUELA*

Bond, Robert D., ed. CONTEMPORARY VENEZUELA AND ITS ROLE IN INTERNATIONAL AFFAIRS. New York: New York University Press, 1977. A Council on Foreign Relations Book. Index. x, 267 pp.

## *MISCELLANEOUS*

Germidis, Dimitri, ed. TRANSFER OF TECHNOLOGY BY MULTINATIONAL CORPORATIONS. Volumes I and II. Paris: OECD, Development Centre Studies, 1977. Annex. Vol. I, 309 pp.; Vol. II, 258 pp. Paper.

OECD. DEVELOPMENT CORPORATION: EFFORTS AND POLICIES OF THE MEMBERS OF THE DEVELOPMENT ASSISTANCE COMMITTEE. 1977 Review. Paris: OECD, 1977. Annexes. 240 pp. Paper.

OECD. GEOGRAPHICAL DISTRIBUTION OF FINANCIAL FLOWS TO DEVELOPING COUNTRIES: DATA ON DISBURSEMENTS 1969 TO 1975. Paris: OECD, 1977. Tables. xiv, 285 pp. Paper.

Palerm, Angel. HISTORIA DE LA ETNOLOGIA: TYLOR Y LOS PROFESIONALES BRITANICOS. México: Centro de Investigaciones Superiores, ediciones de la Casa Chata, 1977. Obras citadas. 174 pp. Paper.

# Advertising Supplement:

## Journal of Interamerican Studies and World Affairs

This supplement has been prepared especially for our readers to bring them information and announcements of professional interest. By placing advertisements in the pages of this journal, our advertisers have indicated a desire to communicate with our readers. We hope our readers will acknowledge their indirect support of the journal and its purposes by mentioning the journal in correspondence with advertisers.

# METROPOLITAN LATIN AMERICA: The Challenge and the Response

Latin American Urban Research, Volume 6

edited by **WAYNE A. CORNELIUS**, *Massachusetts Institute of Technology*
**ROBERT V. KEMPER**, Southern Methodist University

This volume focuses on the most critical problems confronting nine major Latin American and Caribbean cities, and the actual responses of local and national governments to these problems. Each chapter provides a comprehensive overview of urban development problems and government performance in dealing with them in a single metropolitan area. Contributors also discuss the role of the metropolitan area in regional and national development, and the tensions between government policies aimed at the problems of the metropolitan area and policies for national and regional development. The volume provides indispensible source material for scholars doing research on specific cities as well as an empirical base for comparative urban studies. It also includes a 1,600-item bibliography of studies on urban Latin America published during the 1974-1976 period.

CONTENTS

Introduction, WAYNE A. CORNELIUS

**Case Studies**

1. Guadalajara: Creating the Divided City, JOHN WALTON, *Northwestern University*
2. Mexico City: The Emerging Megalopolis, GUSTAVO GARZA, *El Colegio de México* and MARTHA SCHTEINGART, *El Colegio de México*
3. Bogotá: Politics, Planning and the Crisis of Lost Opportunities, ALAN GILBERT, *University College, London*
4. Urban Development and Governmental Response: The Case of Medellin, DAVID W. DENT, *Towson State College*
5. Port-au-Prince: Awakening to the Urban Crisis, SIMON M. FASS
6. Urban Problems and Policy Responses for Metropolitan Guayaquil, RICHARD J. MOORE, *University of Texas, Austin*
7. Metropolitan Lima: Urban Problem-Solving under Military Rule, HENRY A. DIETZ, *University of Texas, Austin*
8. Caracas: The Politics of Intensifying Primacy, DAVID J. MYERS, *Pennsylvania State University*
9. Towards a Development Strategy for Grande Rio de Janeiro, DAVID M. VETTER, *Universidade Federal do Rio de Janeiro* and ANA MARIA BRASILEIRO, *Instituto Brasileiro de Administração*

BIBLIOGRAPHY: RECENT URBAN STUDIES ON LATIN AMERICA (1974-1976)

| | | | |
|---|---|---|---|
| **February 1978** | **ISBN 0-8039-0661-7** | **hardcover** | **$18.50** |
| **352 pages** | **ISBN 0-8039-0662-5** | **softcover** | **$ 7.95** |

SAGE Publications, Inc.
275 South Beverly Drive
Beverly Hills, California 90212

SAGE Publications Ltd
28 Banner Street
London EC1Y 8QE

# LATIN AMERICA AND WORLD ECONOMY: A Changing International Order

edited by **JOSEPH GRUNWALD**

How do nations of Latin America interact with other countries in the world community? This anthology approaches the region's relations with the outside world from both an economic and a political perspective, examining Latin America's desire to integrate with the world economy, as well as its struggle for self-reliance. Latin American and non-Latin American contributors discuss a range of subjects including the character of the "special relationship" between Latin America and the United States, and the ambiguous nature of Latin America's relations with other countries of the Third World.

**CONTENTS**


Preface by JOSEPH GRUNWALD

1. Overview and Perspective, JOSEPH GRUNWALD

**Part I — Economic Relations with Industrial Countries**

2. The Mature Neighbor Policy: A Proposal for A United States Economic Policy for Latin America, ALBERT FISHLOW
3. Britain's Economic Relations with Latin America, LAURENCE WHITEHEAD
4. The Economic Relations Between Germany and Latin America and the Significance of the European Community, ALBRECHT von GLEICH
5. Latin America's Opening to the Pacific, CLAUDIO VELIZ

**Part II — Mexico and Brazil**

6. The External Sector of the Mexican Economy, LEOPOLDO SOLIS
7. The Determinants of Brazil's Foreign Economic Policy, WERNER BAER and CARLOS von DOELLINGER




*"As long as the notion persists that Latin America is unimportant for the United States and other developed countries, it will be difficult to persuade Latin American countries that they are living in an interdependent world. One-sided importance creates a one-sided dependency relationship. Such a perseption results in demands, not cooperation. Cooperation for development becomes meaningful only when there is a recognition of interdependence on both sides of the North-South relationship."*

*— from Chapter 1*


**Volume 2, Latin American International Affairs**

| | | | |
|---|---|---|---|
| **February 1978** | **ISBN 0-8039-0864-4** | **hardcover** | **$18.50** |
| **320 pages** | **ISBN 0-8039-0966-7** | **softcover** | **$ 8.95** |

**SAGE** PUBLICATIONS, INC
275 South Beverly Drive
Beverly Hills, California 90212

**SAGE** PUBLICATIONS LTD
28 Banner Street
London EC1Y 8QE, England

Vol. 20 No. 3
August 1978

# JOURNAL OF INTERAMERICAN STUDIES

# and WORLD AFFAIRS

A Publication of the Center for Advanced International Studies,
The University of Miami

SAGE PUBLICATIONS

*Journal of INTERAMERICAN STUDIES and WORLD AFFAIRS*



The editors and publisher wish to acknowledge with gratitude the assistance and encouragement of the Center for Advanced International Studies, University of Miami, in providing ancillary services and support for this journal.

*Journal of*
INTERAMERICAN
STUDIES
*and* WORLD AFFAIRS

Vol. 20
No. 3
August
1978

# CONTENTS

*Introductory Note* 227

*The Caribbean and the New International Economic Order*
WILLIAM G. DEMAS 229

*The New International Economic Order: Centerpiece Venezuela*
MARKOS MAMALAKIS 265

*Latin America and the Primary Product Trade*
ROBERTO JUNGUITO 297

*Latin America and the World Economy: Some Observations on External Indebtedness and the International Monetary System*
ALDO FERRER 321
(Translated by Marjory Mattingly Urquidi)

*Brazilian External Debt: A Study in Capital Flows and Transfer of Resources*
RAMESH C. GARG 341

SAGE PUBLICATIONS / *Beverly Hills London*

**POLICY: THE JOURNAL OF INTERAMERICAN STUDIES AND WORLD AFFAIRS** reflects the interests of the scholarly community and interested public concerned with the social, economic, political, and cultural aspects of life in Latin America (including the Caribbean); particularly in those instances where the subject is of concern to more than one of the traditional disciplines. As these concerns change, so will the content of the journal.

**ARTICLES** which have special relevance for interrelationships between American nations and of those nations with the rest of the world will be given special consideration. An effort will be made to include occasional articles that state an unusual or even discordant position on a subject of broad interest to be supplemented by critical comments of authorities representing differing positions on the topic. The editors continue to welcome articles by scholars from all parts of the world.

**MANUSCRIPTS** should be submitted in duplicate to: Editor, JOURNAL OF INTERAMERICAN STUDIES AND WORLD AFFAIRS, Box 24-8134, University of Miami, Coral Gables, Florida 33124. Manuscripts should be typewritten, double-spaced, with footnotes, references, tables, and charts on separate pages, and should follow the current journal style. A brief biographical paragraph describing each author's current affiliation, research interests, and recent publications should accompany the manuscript.

**CORRESPONDENCE** regarding book reviews should be sent directly to: Book Review Editor, JOURNAL OF INTERAMERICAN STUDIES AND WORLD AFFAIRS, Box 24-8134, University of Miami, Coral Gables, Florida 33124.

---

**JOURNAL OF INTERAMERICAN STUDIES AND WORLD AFFAIRS** is published four times annually—in February, May, August, and November. 

**Subscriptions:** Regular institutional rate $28.00. Individuals may subscribe at a one-year rate of $15.00. Add $1.00 per year for subscriptions outside the United States. Orders from U.K., Europe, the Middle East, and Africa should be sent to the London office (address below). Noninstitutional orders **must** be paid by personal check.

Second-class postage paid at Beverly Hills, California.

**Inquiries:** Address all correspondence and permissions requests to SAGE PUBLICATIONS, INC., 275 South Beverly Drive, Beverly Hills, California 90212. Inquiries and subscriptions from U.K., Europe, the Middle East, and Africa should be sent to SAGE PUBLICATIONS LTD, 28 Banner Street, London EC1Y 8QE, England. Other orders should be sent to the Beverly Hills office.

**Advertising:** Current rates and specifications may be obtained by writing to the Advertising Manager at the Beverly Hills office (address above).

**This journal is abstracted or indexed in Historical Abstracts, Human Resources Abstracts, Sage Urban Studies Abstracts, International Political Science Abstracts, Public Affairs Information Service, Current Contents, Social Sciences Citation Index, Social Sciences Index, ABC POL SCI and United States Political Science Documents.**

**Back Issues:** Information about availability and prices of back issues may be obtained from the publisher's order department (address above). Write to London office for sterling prices.

**Claims for undelivered copies** must be made no later than three months following month of publication. The publisher will supply missing copies when losses have been sustained in transit and where the reserve stock will permit.

**Change of Address:** Six weeks' advance notice must be given when notifying of change of address. Please send old address label along with the new address to insure proper identification. Please specify name of journal.

## *INTRODUCTORY NOTE*

Two years ago the Associate Editor of this *Journal* suggested that a special issue on the "New International Economic Order" (NIEO) as it affects Latin America would be an important and timely contribution for our readers. The number of topics and areas to be treated, as outlined by Dr. Wogart, proved to be more than the space a single issue of this *Journal* could accommodate and still provide the full treatment that the contributors from their experience believed necessary for their individual essays. Accordingly, to maintain a balance between regional and topical essays, this issue is confined to two area-oriented articles on the Caribbean Archipelago and Venezuela: two topical articles dealing with commodities and finance and concluding with a concise account of the external debt of Brazil.

The commodity and debt issues were selected, as they have been at the center of any discussion of the NIEO. The formation of a commodity fund is supported by all Latin American nations as a mechanism to stabilize and strengthen export earnings, while the idea of debt renegotiations and cancellations is generally opposed by the three largest nations of the region. Venezuela was the initiator of OPEC and has become the champion of the NIEO in Latin America and to a large degree in the Third World generally, while the Caribbean Archipelago as here defined is perhaps unique in the world in its combination of small countries at various levels of political independence and dependence, and is the only geographical region of the Western Hemisphere with nations established since 1960 which also provide highly contrasting as well as common economic problems with their regional political connotations.

The *Journal* expects to extend its treatment of the NIEO in Latin America by publishing in the future a topical article on technology, a regional one on Brazil, an evaluative review essay on recent literature, and possibly others, including a statement as to the extent that the concept of the NIEO is a new format for giving ongoing problems of long standing a more provocative framework for consideration by individual nations, within a context that enhances international cooperation among nations in varying stages of development with their own unique set of political and economic problems.

Three of the authors, William Demas, Aldo Ferrer, and Roberto Junguito, in addition to substantial scholarly research on the economy of Latin America and the Caribbean, have had impressive experience in policy positions in their governments, international organizations, and consultative bodies. It is believed that this adds a significant dimension to their appraisal of the New International Economic Order and the North-South dialogue generally, as does the long experience of Markos Mamalakis in theoretical and applied research on development economics in Spanish America. Ramesh Garg's recent research on the effect of the external debt of Brazil on that nation's rate of growth is in some ways a detailed and specific extension of the preceding essay by Aldo Ferrer.

—*Jan Peter Wogart*
—*John P. Harrison*

**WILLIAM G. DEMAS**
*Caribbean Development Bank*
*St. Michael, Barbados, W. I.*

# *THE CARIBBEAN AND THE NEW INTERNATIONAL ECONOMIC ORDER*

## *Caribbean Political Economy*

### *WHAT IS THE CARIBBEAN:*

Definition of categories is an age-old scholastic and often sterile pastime. But in discussing the Caribbean, definitions are essential, particularly in these days when there is growing fuzziness as to what constitutes the Caribbean.

The fact is that there are three separate but overlapping definitions of the Caribbean in widespread use today.

First, there is the English-speaking Caribbean or the Commonwealth Caribbean or West Indies. Nearly all of these countries and territories are member states of the Caribbean community which comprises the four relatively "more developed countries" of Barbados, Guyana, Jamaica, and Trinidad and Tobago, and the generally smaller eight relatively "less

AUTHOR'S NOTE: Acknowledgments are due to two of my colleagues at CDB: Rupert Mullings, for making useful comments on the first draft of the paper, and Herman Grant, for preparing the statistical appendix.

Journal of Interamerican Studies and World Affairs, Vol. 20 No. 3, August 1978

developed" countries of Antigua, Belize, Dominica, Grenada, Montserrat, St. Kitts-Nevis-Anguilla, St. Lucia, and St. Vincent. Outside the community are the Bahamas (which nevertheless have informal links with the community) and the tiny British colonies of the British Virgin Islands, Cayman Islands, and Turks and Caicos Islands. These are all islands, with the exception of the mainland territories of Belize (in Central America) and Guyana (in South America).

All the member states of the Caribbean community, with the exception of the mainland countries of Belize and Guyana, were united in the West Indies Federation for a short period from 1958 to 1962. The Federation was the first West Indian-wide attempt at political and economic integration but it failed for a variety of reasons, including growing island nationalism and the fear that, in the absence of large amounts of British financial aid, the bigger and slightly less poor islands would have to carry the smaller and poorer islands.

More recently an attempt has been made to achieve economic integration among the English-speaking Caribbean countries through the formation in 1968 of the Caribbean Free Trade Association (CARIFTA), which developed in 1973-1974 into the Caribbean community. The community pursues purely economic integration among its member states through the Caribbean common market. It also pursues so-called "functional cooperation" in many areas, particularly sea and air transport, university and general education, and health. In some cases such cooperation includes common services, as in university education and shipping. Finally, the community seeks to achieve coordination of the foreign policies of its independent member states.

Second, there is the area comprising the first group of countries plus Cuba, Dominican Republic, Haiti, Puerto Rico, the U.S. Virgin Islands, Suriname, the Netherlands Antilles, and the three French departments of Martinique, Guadeloupe, and Cayenne. This area is often referred to as the Caribbean Archipelago. It consists of all the islands in the Caribbean sea together with the mainland countries of Belize, Guyana, Cayenne, and Suriname.

More recently a broader concept of the Caribbean has been advanced in some quarters. This is the so-called Caribbean basin comprising the Archipelago countries as well as those mainland countries whose shores are washed by the Caribbean sea—that is, Mexico, the five Central American Republics, Panama, Colombia, and Venezuela.

In fact, one can depict these three concepts of the Caribbean in terms of three concentric circles. Using mathematical notation, $C_1$ would be the English-speaking Caribbean, $C_2$ the Caribbean Archipelago, and $C_3$ the Caribbean basin, and we would have $C_3 > C_2 > C_1$.

### *THE CARIBBEAN ARCHIPELAGO*

Anyone with even a superficial knowledge of the history of Latin America generally and the area in particular knows that the historically and culturally valid definition of the Caribbean is that of the Caribbean Archipelago, or $C_2$. This essay focuses, therefore, on the Archipelago—although the English-speaking Caribbean, $C_1$, will be dealt with extensively.

The countries and territories of the Caribbean area as here defined have a combined land area of 281,421 square miles and a total population of 28 million, making the area a potentially economically viable one—if the several formidable barriers in the way of integration could ever possibly be overcome.

When we look closely at the countries and territories of the Caribbean Archipelago, we find a variety of levels of constitutional development, types of political systems, economic ideologies, and development strategies, as well as considerable variation in size, population, and endowment of natural resources and linguistic and cultural patterns.

*Constitutional Patterns and External Associations*

The independent countries of the area are (in order of year of achievement of independence) Haiti, Dominican Republic, Cuba in the nineteenth century, and, beginning in 1962, Jamaica, Trinidad and Tobago, Guyana, Barbados, Bahamas, Grenada, and Suriname. (It should be noted that the English-speaking countries and Suriname achieved their independence in the 1960s and 1970s.)

All the other countries of the Caribbean area are politically dependent territories. Puerto Rico has a unique status of Free Associated State with the United States involving a very close political relationship with the United States of whose customs and currency areas it forms part. The same applies to the U.S. Virgin Islands, except that the extent of internal autonomy is less than in Puerto Rico.

The English-speaking politically dependent territories include the British associated states, which have full internal self-government, but with Britain still being responsible for defense and external affairs. There are five colonies—internally self-governing Belize on the Central American mainland and the four very small individual islands or groups of islands of British Virgin Islands, Cayman Islands, Montserrat, and Turks and Caicos Islands.

The Netherlands Antilles consist of a federation of six self-governing islands, with the Kingdom of the Netherlands being responsible for defense and external affairs. The Netherlands Antilles, like the Associated States of Britain, are more fully internally self-governing than Puerto Rico and the U.S. Virgin Islands.

The English- and Dutch-speaking territories were, until recently, involved in reciprocal preferential trade agreements with their respective metropolitan countries, but these preferential agreements have now been replaced by the Lomé Convention on trade and aid between the EEC and the independent countries, and between the EEC and the dependent territories under Part IV of the Treaty of Rome. These new arrangements have abolished the "reverse" preferences which the associated countries and territories formerly granted to the metropolitan countries.

Finally, we should mention the French Overseas departments of Martinique, Guadeloupe, and Cayenne which are juridically parts of metropolitan France and which participate directly in French elections.

*Political Systems and Economic Ideologies*

There is considerable variety in political systems and economic ideologies. Cuba has a centrally planned socialist economy and close economic ties with the Soviet Union and recently became a full member of COMECON. Guyana and Jamaica are moving toward Third World socialism and democratic socialism, respectively. Dominican Republic and Haiti tend to be rather conservative in their economic ideologies. The other independent countries of the area—Bahamas, Barbados, Grenada, Suriname, and Trinidad and Tobago—have more or less "centrist" ideologies, Barbados having a fairly well-developed "Welfare State" and Trinidad and Tobago being somewhat more "left" (in the sense of a larger state-owned sector and conscious policies of income redistribution) than the others.

The politically dependent territories obviously have less freedom of choice in such matters. Puerto Rico and the U.S. Virgin Islands are highly integrated in a very dependent manner into the U.S. economy, with free emigration opportunities to the metropolis, and also receive a high level of welfare-oriented transfer payments from the Mainland. Puerto Rico's development strategy has over the last three decades resulted in a large increase in per capita income and exports of manufactured goods which now exceed the traditional exports of sugar, tobacco, and the needlework industries. But unemployment remains high, the food-producing sector is depressed, and the problem of a more equitable distribution of income remains.

Economic and financial integration between France and her three Caribbean overseas departments goes so far as to make it impossible to talk of the "national economy" of any of the three departments. Their economies are the most highly artificial in an area in which there is considerable artificiality of national economies. There exists nothing even remotely approaching the levels of production in agriculture, industry, and tourism achieved in highly dependent Puerto Rico. The economies produce virtually nothing and rest to an alarming extent on the basis of massive transfer payments from France.

In the remaining British Associated States, colonies, and the Netherlands Antilles there is a smaller degree of dependent integration into the metropolitan economies than in the U.S. territories and the French departments.

*Size, Population, and Natural Resources*

Marked differences in geographical size, population, and natural resource endowment also exist.

The northwest islands of the Greater Antilles are much larger than those of the Lesser Antilles in the east. Cuba, the largest Caribbean island, has a population of over 9 million and a land area of 44,000 square miles. It is not densely populated and is fairly well endowed with large areas of land suitable for agriculture and livestock and with mineral deposits of nickel and copper. Dominican Republic and Haiti have populations of roughly 4½ million each and areas of 19,000 and 11,000 square miles respectively; but Haiti has a much denser population (428 as against 251 persons per square mile) on the smaller and more mountainous and infertile part of the island of Hispaniola, which it shares with the Dominican Republic. Haiti has relatively small deposits of bauxite and copper and some hydroelectric potential, while the Dominican Republic has deposits of bauxite, copper, and nickel. Puerto Rico has no significant mineral deposits (except copper) and a high population density of 900 persons per square mile. Jamaica, the other country forming part of the Greater Antilles, has like Haiti, large areas of mountainous terrain, but is somewhat better endowed for agricultural and livestock production than Haiti. It has a population density of 463 persons per square mile. On the other hand, it is very richly endowed with bauxite, in the production of which it is, after Australia, the world's largest supplier. All the islands of the Greater Antilles have very good tourism potential.

Generally speaking, the islands of the Lesser Antilles are geographically smaller in size, have small and very dense populations and little, if any, by way of mineral resources. Trinidad and Tobago, the largest of the Lesser Antilles, has a population of 1 million; Barbados 250,000; and the seven English-speaking Leeward and Windward Islands have very small populations with the largest, Grenada and St. Lucia, having approximately 110,000 inhabitants. Like those in the Greater Antilles, nearly all the islands of the Lesser Antilles have sun, sea, and beaches which constitute tourist attractions. The only significant producer of minerals in this group is Trinidad and Tobago, which, however, is a minor producer of oil by world standards.

The mainland countries of Belize, Guyana, Suriname, and Cayenne have much bigger land areas, but very low population densities. They all have considerable by no means yet fully exploited agricultural, livestock, and forestry potential and, in the case of Guyana and Suriname, considerable deposits of bauxite and other minerals such as gold. In addition, there are rich fishing and shrimp banks off the three Guianas.

### *Differences in Language and Culture*

Apart from these constitutional, political, economic, and geographical differences between the countries and territories of the Caribbean area, there are certain linguistic and cultural differences—French influence in Haiti; Spanish in Cuba, Dominican Republic, and Puerto Rico; English in the Commonwealth Caribbean; Dutch in Suriname and the Netherlands Antilles; French in the three overseas departments of France.

*UNDERLYING UNITY OF CARIBBEAN DESPITE FRAGMENTATION*

In the face of such bewildering variety, is there any meaning as to whether the countries of the Caribbean Archipelago in any way have much in common with each other? It is possible to highlight many common features of these countries. These common features spring from history and geography.

To students of Caribbean history it is obvious that the Caribbean Archipelago countries have a common historical legacy: the sugar plantation, slavery, indentured labor, monocultural economies producing what they did not consume and consuming what they did not produce, a heavy African input into their populations and many common cultural features associated with this in spite of linguistic differences, and (with the exception of Haiti) perhaps the longest period of external political dependence of any part of the Third World. Finally, there is the fact that, in spite of the sea which separates them, they all belong to a geographically distinct part of the world. (It is this distinctness, this Caribbean identity, which makes for the inclusion of the Mainland countries of Belize, Guyana, Suriname, and Cayenne side by side with the Archipelago islands in the Caribbean area.)

At the same time, historically the economies have been highly dependent on the various metropolitan countries in terms of trade, transport, and communications, technology, direct foreign investment, and, more recently, economic aid as well as outlets for emigration (including the brain drain). In one word, the historical legacy of these countries can be said to be one of extreme external economic dependence and lack of "linkages" between the various sectors of the national economies of each country and between the sectors of the various countries. Intra-area trade and other economic transactions were unable to develop to any significant extent, the individual countries being tied "vertically" to their particular metropolitan country rather than "horizontally" with each other.

Even today the Caribbean remains one of the most highly economically fragmented, dependent, and "balkanized" areas of the Third World, both politically and economically. Very obviously, they are separated by the sea. The islands and the mainland countries of Belize in Central America and Guyana, Suriname, and Cayenne on the South American mainland are geographically separated by the sea—a very effective barrier in the absence of an excellent system of sea and air transportation and of telecommunications, which does not yet exist.

Nevertheless, whatever may be the shortcomings of most of the individual Caribbean countries and territories from the point of view of resources, population size, and markets, it is clear that the Caribbean area, *regarded as a group*, has a reasonably large population of just under 30 million and a fairly good and diversified natural resource base—agricultural land, livestock potential, forestry resources, fisheries, bauxite, nickel, copper, oil, natural gas, hydroelectric power, and the sun, sea, and sand required for a certain type of tourism. (The full mineral potential of the three Guianas is also yet unknown.)

What is true of the 30-million Caribbean area is also true of the 5-million Caribbean community. Regarded *as a group*, they have, in relation to their total population, almost as wide a range of natural resources as the wider Caribbean Archipelago, whatever may be their natural resource and demographic limitations at the individual country level.

### *SIZE, DEPENDENCE, PER CAPITA INCOME, AND DEVELOPMENT*

Nervertheless, one must realistically admit that the individual countries and territories of both the Caribbean community and the wider Caribbean Archipelago countries suffer from certain disadvantages in terms of their autonomous economic development. These disadvantages are the legacy of external dependence combined with small size of population and a narrow range of natural resources at the individual country level.

The historical legacy of dependence is not in dispute. There is, however, a more lively debate concerning the effects of small size on the capacity for autonomous economic developments; questions are even often raised as to whether small island populations of less than 100,000 can with any meaning maintain the substance of their political independence, once they achieve it.

In discussing the legacy and the present reality of external economic dependence, we have to draw immediate attention to an economic fact that is of the highest importance for an understanding of the Caribbean economy today—the existence of per capita incomes in both the politically dependent and independent countries of the area (except for Haiti) that are relatively high by Third World standards. But, paradoxically enough, the extremely long history of Caribbean external economic dependence and close association with the metropolitan countries has resulted in glacially slow and gradual "trickle-down" effects. Nevertheless, the relatively high levels of per capita income are a highly misleading and inappropriate index of the present level of economic development of the countries and territories of the area. They have to be qualified to take account of the very high levels of unemployment and underemployment, of an often high degree of inequality of income distribution, of lagging and backward food-producing sectors, and of an undiversified structure of production and exports. Even more fundamentally, the per capita income figure conceals the true nature of economic underdevelopment, which is a distorted and highly unbalanced economic structure incapable of meeting the basic needs of the rural and urban masses and lacking in internal economic resilience in the face of adverse economic impacts of external origin. Thus, the Caribbean economies, in spite of the relatively high levels of per capita income, are riddled with all the features of "dependent underdevelopment."

In discussing the issue of size, I cannot go into all the ramifications of this debate except to stress that those who do not see any inherent disadvantages in small size stress the political and cultural will of the people of a very small country to survive and the need for indigenous technological innovation in such countries. They sometimes even stress the advantages of small size in terms of greater amenability to economic management and a greater sense of identity and community solidarity among the people of a small nation-state. Finally, the make the valid point that the quality of human resources of a country can more than compensate for a lack of natural resources.

Those who have doubts about the economic viability of very small countries tend to stress the overwhelming significance of economies of large scale in terms of administration, national markets, and the scope for the application of efficient capital-intensive technologies. They also point out that in small countries it is difficult to have the *wide range* of both human and natural resources required for an indigenously motivated pattern of economic development.

One obvious qualification to the simple notion of size is, however, the volume of natural resources, the most outstanding case in point being Kuwait and the United Arab Emirates, which are all richly endowed with petroleum resources in spite of their very small land area and population.

Be this as it may, in terms of the individual countries of both the Caribbean Archipelago and Caribbean community (particularly in the very small islands), natural resources on an individual country basis tend to be either very limited or highly skewed in favor of a certain agricultural or mineral commodity or commodities. Moreover (and again, particularly in the smaller islands), trained human resources are subject to continuous depletion as a result of the brain drain to North America, and, what is more, with populations that are so small in absolute numbers it is extremely difficult to have a sufficiently wide range of the skills required for internally motivated economic and social development.

### *RATIONALE AND PROBLEMS OF CARIBBEAN ARCHIPELAGO INTEGRATION*

We therefore immediately come upon one of the most central issues in Caribbean economic development—the need for meaningful economic integration. Thus, the prospects for autonomous development of the Caribbean Archipelago and the more geographically limited Caribbean community would obviously be enhanced by schemes of integration and economic cooperation bringing a wider market and a wider range of human and natural resources (including low density of population in countries such as Belize, Guyana, Suriname, Cayenne, and Cuba).

One important corollary of this point of view is that the prospects for economic and financial viability in the newly independent and about-to-be independent Caribbean countries that are small in terms of population would seem in large measure to depend in most cases on the successful implementation of realistic schemes of economic and even political integration and cooperation. This proposition holds with particular force for those very small English-speaking and Dutch-speaking Caribbean countries either newly independent, such as Grenada, or on the verge of independence—the British Associated States of Antigua, Dominica, St. Kitts-Nevis-Anguilla, St. Lucia and St. Vincent, and the Holland-affiliated Federation of the Netherlands Antilles. Indeed, some, including myself, would go further and argue that the entire English-speaking group of the Leeward and Windward Islands should have proceeded to independence as a single group, not only for reasons of size of market and human and natural resource endowment, but also because of the need to achieve more economic and effective administrative services and the need, because of their weakness in all spheres, to present a single front in all external relations and contact with the outside world. A smaller number of persons, again including myself, would go even further and urge the view that the only way in which the small English-speaking countries of the eastern Caribbean (not only the Leeward and Windward Islands but also Barbados, Trinidad and Tobago, and Guyana) can achieve meaningful economic and political independence and cultural identity in the face of the powerful external economic, diplomatic, geopolitical, and political forces (emanating from more powerful large and medium-sized states as well as the transnational corporations) is by establishing a political union among themselves. I must, however, admit that in the present climate of West Indian thinking, both these viewpoints would today be regarded as Utopian by all the countries concerned. So the smaller Leeward and Windward Islands are clearly now proceeding to *individual* independence, and only time will tell whether their individual independence will ever be a reality from a substantive rather than a formal point of view.

More generally, the immediate or near-term scope for Caribbean integration would seem to be reduced by many powerful factors (both historical and contemporary) making for Caribbean fragmentation and disintegration.

Because of the present peculiar constitutional and economic ties which Puerto Rico, U.S. Virgin Islands. Martinique, Guadeloupe, and Cayenne have with their metropolitan countries, one cannot at present discuss meaningfully the inclusion of these territories in any scheme of Caribbean economic integration. For technical economic reasons having to do with the existence of a centrally planned economy in Cuba, the inclusion of this country in a comprehensive scheme of Caribbean economic integration must also be ruled out. On the other hand, there are clearly no such compelling economic (as distinct from diplomatic and political) reasons why Haiti, Dominican Republic, Suriname, and (in time) an independent Netherlands Antilles should be ruled out from participating in such a scheme. Comprehensive economic integration is one thing. Loose arrangements for economic cooperation and functional collaboration are another. Therefore, there is great immediate scope for a greater degree of economic cooperation and functional collaboration among *all* the countries and territories of the Caribbean area.

## *NATIONAL DEVELOPMENT PROBLEMS AND STRATEGIES*

Let us now summarily list the main economic problems facing most of the countries of the Caribbean Archipelago in general, and the Caribbean community in particular, and mention briefly the strategies which could be and are in some cases being applied in overcoming these constraints to development.

From the previous discussion in which we dealt with historical legacy and small size, it should not be surprising that the following figure prominently among the development problems of the area:

(a) a very large food import bill amounting for the English-speaking Caribbean countries alone to nearly US $0.5 billion or about US $80 per head of population—perhaps one of the highest per capita food import bills in the Third World;
(b) a heavily undiversified and specialized structure of production, with dependence on a single crop or a limited number of export products such as sugar, bananas, coffee, citrus, oil and natural gas, bauxite and alumina, and tourism;
(c) corresponding dependence on a very wide range of imports, not only of capital goods but also intermediate goods as well as food and other consumer goods (Cuba and to some extent Guyana are exceptions);
(d) the fact that export agriculture is high-cost and on the decline, partly because of low productivity and partly because of the relatively high wage-rates spilling over from high productivity and better paid sectors (minerals and tourism); sugar, bananas, and citrus are the most seriously affected export crops in the countries belonging to the Caribbean community;
(e) an absence of economic linkages between different sectors of the national economy—e.g., agriculture and industry, agriculture and Tourism, mining and manufacturing, and so on; manufacturing and tourism, in particular, rely to an excessive degree on inputs imported from outside the area;
(f) the inability so far of the manufacturing sector to achieve significant levels of extraregional exports;
(g) in spite of relatively high levels of per capita income, economies with a strong lack of resilience in the face of adverse economic developments of external origin;
(h) low levels of national savings (in the household, public, and corporate sectors) and corresponding excessively high levels and inappropriate patterns of consumption;
(i) above all, alarmingly high levels of unemployment (ranging from 14% to 30% of the labor force) and equally high levels of low-earning underemployment.

The development strategies that could be implemented (and which are beginning to be implemented by many countries in the area) can easily be seen:

(a) efforts to increase levels of food production for the domestic and regional markets;
(b) efforts to diversify both the internal composition of economic activities and the composition of exports and imports (there is also need to diversify both the country destination of exports and the country source of imports to the extent that doing these things would be economic in the long run);
(c) efforts to promote more linkages as between various sectors and activities of the individual national economies and as between the various sectors and activities of different countries in the region;
(d) efforts to foster trade specialization and cooperation in production at the regional or area levels;
(e) efforts to make more competitive traditional agricultural export crops;
(f) efforts to increase sales of manufactured goods extraregionally;
(g) efforts at an "incomes and prices" policy; and
(h) efforts to adapt imported technology as well as to encourage the development and use of technologies more appropriate to the countries of the region.

We must note here that many of the apparently purely economic constraints to Caribbean economic development arise from factors usually relevant to political economy rather than to economics proper. The aversion to both peasant and wage-labor agriculture among many sections of the population is a sociological parameter rooted in the historical legacy of slavery and in the low value and status assigned to agriculture as an occupation. High levels and inappropriate patterns of consumption arise again from the impact of the consumption patterns of the affluent North American and West European societies, imported through the advertising in and the images conveyed by the electronic mass media (particularly television), the presence of many tourists in the countries, and the proximity of North America. The high levels of unemployment can be partly explained by the widespread imitative use of inappropriate capital-intensive technologies imported without modification with a view to better suiting local factor endowments. They can also be explained by the deficiencies of a colonial-inherited elitist and often inappropriate system of education, deficient in opportunities and motivations for technical and vocational training and failing miserably in integrating the "world of school" with the "world of work." Finally, "Western" types of trade unionism and generally free collective bargaining processes also facilitate the transmission of high wages from the mineral or tourism sectors into the public and agricultural sectors, making for low or negative public sector surpluses and high costs of agricultural production. But under the political systems existing in most if not all the countries of the area, the application of incomes and prices policies is notoriously difficult.

The existence of these "political economy constraints" on autonomous patterns of development implies that fundamentally the development problems of the area can be tackled effectively only through the political process which would have to undertake the onerous tasks of radically restructuring educational and training systems and initiating changes in values and attitudes in relation to lifestyles, work habits, levels and patterns of consumption, and propensities to technological adaptation and innovation. Let it be noted here that the present political institutions and mechanisms devised to preserve and promote traditional civil and political rights and liberties inherited from the metropolitan powers could, under many circumstances, prove inconsistent (at least in some degree) with the kinds of political processes required to push through the necessary far-reaching changes in values and attitudes.

In the light of the prevailing frailness of economic structures, all the Caribbean countries (with the sole exception of Trinidad and Tobago, a minor exporter and producer of oil by world standards) have been adversely affected by the international economic crisis which had its onset in 1973-1974 resulting in considerably higher prices for oil as well as for imports of manufactured goods and food from the industrialized countries. The subsequent recession in the industrialized countries also added to the impact of these adverse developments on the Caribbean countries which were faced with worsening terms of trade, a slowing down of demand for their exports in the industrialized countries, imported inflation, and consequently very severe balance-of-payments and fiscal difficulties.

## *The Caribbean And The New International Economic Order*

### *ROLE OF CARIBBEAN IN DIALOGUE ON NEW ORDER*

Many of the independent English-speaking Caribbean countries—particularly Guyana and Jamaica—have been in the forefront of the demand for a New International Economic Order. These demands have been made both within the UN system and outside, as in the case of the disappointing North-South dialogue of 1975-1977 in Paris. It would be pointless to list in this essay all of the demands made by the Third World countries in connection with the proposed New International Economic Order. I prefer to list certain broad areas which appear to be of great significance for the Caribbean countries. These are:

(a) stable and remunerative prices for commodity exports of the developing countries;
(b) better access for semimanufactures and manufactures in the markets of the developed countries;
(c) a greater volume of official development assistance, as far as possible on concessional terms, and appropriate action on the debt problems of the individual developing countries;
(d) the need to take into account and act on the special needs of developing island economies;
(e) economic cooperation among developing countries; and

(f) a fairer deal from the transnational corporations in respect of both direct investment and the transfer of technology.

In addition, quite apart from a restructuring of the international economic system, greater internal effort in the fields of food production and the mobilization of domestic financial resources have been stressed by some, as has been the need for the pursuit of "basis needs" development strategies—that is to say, strategies that aim at structural transformation of the economy while also meeting the needs of the poor majority of the population for a more human and less degraded and deprived existence.

*ISSUE OF PARTICULARISTIC OR UNIVERSALISTIC CONCESSIONS*

To begin with, one has to probe deeply and face up to the question of whether for countries such as the Caribbean preferential treatment in protected developed country markets, such as the socialist bloc or European economic community, are not preferable to "universal" schemes such as the UNCTAD proposal. So far as the Caribbean is concerned, this issue primarily centers around the prices and volumes of exports of sugar and bananas, as well as access for semimanufactured and manufactured exports into the markets of the developed countries. But it is not a question of either/or. For to the extent that the Caribbean countries export on the world market outside of these preferential zones, they need both "particularistic" and "universalistic" means of export support.

Indeed, the real significance of the Lomé Convention is that some of the concepts underlying the New International Economic Order have been incorporated into the agreement—for example, mechanisms to avoid or reduce possible political influence on the part of the EEC on the associated developing countries; the removal of the provision in the previous Yaounde Conventions for the granting of "reverse preferences" by the associated developing countries; the recognition of a special category of "least developed" countries; and the encouragement of economic cooperation among the associated developing countries; and the incorporation of a Commodity Export Stabilization Scheme (STABEX).

We also should not forget that the extent of trade and possibly aid advantages conferred on the developing countries party to the Lomé Convention is likely to diminish over time, so that ultimately the Caribbean countries will get the same treatment that Europe gives to other developing countries. Accordingly, one can objectively justify the temporary trade advantages available to some of the Caribbean countries under the present and subsequent five-year conventions as a means of enabling them to retain certain preferential treatment which they formerly had in the markets of the metropolitan countries for certain commodities which they produced either at high cost (such as sugar and bananas) or competitively (such as rum). In terms of the need for at least temporary props for certain important export products, the Caribbean countries concerned constitute a special case among Third World countries.

*COMMODITIES*

The Caribbean certainly has an interest in the integrated program for commodities elaborated by the UNCTAD Secretariat and discussed in both that forum and in the North-South dialogue in Paris. Of the 18 commodities selected for the common fund approach, sugar, bananas, bauxite, cocoa, and coffee are of interest to the Caribbean.

It has been often urged by reactionary writers that many individual developing countries stand to lose to the extent that they would be net importers of many of the 18 commodities. The Caribbean would certainly be among such developing countries. But this point has, from the outset, been recognized in the UNCTAD secretariat's initial proposal on commodities, where it was recommended that the individual developing countries who lose by having to pay higher prices for one or more imported commodities should receive special compensation in various ways both from the proposed common fund and from other sources of external finance. In this connection, one should also take into account the proposal initiated by the Commonwealth group of experts on the New International Economic Order that receipts from tourism (an economic activity of great importance to many of the Caribbean countries) should be taken into account in the operation of the IMF scheme of compensatory financing for export shortfalls in developing countries.

*MANUFACTURES*

The Caribbean, as observed earlier, needs to achieve considerable increases in its level of exports of semimanufactures and manufactures to extraregional markets, and on the face of it would appear to stand to gain considerably from the provision of better access for such products to the markets of the industrialized countries. Many of the countries of the area already have duty-free access for a wide range of manufactures and semimanufactures into the European economic community under the Lomé Convention. As developing countries, they also have favorable treatment under the General System of Preferences (GSP) in the markets of developed countries, such as Canada and the United States of America. On the other hand, because of relatively high wage-rates in the face of considerable unemployment, as well as low volume of exports by individual exporting firms, there is reason to believe that high costs of production and small volumes may not make them as competitive as other developing countries—particularly leading Third World exporters such as South Korea, Taiwan, Singapore, Mexico, Colombia, and Brazil. On these grounds, one can argue that they may not be able to take automatic advantage of the arrangements for duty-free or low-duty access of both the Lomé Convention and the GSP. But this should not be allowed to obscure the long-term interest which virtually all the countries of the area have, along with other developing countries, in preferential access to the markets of the developed countries. After all, no reasonable government or individual in the Caribbean countries concerned would expect these countries to benefit fully from every single new arrangement made in connection with the New International Economic Order. Third World solidarity is essential; for just as any single Third World country may not benefit from any one area as much as others, so are there other areas from which a single country may benefit more than others.

### *OFFICIAL DEVELOPMENT ASSISTANCE*

The Caribbean countries, whatever their size, volume, and range of natural resources or ideological orientation, are heavily dependent on official development assistance and, as small countries, receive as a group one of the highest per capita levels of aid among Third World countries. This applies to Cuba just as much as to Montserrat. This high dependence in the case of any single country is the product of one or more of the following:

—diseconomies of very small scale in administration, public services, public utilities, and infrastructure;
—high rates of consumption and low rates of national saving in relation to Gross National Product;
—in one or two countries, very rapid rates of economic and social transformation desired by the leaders; and
—very tight foreign exchange constraints in the development process.

On the other hand, the larger and relatively more developed countries have been considered "middle-income" countries not deserving of official economic aid on concessional terms. The call in the New International Economic Order for greater volumes of official development assistance for developing countries on concessional terms is therefore clearly to the advantage of all the Caribbean countries.

Some of those Caribbean countries where foreign exchange constraints are very tight are now facing a serious problem of external debt service, because of the relatively short maturities which characterize their recent borrowing from private sources and governmental export credit agencies, because of worsened terms of trade, balance-of-payments, and fiscal deterioration for other reasons, and because in the case of the larger and relatively more developed countries, as a result of their relatively high per capita income, they have not received sufficient levels of official development assistance on sufficiently concessional terms. Clearly, all the Commonwealth Caribbean countries could gain to the extent that the external debt problem is realistically tackled by the international community.

*DEVELOPING ISLAND ECONOMIES*

Nearly all of the Caribbean countries can be characterized as small or disadvantaged developing island economies. The disadvantages in international economic relations faced by these countries have been well analyzed by the UNCTAD Secretariat. These disadvantages are small domestic markets; separation by sea which makes for high transport costs in both international and intraregional trade, even in an integrated market; lack of diversified economic structures; diseconomies of small scale in public services, public utilities, and infrastructure; absence in most cases of natural resources; and extensive economic dependence on the outside world. Any appropriate set of measures which is undertaken by the international community in favor of developing island countries would obviously benefit the Caribbean countries: official lending on highly concessional terms; special assistance of this nature for interisland transport and communications facilities; the use of external financial and technical assistance to promote economic integration and cooperation among groups of neighboring islands; and technical assistance to help such countries to bargain effectively with the transnational corporations so as to improve their terms of access to foreign shipping services, foreign direct investment, and to technology.

One very important aspect of small size and external economic dependence in the Caribbean countries is the issue of economic cooperation among developing countries.

### *ECONOMIC COOPERATION AMONG DEVELOPING COUNTRIES*

So far the economic integration experiment has been limited to the English-speaking Caribbean countries and has taken the form of the Caribbean community, of which the most important part is the Caribbean common market. The share of intra-common market trade in total trade grew from 8% in 1967 (the year before the freeing of trade under CARIFTA in 1968) to 11% in 1973, and then dropped to 7% in 1976. The fact is that the common market is now facing serious difficulties as a result of import restrictions imposed by Guyana and Jamaica against "inessential" products because of their very serious foreign exchange difficulties. Now, as every economist knows, the benefits of economic integration among developing countries are not confined to the benefits arising from trade liberalization. The reason is that in the long run, greater benefits can result from cooperation in production involving the establishment of complementary structures of production and from the establishment of certain common services in areas such as transportation and communications, other infrastructure, research, education, and administration. Member states of the Caribbean common market are now beginning to implement some of the provisions of the treaty, other than those calling for intraregional trade liberalization and the establishment of a common external tariff protective system. A start has been made on the implementation of the regional food plan (including the establishment of the Caribbean Food Corporation to implement the plan), and the first steps are being taken to implement the system of regional industrial programming laid down in the treaty, with priority attention being given to the pulp and paper sector, based on the forestry resources of the region.

Nevertheless, we cannot too lightly dismiss the import restrictions on "inessential" light manufactures; for while it is true that (with the exception of petroleum, fertilizer, and rice) most intraregional trade so far consists of products of the light manufacturing sector not based to any significant extent on local and regional inputs and therefore containing the minimal local and regional value added required to meet the rules of origin, such industries tend to be relatively labor-intensive, with the result that restrictions on intraregional trade can produce serious unemployment in those CARICOM countries whose exports are so restricted. This factor of severe restrictions on intraregional trade has led to a certain amount of demoralization but not despair among certain groups in the member states of CARICOM and particularly among those who advocate regional solutions to the development problems of the region.

The solution to these problems of deep structural disequilibrium in the balance-of-payments is for the two or three countries seriously affected to make the necessary structural adjustments to the large external deficits produced by the international economic crisis and subsequent world recession, and for them to receive balance-of-payments support to help them to adjust quickly and successfully. Fundamentally, full adjustment to this situation can be achieved only by increases of production (of both import substitutes and exports). Trinidad and Tobago, the only oil-producing Caribbean country, has given a significant amount of balance-of-payments support to its less fortunate sister states by making available US$150 million since the onset of the world economic crisis in 1973-1974. It is hoped that Trinidad and Tobago will continue giving such support and that the World Bank, IMF, and interested donor countries will make available adequate amounts of short-term, medium-term, and long-term balance-of-payments support to CARICOM countries such as Barbados, Guyana and Jamaica, and development finance on concessional terms to the less developed countries that, because they have no central bank and limited monetary independence, experience their balance-of-payments problems in the form of large fiscal deficits and shrinkage of both public and private liquidity. To the extent that this is done, and intraregional trade increases to precrisis levels, it should be possible for the regional movement to move increasingly toward more effective cooperation in production and the building up, over time, of more complementary structures of production. At the same time, any efforts among some or all of the smaller countries to establish common services among themselves should be morally and financially supported both within and outside the region. In this way, economic integration will undoubtedly create, in the long run, a considerable level of benefits to the Caribbean countries.

Indeed, one essential prerequisite for a just and durable scheme of Caribbean economic integration is the provision of the maximum feasible range of opportunities for rapid development in the relatively less developed countries. Just as the developing countries throughout the world are seeking from the developed countries the creation of a new and more just international order which would make possible their soundly based development, so must justice and equity prevail in economic integration and cooperation schemes among the developing countries themselves. Fortunately, this need has always been clearly recognized and acted upon within the framework of Caribbean economic integration; for the relatively more-developed countries of the community have always seen that, if it were otherwise, their case for more just and equitable economic treatment by the world's developed countries would have no moral basis.

But there are many, both within the region and outside, who question the effectiveness of the concept of economic integration among such small countries as an aid to development and pin their hopes on much wider economic cooperation among larger numbers of Third World countries. To do this, I submit, is to throw out the baby with the bath water. Economic integration among a group of neighboring Third World countries, however small, and economic cooperation among a much bigger number of Third World countries are not in conflict with, but are complementary to, each other. Indeed, perhaps the best way of setting about economic cooperation among a large number of developing countries is to organize such cooperation on the basis of a gradual development of economic links between subregional integration schemes or between such schemes and individual large developing countries. For if we are to be completely objective, we must face up to the real possibility of relations of dominance and dependence being established, as between Third World countries; for these countries, while they quite definitely have a fundamental unity of interest with each other, vary considerably in size and economic strength. The Caribbean community has a total population of only 5 million persons and consists for the most part of either very small or very weak countries. The community, while seeking to extend the area of economic cooperation with other Third World countries (both in Latin America and outside), should give primary emphasis at this stage to welding itself into a cohesive unit characterized by the closest possible coordination of external economic actions, policies, and relationships. This was, it should be noted, the rationale behind the formation of the Andean group, under which the smaller and medium-sized countries of LAFTA formed a subgroup of their own as a means of cooperating more easily and equitably with Mexico, Brazil, and Argentina, the three giants of LAFTA. Similarly, this type of subregional cohesion provides the only sensible basis on which the Caribbean community countries should enter into very desirable closer economic relationships with the other countries and territories of the Caribbean Archipelago as well as with the large and relatively more developed and powerful Mainland countries of Mexico, Colombia, and Venezuela. The Caribbean community as a group must also maintain its position of negotiating as a group in its developing relations with other Third World countries both within and outside the African, Caribbean, and Pacific group which have entered into the Lomé Convention with the EEC.

To say this is not to deny the need for CARICOM to "widen" itself in the medium term to include other Caribbean Archipelago countries such as the Dominican Republic, Haiti, and Suriname and to develop cooperative relationships with countries such as Cuba, the Netherlands Antilles, and even conceivably the French Antillean departments. This process can be initiated by the Caribbean community negotiating either trade or economic complementarity agreements and even associate membership with other Caribbean Archipelago countries. An important step was recently taken toward greater economic cooperation among most of the countries of the Caribbean Archipelago through the establishment in 1975 of the Caribbean Development and Cooperation Committee (CDCC) of the UN Economic Commission of Latin America (ECLA). The CDCC of ECLA has the following memberships: Bahamas, Barbados, Cuba, Dominican Republic, Grenada, Guyana, Haiti, Jamaica, Suriname, and Trinidad and Tobago, with the British Associated States, Belize, and the Netherlands Antilles being associate members.

Another possible route to greater economic cooperation among the Caribbean Archipelago countries could emerge to the extent that the proposal for the creation of a Caribbean Group for Economic Cooperation in development comes about. The intention here is that some of the industrialized countries with special links with the Caribbean and some of the mainland countries whose shores are washed by the Caribbean sea join with the CARICOM state of Trinidad and Tobago in cooperating with the majority of the Caribbean Archipelago countries by providing them with additional official development assistance within a multi-lateral framework, whilst encouraging and promoting present integration and new cooperation efforts among the potential beneficiaries of such aid. Such additional economic aid is intended to be for a limited period of time to help the recipient countries, which as a result of external international economic factors are now faced with considerable economic and financial difficulties.

Indeed, the well-organized need for the Caribbean countries to have closer economic relationships with the Latin American countries, while preserving their Caribbean economic and cultural identity and increasing the degree of their external economic and diplomatic solidarity, can best be accommodated within a framework under which:

(a) multilateral financial assistance is made available to some or all of the Caribbean Archipelago countries by the bigger Caribbean basin and other Latin American countries, through subregional financial institutions controlled by the Caribbean countries, such as the Caribbean Development Bank;

(b) the countries of the Caribbean community *as a community and not on an individual basis* should enter into trade and economic complementarity agreements with other countries of the Archipelago, with the larger neighboring Caribbean basin and with other Latin American countries. (This is so both because it would strengthen the bargaining power of the individual Caribbean community countries and because it would prevent the preemption by third countries of opportunities for intra-CARICOM trade and economic complementarity and so strengthen the Caribbean community.) One such agreement between Mexico and the Caribbean community has recently been entered into.

### *FOREIGN INVESTMENT, TECHNOLOGY TRANSFER, AND THE TRANSNATIONAL CORPORATION*

Because of the long centuries-old history of economically dependent association of nearly all the countries of the Caribbean Archipelago with developed metropolitan countries, resulting in still too many cases of domination of many key sectors of their economies by the giant transnational corporations, most of the Caribbean countries have an interest in the demands in the New International Economic Order for an elimination of the unhealthy economic and political effects of the transnational corporations on the sound and balanced development and sovereign integrity of Third World countries and for an improvement in the terms under which the technology developed by these corporations is "transferred" (or, more precisely, sold) to developing countries. Moreover, the call for the development and use of more appropriate technology in Third World countries suffering from heavy structural unemployment is highly relevant to all the countries of the Caribbean.

Many of the English-speaking Caribbean countries—particularly Guyana and, to a lesser extent, Jamaica and Trinidad and Tobago—have over the last few years been seeking to reduce dependence on the transnational corporation. Although the need for foreign exchange will continue to be very acute and may well slow down the pace of bringing key sectors of the economies under national control, it would be extremely naive to believe that those Caribbean countries with radical or nationalist economic policies will make a complete about-face and open up their economies indiscriminately to direct foreign investments. What is more likely is the adoption by these countries of more selective and flexible and less dogmatic policies on direct foreign investment and the transnational corporations. Both the improvement of the terms under which technology is "transferred" by the transnational corporations and the local and regional development and application of more appropriate technologies would seem to be tendencies that are likely to be strengthened in the future in all the Caribbean countries.

### *INTERNAL EFFORTS FOR ECONOMIC TRANSFORMATION*

The New International Economic Order deals fundamentally with the deep-seated imbalances in international economic relationships between developing and developed countries. But very few serious Third World advocates of the New International Economic Order would ignore the need for serious internal efforts at mobilization of resources and transformation of economic and social structures. These efforts and transformations, it is generally agreed, should be pursued through vigorous programs for developing food production, for mobilizing internal financial resources, and more generally for pursuing a "basic needs" development strategy.

Fortunately, in most of the countries of the Caribbean Archipelago, the need for such internal efforts and such transformations aiming at a socially just pattern of economic growth and development is clearly recognized irrespective of size, economic and political orientation, level and ranges of human and natural resources, and stage of development of the various countries. There are now very few governments in the Caribbean area who would dare to support explicitly the pursuit of economic and social elitism in their development strategies.

### *CONCLUDING OBSERVATION*

To conclude: all the Caribbean countries have a vital interest in the realization of most of the fundamental proposals for a New International Economic Order. They tend to see the achievement of such an order as widening their development options and so contributing, if not to the ending, at least to the diminution of the area's historical legacy of external economic dependence and fragmentation.

## REFERENCES CONSULTED

American Assembly (1971) The United States and the Caribbean. Tad Szulc (ed.). Englewood Cliffs, NJ: Prentice Hall.

BEST, L. (1970) Black Power and National Reconstruction. Port-of-Spain, Trinidad: Tapia.

——— (1967) The Economy of the British Commonwealth Caribbean: An Overview—West Indies-Caribbean Economic Relations. Mona, Jamaica: University of the West Indies, Institute of Social and Economic Research (ISER).

——— (1966) "Size and survival." New World Q. (Barbados Independence issue).

BREWSTER, H. and C. THOMAS (1967) The Dynamics of West Indian Economic Integration, Studies in Regional Economic Integration, Vol. 1. Mona, Jamaica: University of the West Indies, ISER.

Caribbean Community Secretariat (1973) The Caribbean Community, A Guide. Georgetown, Guyana: Caribbean Community Secretariat.

Commonwealth Experts' Group (1977) "Towards a new international economic order." A final report by the Commonwealth Experts' Group. London: Commonwealth Secretariat.

DEMAS, W. G. (1976a) "Commitment, skill, and organization." May address at Sixth Annual Board of Governors' meeting in St. Kitts. Barbados, West Indies: Caribbean Development Bank (CDB).

——— (1976b) Essays on Caribbean Integration and Development. Mona, Jamaica: University of West Indies.

——— (1974) "West Indian nationhood and Caribbean integration." No. 1 in a collection of papers published in the series, Challenges in the New Caribbean, David I. Mitchell (ed.). Barbados: CCC Publishing House.

——— (1965) Economics of Development in Small Countries. Montreal: McGill University.

EMMANUEL, P., V. LEWIS, and A. McINTYRE (1975) "The political economy of independence for the Leeward and Windward Island." Mona, Jamaica: University of the West Indies, ISER. (mimeo)

GIRVAN, N. (1967) The Caribbean Bauxite Industry. Mona, Jamaica: University of the West Indies, ISER.

——— and O. JEFFERSON [eds.] (1971) Readings in the Political Economy of the Caribbean, Mona, Jamaica: New World Group, Ltd.

HAWKINS, I. (1976) The Changing Face of the Caribbean. Bridgetown, Barbados, West Indies: Cedar Press.

HUBERMAN, L. and P. M. SWEEZY (1970) Socialism in Cuba. New York and London: Monthly Review Press and Modern Reader Paperbacks.

LEWIS, A. (1972) Statement at the Second Annual Meeting of the Board of Governors of the Caribbean Development Bank, given in Jamaica. Barbados: CDB.

LEWIS, G. K. (1974) Notes on the Puerto Rican Revolution: An Essay of American Dominance and Caribbean Resistance. New York: Monthly Review Press.

——— (1972) The Virgin Islands: A Caribbean Lilliput. Evanston, IL: Northwestern Univ. Press.

——— (1968) The Growth of the Modern West Indies. London: MacGibbon & Kee.

LEWIS, V. (1973) "The Caribbean community: a political analysis." Barbados Advocate-News (June 14).

McINTYRE, A. (1977) Statement at the Seventh Annual Meeting of the Board of Governors of the Caribbean Development Bank, given in Trinidad. Barbados: CDB.

——— (1975) Statement at the 16th Session of the Economic Commission for Latin America (ECLA) held in Port-of-Spain, Trinidad. Santiago, Chile: ECLA.

——— (1965) Decolonisation and Trade Policy in the West Indies: The Caribbean Transition. Rio Piedras, Puerto Rico: University of Puerto Rico, Institute of Caribbean Studies.

——— and B. WATSON (1970) Foreign Investment in the Commonwealth Caribbean. Mona, Jamaica: University of the West Indies, ISER.

MATTHEWS, H. L. (1970) Castro. London: Penguin.

MUNRO, T. and R. LEWIS [eds.] (1971) Readings in Government and Politics of the West Indies. Mona, Jamaica: University of the West Indies. Department of Government.

RAMPHAL, S. S. (1975) "To care for CARICOM." Speech given in Jamaica, July 5.

——— (1971) Dialogue of Unity: A Search for West Indian Identity. Georgetown, Guyana: Ministry of External Affairs.

RUBIN, R. and R. P. SCHAEDEL [eds.] (1975) The Haitian Potential: Research and Resources of Haiti. New York: Teachers College Press.

SEGAL, A. (1968) The Politics of Caribbean Integration. Rio Piedras, Puerto Rico: University of Puerto Rico, Institute of Caribbean Studies.

VEGA, B. (1978) "The Caribbean—yesterday and today." Opening address of the Annual Conference of Caribbean Studies Association, Santiago, Dominican Republic.

WILLIAMS, E. (1973a) "The foreign policies of the Caribbean states." Commonwealth J. of Int. Affairs 249.

——— (1973b) "A new federation for the commonwealth Caribbean?" Pol. Q. 44 (July-September): 242-256.

——— (1970) From Columbus to Castro. London: Deutsch.

——— (1944) Capitalism and Slavery. Chapel Hill: Univ. of North Carolina Press.

*William G. Demas has been President of the Caribbean Development Bank since 1974. Earlier he was Secretary-General of the Commonwealth Caribbean Regional Secretariat (1970-1974) and Permanent Secretary in the Ministry of Planning and Development for his native Trinidad and Tobago and Economic Advisor to its Prime Minister. He studied economics at Cambridge University and is the author of* Economics of Development in Small Countries with Special Reference to the Caribbean *(McGill University Press, 1965) and* Essays on Caribbean Integration and Development *(University of the West Indies, 1976). As both a student and practitioner of economic development, he has participated in and followed closely discussions over the last two years on proposals for a New International Economic Order.*

## APPENDIX I

Selected Economic Data on Caribbean Area

| COUNTRIES | POPULATION ('000) (c) | AREA Sq. Mi. | GNP (US$m) (b) | POPULATION DENSITY (h) | GNP PER CAPITA (b) | EXPORTS FOB (e) | IMPORTS CIF (e) |
|---|---|---|---|---|---|---|---|
| 1. Barbados | 247(a) | 166 | 379(d) | 1,488 | 1,534 | 86 | 79 |
| 2. Guyana | 770 | 83,000 | 400 | 9 | 510(d) | 298 | 357 |
| 3. Jamaica | 2,042 | 4,411 | 2,270 | 463 | 1,110 | 608 | 689 |
| 4. Trinidad & Tobago | 1,082 | 1,980 | 2,170 | 546 | 2,000 | 2,213 | 2,158 |
| 5. Bahamas (j) | 204 | 4,404 | 630 | 46 | 3,110 | 1,094 | 972 |
| ENGLISH-SPEAKING MORE DEVELOPED | 4,345 | 93,961 | 5,849 | 46 | 1,346 | 4,299 | 4,255 |
| 6. Antigua (& Dependencies) | 71 | 171 | 60 | 415 | 840 | 24(k) | 53(k) |
| 7. Belize | 140 | 8,867 | 90 | 16 | 670 | 37 | 40 |
| 8. Dominica | 75 | 290 | 40 | 259 | 560 | 9(i) | 17(i) |
| 9. Grenada | 110 | 133 | 40 | 827 | 390 | 10(i) | 20(i) |
| 10. Montserrat | 13(g) | 38 | n.a. | 342 | n.a. | 0.4(i) | 6(i) |
| 11. St. Kitts/Nevis/Anguilla | 49 | 155 | 30 | 316 | 640 | 6(i) | 13(1) |
| 12. St. Lucia | 107 | 238 | 60 | 450 | 580 | 13(i) | 37(i) |
| 13. St. Vincent | 90 | 150 | 40 | 600 | 420 | 5(i) | 20(i) |
| 14. British Virgin Islands (j) | 10(f) | 59 | n.a. | 169 | n.a. | n.a. | n.a. |
| 15. Cayman Islands (j) | 10(f) | 100 | n.a. | 100 | n.a. | n.a. | n.a. |
| 16. Turks & Caicos (j) | 6 | 166 | n.a. | 36 | n.a. | n.a. | n.a. |

APPENDIX I (Continued)

| | | | | | | | |
|---|---|---|---|---|---|---|---|
| ENGLISH-SPEAKING LESS DEVELOPED | 681 | 10,367 | n.a. | 66 | n.a. | n.a. | n.a. |
| 17. Dominican Republic | 4,695 | 18,703 | 3,390 | 251 | 720 | 716 | 730 |
| 18. Haiti | 4,584 | 10,714 | 850 | 428 | 190 | 190 | 209 |
| 19. Cuba | 9,332 | 44,218 | 7,460 | 211 | 800 | n.a. | n.a. |
| 20. Puerto Rico | 3,090 | 3,435 | 7,120 | 900 | 2,300 | n.a. | n.a. |
| 21. U.S. Virgin Islands | 63(f) | 133 | n.a. | 474 | n.a. | n.a. | n.a. |
| 22. Netherland Antilles | 242 | 394 | 410 | 614 | 1,680 | 2,111 | 2,155 |
| 23. Martinique | 325 | 425 | 770 | 765 | 2,350 | 124 | 120 |
| 24. Guadeloupe (& Dependencies) | 325 | 685 | 490 | 474 | 1,500 | 88 | 89 |
| 25. Cayenne | 56 | 35,135 | 100 | 2 | 1,680 | 4 | 6 |
| 26. Suriname | 368 | 63,251 | 500 | 6 | 1,370 | 275 | 303 |
| GRAND TOTAL | 28,106 | 281,421 | n.a. | 100 | n.a. | n.a. | n.a. |

NOTES: n.a. – not available; (a) – mid-1976; (b) – GNP at market prices 1975; (c) – mid-1975; (d) – 1976 data; (e) – U.S. $m 1976; (f) – 1970 Census; (g) – 1972 Census; (h) – population per square mile; (i) – 1975 data; (j) – non-CARICOM country; (k) – 1974 data; (l) – 1973 data.

SOURCES: *World Bank Atlas 1977* (World Bank); *The Times Atlas of the World* (Comprehensive Edition, 1975); *International Financial Statistics* (IMF, February 1978); *Direction of Trade* (IMF, 1970-1976); *Annual Digest of Statistics 1975* (ECCM Secretariat); *Digest of Trade Statistics of CARICOM Member States* (CARICOM Secretariat, September 1976).

# APPENDIX II

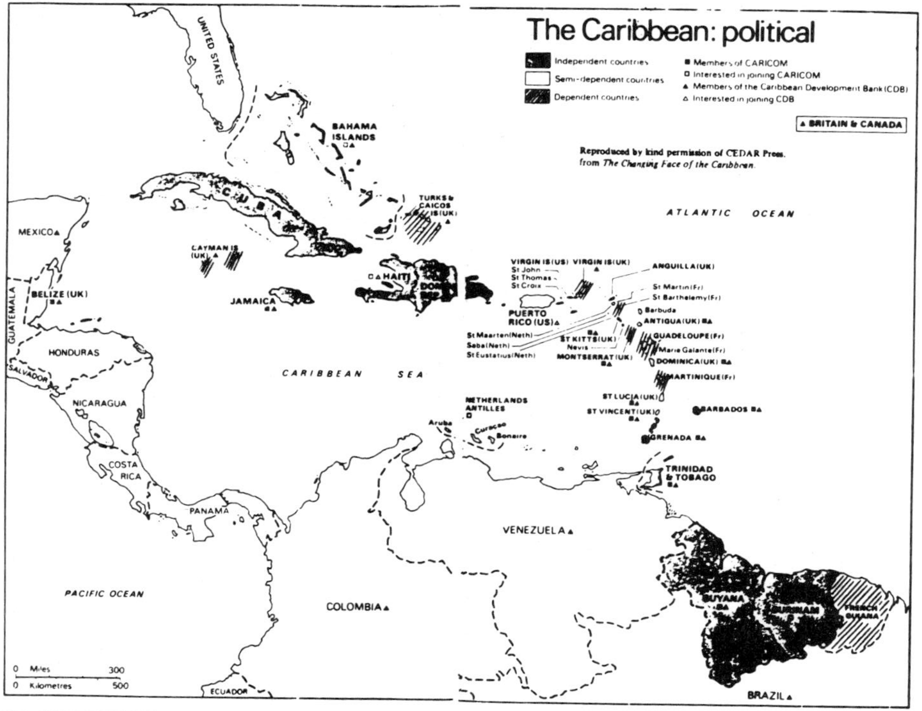
The Caribbean: political
Independent countries
Semi-dependent countries
Dependent countries
Members of CARICOM
Interested in joining CARICOM
Members of the Caribbean Development Bank (CDB)
Interested in joining CDB
BRITAIN & CANADA
Reproduced by kind permission of CEDAR Press, from The Changing Face of the Caribbean.
UNITED STATES
BAHAMA ISLANDS
TURKS & CAICOS IS(UK)
ATLANTIC OCEAN
MEXICO
CUBA
CAYMAN IS (UK)
JAMAICA
HAITI
VIRGIN IS(US)
VIRGIN IS(UK)
St John
St Thomas
St Croix
ANGUILLA(UK)
St Martin(Fr)
St Barthelemy(Fr)
Barbuda
ANTIGUA(UK)
PUERTO RICO (US)
St Maarten(Neth)
Saba(Neth)
St Eustatius(Neth)
ST KITTS(UK)
Nevis
MONTSERRAT(UK)
GUADELOUPE(Fr)
Marie Galante(Fr)
DOMINICA(UK)
MARTINIQUE(Fr)
GUATEMALA
BELIZE (UK)
HONDURAS
SALVADOR
CARIBBEAN SEA
NICARAGUA
NETHERLANDS ANTILLES
Aruba
Curaçao
Bonaire
ST LUCIA(UK)
ST VINCENT(UK)
BARBADOS
GRENADA
TRINIDAD & TOBAGO
COSTA RICA
PANAMA
VENEZUELA
GUYANA
SURINAM
FRENCH GUIANA
PACIFIC OCEAN
COLOMBIA
0 Miles 300
0 Kilometres 500
ECUADOR
BRAZIL

## ERRATUM

In the May 1978 issue of the *Journal of Interamerican Studies* (Volume 20, Number 2) in the first paragraph of the Review Essay "Argentina at the Crossroads" by Alberto Ciria, pages 211-212 should have read.

Argentina has been, for many decades, the "odd man out" of Latin American politics. A marginal area of the Spanish colonial empire, at least up to the eighteenth century, it progressed in the nineteenth century from a backwoods region to central importance in South America. This, of course, was due mainly to its early specialization in meat and cereals production, which consolidated the country's comparative advantages in the "international division of labor" then present on a world scale. By 1900 massive injections of capital and manpower (mostly from Italy and Spain) had already patterned Argentina's outward-oriented development of its economy vis-à-vis the leading power of the day, Great Britain. Furthermore, the early development of an indigenous landowning-commercial elite with its center in the port city of Buenos Aires and the pampas' hinterland, managed to survive internecine struggles by local or national caudillos (Juan Manuel de Rosas) and ended up by strengthening the economic, political, and social hegemony of a city over a nation.

**MARKOS MAMALAKIS**
*Department of Economics*
*University of Wisconsin—Milwaukee*
*Milwaukee, Wisconsin 53201*

# *THE NEW INTERNATIONAL ECONOMIC ORDER*
## *Centerpiece Venezuela*

"A new economic order is essential for world peace," proclaimed President Carlos Andrés Pérez of Venezuela (1976) on November 16, 1976, at the UN General Assembly in fulfilling "the mandate which Simon Bolívar gave [the Venezuelans] more than 150 years ago" (Pérez, 1976: 28). Responding to this call of destiny and reaffirming Venezuela's claimed Bolivarian tradition

---

AUTHOR'S NOTE: The author extends his appreciation to Professor Helmut Hesse, Director of the Ibero-American Institute for Economic Research of the University of Göttingen for his intellectual stimulation, the German Research Foundation, the University of Wisconsin—Milwaukee for its support of his research at Göttingen, officials of the Venezuelan Mission to the UN, the Venezuelan embassies in Bonn and Washington, the Central Bank and Ministry of Mines of Venezuela for their generosity in providing documentary sources, and Professor Howard Ellis of the University of California—Berkeley for his assistance in revising the manuscript.

---

EDITOR'S NOTE: This article contains a number of acronyms pertaining to the International and Domestic Economic Orders and their components. The complete name for each acronym is given the first time it is used. For reference purposes, the reader may fully identify each acronym wherever used by referring to Figure 1, a diagram of the economic orders and their components, compiled by the author.

Journal of Interamerican Studies and World Affairs, Vol. 20 No. 3, August 1978

of placing "its resources at the service of its people, at the service of Latin America, at the service of humanity" (Pérez, 1976: 28), President Pérez (nicknamed Simonsito) sought in and through the New International Economic Order (NIEO) a new Lebensraum, not of destructive territorial expansion, but of increased purchasing power, dignity, equality, and independence for the poor, weak, underprivileged countries (Pérez, 1976: 7, 11). The NIEO, "a moral obligation of all nations," "is required as a desideratum of peace," especially since the disintegrating "old international economic order which emerged from the Second World War . . . was an unjust system of relations based on inequality . . . designed to benefit those countries which had accumulated the fruits of technical progress" (Pérez, 1976: 9).[1] To President Pérez, achievement of a NIEO was, thus, a moral obligation and ideological commitment as well as a matter of emotional involvement and Bolivar-sized personal ambition of global leadership.

How profoundly has Venezuela reshaped the old and forged a NIEO in fulfilling its Bolivarian mandate? What have the major global, regional, and domestic effects and reactions been to Venezuela's initiatives? What basic economic factors have motivated its leaders, and what benefits has or does Venezuela expect to derive from the NIEO? By answering these questions as well as possible, this article hopes to define Venezuela's role and goals in shaping the NIEO.

To respond to these questions, trace the features, and examine the two-way interactions between the global and Venezuelan orders, the international economic order (IEO) is organized into (1) an international production order (IPO), which deals with global production and exchange of goods and services; (2) an international distribution order (IDO), which deals with the international distribution of income from and expenditures on goods and services; and (3) an international capital formation order (ICFO), which is shaped by the endowments and accumulation of various capital forms. The ICFO has been subdivided, in turn, into the international saving order (ISO), the international financial intermediation order (IFO), and the international investment order (IIO).[2]

Furthermore, the *old* IEO (OIEO), with which Venezuelan leaders were so dissatisfied, is contrasted to the *new* IEO (NIEO), which proposes to eliminate global poverty in any absolute sense and to reduce relative poverty. The normative concept of the desired, ideal NIEO is distinguished from the positive concept of the actual NIEO which refers to the order established by the configuration of events following the post-1973 oil price increases.

The domestic economic order (DEO) of Venezuela has been restructured into a domestic production order (DPO), a domestic distribution order (DDO), and a domestic capital formation order (DCFO). In turn, the DCFO is subdivided into domestic saving (DSO), financial intermediation (DFO), and investment (DIO) orders. Also contrasted are the old and new, actual and desired forms. A schematic summary of the analytical framework of this article is presented in Figure 1.

Distinguished Venezuelan leaders such as President Carlos Andrés Pérez, Foreign Minister and former Ambassador to the United Nations Simón Alberto Consalvi, Minister of Energy and Mines Valentin Hernández, and Minister of State for International Economic Affairs Manuel Pérez-Guerrero, all with the most impressive credentials of public service, recognized fully that the IEO influences, reflects, and is shaped by interactions (the so-called interdependence) of a multitude of domestic economic, political, and social orders.[3] Emergence of a NIEO required a previous or simultaneous transformation of Venezuela's DEO while IEO forces were expected to shape its own DEO. The goal was to correct the perceived defects of the domestic order and seek a transformation of an IEO considered as unjust. Changes in global and domestic production orders are examined first.

*The Production Order*

The IPO has undergone basic changes since 1973—inflation combined with rising global unemployment (stagflation), falling rates of income growth, and highly volatile foreign exchange rates. With only these features considered, it is extremely difficult to accept the fact that 1973 is a benchmark year separating a new from the old order rather than just another turning point in a continuum of economic cycles. What, however impregnates the year 1973 with irreversible historical significance is the unprecedented oil price shock released by the Organization of Petroleum Exporting Countries (OPEC), which has established new regional as well as global oil-sector-based strategic, political, and economic power balances. Hardly less significant, the OPEC trident of price rises, output controls, and nationalization of oil had been forged by Venezuela over the last twenty years (Fuad in Bond, 1977a: 121-145).

Venezuela's pre-1973 domestic production order (DPO) was dominated by private mineral and mixed ownership service capitalism. In 1970, mining and services combined contributed 79.2% of gross domestic product—mining 20.5%, services 58.7%—while employment in mining as a percentage of the labor force was 2.0% and in services was 53.2% (Mamalakis, 1977a: 280, 346). Within this mineral-service capitalism, it was mining that laid most of the golden eggs (exports, foreign exchange, saving, government revenues) and services that reaped most of the benefits. Extreme poverty for some groups, low income growth rates, and economic dependence were, however, also hallmarks of the old order.

The desired new DPO, so strongly advocated and pursued by President Carlos Andrés Pérez, was considered a central instrument in removing the stigma of underdevelopment. Within a stable and vigorous political democracy (Bond, 1977a: 231), it would be a major lever in erasing poverty and accelerating growth. A strategic role would be played by an employment-creating, import-substituting as well as export-promoting, industrial (and to a lesser extent agricultural) capitalism, in

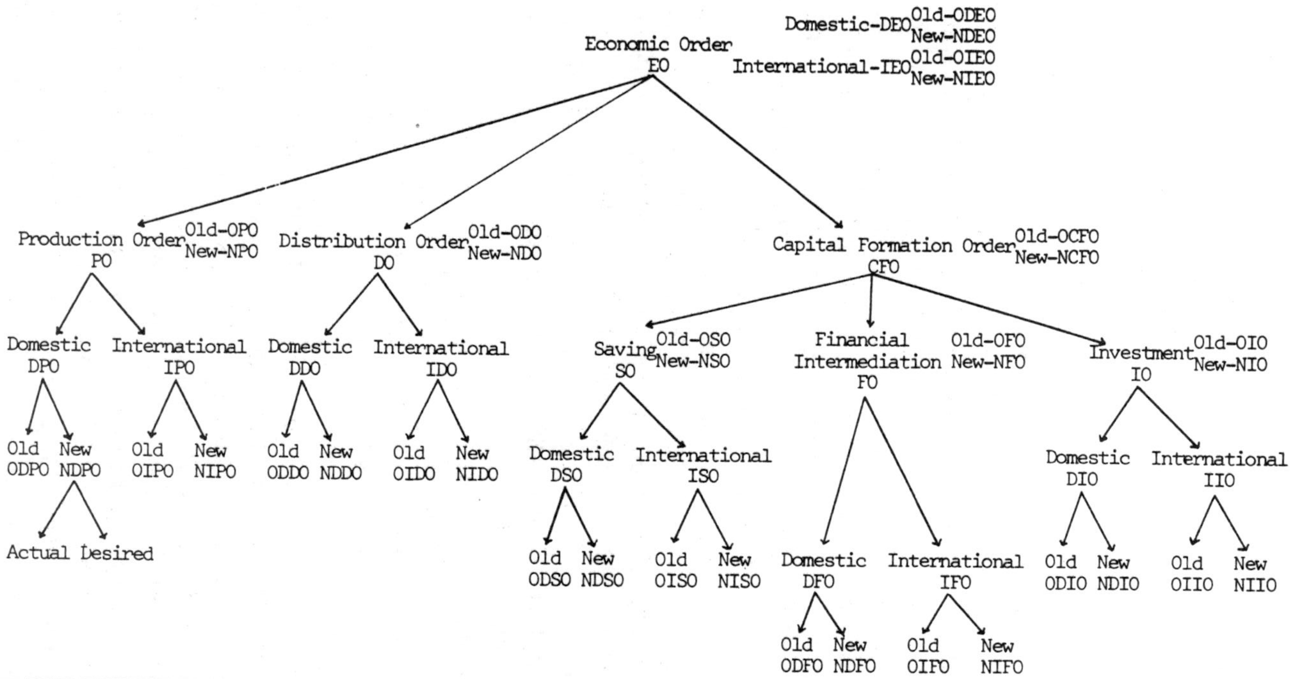


**Figure 1: International and Domestic Economic Orders and Their Components**

forming a NDEO capable of cushioning Venezuela from the inevitable demise of mineral capitalism as oil reserves became exhausted.

The DPO, which emerged immediately after the global shock of the 1973 oil price rise, can be considered transitional. This new DPO, shaped by the configuration of events triggered by OPEC, fell short of some and exceeded other goals contained in the blueprint for the desired new DPO.

The new international production order with its oil price bonanza was good, pragmatic politics and excellent economics for Venezuela. The master stroke shaping its foundations was the Venezuela-inspired solidarity among the OPEC nations. To Venezuela's leaders, support for the NIEO was a clear precondition for "the continued political effectiveness of OPEC" (Bond, 1977a: 244). Thus, Venezuela's NIEO campaign emerged as a natural extension of its oil diplomacy.

As oil prices more than quadrupled and the income share of mining spurted to 37% of GDP in 1974 (BCV, 1975: A-142), mineral capitalism seemed to take hold of Venezuela's destiny even more, not less, than before. Dependence on oil exports, saving, and government revenues became literally total. The present NIEO, especially production, emerged more mineral-based than the old.

The initial contribution of the 1973-1974 mineral boom to income generation and growth was formidable and unprecedented. GDP in curent prices rose from US$14.8 billion in 1972 to US$17.8 billion in 1973, soaring in 1974 to US$26.6 billion (BCV, 1975: A-131, table A-IV-1 converted).[4] Per capita income (GDP divided by population) rose by 17.0% from US$1,352.0 in 1972 to US$1,581.3 in 1973, then leaped upward in 1974 by an unprecedented 60.1% to US$2,545.0 (BCV, 1975: A-131, table A-IV-1; and IMF, 1976a: 408). Any doubts about the ability of mineral depletion and exports to contribute massively to extensive (aggregate) and intensive (per capita) income growth were dispelled by the events of 1973 and 1974.

The link between the existing and the desired domestic and international production orders is found in the price of oil.

For Venezuela, the desired NIEO would contain "just" and realistic prices for mineral exports. This goal of "just prices" (FIV, 1976: 4) had been fulfilled by 1974. The export price of a barrel of Venezuelan oil skyrocketed from US$2.93 in 1972 to US$14.06 in 1974 (MMH, 1975: 143). The oil price shock undermined the foundations of the OIPO, characterized by dominance of industry in the industrial nations, with their former stable but low oil prices. The new, "just" oil prices also laid the foundations of an interim NIPO characterized by global dominance of OPEC nations, dominance (political as well as economic) of Venezuela within Latin America, and international as well as domestic dominance of petroleum extraction (Mamalakis, 1971).

The actual NIPO has not been uniformly favorable to Third World countries. While the terms of trade for major oil exporters improved by 138% in 1974 (they had improved by 14% in 1973), for the non-oil developing countries they fell by 8% in 1974 and by 13% in 1975, for the major developed countries they deteriorated in each year between 1974 and 1976 (IMF, 1977: 11). The NIPO created by the post-1973 improvement in the terms of trade of oil is thus marked by a schism of the South, with the petroleum exporting nations enjoying just prices and the rest of the developing countries being told that the current petroleum golden age, which is financially intolerable to them, marks the transition to their own affluence and prosperity. However, this schism is real and pervasive, and most economic evidence suggests that high oil prices hinder rather than strengthen the development prospects of the nonpetroleum Latin American and other Third World nations. Massive worldwide unemployment, accelerated inflation, lower income growth rates, and a sharply declining value of the dollar, all largely but not exclusively caused by OPEC's oil price policies and a part of the actual NIPO, have only hindered economic recovery in the nonpetroleum Third World and solidified the income schism within the South.

These interim oil-based domestic and international production orders are viewed in Venezuela as the first step leading to its emancipation from external—political and economic—domination. In OPEC, according to President Pérez, Venezuela has found "a new negotiating power" which it intends to use as "an instrument . . . for the construction of this New International Economic Order. The increase in petroleum prices . . . represents . . . an irrevocable decision to dignify trade relations and to increase the value of goods and other basic products from Third World countries" (Pérez, 1976: 9-10).

Potential features distinguishing the desired new from the old international production order are many. They include, for the Third World, increased purchasing power, just and stable raw materials prices, self-sufficiency in—or at least increased—food production, a new global monetary order, a new legal order for the exploitation of the world's commons, and an integrated regional growth in Latin America.

Carlos Andrés Pérez views this desired NIPO to be a future certainty: "The New International Economic Order . . . has to be, and indeed will be the inevitable consequence of the new world political order" (Pérez, 1976; 10).

To turn this into a reality, Venezuela has helped in the creation and contributed to the International Fund for Agricultural Development; advocated a new global monetary system based on Special Drawing Rights (Pérez, 1976: 12); supported "UNCTAD's integrated program on raw materials" (Pérez, 1976: 11) and the common reserve fund; pursued the goal of nuclear disarmament and reduced production of armaments; promoted regional cooperation and integration in Latin America by strengthening the Latin American Economic System (SELA), the Cartagena Accord, and the Andean Pact (Pérez, 1976: 26-27). It strongly advocates the formulation of a new Law of the Sea with "a new judicial order governing the ocean depths outside the limits of national jurisdiction, areas which are the common heritage of mankind" (Pérez, 1976: 21); favors access to the sea for landlocked Bolivia (Pérez, 1976: 22); and has given total support to "wiping out the last traces of colonialism" by promoting "the signing of a new treaty between the United States and our Latin American sister republic which would fully restore the latter's sovereignty over the Canal Zone" (Pérez, 1976: 23).

Many, if not most, of the non-OPEC developing countries are worse off (sometimes considerably) in terms of income growth, balance of payments deficits, inflation, and external dependence under the new post-1973 IPS than under the old one. The damage caused to the truly poor nations by Venezuela's oil price policies has been rarely offset, and then only partially, by Venezuela's contributions to OPEC's Special Fund, the subsidy account of the International Monetary Fund (IMF), and loans to the oil facility of the IMF.

Economic development, political independence, and human dignity have seemed to require control over and mobilization of external as well as internal forces. The NIEO was the mechanism through which President Pérez and his government hoped to transform these external forces from causes of deprivation and exploitation into a base for achieving universal prosperity. In a narrower sense, the NIEO would help transform Venezuela's domestic production order. The post-1973 oil price increases turned a wild dream into an unexpected reality. The NIEO, with its spectacular increase in the value of oil exports, became an instrument of social, economic, and political change far more powerful than ever expected.

Carlos Andrés Pérez's government launched an ambitious program to augment industrial production, diversify exports, and enter new bilateral as well as multilateral trade agreements. Internal diversification of production in terms of sectors, regions, and inputs became a goal as well as an instrument for acquiring the modernization and self-transformation capacity indispensable for sustained growth. Venezuela's leaders were fully aware from the mineral experiences of guano in Peru, tin in Bolivia, and nitrate in Chile that lasting changes in the IPO could not occur without a major transformation in Venezuela's DPO through a modernizing industrialization as well as agricultural and service revolutions (educational, transportation, nutritional, institutional).

Venezuela did not aspire to be, nor could it prosper or even survive as, a rich democratic oil oasis surrounded by a hemispheric desert of poverty, narrow nationalism, dependence, and limited political and human rights. Carlos Andrés Pérez's dream, like Bolivar's, has been to create a Great Latin American Fatherland (Pérez, 1977: 14), a "Nation of Republics" (Pérez, 1977: 9), by integrating the small and the big, the poor and the rich. President Pérez proposed and hoped that the newly created (1975) Latin American Economic System (SELA) would serve as the pivotal instrument turning Latin America into the regional giant matching those of the North (USA), the West (European Economic Community), and the East (USSR; Pérez, 1977: 9) in strength, aspirations, and capacity to improve economic welfare of all its peoples.

SELA would serve (Bond, 1977b) as the jointly controlled vehicle for establishing the new, regionally integrated Latin American Economic Order (NLAEO) which would be capable of removing centuries-old bottlenecks inhibiting growth and also capable of cleansing Latin America of the inherited Old World vices (Pérez, 1977: 14) that are strangling sociopolitical progress. SELA would provide the umbrella for establishing Latin American multinational enterprises and projects in fertilizers, social housing for the underprivileged, technology networks, artisan development, and agricultural self-sufficiency (Pérez, 1977: 6-9).

Establishment of a new Venezuelan production order is regarded by Pérez as a precondition for the creation of a new Latin American economic order; and a NLAEO is in turn a precondition for a truly NIPO and NIEO. To President Pérez, the reverse was also true—that a NIEO was a precondition for a NLAEO and for a new Venezuelan domestic order.

A commonality of Latin American interests in establishing a NLAEO does, in fact, exist. Disagreement prevails, however, over the instruments to be used in creating the NLAEO. SELA is accepted by all, Venezuela's oil policy is not.

In a truly Venezuelan tradition, President Pérez is a pragmatic visionary. In his mind, when seeking to establish the NIEO, independence is the foremost goal not of each region, province, or country, but of Latin America as an integrated continent within an interdependent cosmos (Pérez, 1977: 12). Also, pragmatically, he envisages turning the New Order into reality, first within Venezuela and then within Latin America (Pérez, 1977: 13), without waiting for it to first become a "planetary reality" (Pérez, 1977: 13).

*The Distribution Order*

Nothing has changed since 1973 as sharply, profoundly, and decisively by actions of Venezuela as the IDO. As will be seen below, the actual NIEO has also had a major impact on the domestic distribution order.

As a consequence of the oil price increases, the distribution of world income between the First or Industrial World and the Third or Nonindustrial World was changed drastically after 1973 in favor of the latter. This North-South redistribution of income is measured by, as well as reflected in, a sharp and continuous rise in the volume of imports and value of exports by the Third World (IMF, 1977: 9).[5] The interworld redistribution coincided with, reflected, and followed a global sectoral redistribution of income from northern industry, services, and agriculture to southern oil mining.

This redistribution of global income has coincided with an intra-Third World income redistribution in favor of major oil exporters and against most other developing countries. The volume of imports by major oil exporters rose by an average of 26% per year between 1973 and 1976 (by an astonishing 42.5% in 1975), while it increased by only a meager 4.5% per year in the same period for the other developing countries (and actually fell by 6% in 1975; IMF, 1977: 9). Whether per capita income, real imports, value of exports, terms of trade, or their respective rates of growth are used as criteria, the old pre-1973 Third World has been split into the Rich South, composed of a privileged caste of oil exporting nations with Venezuela as a leader, and another world of paupers and outcasts composed of the other developing nations, also known as the Poor South or Fourth World. A less pronounced but still pervasive intra-First World or intra-north, redistribution of global income has also occurred (IMF, 1977: Table 1, p. 3).

Thus, in terms of the distribution of global income, the NIEO—more specifically, the NIDO—has been both good economics and good politics for Venezuela. However, it has been poor politics and dismal economics for most other Latin American countries which are suffering from deteriorating terms of trade for their exports.

Furthermore, since 1973, real, intraregional, intercountry resource flows have been redistributed within Latin America as a consequence of oil price increases and investment income from petroleum-consumption loans in favor of Venezuela (and to a much lesser extent in favor of Ecuador). The Intra-Latin American Redistribution of Income is manifested by a more than quadrupling in the value of Venezuelan exports (FOB) between 1972 ($3,782) and 1974 ($15,197), and a more than doubling of its imports (FOB) between 1972 ($2,222) and 1975 ($5,462; BCV, 1975: A-251).

Both the income and expenditure aspects of the IDO have been revamped since 1973, though not synchronously. The spectacular rise in the value of Venezuela's exports (primarily oil) was largely matched in 1973 and 1974 by an equally spectacular increase in its international financial assets of varying degrees of liquidity. Initially, Venezuela could not absorb all real resources commanded by its petrodollars, nor could the oil importing nations pay with real resources. Petrodollar accumulation was the first highly visible change in the international distribution order. Net international reserves of Venezuela's Central Bank snowballed from Bs.6,155 million in 1972 to Bs.36,429 million in 1975 (BCV, 1975: A-27). Initially, therefore, it was primarily monetary and real *income*, and only to a lesser extent monetary and real global *expenditures* (resource absorption), that was redistributed in favor of Venezuela. The change in the global monetary *income* distribution order ushered in the rise in Venezuela's real imports in 1975, 1976, and 1977, signifying a lagged adjustment in the money and real *expenditure* (resource flow) distribution order.

The NIDO had initially, therefore, a paradoxical, apparently contradictory impact depending on whether the income earned or expenditure-incurred distribution criterion is considered. The international distribution of monetary and real income turned decisively in favor of Venezuela since 1973 as improved terms of trade augmented the value of exports. Real global expenditures were also redistributed in favor of Venezuela, but hardly as much as income earned. Higher real imports still fell billions short of export values, or far below potential of export-based levels. The redistribution of money income in favor of Venezuela gave rise to spectacular export surpluses or an apparent release of resources (unfavorable to Venezuelan expenditure distribution) to the nations importing oil on a deferred-payment basis. All this happened because Venezuela's monetary gross domestic product rose sharply. This permitted an increase in the nation's real expenditures as manifested in rising real imports (favorable to Venezuelan international income distribution due to improved terms of trade). However, it also gave rise to a "temporary" release of a substantial part of the income increment to other nations (unfavorable to Venezuelan distribution of international income-expenditures). This, in turn, was manifested in large export and current account of a balance of payments surpluses.

The actual NIDO had a major impact on the DDO of Venezuela. Characteristically Venezuela has been a rentier country, but since 1973 it has become a par excellence rentier, or more accurately a minerals rentier country. It has raised its monetary and real income since 1973 not by producing and exporting more oil (quantity of production and exports of oil declined between 1973 and 1975), but by collecting increased oil consumption taxes from non-Venezuelan oil consumers. Oil depletion rents, which had a value proportional to oil consumption taxes collected from the rest of the world, were distributed in ever-increasing amounts to each and all of the Venezuelans, even favoring the poor (Urdaneta de Ferrán, 1977: 2, 3, 22).

Oil depletion rents have become a major determinant of aggregate as well as individual welfare and income overshadowing each of the classical determinants of income—land, labor, and physical capital. Using the surplus of exploitation in mining as a proxy for mineral rents, these rose from $2 billion or about 16% of GDP in 1971, to $10.7 billion and 35% of GDP in 1974 (calculated from data found in BCV, 1975: A-IV-2), by which date Venezuela's domestic distribution order was dominated by mineral rents.[6] A domestic minerals distribution order has emerged with all the class, sectoral, and regional features described by Mamalakis (1976a: 354-357; 1977b: 12-35; 1978: section on distribution). However, absolute poverty still exists, while relative poverty continues at a socially explosive level.

Assumption of world taxing power by Venezuela, as a leader of the petroleum exporting nations, has had a major catalytic impact, setting in motion forces which replace the old international distribution order. In the past, collecting taxes from foreign nations through the imposition of export levies was commonplace. Since 1973 the speed, magnitude, and collusive nature of oil taxes imposed upon and collected from the rest of the world by Venezuela have been unprecedented. Ordinary petroleum revenues of the Venezuelan central government rose from Bs.7,940 million in 1972 to Bs.36,508 million in 1974, before receding to Bs.31,648 in 1975 (BCV, 1975: A-V-14), almost all collected from foreign oil consumers.

Venezuela's global taxing authority, with its new-found strength, remains intrinsically linked to oil exports and oil consumption by foreign nations at continuously favorable terms of trade. It is product-based (oil) as well as sector-based (mining) and could be eroded by oil depletion, oil substitution, and diminishing collusion with other oil exporters, or it equally could be strengthened by concentrated expansion of the product base, exhaustion of alternative energy sources, or increasing collusion with other oil exporters. The current oil-tax-based international distribution order can thus only be as permanent and stable as the underlying collusive, product, and sectoral base.

It is impossible for all countries to have improved terms of trade for their export products. Any attempt, therefore, to generalize and extend Venezuela's highly selective and successful oil-linked global taxation system to most or all other exports of developing countries would lead to a deterioration in oil's terms of trade and therefore be self-defeating.

Venezuela has taken further steps in reshaping the world distribution order. Its action of reducing petroleum production from 3.366 million b/d (barrels per day) in 1973 to 2.294 million b/d in 1976 (BCV, June 1977: 77) has buttressed its oil price policy, solidified its global taxing power, and sustained the redistribution of income and to a lesser extent expenditures in its favor. It has been giving up less and getting much more. Real global welfare can hardly be improved, however, by either isolated or universal output-reducing policies, and Venezuela's action cannot serve as a positive paradigm—not even for depletable mineral exports—or provide a lasting pillar to any economic order. Further oil output reductions will reduce Venezuela's global role and can hasten the demise of the present, heavily oil-tax-based international economic order.

Many, if not most, of the events already described in the present section are byproducts of a selective nationalization policy leading to an internal as well as international ownership transformation. According to this policy, mineral resources and strategic industrial, service, and mining activities were reserved for government and/or national ownership. As the domestic ownership-distribution order was altered and this NDEO became an instrument in building the NIEO, the national (as against foreign) income share rose, mineral rents skyrocketed, and the already described redistribution of global, aggregate, sectoral, and factor income took place.

Ownership of oil and gas gave government the power to act as a world price maker rather than price taker, in collusion with other petroleum exporting nations. Furthermore, the tables were turned on the multinational oil corporations as well as the industrial giants of the North. It was now the Venezuelan state that manipulated the multinational corporations (which allegedly had controlled it in the past), using their worldwide marketing and distribution network to collect oil sales taxes from the remotest corners of the globe and from the "strongest" governments of industrialized nations. Without the multinational oil companies acting as extraterritorial tax-collecting agencies for the Venezuelan government and other OPEC members, the fabulous pro-OPEC income redistribution between 1973 and 1978 would never have materialized. The NIEO's stability, therefore, heavily rests on the continued ability of the Venezuelan government to use oil multinationals as its global tax collecting agencies. Thus, even though the tax power (or price decision) rests with OPEC, without the enforcement, implementation, and collection of oil taxes by foreign or Venezuelan-owned multinationals, the OPEC tax authority would mean little.

Some may call the OPEC-dominated era one of oil consumer exploitation by oil exporters. Others may label it the era of oil hegemony and imperialism. Either way, some trends of this era cannot continue. Changing the international distribution order through ever-improving terms of trade for petroleum eventually would be self-destructive. The underlying sectoral conflicts and income redistribution cannot be ignored. Superdominance of oil mining is bound to make the oil-tax-paying agriculture, industry, and services of the First and Fourth Worlds so anemic that they will either be forced to find a substitute for OPEC oil or languish into the deep depression capable of destroying the external dominance of Venezuela's oil sector.

The NIDO has changed global income distribution, but it cannot be argued convincingly that it has improved it. Global income inequalities are actually deeper in the new than under the old order. And no order has long-term survival probabilities unless it reduces, not merely changes, global per capita income inequalities.

Furthermore, although Venezuela's rent distribution pattern is equitable in that it favors the poor, the rampant absolute poverty in its own back yard is still intolerable. No new DDO can be in the projected Bolivarian image of justice or compassion when the poorest 30% enjoy less than 5% of income. Long-term progress cannot be achieved unless both the income and mineral rent distribution patterns are such as to provide strong stimuli for the global, regional and domestic accumulation of scarce, growth-promoting capital forms.

## *The Capital Formation Order*

The capital formation order consists of and is shaped by the national and international saving, financial intermediation, and investment suborders (Mamalakis, 1976a: 244-290, 358-365). The shocks unleashed by Venezuela and OPEC since 1973 have changed visibly and profoundly each of these capital formation suborders.

### *THE SAVING ORDER*

The oil price increases of 1974-1977 have ushered in a new era of the world saving process. A new international saving order (ISO) has been established, characterized by a massive increase in national saving by Venezuela (and other OPEC countries), a lagged, largely partial increase in domestic saving (investment), and lending of the surplus (excess of national over domestic) savings by the Venezuela-OPEC bloc to the rest of the world. The surplus national savings of the OPEC group (measured by their balance of payments current account surplus), which was largely lent to other nations, rose tenfold from US$6.2 billion in 1973 to US$66.7 billion in 1974 (IMF, 1976b: 13). The major oil exporting nations thus became the largest international lenders and aid donors to the rest of the world in history.

The domestic saving order (DSO) of Venezuela has also been transformed. The phenomenal rise in petroleum revenues, income, resource surpluses, and saving have increased aggregate saving to levels that could not be absorbed, at least in the short run, by domestic investment (saving). As the surplus of exploitation (nonwage income) in Venezuela climbed from US$9.2 billion in 1973 to US$19.1 billion in 1974 (BCV, 1975: table A-IV-1, p. A-

131, converted), national saving almost doubled from US$5.9 billion in 1973 to US$11.7 billion in 1974 (BCV, 1975: table A-IV-1, p. A-131, converted). Of this increase in national saving, 83% can be explained by the rise in government saving, which spurted by more than 400% from US$1.4 billion in 1973 to US$6.3 billion in 1974 (BCV, 1975: table A-V-8, p. A-202, converted; Mamalakis, 1976b). Venezuela's new, actual DSO was totally oil-based and government controlled.

To harness the masses of black gold pouring into the coffers of the Venezuelan government, on June 21, 1974, President Carlos Andrés Pérez created the Venezuelan Investment Fund (Fondo de Inversiones de Venezuela—FIV) with an initial capital endowment of US$3.0 billion.[7] The Fund's fabulous investable resources were generated by mining (oil and gas) exports, not agriculture or industry. The Investment Fund became the depository and manager of global oil sales taxes imposed and collected by the Venezuelan government in collusion with the other OPEC nations.

In the divided South of the post-1973 era, the rich South relishes massive surplus national (oil-derived) savings, while the petroleum-poor South reels under the impact of (oil-reinforced) deficit national savings, i.e., national savings falling significantly short of domestic investment. The saving surplus of Venezuela, which was equal to US$851 million or 14.5% of national saving in 1973, skyrocketed to US$6 billion or 51.7% of national saving in 1974 (BCV, 1975: table A-IV-1, p. A-131, converted), and was lent abroad largely through the Venezuelan Investment Fund. Venezuela's surplus of the nation on current account (negative foreign saving) was also equal to US$6 billion in 1974 (BCV, 1975: table A-IV-1, p. A-131, converted), but has been reduced drastically in 1976 and 1977.

Venezuela's actual new DSO is also totally dependent on oil depletion, continued favorable terms of trade for oil, and global acceptance of oil consumption taxes. It is a saving order controlled by sectoral (oil) savings where the volition of income classes or groups (households, firms, and foreigners) carries secondary weight. Its life expectancy is likely to be equal to that of petroleum depletion saving, which is nonreproducible. Venezuela's desired new DSO envisages a rising importance of reproducible savings by agriculture, industry, and services as well as by households and firms, but not by foreigners.

The actual new ISO is also heavily dependent on mineral savings, national and foreign, which have largely displaced the traditional savings by industry, agriculture, and services. The national savings shortfall of the "other primary producing countries," which was equal to US$8.7 billion in 1973 and was largely covered by surplus savings of the industrial West, climbed to US$42.9 billion in 1974 and was totally filled by OPEC's surplus petrosavings (IMF, 1976b: 13). Even the industrial countries developed a national saving deficit in 1974 (but not in 1975), covering it with surplus mineral savings from the rich petroleum South (IMF, 1976b: 13).

Venezuela redistributed some of its oil riches and savings to needy countries. It contributed $224 million to OPEC's Special Aid Fund of $1.6 billion, which was established at Venezuela's initiative in 1977 to provide interest-free loans to developing countries with resources that would amount to "about 8% of each OPEC member's expected oil revenues" for that year (FIV, 1977b: 21). Venezuela also granted $100 million to the UN Emergency Program, which assisted weaker countries of the international community (FIV, 1977b: 22). President Pérez's rationale for this minimal international sharing is found in his statement that "International economic hypocrisy has a name: Aid. It will never be a source of revenue necessary for development—that can only be obtained by just and equitable terms of trade" (Pérez, 1976: 13).

### *THE FINANCIAL INTERMEDIATION ORDER*

In terms of financial intermediation, a new international economic order was born in 1973. On a global level, the existing intermediation of NIFO is characterized by the overwhelming presence of petrocredits and petroaid ($67 billion in 1974, $41 billion in 1976), by the rich petroworld to non-oil-developing countries ($44 billion in 1974, $40 billion in 1976), as well as industrial countries ($10 billion in 1974, $1 billion in 1976; IMF, 1977: 13).[8] At the regional level of Latin America and the Caribbean, petrocredits had to be extended to cover their phenomenal current account deficits: $13.1 billion in 1974, $16.3 billion in 1975, and $11.2 billion in 1976, as compared tc $4.5 billion in 1973 (IMF, 1977: 15), largely but not exclusively caused by Venezuela's and OPEC's oil price policy.

In part forced by circumstances, in part on its own volition, Venezuela has assumed a major role in international financial intermediation since 1973. As world money and real income were redistributed in its favor, with money and real domestic expenditures lagging significantly behind,[9] large current account surpluses emerged. Venezuela had a choice of either giving back unrequited transfers or lending back the nonabsorbable oil consumer taxes it had collected. It opted for the latter.

As we have already seen, the government owned and controlled Investment Fund became the guardian and distributor-lender of most of the government's surplus oil taxes. With the lion's share held abroad to prevent domestic inflation, Venezuela launched its "International Financial Cooperation" program and emerged as a lender-creditor to the United States, the World and Inter-American Development Banks, and the International Monetary Fund, not only through the Venezuelan Investment Fund but also through its Central Bank, the Treasury, and the Ministry of Foreign Affairs (FIV, 1977a: 41-58; FIV, 1977b: 1-25). Above all, a novel network of inter-American financial interaction mechanisms has been created in which Venezuela as a creditor in the center is surrounded by the multitude of petrocredit-dependent Caribbean, Central and South American countries. A credit dependence, derived from the original oil dependence, has emerge as a central feature of the NIFO.

Within the NIFO, which was largely shaped by and served Venezuela's objectives, financial cooperation assumed multiple goals. First, financial assistance became an instrument promoting Venezuela's petroleum price policy (FIV, 1977b: 4) which was a cornerstone of the new international income distribution order, so favorable to Venezuela. Oil credits were to be recycled to those paying or promoting the payment of oil taxes to Venezuela. According to the second goal, which at least in part contradicted the first, financial assistance would be used "to encourage international solidarity" and "to build a common front" among developing countries "to defend the prices of raw materials" (FIV, 1977b: 4). An international economic order in which prices of all or most nonoil raw materials were to be raised would, by definition, at least partially reverse the prevailing terms of trade and be less advantageous to Venezuela than the current oil-based order. There is not much evidence that this second goal has been pursued beyond the verbal stage.

The third and most ambitious goal was to use financial assistance to transform the global and regional production orders. Part of the global income redistributed to Venezuela would be used to bring forth a new Latin American production order by increasing productive capacity, strengthening Latin American integration, and promoting commercial interchange between Venezuela and the other Central and South American countries (FIV, 1977b: 4). This goal has been vigorously pursued. The Venezuelan Investment Fund, emerging as a global investment bank, has engaged in lending through bank-to-bank, bank-to-state, bank-to-state agencies, bank-to-development institutions, bank-to-multistate agencies, and bank-to-regional agencies.

Through the Inter-American Development Bank, the Fund has recycled petrodollars to Costa Rica (fishing), Ecuador (cement), Guatemala (hydroelectric power), Peru (industry), and Jamaica, Argentina, Chile, Brazil, and Mexico (export credits; FIV, 1977b: 9). It has financed the development of resources, agriculture, industry, agroindustry, agroforestry, tourism, and export promotion through the Central American Bank for Economic Integration (FIV, 1977b: 12). Through the Caribbean Development Bank it has channeled surplus oil funds to Guyana (small industries), Jamaica (development bank), and the Bahamas (water sewerage; FIV, 1977b: 11). It also agreed, through Economic Cooperation Agreements with the Central American

Central Banks, to "provide them with the financing of Balance of Payments deficits," with the respective credits to be used in turn to finance economic development programs and projects.[10] It has also promoted regional development through the Bank of Jamaica and the Interamerican Savings and Loans Bank (IASLD).[11]

Between January 1, 1974 and December 31, 1977, Venezuela had extended credits abroad equivalent to $2.5 billion (FIV, 1977b: 25) through its international financial cooperation program. These credits accounted for only a part of its current account surplus. It was expected that the petrodollars converted into petrocredits abroad would be ultimately converted into scarce domestic capital forms.

Noneleemosynary in nature, these credits had earned for Venezuela more than half a billion dollars (FIV, 1977b: 23) by January 1977 as they commanded the almost usurious and often minimum rate of 8% (FIV, 1977b: 6, 8, 10, 12, 14). I say usurious not only because of its high level, but primarily because these credits support oil consumption, which sustains but hardly augments productive capacity. By not being self-liquidating, these loans postpone but do not solve the oil-payment problem. NIFO, so onerous to oil consumers, has not emerged because Venezuela aimed to exploit the already helpless oil buyers, but because its leaders, so new in the game of global credits and aid, wanted to protect the new-found wealth. The fund was a manager and creditor, not an aid donor. Many recipients could not afford credits, however; they needed outright gifts.

The Investment Fund enabled Peru to defer oil-tax payments by financing at an 8% interest rate through the Banco de la Nación del Perú "the excess over US$6.00 in the price of every 10.000 barrel daily of oil imported" from the state-owned petroleum corporation of Venezuela or Ecuador (FIV, 1977b: 19). But unless Peru strikes it rich in oil, payment of these deferred taxes appears most unlikely.

The "minerals financial intermediation system" of the NIEO, where petro current account surpluses finance the deficits of oil importing nations, is promoted by all nations (both oil-tax collecting and paying) in an effort to minimize the dislocations, including possible bankruptcy, of the victims of this taxation. Both Venezuela and the other OPEC nations are returning in the form of credits, within and as part of the NIFO, part of the global oil taxes collected to the payors to prevent their default and enable them to continue making their tax payments. Sooner rather than later, however, the NIFO may have to accommodate the conversion of noncollectable petrocredits into outright petrogrants.

### *THE INVESTMENT ORDER*

Central features of Venezuela's pre-1973 investment order were a relative abundance of mineral and unskilled human and —since 1958—political capital; a shortage of physical, skilled human, and even social capital; and an inadequate conversion of the abundant oil into strategic scarce capital forms. The defects in the domestic investment order resulted in part from a low investment absorption and oil conversion capacity as a consequence of a human factor bootleneck, and in part from an allegedly unjust international investment order dominated by physical capital produced by industry in the modern, advanced countries and in which valuable, nonrenewable mineral capital was delivered by the South to the North at very low prices. Venezuela, whether or not ruled by a mineral-based plutocracy, had remained for too long a consumption-oriented society.

Recent Venezuelan leaders aspired (a) to bring about a new IIO which assigned an increased value to mineral (oil) capital, (b) to use this IIO as a springboard to transform the old DIO into a new one, and (c) to exert through Venezuela's new DIO continued influence and control over the ever-changing IIO.

The external bottleneck had been removed by 1974. Within a drastically changed IIO, the industrial North paid dearly for Venezuela's oil capital, which had more than quadrupled in value, and the rate of decumulation of oil capital had become the world's pivot. Internally, Venezuelan leaders faced three choices: to squander their petrowealth on (luxury) consumption (of imports), drown in a sea of petrodollars, or increase the conversion of petrocapital into scarce capital forms.

The "Sow the Oil" manifesto became the Magna Carta of the desired new domestic investment order. Formulated by Juan Pablo Perez Alfonso, the father of OPEC, using an expression coined by Arturo Uslar Pietri in 1936 (VN-DOC, 1977: 130), "sowing the oil" became a declaration of intentions as well as a symbol of hope. It proclaimed, above all, the necessity of accelerated conversion of oil capital depleted into investment in strategic inputs, sectors, and regions, including reinvestment in the oil sector.

Investment in human capital became the cornerstone of a manpower policy concentrating on the conversion of petrocapital into those scientific and technical skills essential for the government's development strategy. The goal was to improve the quality of a rapidly rising population. Under the celebrated multimillion-dollar *Gran Mariscal de Ayacucho* fellowship program, some 11,000 students were being trained in 1977: 43% in Venezuelan universities and the remainder in foreign universities—the United States, 32%; France, 4%; Mexico, 3%; Italy and Canada, 2%. They were enrolled in such priority fields as petroleum engineering, geology, and agriculture. Not since Peter the Great has a country launched such a Promethean effort of sending its youth to master the elements of progress in Western civilization.

A program to increase sharply the stock of physical capital in selected branches of agriculture, mining (hydrocarbons), industry, transportation (cargo carriers), storage (silos), and so forth was formulated and is being gradually implemented. Criteria listed as having been used in setting priorities were the traditional ones of maximum social productivity, import substitution, and employment creation as well as those of decentralization, export promotion, and regional diversification (FIV, 1977a: 18, 20, 22, 24, 25, 35). Novel but not surprising was largely implicit reliance on the "new international economic order investment criterion" which ranked projects according to their ability to create a new domestic and international (production, distribution, capital formation) economic order (FIV, 1977a:

20, 29-31). Scrupulously avoided were the unbalanced growth strategies which had given rise to destructive sectoral and regional conflicts elsewhere in Latin America.

However, unemployment and underemployment, as well as urban misery belts and income inequality, are likely to persist since the effective investment criteria revealed by actual projects (FIV, 1977a: 17-36) as having been used are those of capital, technology, and materials intensity and large-scale rather than labor absorption. A heavy dependence on capital goods imports will also emerge, while emphasis on government ownership definitely does not stimulate the indispensable private initiative (see also Bond, 1977a: 240).

In sectoral terms, the blueprint for the new DIO gave mild preference to an accelerated industrialization, with the Venezuelan Investment Fund "sowing the oil" in the basic mineral- and oil-based iron and steel, cement, chemical, petrochemical, and even metallurgical branches in which Venezuela had a comparative advantage. Preference was given during the 1975-1976 biennium to the iron and steel, aluminum, shipping, and cement industries (FIV, 1977a: 17-18).

The giant-to-be iron and steel industry was assigned the multiple role of reducing dependence on steel imports, satisfying the requirements of a rapidly growing industry (automotive, petroleum, combustion engine, electrical machinery, and metal mechanical) and construction, creating employment, diversifying exports, and placing Venezuela's steel producers in the frontier of Andean Pact countries, as well as among the world's top 20. Similar tasks, on only a slightly less grandiose scale, were given to the aluminum, cement, and maritime transportation industries (FIV, 1977a: 22-24, 27, 32).

Already plagued by regional imbalances and in order to avoid the internal North-South, urban-rural ruptures tearing at the foundations of so many developing nations, a blueprint for a regionally balanced new DIO was also formulated and is being implemented. Regional growth poles have been seeded in outlying provinces, regions, and cities in an effort to stem, if not reverse, the human and capital flight that had turned Caracas into a hydrocephalic service—industry living off the oil metropolis. Oil savings were being plowed into a rapidly growing iron and steel complex in Zulia and Táchira (FIV, 1977a: 22), a metal-mechanic complex was emerging in the region of Guayana (FIV, 1977a: 30), aluminum plants were located in Guacara and the city of Guayana, and a complex of yards for the maintenance, repair, modification, and construction of ships and their machines was being built in the peninsula of Paraguaná in the state of Falcón (FIV, 1977a: 25-26). As these investments established a new DEO, Venezuela was expected to become a major competitor in Latin American and global markets, not only to Colombia and Chile but also to the United States.

Multibillion petroinvestments were also channeled toward nationalization of the thorn-in-the-eye, primarily American-owned, multinational oil and iron ore producers, along with Canadian-owned electric energy generating companies. Together they had allegedly exercised in the past a controlling influence over the nation's political, social, and economic destiny (FIV, 1977a: 31). Only thus could Venezuela achieve its goal of controlling global interdependence rather than just managing it.

## *Concluding Remarks*

The NIEO issues are complicated, diverse, and often unclear (Hesse, 1977). Thus, in a world as heterogeneous and diverse as ours, a variety of perceptions of the actual, and especially the desired, economic orders is most likely.

In order to examine Venezuela's role and goals vis-à-vis the NIEO, the international and domestic orders were subdivided into production, distribution, and capital formation suborders; their old and new, actual and desired forms were defined and contrasted; and the interactions among them were explored.

Even though many NIEO issues or events have multiple, interrelated, and complicated effects on production distribution and capital formation, I have tried to distinguish these as clearly and carefully as possible in the various sections. Where I have been successful or not, only the reader can decide.

Whether initiative or impact of action is the criterion used, Venezuela has played an unmistakable role in destroying the OIEO and creating a new one. In summary, the highly visible impact of its actions (the more relevant measure) on the production, distribution, and capital formation dimensions of the international and domestic orders is as follows.

*Production Order: improved terms of trade for oil, but only slow, selective progress elsewhere.* Achievement of "just" oil prices for Venezuela and other oil exporters is the earmark of both NIEO and NIPO. Oil-based and oil-oriented, the NIPO has massively improved the economic welfare of Venezuela and other oil exporters. However, it is only the potential to achieve economic development that Venezuela has acquired as a consequence of higher oil export prices, oil consumption taxes and mineral depletion rents, not economic development itself. Soaring oil purchasing power (a higher budget) permits but does not guarantee acquisition and absorption of technology and human (skills, education) and physical capital which are the basic determinants of lasting welfare.

The actual gains in transforming and diversifying domestic production are still understandably modest, but promise to accelerate. From the perspective of the non-OPEC world, which is plagued by inflation, unemployment, balance of payments disequilibria, mounting inequalities, and slow growth, Venezuela's order-building oil price actions can hardly be considered as constructive or progressive, but also not, by any means, intentionally malevolent.

*Distribution Order: spectacular gains for Venezuela as oil tax revenues and rents balloon.* As a consequence of the sharply higher oil rents collected by Venezuela within OPEC, world income and, to a lesser extent, expenditures have been redistributed from the North to the South, from the petroleum-poor to the petroleum-rich South, and from almost all other Americas to Venezuela and Ecuador. Venezuela has only minimally shared its petrorents and prosperity with other Latins or the least developed nations.

The prevailing global as well as domestic Venezuelan oil rent distribution orders can function as the steppingstone to unbounded progress and prosperity or as a trap for a parasitic, wasteful, and profligate existence. Although Venezuelan leaders have opted for the path of progress, success depends on the obstacle-surrounded development plan implementation phase currently underway.

*Capital Formation Order: some bottlenecks removed, but the Promethean challenges still lie ahead.* Removal of the saving constraint for the privileged oil exporting nations (and a correspondingly stronger saving bottleneck for most Fourth World countries) is the central feature of NICFO and NISO. Furthermore, within the NIFO Venezuela, along with most other OPEC nations, has emerged as an international petrocreditor, returning part of oil taxes to the payors in the form of credits and, less frequently, as grants.

The unresolved challenge is to achieve a maximum and continuous conversion of petroleum capital being depleted into scarce human, physical, and technological capital and to achieve a permanent petroboom through the development of its oil resources, especially in the Orinoco Oil Belt.

Fortune rarely strikes twice in a generation. Venezuela capitalized fully on the Arab-Israeli conflict and the 1969-1973 prosperity to extract fabulous riches from oil consumers through taxes. Although Venezuela's projects and plans are, as we have seen, almost overambitious, it is still not clear whether its fabulous mineral rents will serve as the Promethean source of long-lasting Venezuelan prosperity or a fatal siren song luring the recipients into inactivity or wrong activity in critical bottleneck areas.

The illusion of permanent prosperity radiating from ephemeral mineral booms, which in the past lulled nitrate-rich Chile and guano-rich Perú into relative inaction or wrong type of action, still poses the main obstacle in fulfilling Venezuela's dreams. President Carlos André Pérez's call is for action. The political, social, and external winds are favorable. If implementation fails, even should external factors continue to be blamed, such voices, like those of the sirens' victims, will not be believed nor heard, and the Venezuelan government will have defaulted on what it has perceived to be the mandate of Bolívar. The New International Economic Order, with its payment of fabulous oil taxes by oil consumers, will not have served Venezuela, Latin America, or humanity.

## NOTES

1. Highly informative and balanced political, historical, and, to a lesser degree, economic background information about Venezuela is found in Tugwell (1975) and in the essays by Levine, Kuczynski, Tugwell, Fuad, Martz, and Bond in Bond (1977a).

2. The production-distribution-capital formation framework, given global scope here in order to investigate the role of Venezuela in the IEO, was developed by Mamalakis (1976a: 345-365) to analyze the domestic economic order and growth of Chile.

3. The terms used for these orders, except those of the OIEO and the NIEO, are newly minted here to examine the views and strategies of Venezuelan leaders. They have not been used by them and are not attributed to them.

4. The term "converted" is used in citations to indicate that the original statistical information was expressed in Venezuelan bolivars (Bs) and was converted into U.S. dollars for purposes of this essay at the official and free exchange rate of US$1 = Bs 4.285.

5. For a more detailed analysis of the various definitions of international distribution of income, see Mamalakis (1976a: 228-232; 1977b: 18-31).

6. I have used the surplus of exploitation in mining as the proxy for mineral rents.

7. The Venezuelan Investment Fund will also be referred to as FIV, Fondo de Inversiones de Venezuela, the fund, and the Investment Fund. See also Pérez (1975).

8. The older international financial intermediation order (OIFO) was characterized, in contrast, by industrial country credits of much smaller scale (an average of $10.2 billion during 1967-1972), primarily to less developed nonoil countries (an average of $8.1 billion during 1967-1972), but also to more developed nonoil nonindustrial countries (an average of $1.7 billion during 1967-1972; IMF, 1977: 13). Petrocredits (always measured by the surplus of current account in the balance of payments of major oil exporting countries) were only a miniscule annual average of $10.7 billion during 1967-1972 (IMF, 1977: 13).

9. Domestic expenditures were either deliberately constrained, due to low domestic investment absorption capacity in an effort to prevent inflation and wasteful consumption, or because oil consumers could not release resources to pay for their oil imports.

10. In Costa Rica—highways, fishing, docks, roads, agriculture; El Salvador—hydro-

electric power sugar mills, Guatemala—hydroelectric power; Honduras, Nicaragua—light and energy; Panama—electrification (FIV, 1977b: 13-16).

11. In Jamaica, support was provided for investments in roads, highways, rural electrification, airports, sites and services, and water supplies (FIV, 1977b: 17-18). Through IASLD, funds were provided to the Agricultural Credit Bank of Cartago (Costa Rica), the Ecuadorian Housing Bank, and Central Saving and Loan Cash for Housing (Bolivia; FIV, 1977b: 20).

## REFERENCES


BCV [Banco Central de Venezuela] (1977) Boletin Mensual 401 (Junio). Caracas: BCV.

——— (1976) Informe Economico 1975. Caracas: BCV.

——— (1975) Informe Economico 1974. Caracas: BCV.

BOND, R. D. [ed.] (1977a) Contemporary Venezuela and Its Role in International Affairs. New York: A Council on Foreign Relations Book, New York University Press.

——— (1977b) "Regionalism in Latin America: prospects for the Latin American Economic System (SELA)." Paper prepared for the research project on "Conflict and cooperation in the Americas." Washington, DC: Woodrow Wilson International Center for Scholars, funded by the External Research Office of the Department of State.

CLERC, J. P. (1977) "The difficult art of 'sowing oil'." Documentación, Venezuela Now (May 30): 130. New York: Venezuelan Mission to the United Nations. [Reprint from Le Monde]

FIV [Fondo de Inversiones de Venezuela] (1977a) Memoria y Cuenta 1976 (March). Caracas: FIV.

——— (1977b) International Financial Cooperation. Caracas: FIV.

——— (1976) Fondo de Inversiones de Venezuela. Caracas: FIV.

HART, J. (1977) "Latin American policies toward the New International Economic Order." Paper prepared for the research project on "Conflict and cooperation in the Americas." Washington, DC: Woodrow Wilson International Center for Scholars.

HESSE, H. (1977) "The New International Economic Order—the discussion in outline." German Econ. Rev. 15: 1-11.

IMF [International Monetary Fund] (1977) Annual Report 1977. Washington, DC: IMF.

——— (1976a) International Financial Statistics XXIX (January).

——— (1976b) Annual Report 1976. Washington, DC: IMF.

MAMALAKIS, M. (forthcoming) "La teoria mineral de crecimiento: la experiencia Latinoamericana." El Trimestre Economico.

——— (1977a) "Urbanizacion y transformaciones sectoriales en Latinoamerica. Antecedentes e implicaciones para una reforma urbana," pp. 269-347 in J. E. Hardoy and Richard P. Schaedel (eds.) Asentamientos urbanos y organizacion socioproductiva en la historia de America Latina. Buenos Aires: Sociedad Interamericana de Planificacion (SIAP).

——— (1977b) "The minerals theory of growth: the Latin American evidence." Paper presented at Fifth World Congress of the International Economic Association, Tokyo, 29 August-3 September.

——— (1976a) The Growth and Structure of the Chilean Economy: From Independence to Allende. New Haven and London: Yale Univ. Press.

——— (1976b) "A mineral creation: the Venezuelan investment fund." Discussion paper 14. Göttingen, Germany: University of Göttingen, Ibero-Amerika Institut.

——— (1971) "The theory of sectoral clashes and coalitions revisited." Latin American Research Rev. 6 (Fall): 89-126.

MMH [República de Venezuela, Ministerio de Minas e Hidrocarburos, Dirección General, Oficina de Economía Petrolera] (1975) Petroleo y Otrós Datos Estadísticos 1974. Caracas: Ministerio de Minas e Hidrocarburos.

PEREZ, C. A. (1977) EL SELA. Afortunado Complemento de la Integración Latinoamericana. Discurso pronunciado en la instalación de la tercera reunión del Sistema Económico Latinoamericano. Caracas: Ministerio de Información y Turismo, 22 de marzo.

——— (1976) "A new economic order is essential for world peace." November 16 address to the UN General Assembly. Caracas: Ministerio de Información y Turismo.

——— (1975) Message to Congress by Venezuelan President Carlos Andrés Pérez on Completion of the Year of Special Powers, June 4. Caracas: Oficina Central de Información.

TUGWELL, F. (1975) The Politics of Oil in Venezuela. Stanford, CA: Stanford Univ. Press.

TREVERTON, G. F. (1977) "Economic interest and political ambition in Latin America's external relations: Brazil, Mexico, and Venezuela." Paper prepared for the research project on "Conflict and cooperation in the Americas." Washington, DC: Woodrow Wilson International Center for Scholars.

URDANETA DE FERRAN, L. (1977) "Effect of public expenditure on income distribution in Venezuela." Paper prepared for the York Conference of the International Association for Research in Income and Wealth. Caracas: Central Bank of Venezuela.

VN-DOC [Documentacion, Venezuela Now] (1977) "The difficult art of 'sowing oil'."

*Markos Mamalakis, a native of Greece, received his training in law, politics, and economics at the Universities of Salonica, Munich, and California—Berkeley. Currently a professor of economics at the University of Wisconsin—Milwaukee, he has held previous appointments at the Universities of California—Berkeley, Yale, Chile, and Göttingen. His first monograph on economic growth in Latin America,* The Theory of Sectoral Clashes *and* Coalitions in Essays on the Chilean Economy, *was published in 1965, and his latest book is* The Growth and Structure of the Chilean Economy: From Independence to Allende *(Yale, 1976). For these and other books and many articles, Dr. Mamalakis has received numerous awards and honors.*

**ROBERTO JUNGUITO**
*FEDESARROLLO*
*Apartado Aéreo 20513*
*Bogotá, Colombia*

# *LATIN AMERICA AND THE PRIMARY PRODUCT TRADE*

The impact on Latin American economies stemming from recent developments of the primary product markets is analyzed in this article. Brief comments are also offered on the political stands these countries have adopted or are considering adopting as a result of the ongoing dialogue taking place at both the academic and political levels on the new international economic order.

Rather than pursue the traditional route of first reviewing major problems that primary product trade has imposed on economic development efforts and then recounting alternative control schemes adopted in primary trade, this article focuses primarily on the degree to which Latin America is dependent on primary products as a source of foreign exchange earnings, and second on the influence, relative to other developing countries (LDCs), that primary products have had on foreign earnings, export instability, and terms of trade.

Journal of Interamerican Studies and World Affairs, Vol. 20 No. 3, August 1978

### *Primary Products and Their Importance in Latin American Exports*

Primary products have been extremely important not only in Latin American trade but also in the trade flow of all developing countries. Some authors argue that the problem of trade in LDCs is synonymous to the problem that primary products face in world markets, in that these countries are heavily dependent on primary products as a major source of exports (Singh, 1976: 87). What requires analysis, then, is not simply a definition of whether or not primary products are important to international trade, but whether Latin America depends to a greater extent than expected on the international trade of these products.

To answer this question, the methodology first focuses on the expected dependency share of primary products at different per capita income levels and then compares the actual behavior of each Latin American country (LAC) with the norm.

Levels of the expected "normal" patterns are derived from a recent study identifying both the typical patterns of total good and nonfactor service export shares as a proportion of the Gross Domestic Product (GDP), as well as the actual share of primary exports on GDP at different per capita income levels (Chenery and Syrquin, 1975: 20).[1] By dividing the actual by the normal shares, it is possible to obtain a measurement of the extent a country or region deviates from the international average.[2]

The second step is to estimate both the primary export share and the per capita income level for every LAC (Table 1) and compare it with the expected norm (Figure 1).[3] The table presents two alternative concepts of the primary share as well as the GDP per capita data for each country. Column 1 shows the primary share as a proportion of total merchandise exports, while the second column, strictly comparable to the norm, presents the primary share in regard to total goods and nonfactor service exports.

The results reflect the expected course to the extent that the higher income countries (except Venezuela) tend to show lower primary export shares. The majority of the LACs, however, show

TABLE 1
Export Shares of Primary Products in Latin American Trade, 1973-1975

| COUNTRY | PRIMARY SHARE IN MERCHANDISE EXPORTS (1) | PRIMARY SHARE IN TOTAL GOOD AND NFS EXPORTS (2) | GDP PER CAPITA (U.S. DOLLARS) (3) |
|---|---|---|---|
| Argentina | 44.6 | 38.1 | 1.550 |
| Bolivia | 87.0 | 79.7 | 360 |
| Brazil | 48.2 | 45.4 | 1.030 |
| Chile | 74.7 | 68.5 | 990 |
| Colombia | 71.5 | 58.6 | 580 |
| Costa Rica | 71.1 | 58.2 | 960 |
| Dominican Republic | 74.2 | 64.0 | 720 |
| Ecuador | 84.8 | 79.7 | 590 |
| El Salvador | 62.5 | 56.4 | 460 |
| Guatemala | 59.4 | 49.3 | 570 |
| Haiti | 56.1 | 38.3 | 190 |
| Honduras | 84.2 | 76.4 | 360 |
| Mexico | 40.7 | 19.4 | 1.050 |
| Nicaragua | 65.4 | 48.5 | 700 |
| Panama | 81.5 | 26.0 | 1.290 |
| Paraguay | 46.1 | 39.6 | 580 |
| Peru | 84.9 | 70.6 | 760 |
| Uruguay | 62.4 | 49.8 | 1.300 |
| Venezuela | 97.8 | 92.4 | 2.280 |

SOURCES: Col. 1: IBRD, *Community Trade and Price Trends* (1977).
Col. 2: Col. 1 x merchandise to total good export share, IBRD, *World Tables 1976*.
Col. 3: IBRD, *World Bank Atlas 1977*.

that the primary shares are above the corresponding expected norm. The major conclusion is that Latin America as a group tends to be overly dependent on primary commodities as a source of export earnings.

Whether such excessive dependence in primary exports is inherited from the past or whether it is a recent development is a question worth asking. The easiest procedure is to compare how fast primary shares decline for the LACs as a group related to increased income levels, with the expected decline derived from the international sample of countries.

The norms derived from the Chenery-Syrquin study suggest that the income elasticity of decline of the primary export share for countries with income per capita of around US$500 (1975 dollars) should be around –.25. The LAC figures, on the other hand, indicate that the average primary export share has passed from 74.2% to 68.7% between 1968 and 1974, while the annual

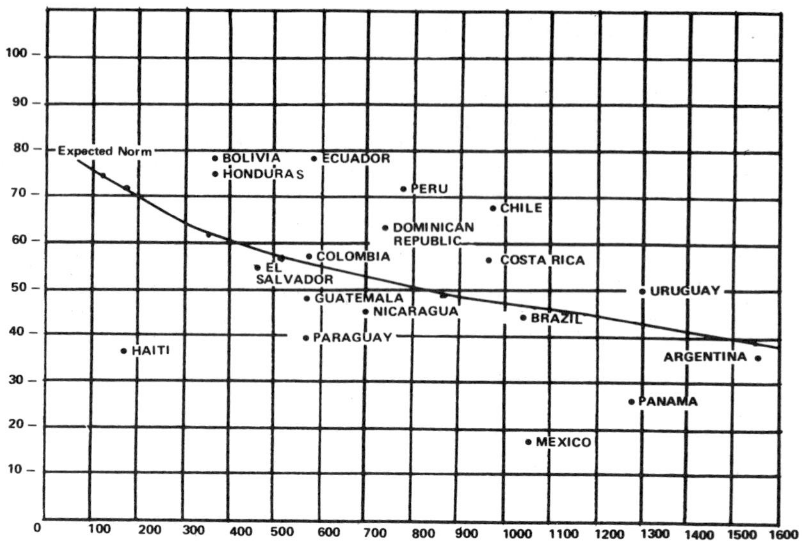


**Figure 1: Export Shares and Income Per Capita (U.S. dollars per capita)**

GDP per capita growth in such a period has been around 3.3%.[4] These figures yield an implicit elasticity of decline of the primary share of –.39. This illustrates that the Latin American countries have recently adjusted their export activities, consequently closing the gap between the two averages.

Before passing on to the implications of the large Latin American dependency on primary exports, a last point should be made regarding the imports of primary products to the Latin American countries. The most important primary commodity import has been oil; the principal importing country, Brazil. For Latin America as a whole, exports of petroleum, however, outweigh imports because of such oil rich countries as Venezuela, Ecuador, and, increasingly, Mexico. Nevertheless, LACs continue to have a favorable oil trade balance, since exports overcompensate for imports.[5] Wheat has been the second most important primary commodity imported and stands as the only major primary good that shows an unfavorable trade balance.[6] It is estimated currently that total primary imports comprise less than 20% of the gross value primary exports from Latin America.

### *Trade in Primary Products and Export Instability*

Having classified LACs as a group of countries more than normally dependent on primary products as a source of export earnings, the first question which naturally comes to mind is the impact of such dependency on export instability. The argument traditionally made in the primary commodity literature is that the high price instability of primary products, together with the high dependency of LDCs on primary exports, are jointly responsible for the high export earnings instability.[7] In this context, two main aspects should be analyzed. The first is whether the large LAC dependency and concentration on primary trade has had a more than proportional impact on the instability of export earnings when compared to the other LDCs. The second issue is to what extent Latin America is involved in the export trade of the more unstable primary commodities.

Some evidence of the relative instability of Latin American export prices is summarized in a recent World Bank study; see Table 2 (IBRD, 1976: Table 14). The first column shows a measurement of export instability for each Latin American country; the second column establishes the ranking of 117 countries in a worldwide context.[8] Results indicate that Latin America as a region has not registered any greater export instability than that observed in other less developed countries. LAC behavior has been strictly average. The average ranking of the Latin American countries in the world data sample has been estimated as 58th place, which corresponds to the mean value of the 117 countries involved in the analysis. Moreover, the table shows that export instability indices for nine Latin American countries are above the average; for nine, below the average; and one stands precisely at the worldwide average.

The last two columns in Table 2 show a primary export concentration index and its corresponding world ranking for each Latin American country.[9] Then, in order to find out if those LACs showing a more concentrated primary export share also showed larger export instability, the concentration index

TABLE 2
Primary Concentration and Instability Index in Latin American Trade

| COUNTRY | INSTABILITY INDEX | | PRIMARY CONCENTRATION | |
|---|---|---|---|---|
| | LEVEL | WORLD RANKING (117 COUNTRIES) | SHARE OF THREE MAJOR PRODUCTS | WORLD RANKING (113 COUNTRIES) |
| Argentina | 10.3 | 85 | 35.7 | 29 |
| Venezuela | 6.2 | 37 | 93.9 | 104 |
| Uruguay | 10.0 | 78 | 59.0 | 58 |
| Panama | 3.3 | 8 | 79.9 | 86 |
| Mexico | 8.1 | 60 | 17.8 | 13 |
| Brazil | 11.1 | 90 | 43.7 | 42 |
| Chile | 11.8 | 93 | 81.4 | 87 |
| Costa Rica | 6.4 | 41 | 65.3 | 64 |
| Peru | 7.6 | 58 | 58.1 | 57 |
| Cuba | - | - | 83.1 | 93 |
| Nicaragua | 6.9 | 49 | 54.0 | 49 |
| Dominican Republic | 8.9 | 66 | 69.7 | 68 |
| Colombia | 8.6 | 64 | 76.4 | 80 |
| Paraguay | 9.9 | 77 | 33.7 | 27 |
| Ecuador | 12.6 | 97 | 73.1 | 75 |
| El Salvador | 6.3 | 39 | 57.4 | 56 |
| Honduras | 5.5 | 23 | 70.4 | 69 |
| Bolivia | 7.4 | 57 | 71.4 | 71 |
| Haiti | 5.7 | 27 | 64.7 | 62 |
| Guatemala | 6.9 | 48 | 50.1 | 47 |
| TOTAL | | 58 | | 62 |

SOURCE: IBRD, *World Tables 1976,* Table 14. The instability index refers to the percentage square root of deviations from a four-year moving average. It covers the period 1968-1973.

(column 3) is compared to the instability index (column 1). Results show that there are innumerable combinations between export instability and primary export concentration, and that, in general, among Latin American countries there is a low correlation between the two variables under analysis.

Figure 2 plots observations shown in Table 2. Those countries characterized by high export instability and high primary export shares appear in the first quadrant. The majority of these countries correspond to the Andean republics—Chile, Peru, Ecuador, Bolivia, and Colombia. On the other hand, there is a group of countries with medium or high primary export concentration but with low instability indices (quadrants II and III); they correspond to the Central American republics. Finally, there is a group of countries with low primary dependency which register

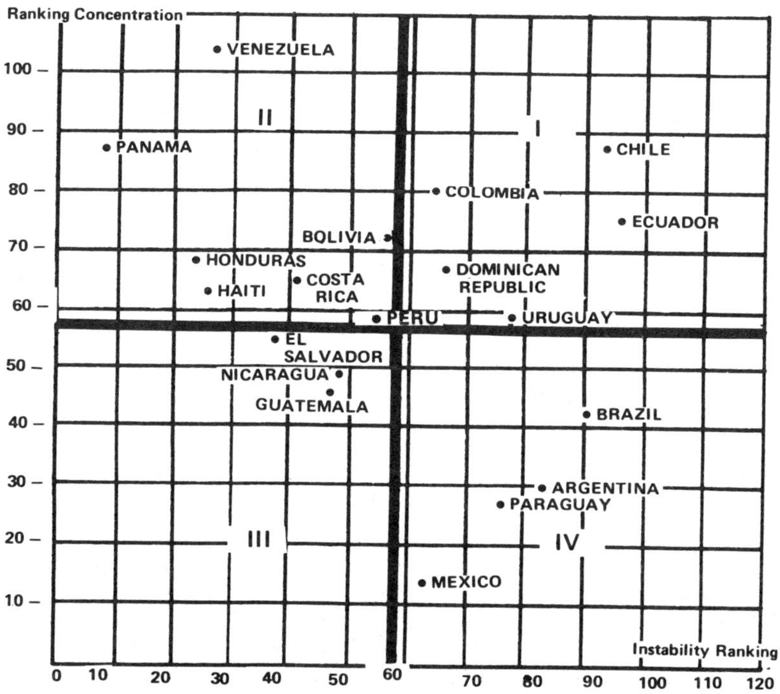


**Figure 2: Commodity Concentration and Export Instability**

high levels of instability. This group includes the most important Latin countries—Argentina, Brazil, and Mexico.

Consequently, the results indicate that in Latin America there has not been a high degree of correlation between export instability and the high dependency and concentration of those countries in primary products. To the contrary, there seems to be some evidence that in the larger countries, the observed export instability resulted more from domestic economic management than from dependency on primary products.

Although concentration on every primary export may not be the prime reason for export instability, it is clearly possible that certain specific primary exports have had an important impact on overall export performance in the past.

To examine this hypothesis, the first two columns in Table 3 illustrate the value and share of the major primary products

TABLE 3
Latin American Primary Exports and Commodity Instability Indices (millions of U.S. dollars)

| COMMODITY | LATIN AMERICAN EXPORTS | | PRICE INSTABILITY | |
|---|---|---|---|---|
| | VALUE (1) | SHARE (2) | INDEX A (3) | INDEX B (4) |
| Oil | 14,003 | 51.96 | 8.4 | 23.9 |
| Coffee | 2,532 | 9.34 | 7.6 | 8.3 |
| Sugar | 2,487 | 9.17 | 13.2 | 26.7 |
| Copper | 1,485 | 5.48 | 15.5 | 18.2 |
| Iron ore | 975 | 3.60 | 5.6 | 6.8 |
| Cotton | 692 | 2.55 | 5.0 | 7.6 |
| Beef | 640 | 2.36 | 10.2 | 13.2 |
| Maize | 612 | 2.26 | 7.0 | 9.8 |
| Banana | 525 | 1.94 | 3.8 | 4.5 |
| Wheat | 294 | 1.08 | 7.3 | 13.2 |
| Cocoa | 292 | 1.08 | 17.1 | 20.4 |
| Silver | 272 | 1.00 | * | * |
| Bauxite | 250 | .92 | 6.1 | 9.8 |
| Zinc | 252 | .93 | 15.1 | 24.9 |
| Timber | 245 | .90 | 7.2 | 6.9 |
| Tobacco | 220 | .81 | 5.3 | 6.5 |
| Wool | 218 | .80 | 11.9 | 20.2 |
| Fishmeal | 213 | .78 | 16.2 | 27.0 |
| Tin | 199 | .73 | 7.3 | 10.8 |
| Rice | 129 | .47 | 13.9 | 9.8 |
| Vegetable oils | 116 | .43 | 14.0 | 18.0 |
| Lead | 124 | .46 | 12.9 | 14.8 |
| Sisal | 80 | .29 | 19.2 | 30.3 |
| Hides and skins | 60 | .22 | * | * |
| Manganese ore | 56 | .21 | 7.0 | 11.6 |
| Peanuts | 28 | .10 | 8.1 | 12.4 |
| Tea | 20 | .07 | 3.5 | 4.3 |
| Rubber | 7 | .02 | 12.8 | 14.2 |
| Abaca | 4 | .01 | * | * |
| Phosphate rock | 3 | .01 | 10.1 | 23.3 |
| | 27,122 | 100.41 | | |

SOURCES: Col. 1: IBRD, *Commodity Trade and Price Trends,* 1977. Refers to average annual 1973-1975 values.
Col. 2: Percentage share of Col. 1.
Cols. 3 and 4: IBRD *Price Prospects for Major Primary Products*, Table 15. Index A refers to the absolute average percentage deviation from the five-year moving average. Index B corresponds to the standard deviation (root mean square of deviations) from a similar moving average.

exported from Latin America, while the other two columns present two alternative indices of individual product price instability. Using the individual product export share and its instability index, the correlation is very low and not significant.

One last exercise to illustrate the effects of primary products on LACs' export instability is to work out an appropriate individual country primary product price instability index and to compare it with its corresponding export value instability index. Thus, the left column of Table 4 shows the export instability index, while the right side presents the weighted primary price index. The data shown in the table, as well as the correlation analysis made between the two series, indicate once again a very low relationship between the primary product instability and overall export instability. This result confirms the findings of previous paragraphs in that primary product behavior explains on only a very small scale the fluctuations observed in LAC exports. It thus supports previous findings that Latin America's unstable export behavior may have been less a consequence of external market instability than possibly domestic policy changes.

### *Export Behavior and Terms of Trade*

Traditionally, Latin American economists have argued that primary product exports have received lower prices than manufactured goods, most of which Latin America had to import. In other words, the terms of trade tend to go against the primary exporting countries, given the low income elasticities of demand for primary goods versus the high income elasticity compared to those for manufactured goods, and also because the supply response of primary goods to price incentives tends to be excessive and delayed (Singh, 1976: 88).

Recent studies of terms of trade show that indeed there had been a long declining trend from the second half of the 1950s to the beginning of the 1970s. Since then, an upward trend has been

TABLE 4
Export and Price Instability Indices
of Primary Products

| COUNTRY | INSTABILITY INDICES | |
|---|---|---|
| | EXPORTS (1) | PRIMARY PRICES (2) |
| Argentina | 10.3 | 13.49 |
| Bolivia | 7.4 | 13.45 |
| Brazil | 11.1 | 10.77 |
| Colombia | 18.6 | 10.24 |
| Costa Rica | 6.4 | 9.24 |
| Chile | 11.8 | 17.44 |
| Ecuador | 12.6 | 7.93 |
| El Salvador | 6.3 | 9.95 |
| Guatemala | 6.9 | 9.34 |
| Haiti | 5.7 | 12.60 |
| Honduras | 5.5 | 10.43 |
| Mexico | 8.1 | 13.44 |
| Nicaragua | 6.9 | 8.40 |
| Panama | 3.3 | 11.41 |
| Paraguay | 9.9 | 9.15 |
| Peru | 7.6 | 19.00 |
| Dominican Republic | 8.9 | 19.88 |
| Uruguay | 10.0 | 17.18 |
| Venezuela | 6.2 | 27.97 |

SOURCES: Col. 1 = Col. 1, Table 2.
Col. 2 = Estimated as each country's weighted average of the instability Index B from Table 3. The weights used were the shares of each primary product in the total country's commodity exports.

taking place which was especially strong during 1973-1974, a period which became known as the "commodity boom" (CEPAL, 1976: 37-39). In the recession year of 1975 prices of primary exports, primary products, and manufactured products declined, but show a moderate recuperation since 1976. Projections on the possible future course of primary prices indicate that they will increase in nominal but decline in real terms, by approximately 35% between 1978 and 1985 (IBRD, 1977b: 34-35).

Having reviewed the issues and trends in primary trade, the point that should be examined is whether the terms of trade and, in particular, the prices of primary products, have been relatively more favorable to the LACs than to the entire group of LDCs, and what the impact of the terms of trade behavior on export and output performance has been.

In terms of the trends shown by primary product prices in the LACs and LDCs, it is conceivable that they could differ given the diversity of the export mix between the two groups of countries. To pinpoint such differences, Table 5 shows the value and share of exports both for LACs and LDCs. When the two export mixes are compared, fundamental differences can be seen. The relative importance of Latin American exports tends to be higher in almost all agricultural-based products and less important in oil exports. Given the different price pattern of oil products and agricultural commodities since 1973, this sole factor should by itself produce important differences in primary product price indexes and even in the terms of trade.

In addition to the differences observed in the export mixes, the terms of trade may differ among regions for several other reasons. On the one hand, price indices based on international posted prices may not adequately reflect the true effective sale prices of each country (CEPAL, 1976a: 4). This situation is rather common, since most of the other LDCs are members of the Lomé Convention through which they obtain more favorable prices for their primary goods (CEPAL, 1976b: 12). In this regard, it is important to note that "Latin America is the only one of the larger regions of the developing world which has not made preferential arrangements, explicit or implicit, with the developed countries either in the individual or in a collective fashion for the trade of basic or primary products, different naturally from those obtained by all developing countries in virtue of the Generalized Preference System" (CEPAL, 1975: 39).

Moreover, differences in the development of the terms of trade between Latin America and other LDCs may also be caused by different combinations of primary exports and differences in import prices. After all, the terms of trade, in their strictest

TABLE 5
Annual Export Values of Primary Products,
1973-1975

| EXPORTS | LATIN AMERICA VALUE (Millions of U.S. Dollars) | LATIN AMERICA SHARE | DEVELOPING COUNTRIES VALUE (Millions of U.S. Dollars) | DEVELOPING COUNTRIES SHARE |
|---|---|---|---|---|
| A. FOODSTUFFS | 7,887 | 29.1 | 21,175 | 16.7 |
| 1. Beverages | 2,845 | 10.5 | 6,056 | 4.8 |
| Cocoa | 292 | 1.1 | 1,364 | 1.1 |
| Coffee | 2,532 | 9.3 | 3,998 | 3.1 |
| Tea | 20 | .1 | 694 | .5 |
| 2. Cereals | 1,035 | 3.8 | 2,125 | 1.7 |
| Wheat | 294 | 1.1 | 327 | .3 |
| Rice | 129 | .5 | 880 | .7 |
| Maize | 612 | 2.3 | 918 | .7 |
| 3. Other Foodstuffs | 4,008 | 14.8 | 7,622 | 6.0 |
| Sugar | 2,487 | 9.1 | 4,279 | 3.4 |
| Banana | 525 | 1.9 | 649 | .5 |
| Beef | 640 | 2.4 | 708 | .6 |
| Fishmeal | 213 | .8 | 263 | .2 |
| Oil and fats | 144 | .5 | 1,723 | .1 |
| B. AGRICULTURAL NON-FOOD | 1,218 | 4.5 | 5,372 | 4.2 |
| Cotton | 692 | 2.6 | 2,173 | 1.7 |
| Jute | 1 | - | 182 | .1 |
| Sisal | 80 | .3 | 204 | .2 |
| Wool | 218 | .8 | 277 | .2 |
| Rubber | 7 | - | 1,859 | 1.4 |
| Tobacco | 220 | .8 | 677 | .5 |
| C. TIMBER | 245 | .9 | 2,527 | 2.0 |
| D. MINERALS | 3,310 | 12.2 | 8,990 | 7.1 |
| Copper | 1,485 | 5.5 | 3,965 | 3.1 |
| Lead | 123 | .5 | 206 | .2 |
| Tin | 199 | .7 | 1,010 | .8 |
| Zinc | 218 | .8 | 354 | .3 |
| Bauxite | 250 | .9 | 376 | .3 |
| Iron ore | 975 | 3.6 | 1,701 | 1.3 |
| Phosphate rock | 3 | - | 1,200 | .9 |
| Manganese ore | 56 | .2 | 178 | .1 |
| E. OIL | 14,093 | 52.0 | 93,863 | 73.8 |
| F. OTHER PRIMARY EXPORTS | 1,583 | 5.8 | 582 | .5 |
| G. TOTAL (35 Commodities) | 27,123 | 100.0 | 127,137 | 100.0 |

SOURCE: IBRD, *Commodity Trade and Price Trends* (1977).

definition, measure the ratio between unit export and import value (CEPAL, 1976a: 3-22).[10] In order to visualize the precise

TABLE 6
Terms of Trade for Latin America and for Total Developing Countries

| YEAR | DEVELOPING COUNTRIES (1) | LATIN AMERICA (2) |
|---|---|---|
| 1950 | 111 | 129 |
| 1951 | 117 | 128 |
| 1952 | 106 | 117 |
| 1953 | 105 | 126 |
| 1954 | 111 | 129 |
| 1955 | 109 | 119 |
| 1956 | 107 | 117 |
| 1957 | 103 | 118 |
| 1958 | 103 | 110 |
| 1959 | 105 | 102 |
| 1960 | 103 | 102 |
| 1961 | 100 | 100 |
| 1962 | 98 | 94 |
| 1963 | 99 | 95 |
| 1964 | 101 | 97 |
| 1965 | 99 | 93 |
| 1966 | 100 | 95 |
| 1967 | 99 | 93 |
| 1968 | 100 | 95 |
| 1969 | 101 | 96 |
| 1970 | 100 | 100 |
| 1971 | 104 | 99 |
| 1972 | 102 | 102 |
| 1973 | 112 | * |
| 1974 | 156 | * |
| 1975 | 139 | * |
| 1976 | 145 | * |

SOURCE: Terms of trade figures refer to the quotient of unit export and unit import prices.
Col. 1.: IBRD, *Commodity Trade and Price Trends,* August 1977.
Col. 2: CEPAL, *América Latina: Relación de Precios del Intercambio,* Chile, 1966.

relative behavior of the terms of trade in Latin America vis-à-vis the developing world at large, Table 6 presents both sets of values during the period 1950-1972. The figures clearly show that the terms of trade suffered from a declining trend, which was more severe in Latin America than in other LDCs.

Although comparable information is lacking after 1972, it may be presumed that the terms of trade have continued to be less favorable to the Latin American countries in respect to the world's rapid jump in oil prices.[11]

To learn why the terms of trade have been less favorable to the Latin countries than to other LDCs, commodity prices and unit import prices are presented in Table 7. This information shows that it was the unit import prices which rose, rather than the unit export prices. This explains the observed terms of trade differences. This result seems to have been due to the intensive and costly import substitution process which characterized Latin American development during the 1960s, a process which was carried through far less in other LDCs.

The outstanding factor, and one which explains to a larger extent the terms of trade effect discussed, remains, however, the difference of oil prices since 1973. Even more, the primary product projections suggest that the widening gap will increase in the coming years. This point may be clearly appreciated in column 5, which shows the quotient of the price index of primary products of the LACs in relation to those of the LDCs. Such value presents a permanent decline since 1970, and it is expected to continue until 1985.

In brief, the major result of the statistical analysis can be summarized as follows. Latin America is subject to more unfavorable terms of trade behavior than the other developing regions, a situation which is likely to continue in the foreseeable future, given the price projections of primary products and, in particular, the oil price trends. This unfavorable terms of trade effect may be explained partly as a result of the import substitution process which characterized the Latin American development of the 1960s, and, more important, the result observed is due

TABLE 7
## Primary Product Prices

| | LATIN AMERICA | | DEVELOPING COUNTRIES | | LAC'S BASIC PRODUCTS | LAC'S UNIT IMPORTS |
|---|---|---|---|---|---|---|
| YEAR | PRIMARY PRODUCTS (1) | UNIT EXPORTS (2) | PRIMARY PRODUCTS (3) | UNIT EXPORTS (4) | LDC'S BASIC PRODUCTS (5) | LDC'S UNIT IMPORTS (6) |
| 1950 | 110 | 108 | 120 | 94 | 92 | 87 |
| 1951 | 117 | 140 | 125 | 117 | 94 | 88 |
| 1952 | 114 | 117 | 122 | 107 | 93 | 89 |
| 1953 | 115 | 117 | 126 | 99 | 91 | 89 |
| 1954 | 123 | 101 | 134 | 101 | 92 | 95 |
| 1955 | 122 | 104 | 133 | 102 | 92 | 93 |
| 1956 | 122 | 94 | 133 | 101 | 92 | 93 |
| 1957 | 116 | 92 | 132 | 101 | 88 | 87 |
| 1958 | 105 | 86 | 125 | 96 | 84 | 94 |
| 1959 | 101 | 86 | 114 | 94 | 88 | 94 |
| 1960 | 100 | 92 | 107 | 94 | 93 | 95 |
| 1961 | 94 | 91 | 106 | 91 | 89 | 97 |
| 1962 | 93 | 82 | 101 | 89 | 92 | 99 |
| 1963 | 92 | 93 | 102 | 91 | 90 | 98 |
| 1964 | 96 | 98 | 98 | 94 | 98 | 101 |
| 1965 | 97 | 94 | 98 | 93 | 99 | 100 |
| 1966 | 97 | 97 | 99 | 95 | 98 | 101 |
| 1967 | 94 | 95 | 97 | 94 | 98 | 101 |
| 1968 | 95 | 93 | 97 | 94 | 98 | 101 |
| 1969 | 97 | 97 | 99 | 97 | 98 | 100 |
| 1970 | 100 | 100 | 100 | 100 | 100 | 100 |
| 1971 | 114 | 113 | 122 | 108 | 93 | 97 |
| 1972 | 130 | 130 | 135 | 116 | 96 | 100 |
| 1973 | 184 | * | 196 | 158 | 94 | * |
| 1974 | 496 | * | 613 | 318 | 81 | * |
| 1975 | 517 | * | 657 | 311 | 79 | * |
| 1976 | 555 | * | 705 | 330 | 79 | * |
| 1977 | 623 | * | 775 | * | 80 | * |
| 1978 | 657 | * | 832 | * | 79 | * |
| 1979 | 702 | * | 892 | * | 79 | * |
| 1980 | 752 | * | 955 | * | 79 | * |
| 1985 | 1,050 | * | 1,339 | * | 78 | * |

SOURCES: Col. 1 and Col. 3: Refer to each region's weighted primary price indices. The individual product price indices are obtained from IBRD, *Price Prospects for major primary products.* The weights for each group of countries' trade are shown in Table 6.
Col. 2: Unit export prices, CEPAL *América Latina: Relación de Precios del Intercambio.* The base period was changed from 1965 to 1970.
Col. 4: Unit LDC's export prices, IBRD, *Price Prospects for Major Primary Products.*
Col. 5: Col. 1 ÷ Col. 3.
Col. 6: Ratio of Latin American and LDC's unit import prices obtained from the sources indicated in other columns.

to the relative commodity price behavior given Latin America's primary export mix.

## *Latin America and the Commodity Dialogue*

The previous sections have shown Latin American dependency on primary exports as a source of export earnings, as well as the problems that such dependency has produced in terms of export instability and export price behavior. In conclusion, this section will outline the Latin American response toward primary product control schemes and policies that have been proposed and adopted in the realm of primary product trade.

Brazil has been one of the leading countries of the world in adopting export restrictions to increase its export earnings. In fact, the so-called coffee valorization scheme executed by the state of São Paulo early in this century was the first recorded effort of this kind (Rowe, 1965: 122). Toward the middle of the 1920s, Cuba, already the world-leading sugar exporting nation, started to exercise unilateral control on the world supplies (Rowe, 1965: 125). It is also well known that Chile, at certain periods, has attempted to exercise unilateral control to stabilize copper prices with much less impact than in the cases of Brazil and Cuba, because of its minor share in the world market (Waite, 1975: 43).

Active Latin American participation in stabilizing primary prices in the hope of increasing its export revenues has, however, not been limited exclusively to unilateral individual country actions. It may be argued that LACs have been the best of friends and have always been among the principal promoters of multinational schemes directed to control primary product markets.

In the area of producer and producer-consumer agreements, one finds that Latin America, mainly through Cuban action, was the promoter of the first sugar exporting agreement signed in 1931 (Rowe, 1965: 125). Since then, most of the LACs have entered the several International Sugar Agreements. More recently, the sugar-exporting Latin American nations have associated themselves with a group of Caribbean countries called GEPLACEA (Grupo de Países Latinoamericanos y del Caribe exportadores de azúcar) to increase the region's negotiating power in drafting the new International Sugar Agreement, establishing themselves as a permanent forum for market analysis and providing a subsidiary market control mechanism (United Nations, 1977).

In regard to copper, Latin America, with the agreement of Chile and Peru, became an active member in the efforts of the 1930s to control output (Rowe, 1965: 154).[12] Also, in the 1960s these two countries became members of the still active Conseil Intergovernmental Des Pays Exportateurs de Cuivre (CIPEC), which was conceived as a mechanism to stablize copper (Waite, 1975: 44).

In the case of coffee, the LACs' initiatives to undertake common commercialization policies on the part of producing countries have been a permanent endeavor. The first international coffee assembly took place in Mexico in 1901 and 1902 under the auspices of the second Pan American Conference (Rochac, 1965: 124-125, 470-471). There were also producer countries' meetings at Cartagena in 1924, at New York in 1930, São Paulo in 1931, and Bogotá in 1936 (FEDESARROLLO, 1976, 4: 1-28). Since 1940 and up to the negotiation of the first International Coffee Agreement in 1962, there were a number of agreements which took place among the LACs, out of which the following can be named: the 1940 Quota Agreement, the 1953 Gentlemen's Agreement, the 1957 Mexico Agreement, and finally the so-called Interamerican Coffee Agreement of 1959 (FEDESARROLLO, 1976: 28).

Since 1962 the LACs have been full participants of the several International Coffee Agreements (International Coffee Organization) and even, for a short time, because of the United States' negative attitude, some of the LACs promoted a producers' alliance in 1972 to adjust upward the reference price for quota purposes, as a result of and in proportion to the devaluation rate of the dollar.[13]

Argentina, on the other hand, has also been an active, if not a permanent and reliable, member of the wheat agreements. It was one of the four countries which signed the 1942 Memorandum of Agreement[14] and a participant in the International Quota Agreements of 1949, 1956, 1959, and 1962 (Rowe, 1965: 163-169).

Moreover, in the area of producer pacts in which Latin American countries have had an active role, the case of bananas should be stressed. This commodity has been produced largely in the LACs (Ecuador, Costa Rica, Honduras, Panama, Colombia, and Guatemala), but its production, especially its commercialization and transportation, have been in the hands of a few and a powerful group of multinational enterprises.[15] Therefore, to increase the producing countries' position and income share, the Latin American governments involved have decided to exercise a larger official action in the banana market. To increase the countries' direct grasp of the market, they created the Unión de Productores y Exportadores de Banana, UPEB (Union of Banana Producing and Exporting Countries), in 1974. To date, its major action has been the establishment of a commercialization enterprise, COMUNBANA. At the present time it is precisely in this area that the oligopolistic transnational issue has been most important (UPEB, 1977: 30-38).

To conclude the description of the LAC's engagments in the commodity control schemes, it should be added that Ecuador and Venezuela have become active members of OPEC (BID, 1974: 33-36),while the large Latin producing nations are members of the Cocoa Agreement (Singh, 1976: 91). Therefore, the Latin American nations have had a clear historical record of active participation in commodity arrangements, especially in those products where the LACs have had an important share in the world market, and thereby a higher potential likelihood to obtain some gains from commodity control schemes.[16]

With the previous descriptions and analysis of the LACs' historical problems and actions in the world of primary trade, it is possible to tackle one final question in regard to the recent and prospective Latin American attitudes toward the new developments in the primary product dialogue. In order to perceive and interpret correctly the Latin American attitudes and possible future actions, it should be recalled that LACs are countries which historically have been and still remain "overly" dependent on primary products as a source of export earnings. More than other LDCs, they have been subject to the fluctuation of primary product prices, which will probably continue to be unfavorable. Nevertheless, they have shown a marked tradition to defend their interests by (1) unilateral action, (2) agreements with other producers, and (3) cooperation with consumers and producers.

With this in mind, it should not come as a surprise to find that the Latin American nations have supported all the proposals and schemes which interfere with the ongoing workings of the primary products marked in order to reduce price fluctuations and to improve terms of trade. Their final goal has been to increase and stabilize foreign exchange earnings and influence policies that improve the share of the producing countries in the value of the final sales of primary commodities.

Besides the positive response shown by the LACs toward all types of producers' arrangements,[17] their attitude has also been to support the initiatives that have taken place at UNCTAD. First, the LACs supported the Manila Declaration, in which the developing world specified in a clear-cut manner its proposed program of action in the trade of primary products.[18] Most of the LACs have also supported the multicommodity approach and the establishment of a common fund for financing stocks. In the words of the Executive Secretary of the UN Economic Commission for Latin America, the LACs' position has been that:

> In order to face in a definitive way the old problem of equitable prices and that of the stability of export earnings, it is required to

design new approaches that could improve the scarce advances realized to the present. It is only in this fashion that the region will be able to develop its total productive capacity. The multicommodity approach is a step that opens up a systematic and continuous action, covering a wide range of products and using a multidimensional set of instruments applicable to each commodity. In order to reach such an objective, one cannot expect that the market forces will be able, by themselves, to create the necessary corrections or to resolve the problem. The creation of a common fund to finance buffer stocks continues to be the cornerstone in the scheme [UNCTAD, 1976].

## *Concluding Remarks*

The findings of this paper indicate that the LACs' permanent concern for the primary product trade is quite well founded. The Latin American region continues to be overly dependent on commodities as a source of foreign exchange earnings. However, while the statistical results show that export instability in the LACs is "average" among the LDCs and that commodity trade has not been the decisive factor in overall export instability, political actions seem to have been geared excessively toward stabilization goals in multinational agreements, even at the level of UNCTAD. Perhaps a larger domestic effort in the control of export fluctuations and a more important drive at the diplomatic tables toward improving the terms of trade and the real prices of commodities would bring net social benefits to the Latin American countries. In fact, the results from this analysis suggest that LACs have suffered and will probably continue to register a terms of trade decline even more severe than that of other LDCs. Producers' alliances, indexing of primary products in international producer and consumer agreements, and restrictive production and export quota systems seem to be the LACs most effective available options over and above UNCTAD's efforts in favor of establishing multicommodity buffer stock mechanisms.

# NOTES

1. The two coefficients corresond to lines 6 (a) and (b) from table 3, p. 20.

2. It can be shown by the definition of the two coefficients in Chenery and Syrquin's statistical index that its quotient applies strictly to the proportion of primary exports to total goods and nonfactor service exports.

3. It should be noted that the Chenery-Syrquin study relates its expected coefficients to specific per capita income levels measured in 1964 dollars. In order to apply the norm to the income levels shown in the table, appropriate correction factors (the implicit U.S. GDP deflators) were used to transform the 1964 to 1975 income levels. Such correction factors were obtained from IBRD (1977a: 26) Selected Price Indices.

4. The primary export shares refer to primary exports as a percentage of total merchandise exports and were obtained from IBRD (1973 and 1977a). The GDP per capita growth figure was estimated from BID (1976), Cuadros 1-2, p. 9; and Cuadro 1, p. 439.

5. The 1976 figures show a favorable balance of $5.1 billion (BID, 1976).

6. The latest available figures show that in 1975, LAC wheat imports amounted to US$1.235 million, while exports were $309 million (FAO, 1975: Vol. 29, Tables 36 and 37).

7. Given the characteristically low price elasticities of demand, fluctuating prices should have a large impact on export earnings (Singh, 1976: 88-89; Perry, 1977: 72).

8. The definition used in the export instability index was the root-mean square of deviations from a four-year moving average.

9. It should be noted that the primary export share or concentration index differs from that shown in Table 1, since it refers to a different time period and its definition includes the primary exports of the three principal commodities as a proportion of total good and nonfactor exports.

10. This corresponds to the definition of barter terms of trade. There is a large variety of concepts and definitions.

11. It should be recalled that the oil export share in Latin America is much less important than that observed in the LDCs as a group, while the oil prices have shown the largest relative increases.

12. The agreement was signed by Chile, Peru, Belgian Congo, and Rhodesia.

13. The Group of Bogotá, which included Brazil, Colombia, Ivory Coast, and Portugal (Angola), acted as a catalyst to engage and coordinate actions between 1972-1974 by 22 coffee-producing nations, including most of the LACs' coffee exporters.

14. The agreement was signed by the United States, Canada, Australia, and Argentina.

15. Clairmonte's (1975) "Bananas" article describes how three multinational companies, Castle and Cook, Del Monte, and United Brands, account for 70% of the world exports.

16. The export share is the most important, but only one, of the elements required for fruitful action. The other elements are that the good is essential, there are few producers, income elasticity is high, and that storage costs are low (Singh, 1976: 90). Nevertheless, it should be noted that the LACs and Caribbean world export percentage shares are: 75, bananas; 47, bauxite; 21, cocoa; 59, coffee; 33, fishmeal; 13, oil; 29, sugar; and 14 as an average for 35 commodities (IBRD, 1977a: 19).

17. The LACs have not only taken positive objective actions toward producers' alliances, but they have also taken a philosophical stand toward them:

> The Latin American nations propose to explore, with the participation principally of other developing regions, all the possibilities to form producers' associations, and they express their decision to transform them into useful instruments to design and apply pricing policies for primary products that respond to the principles of a just redistribution towards producers and the necessary increase of revenues towards the exporting nations [Paragraph 73, Evaluación de Chaguaramas, approved by resolution 347 (XVI) by ECLA].

18. Among UNCTAD's proposed goals ("Declaración y Programa de Acción de Manila," TD/195, February 12, 1976), LDCs agreed to look for an improvement in trade, adopt measures to reduce primary price fluctuations, increase and stabilize the real value of export earnings, and increase the share of developing countries in the transportation, commercialization, and distribution of primary products to improve its share in the income from final sales of its commodities.

## REFERENCES

BID [Banco Internacional de Desarrollo] (1976, 1974) Progreso Económico y Social En América Latina. Informes. Washington, DC: BID.

CEPAL [Comisión Económica para América Latina] (1976a) América Latina: Relación de Precios del Intercambio. Santiago, Chile: CEPAL.

——— (1976b) Temas del Nuevo Orden Económico Internacional. Santiago, Chile: Cuadernos de la CEPAL.

——— (1975) La Coyuntura Internacional y el Sector Externo. Santiago, Chile: Cuadernos de la CEPAL.

CHENERY, H. and M. SYRQUIN (1975) Patterns of Development 1950-1970. London: Oxford Univ. Press.

FAO [Food Agricultural Organization] (1975) Trade Yearbook. Rome, Italy: United Nations, Statistics Division of the Economic and Social Policy Department, FAO.

FEDESARROLLO [Fundación para la Educación Superior y el Desarrollo] (1976) "La política internacional del café." Economía Cafetera Colombiana (Octubre).

IBRD [International Bank for Reconstruction and Development—World Bank] (1977a, 1975, 1973, 1972) Commodity Trade and Price Trends. Washington, DC: IBRD.

——— (1977b) Price Prospects for Major Primary Commodities. Report 814/77 (June). Washington, DC: IBRD.

——— (1976) World Tables, 1976. Baltimore and London: Johns Hopkins Press (published for the World Bank).

International Coffee Organization (1976, 1973, 1968, 1962) International Coffee Agreements. (Published in various locations.)

PERRY, G. (1977) "El nuevo orden comercial internacional y el desarrollo." Coyuntura Económica (December).

ROWE, J.W.F. (1965) Primary Commodities in International Trade. London: Cambridge Univ. Press.

ROCHAC, A. (1965) Diccionario del Café. New York: Pan American Coffee Bureau.

SINGH, S. (1976) "The international dialogue on commodities." Resources Policy (June).

UNCTAD (1976) "Exposición del Secretario Ejecutivo de la Comisión Económica para América Latina, en el Cuarto Período de Sesiones de la UNCTAD." Nairobi, Kenya (May).

United Nations (1977) Convenio Internacional del Azúcar, TD/Sugar, 9/10 (October).

UPEB [Unión de Países Productores y Exportadores de Banasa] (1977) "Papel de la UPEB y COMUNBANA." Informe UPEB 1 (December): 1.

WAITE, D. (1975) "Copper," in C. Payer (ed.) Commodity Trade and the Third World. London: Macmillan.

*Roberto Junguito, an economist from the University of Los Andes, Bogotá, Colombia, did graduate work at Princeton University, where he obtained a diploma in Demography and an M.A. in Economics. He has been Colombia's delegate to the International Coffee Organization in London and, more recently, Director and researcher at FEDESARROLLO (Fundación para la Educatión Superior y El Desarrollo), a nonprofit research center in Bogotá.*

Group of Ten and, once again, the interests of the developing countries were put aside. The basic problem facing the developed countries was to establish new conditions for adjusting their balance of payments, which implied, chiefly, eliminating the balance-of-payments deficit of the United States and the surpluses of West Germany and Japan. During those years, the debate over reform centered on the conditions of adjustment and whether they should focus on trade transactions, as recommended by the United States, or on capital movements, as proposed by France and other industrial countries. Again, it was an internal problem of the bloc of industrial countries and of how they should divide the costs of the adjustment process. The refusal of the industrial countries to link the creation of Special Drawing Rights to the transfer of resources to the developing countries showed, once more, that the concern of the former was to solve the problems of their reciprocal relations before seeking solutions that would take into account the global problems of the world economy.

After 1973 the increases in oil prices, the jump in the rate of inflation, and the recession in the industrial countries shifted the attention of the major countries from a sweeping reform of the international monetary system to the more urgent problems of the international economic crisis. Under such conditions, the reform process was limited basically to accepting the new system of floating exchange rates adopted by the major countries, and to assuming reciprocal obligations "to avoid manipulating exchange rates or the international monetary system in order to prevent effective balance-of-payments adjustment or to gain an unfair competitive advantage over other members" (IMF Survey, 1976b: 20). This agreement, endorsed in Jamaica in January 1976 by the Interim Committee of the Board of Governors of the IMF, was new proof of the interdependence of the industrial economies and of their ability to put aside their differences in order to protect their fundamental interests. But at the same time, the proposed reforms showed that the developing countries continued to be left out of the decisions of the system. As stated in the press release of the Group of 24 representing the developing countries, "the Ministers [of the Group of 24] also expressed their strong disappointment that the interests and concerns of developing countries have received so little attention in the negotiations on international monetary reform, and that decisions affecting all countries continued to be taken in restricted groups of countries. They emphasized that unless there was a fundamental change in the attitude of the developed countries, the dialogue on international economic cooperation now under way in many forums is unlikely to produce any constructive results" (IMF Survey, 1976a: 28). The expansion of the IMF credit tranches and the establishment of a trust fund with the profits from the sale of gold by the Fund were marginal concessions made by the developed countries and of little significance.

The experience of the functioning of the international monetary system indicates that the developing countries can either go on protesting in vain at international meetings, or they can take concerted action that will strengthen their negotiating position and enhance their ability to administer independently their financial potential.

### *THE EXTERNAL DEBT*

The extent of the external disequilibrium of the developing countries and the burden of debt servicing on their balances of payments has aroused serious concern in the monetary authorities of the major countries and in the International Monetary Fund. These concerns stem from two problems: first, the growing risk of an eventual payments moratorium; second, the weakening of the disciplinary rules set by the IMF, when financing is shifted from this international agency to private banks that operate on commercial bases, without imposing conditions of economic policy on the borrowing countries. The IMF and some central banks and financial circles have proposed that the

Fund become the principal lender to the developing countries; that is, that the recycling of petrodollars be shifted from private banks to the IMF, an institution that, furthermore, would channel funds specifically allocated for this purpose by developed countries. This is the purpose of the so-called "Witteveen facility." When the Interim Committee of the Board of Governors of the IMF proposed creating this supplementary financing facility at its meeting the end of April 1977, it emphasized the importance of the Fund as a "financial intermediary" (IMF Survey, 1977: 130).

The proposed application of rules of international discipline to the national policies of the developing countries should be related to the experience in the reform of the international monetary system. In the Jamaica Agreement of January 1976, the Interim Committee of the International Monetary Fund revealed the limits to the reform that the major industrial countries are prepared to carry out. The reform of the three basic problems of the monetary system—a symmetrical system of adjusting the disequilibria in balances of payments, creation of international reserves through supranational decision, and regulation of the disequilibria that arise from short-term capital movements—has remained suspended, at least while the present conditions of instability in the world economy continue. The position of the major countries reflects their resistance to any kind of supranational discipline and their decision to cope with the immediate problems through understandings among themselves. These countries keep their freedom of action in adjusting their balance of payments. In any case, the limitations that have been imposed arise from considerations of their interdependence and not from instruments or agreements that take into account a broader spectrum of the interests involved, in particular those of the developing world. Therefore, the concern expressed in some circles about the need to impose greater international discipline on the economic policy of the developing countries should not be accepted uncritically. In any case, the criteria of international discipline on national policies affecting the adjustment process should be symmetrical in a way that embraces both the developed world and the developing countries.

In any event, the problem of external indebtedness should be placed in its proper perspective by pointing out some facts.

In recent years the external disequilibrium of the developing countries has intensified. The total deficit on current account of these non-oil-exporting countries was more than US$40 billion in the four-year period 1970-1973 and approximately US$110 billion in 1974-1977. In Latin America the average annual deficit on current account went from US$1 billion in 1965-1970, to US$4 billion in 1971-1973, to US$14 billion in 1974-1976. The ratio of deficit to exports rose from 15%, to 22%, to 45% for the same periods (ECLA, 1977). After 1973 the rise in the price of oil dramatically increased the current account deficit of several developing countries. For these countries as a whole, however, this fact explains only a small part of their additional external disequilibrium. According to a recent study made by the IMF economic adviser, in 1977 only 20% of the estimated balance-of-payments deficits on current account of the non-oil-exporting developing countries could be attributed to the effect of higher oil prices (Economist, 1977a). Therefore, the basic cause of the external disequilibrium of these countries continues to be the kind of relations they maintain with the developed world.

Mobilizing funds to finance the disequilibrium of the developing countries has, in recent years, been one of the dominant factors in international payments. In this context, the participation of private banks in this financing has increased greatly. While in 1967 only 5.5% of the external financing of these countries was provided by private banks, the proportion rose to almost 50% in 1976 (Economist, 1977b). Two major factors explain the sharp increase in financing from private sources: first, the abundance of funds held by international private banks that derived chiefly from mobilization of the financial surpluses of the oil-exporting countries; second, lessened demand for credit by the transnational corporations due to their reduced rate of capital formation and their greater ability to finance themselves.

Consequently, private banks have sought new operations for placing their funds to meet increased demand from the developing countries for financing. The Morgan Guaranty Trust Company of New York estimates that U.S. banks have provided two-thirds of the US$60 billion loaned by private banks to the non-oil-exporting developing countries. These loans are concentrated in a small group of countries. According to the U.S. Federal Reserve, by mid-1976 Argentina, Brazil, Peru, Mexico, and Indonesia had received loans amounting to US$32 billion from U.S. banks; Brazil and Mexico alone received US$19 billion. The importance of this type of business to international private banks is seen in the size of their operations and in the growing competition among the leading banks. The spread over the inter-bank rate has tended to narrow for these kinds of operations.

International private banks have lately been an instrument in the recycling of part of the financial surpluses of the oil-producing countries toward the developing countries in need of credit. This function has therefore come to cover a broader geographic area that includes not only the developed countries in deficit but also the developing world.

A few observations will help determine the real degree of risk assumed by private banks when they channel funds to developing countries. First, approximately two-thirds of the loans are concentrated in six countries—Brazil, Mexico, Argentina, South Korea, Peru, and the Philippines—which are among the most advanced economies in the developing world and which have substantial resources and possibilities of meeting their obligations abroad. These countries, apart from their short-term difficulties, are good clients thanks to their development potential and medium- and long-term prospects. On the other hand, some petroleum producers (Algiers, Indonesia, and, more recently, Venezuela) are important recipients of credit from the private banks. These oil-exporting countries have a sound external financial position. Second, the origin of the loans shows that only part of the operations is carried out in dollars and the rest is in other currencies. For example, in the operations of the Chase Manhattan, 30% of its loans are in currencies other than the dollar and, of these, 50% represent loans in the local currency of the borrowing countries. Only 50% of the operations of the Bank of America have been financed in dollars. Two-thirds of the operations of Citycorp are in local currency. In these cases, private banks have acted as mobilizers of local resources in the borrowing countries, and there is therefore no risk of suspension of external payments. Furthermore, one-third of the portfolio of the U.S. banks is in short-term, self-liquidating, low-risk loans. Third, loans to developing countries represent only 5.5% of the consolidated assets of the 21 major U.S. banks. In brief, there is a risk, but it does not appear to be excessive.

External financing via international private banks, which in recent years has been used on a large scale by several countries of Latin America and other areas, unquestionably poses some problems—for example, the relatively short term of the operations. But in general, access to this source of financing is an important factor in expanding available resources and in strengthening the freedom of action of these countries abroad. The experience of Latin America suggests that it would not be desirable to channel all loans through official organizations oriented to apply rules of economic policy that do not always coincide with the real interests and problems of the developing countries. Within a given reality, the principle of freedom of action is a basic requirement for formulating national policies. In this sense, it seems important that developing countries strengthen their links with international private banks, although they should also mobilize additional resources from public sources through the International Monetary Fund and other international agencies.

In any event, it should be recalled that a large part of the funds channeled to developing countries through international banks originates in the developing world, especially the OPEC members. Private banks act as an intermediary to guarantee these funds and, to some extent, to accept sight deposits or short-term funds and place them at medium-term. Within the schemes of horizontal cooperation, it would be advisable to create suitable instruments for financial cooperation within Latin America and the Third World to channel the mobilization of resources from and to the developing world.

### *Prospects for External Relations of Latin America*

In the long-run, center-periphery relations acquire a new meaning even for the developed countries. Expansion of Third World markets, political stability and lowered tensions, and expansion of the supply of energy sources, food, and raw materials are all factors that have a positive effect on the functioning of the world system, détente, and the reduction of military expenditures. If the planet is thought of as a single unit, the interests of the center countries seem to be closely linked to the elimination of underdevelopment and poverty in the periphery. But these are long-run considerations that do not necessarily have an immediate influence on the policies of the developed countries. There are, of course, exceptions like the recent position taken by the United States on the Panama Canal and its agreement to turn the Canal over to Panama. This is an example of an intelligent political response to relations between a great power and a developing area. But it must be stressed that the overall policy of the great powers is definitely conditioned by their immediate problems. These attitudes do not operate only at the government level. Recent surveys in these countries show the low priority given by public opinion to the developing world and to relations with it. The results of the North-South Conference are the most recent version of the response of the developed countries to the Third World.

But is this response an insuperable obstacle to the elimination of underdevelopment and poverty in the periphery? Do the developing countries have no other alternatives for solving their problems than an enlightened and generous response from the center? This is certainly not so. Much of the Third World, especially Latin America, has reached a level of development and available resources that enables them to cope successfully, over reasonable periods of time, with the basic problems of backwardness and poverty. Annual per capita income in Latin America is about 800 dollars, and there is a considerable resource potential and the ability to administer these resources. In any case, the fact that 40% of the Latin American population lives in severe poverty is due more to unequal income distribution than to lack of resources. It should be remembered that 50% of the Latin American population receives 14% of total income, whereas the upper 10% receives 44%. The solution to these problems does not depend primarily on the responses of the advanced countries to the Third World, but on "far-reaching internal changes of a social, political, and institutional character in the developing countries" (Leontieff, 1977: 11). It is obvious that the internal transformation of these countries cannot be achieved within the North-South dialogue.

On the other hand, many of the conflicts that arise between the industrial world and the underdeveloped countries are not negotiable; their solution depends on the latter's taking rational and effective political decisions. For example, a change in the conditions for incorporating investment and foreign technology depends on internal decisions. OPEC illustrates this most vividly. In the present conditions of many developing countries, it actually creates less problems to nationalize a foreign enterprise than to introduce a tax reform that affects the high-income groups within the country.

Furthermore, the dispersion of economic power within the bloc of industrial countries, and the increased number of sources of supply of technology, capital goods, and financing, have greatly improved the Third World's freedom of action abroad. Even with all the problems posed by the present level of external indebtedness of several developing countries, there is little doubt that having broader access to the international financial markets in recent years has strengthened their hand. Another recent example is the Brazilian-German nuclear agreement, which was concluded in the face of opposition from the United States.

Contemporary experience shows that while Latin American countries are more and more affected by international events, their development depends primarily on their own internal decisions on resource allocation, income distribution, and the elimination of their dependency on the center countries. In a new historical perspective, "inward development," the integration of national systems, the incorporation of technological change into internal conditions, and national control of resources are essential elements in a strategy to cope with underdevelopment and dependency.

The response of the developed countries to Latin America and the Third World will depend primarily on the initiatives taken by the latter. Again the example of OPEC comes to mind. In any event, the idea of a new international economic order has not arisen from a generous and enlightened proposal by the major countries, but from recommendations made by the developing world. It is suggested here that the direction taken by relations between the two groups of countries depends basically on Third World initiatives. These include closer ties among the developing countries. In Latin America, the success of the industrial integration of the Andean Group, the effective use of the instruments of action of the Latin American Economic System (SELA), and the Argentine-Brazilian agreement on the exploitation of energy resources in the Paraná basin exemplify the actions essential to the development of the countries of the region and to the creation of new conditions in their relations with the developed capitalist countries and the rest of the world.

From the Latin American standpoint, it is not likely that there will be significant changes in the responses of the developed world to the fundamental problems facing the region. On the other hand, the internal evolution of the United States and the major industrial economies will be very important to Latin America. As long as the developed countries continue to be trapped in the unemployment-inflation trade-off, the adjustment process of the Latin American economies will be more difficult.

The continuation of the conditions of slow growth, high unemployment, and steep price rises in the industrialized world is frankly negative. Therefore, the center's orthodox policies also cost the Latin American countries dearly in terms of weak demand for the primary products traditionally exported by Latin America, increased protectionism against Latin American manufactures that compete in critial sectors of the developed economies, and a worsening of the chronic external disequilibrium of most of the countries of Latin America. In such circumstances, it is difficult to find a solution to the problems of external financing and of debt servicing. There is little doubt that Latin American policies, to cope with their basic development problems and their process of integration and cooperation, will continue to be strongly affected by the economic evolution of the major industrial countries. It is therefore important for Latin America to follow carefully the way in which these countries are dealing with the current crisis and to understand the theoretical framework of their economic policies.

It may be said that Latin America should be more concerned about what the United States can do for itself than what the United States can do for Latin America.

## REFERENCES

ECLA (1977) The Economic and Social Development and the External Relations of Latin America. Santiago, Chile: ECLA. (mimeo)

Economist (1977a) "Aiding the deficits." April 30-May 6: 90-91.

——— (1977b) "A survey of American financial institutions." January 22-28: 5-60, Survey.

FERRER, A. (1976) Economía internacional contemporánea; texto para latinoamericanos. México, D.F.: Fondo de Cultura Economica.

——— (1975) Tecnología y política económica en América Latina. Buenos Aires: Paidos.

IMF Survey (1977) Communiqué of the Interim Committee, May 2. Washington, DC: IMF.

——— (1976a) Communiqué of the Group of 24, January 19. Washington, DC: IMF.

——— (1976b) Press release of January 19 by U.S. delegation. Washington, DC: IMF.

LEONTIEFF, W. (1977) The Future of the World Economy. United Nations Study. New York: Oxford Univ. Press.

*Aldo Ferrer, a former Minister of Economy and Labor of Argentina, is Director of the Centro de Estudios de Coyuntura at the Instituto de Desarrollo Económico y Social, Buenos Aires. A graduate of the University of Buenos Aires, he is also former Executive Secretary of the Latin American Social Sciences Council, author of* The Argentine Economy *(University of California Press, 1967),* Tecnología y Política Económica en América Latina *(Paidos, Buenos Aires, 1975) and* Crisis y Alternativas de la Política Económica Argentina *(Fonda de Cultura Económica, Buenos Aires, 1977).*

**RAMESH C. GARG**
*School of Business Administration*
*Philadelphia College of Textiles and Science*
*Philadelphia, Pennsylvania 19144*

# *BRAZILIAN EXTERNAL DEBT*
## *A Study in Capital Flows and Transfer of Resources*

In recent years the problem of the external indebtedness of non-oil-exporting countries has gained significant weight in public discussion.[1] With the quadrupling of oil prices since the end of 1973, a rapid increase in the borrowing of LDCs has occurred. The standard of living in these countries is extremely low to begin with; any further room for downward adjustment to offset higher cost of oil imports through a slowing down of economy is simply an unacceptable possibility. Moreover, any further economic restraint on the already slower pace of development would be politically unpopular for the leaders in developing countries. Consequently, many LDCs have resorted to increasing external borrowings to pay for the oil bill, as well as to maintain a minimum rate of economic growth. The total external public debt[2] of these countries is now estimated at around $200 billion (U.S. Senate, 1977: 51). This paper examines the debt servicing experience of Brazil. Lately, Brazil has been the center of attention because it owes some $25-$30 billion to foreign creditors. Its debt servicing burden for 1977 would be approximately $5.3 billion, or 40% of an estimated $12 billion in export earnings.

Journal of Interamerican Studies and World Affairs, Vol. 20 No. 3, August 1978

TABLE 1
Brazil: Selected Data on External Public Debt

| YEAR | TOTAL DEBT OUTSTANDING (US $ mn) | TOTAL DEBT SERVICE (US $ mn) | SERVICE PAYMENTS AS P.C. OF EXPORTS (%) | BALANCE ON CURRENT A/C. (SDRs mn) |
|---|---|---|---|---|
| 1967 | 3,533 | 280 | 15.6 | -276 |
| 1968 | 3,908 | 317 | 15.6 | -526 |
| 1969 | 4,153 | 402 | 15.6 | -336 |
| 1970 | 5,080 | 439 | 14.3 | -561 |
| 1971 | 6,295 | 534 | 16.2 | -1,313 |
| 1972 | 8,002 | 716 | 16.4 | -1,372 |
| 1973 | 9,557 | 885 | 13.2 | -1,475 |
| 1974 | 12,022 | 1,125 | 13.0 | -5,971 |
| 1975 | 14,121 | 1,435 | 15.0 | -5,558 |

SOURCES: Data on external public debt taken from IBRD (1977 and 1976) *World Debt Tables*. The data on "Balance on Current A/C" from IMF (1977 and 1976) *Balance of Payments Year Book*.

Even with the 400% increase in the price of coffee, which is Brazil's most important export, the country may have to raise an additional $6 billion to finance the 1977 payment deficits (U.S. Senate, 1977: 54). The problems associated with the balance of payments and external debt management have proved to be serious constraints on the growth of the Brazilian economy in the past few years. An analysis of the data might suggest that Brazil's debt problem was caused not so much by the magnitude of the outstanding debt, but by the stringent terms of borrowing. Debt structure has been heavily concentrated in short-term maturities. Brazilian firms have frequently borrowed in the international market to supplement domestic credits. Borrowing abroad has been considered an attractive proposition even though the borrower must bear the risk of exchange rate fluctuations. Most of these financial credits had maturities of less than one year.

According to the World Bank's recent estimates, the total external public debt outstanding for Brazil increased from $3.5 billion in 1967 to just over $14.0 billion in 1975 (Table 1). This represents an increase of over 400% in eight years. The estimated payments of interest and amoritization, however, increased by 512% during the same period (from $0.280 billion in 1967 to $1.435 billion in 1975).

Since 1971, the debt has been growing at an annual rate of 22%. The debt service payments, on the other hand, have been growing at a much faster rate—more than 28%—for the same period. At the end of 1975, the total debt outstanding for the country represented 10.7% of its GNP and 120% of its exports. The ratios of debt service payments to GNP and exports were 1.3% and 15%, respectively (IBRD, 1977: 219 and 223). Brazil experienced a number of years of substantial balance of payments current account deficits (see Table 1). In 1974, the deficit reached its peak to date at almost $6 billion. Such deficits primarily raised the country's dependence on external capital to fill in the resource gap.[3] The domestic economic policies were geared to achieve relatively rapid industrialization by accelerating the rate of investment in the economy. The beginning of 1968 marked a period of high growth rates for the Brazilian economy. As per the ECLA estimates, the average growth rate of the gross domestic product increased from around 7% for the years 1965-1969 to 11% for 1970-1973 (ECLA, 1976: 53). As far as the financing aspect of this high growth rate is concerned, a policy of complementing domestic credit with liberal external financing was followed by the Brazilian Government (ECLA, 1976: 54-55). The growth policy also called for liberal allocation on the import front.

Because of the measures adopted to pursue the growth policy and the improved creditworthiness of the country abroad, Brazil received massive doses of external capital. This phenomenon explains the significant growth in the Brazilian external public debt. It should be noted that the large commitment of external resources dangerously increased the vulnerability of the Brazilian economy both externally and internally. The resultant increase in the service payments on external debt constitutes a fixed charge on the external earnings. Internally, a large intake of the external resources has provided a constant source of inflationary conditions. In this context, it should be further noted that public sector deficits were primarily financed through monetary expansion, which explains Brazil's almost continuous state of inflation.

TABLE 2
Brazil: Structure of External Public Debt
and Debt Service Payments—1975
(US$ million)

| CATEGORY OF LENDER | EXTERNAL DEBT | | DEBT SERVICE | | DEBT SERVICE AS P.C. OF DEBT OUTSTANDING |
|---|---|---|---|---|---|
| | Outstanding Amount | Percent Distribution | Outstanding Amount | Percent Distribution | |
| Governments | 2,864 | 20 | 224 | 16 | 7.8 |
| International Organizations | 3,069 | 22 | 145 | 10 | 4.7 |
| Financial Markets | 6,671 | 47 | 738 | 51 | 11.0 |
| Other Private Creditors | 168 | 1 | 19 | 1 | 11.3 |
| Suppliers' Credits | 1,349 | 10 | 309 | 22 | 22.9 |
| TOTAL | 14,121 | 100 | 1,435 | 100 | 10.2 |

SOURCE: IBRD (1977) *World Debt Tables.*

Who are the major creditors of Brazil? The most important one is the borrowing from financial markets. This single source represents 47% of the total outstanding external debt in 1975 (Table 2). Credits from the financial markets consist of loans from overseas private banks and other financial institutions, publicly and privately placed bonds, and credits from official commercial banks. Brazil, being a relatively high income LDC with significant export base, has enjoyed a good credit rating in the international financial markets. A recent study by the International Monetary Fund estimates that at the end of December 1976 Brazil and Mexico accounted for 44% of identified gross outstanding debts to banks by non-oil-exporting developing countries and for 86% of their net bank debt (IMF Survey, 1977: 182).[4] Morgan Guaranty Trust Company estimates that by the end of 1976 Brazil owed some $21.22 billion to overseas private banks, out of which $13.86 billion came from the U.S. multinational banks (Morgan Guaranty Trust Co., 1977). Thus, Brazil has been one of the best customers for private international banks.[5] However, the cost of borrowing from the external financial market has been very high for Brazil. For example, in 1975 the average debt service cost from this source was 11.0%, which is well above the accepted bench mark of 10% (Table 2).[6]

International organizations constitute the second rank in the league of creditors for Brazil. In 1975, this source accounted for 22% of the total outstanding debt for Brazil. Loans from this category include credits from the World Bank group, Inter-American Development Bank, and other multilateral and inter-governmental agencies. The average cost of borrowing for Brazil has been the lowest from this source. For example, in 1975, the average cost of borrowing from the international organizations was only 4.7% (see Table 2). Next in importance of Brazil's creditors are the various governments. This source represented 20% of the external debts in 1975. A major portion of the loans from this category is borrowed from the member countries of the Development Assistance Committee (DAC).[7] As Table 2 shows, the average cost of borrowing from government sources was 7.8% in 1975.

The final category of creditors remains that of Suppliers' Credits. They represent credits from manufacturers, exporters, or other suppliers of goods (mostly located in developed countries). In 1975, their share of debt was 10% of the total outstanding debt. However, the percentage of total debt service payments absorbed in servicing suppliers' credits was 22%. The average cost of borrowing from this source has been the highest. For example, in 1975, the average cost of borrowing was 22.9%, which represented the highest percentage cost of borrowing for the year (Table 2).

Everything considered, the Brazilian debt structure has not been a favorable one. It is the relatively higher proportion of loans from the financial markets and the suppliers' credits which distinguishes Brazil's debt problem from that of other developing countries.[8] Official loans from the multilateral institutions constitute only one-fifth of the total Brazilian debt. In recent years, significant welcoming efforts have been made to reduce the share of suppliers' credits, which had reached as high as 23% in 1970.

TABLE 3
Brazil: Total Debt and Debt Service Payments by Source
(percent distribution)

| YEAR | DEBT OUTSTANDING | | DEBT SERVICE | | DEBT SERVICE AS % OF DEBT | |
|---|---|---|---|---|---|---|
| | Total Official | Total Private | Total Official | Total Private | Official | Private |
| (1) | (2) | (3) | (4) | (5) | (6) | (7) |
| 1967 | 74 | 26 | 76 | 24 | 8.1 | 7.5 |
| 1968 | 73 | 27 | 66 | 34 | 7.4 | 10.1 |
| 1969 | 69 | 31 | 59 | 41 | 8.3 | 12.9 |
| 1970 | 60 | 40 | 58 | 42 | 8.4 | 9.0 |
| 1971 | 55 | 45 | 51 | 49 | 7.8 | 9.3 |
| 1972 | 54 | 46 | 38 | 62 | 6.3 | 12.1 |
| 1973 | 49 | 51 | 33 | 67 | 6.2 | 12.3 |
| 1974 | 44 | 56 | 25 | 75 | 5.4 | 12.5 |
| 1975 | 42 | 58 | 26 | 74 | 6.2 | 13.0 |

SOURCE: Calculated from the data on external debt.

## *Debt Structural Analysis*

Table 3 indicates the percentage distribution of debt between the official and private borrowings for the years 1967 through 1975. The official source includes borrowing from various foreign governments and international organizations. The private source, on the other hand, includes suppliers' credits, financial markets, and other private lenders. As can be seen from column 2 of the table, the percentage share of official capital has consistently been declining, from 74% in 1967 to 42% in 1975. At the same time, the role of private borrowing has increased in the Brazilian debt structure. The percentage distribution of the total debt service payments among the official and private debts is shown in columns 4 and 5. It can be observed that the percentage share of the total debt service payments to finance private borrowing has increased at a much faster rate compared to the corresponding increase in the share of such borrowings themselves. The share of total debt service absorbed to service private borrowing has increased from 24% in 1967 to 74% in 1975—an increase of 308%; whereas the share of private borrowing increased from 26% in 1967 to 58% in 1975—an increase of 223%.

The debt servicing experience for Brazil on account of the official capital has been just the reverse; i.e., the percentage of total debt service needed to finance the official borrowing declined from 76% in 1967 to 26% in 1975. The share of official debt, during the same period, declined from 74% to 42%, respectively. This analysis leads to the following conclusions. The share of private borrowing has been historically increasing in the Brazilian debt structure. At the same time, the cost of servicing private borrowing is increasing at a much faster rate. The historical share of official borrowing, on the other hand, is decreasing in the Brazilian debt structure, while the cost of servicing such capital is also decreasing at a faster rate. These adverse movements in the debt structure of Brazil by no means indicate a desirable trend. Columns 6 and 7 of Table 3 provide the data for the percentage cost of borrowing from the official and private sources, respectively. It leads one to believe that Brazil has been able to borrow official capital on increasingly concessional terms whereas the terms on private borrowing have become stiff in recent years.

*Resource Transfer Analysis*

What has been the impact of the above-mentioned shift in the external debt structure on Brazil's transfer of resources? The resource transfer analysis provides a suitable mechanism to ascertain the extent of resource transfer that a country has realized over a period of time. Literature pertaining to the field of international capital movements generally discusses the concept of resource flows. Three variations of capital flows are involved: gross capital inflow, net capital inflow, and resource transfer. Gross capital inflow is defined as all receipts on capital account, without any offsets. Net capital inflow is defined as gross inflow less amortization of loans in case of external debt. Resource transfer on account of external public debt is defined as net capital inflow less interest charges on such debts. The resource transfer concept essentially indicates how much of the

TABLE 4
Brazil: Capital Inflow, Service Payments, and Resource Transfer Analysis, 1967-1975
(US$ million)

| YEAR | DEBT DISBURSEMENT DURING THE YEAR | DEBT SERVICE | | | NET FLOW | NET TRANSFER | IN P.C. OF DEBT DISBURSEMENT | |
|---|---|---|---|---|---|---|---|---|
| | | Amortization | Interest | Total | | | Net Flow | Net Transfer |
| 1967 | 576 | 206 | 74 | 280 | 370 | 296 | 64 | 51 |
| 1968 | 484 | 238 | 79 | 317 | 246 | 167 | 51 | 35 |
| 1969 | 572 | 288 | 114 | 402 | 284 | 170 | 50 | 30 |
| 1970 | 992 | 316 | 124 | 439 | 676 | 552 | 68 | 56 |
| 1971 | 974 | 381 | 153 | 534 | 593 | 440 | 61 | 45 |
| 1972 | 1,611 | 493 | 223 | 716 | 1,118 | 895 | 69 | 56 |
| 1973 | 1,923 | 589 | 296 | 885 | 1,334 | 1,038 | 69 | 54 |
| 1974 | 2,745 | 635 | 490 | 1,125 | 2,110 | 1,620 | 77 | 59 |
| 1975 | 3,434 | 818 | 617 | 1,435 | 2,616 | 1,999 | 76 | 58 |
| 1967-1975 | 13,311 | 3,964 | 2,170 | 6,133 | 9,347 | 7,177 | 70 | 54 |
| 1967-1970 | 2,624 | 1,048 | 391 | 1,438 | 1,576 | 1,185 | 60 | 45 |
| 1971-1975 | 10,687 | 2,916 | 1,779 | 4,695 | 7,771 | 5,992 | 73 | 56 |

SOURCE: IBRD (1977 and 1976) *World Debt Tables* and calculations made by the author.

gross capital inflow is left over to the borrowing country after it pays for the service items.[9]

Table 4 provides the data on resource transfer for Brazil. The data are being compiled by the World Bank based on the reporting made to it by individual countries. The calculations for the net capital flow and resource transfer per unit of external debt disbursement are made by this author. The data cover the latest available statistics for a period of nine years, from 1967 through 1975. It may be observed that Brazil has, on the average, realized a net transfer of resources in the magnitude of 54% of its total borrowings during 1967-1975.[10] From this observation it follows that it takes almost two dollars of fresh borrowings to materialize one dollar of net transfer of real resources. Since 1972, however, the transfer of foreign resources has been increasing. This welcome trend can partially be explained by a simultaneously decreasing share of the suppliers' credits in the Brazilian debt structure.

What can be done in the future about the country's debt problem? Brazil's ability to avoid service payment difficulties depends primarily upon the maintenance of an adequate export base. The country must also reduce its dependence on imports and, thus, on foreign capital to finance its trade deficits. An elaborate policy of import substitution must be instituted by the planners in the country. Given the natural geographical protection and its effect on transportation costs, a great deal of import substitution can be sustained by the economy as it grows in size. Efforts should be continued to reduce the share of suppliers' credits in the total borrowings of the country. At the same time, the worsening trend in the debt structure, as noted above, should be corrected. Planning authorities must devise a long-term plan for substituting high-cost private borrowings with low-cost official borrowings. At the end of 1974, the debt maturity structure of Brazil called for 75% of the total borrowings to be repaid in less than ten years, out of which 39% was due in less than five years (IBRD, 1976b: 51). This suggests a heavy concentration of maturities in earlier years.[11] The future of coffee crops, along with any significant switch among coffee consumers in developed countries in favor of its substitutes because of higher coffee prices, are areas of major concern which require immediate attention and planning. Much will depend upon the cooperation between the coffee-producing countries to avoid maldistribution in order to prevent any further collapse of the market. Any improvement in liquidity during the next several years will greatly strengthen the Brazilian economy's ability to confront its debt servicing problems.

A detailed analysis of the Brazilian case should not detract from the fact that most of the non-oil-exporting LDCs are in a similar boat today, with external debt and service payment demands increasing at an alarming rate. A reasonable limit exists in regard to the amount of credit which will be extended to LDCs by many lending institutions, whose portfolios already carry significant investments in such loans.

Recent publications and conference topics about this situation suggest increased recognition and concern that some LDCs may be approaching their credit limits. A shortsighted reaction leading to a significantly reduced transfer of resources to LDCs might have repercussions beyond the debtor countries involved.

The pursuit of international cooperation leading to increased disclosure, development of better debt service capability measurements, and an international debt management policy with a view to seeking new loans on the basis of both favorable maturity structures and concessional terms will result in a lessening of the future debt service burden for all developing countries and a strengthening of the international economic structure.

## NOTES

1. See in particular IBRD (1976a: 17-26), Avramović (1970), Garg (1977), IBRD (1976b), New York Times (1977), U.S. Senate (1977), and *Wall Street Journal* (1977).

2. External public debt is defined as the debt incurred or guaranteed by government repayable to nonresidents in foreign currency, with an original or extended maturity of more than one year.

3. Literature on economic development explains the concept of resource gap by using a model of two gaps: trade gap and saving gap. Analysis of gaps makes it possible to determine the capital requirements which must be met in order to attain a desired rate of growth. The method of using two gaps is already well known in developing countries through the application of similar procedures in recent years by UNCTAD, ECLA, ISPES, AID, and Professor Hollis B. Chenery, in addition to calculations made by national experts or foreign consultants in individual countries.

4. Net figures after these countries' claims (deposits) on banks are subtracted.

5. For example, 13% of Citybank's worldwide consolidated operating earnings came from Brazil (compared to 28% from the United States). Brazil is also Chase Manhattan's fourth largest loan exposure after Japan, the United States, and United Kingdom (U.S. Senate, 1977: 56).

6. See, for example, Avramović (1970: 130). Avramović maintains that if the debt were contracted on a 25-year repayment schedule with an average interest rate of 6%, the percentage of total debt service on debt outstanding would be 10%—4% for amortization, plus 6% for interest. To justify the benchmark of 10%, according to Avramović, it is hardly conceivable that development can be financed by any terms worse than the terms this number would suggest.

7. For example, in 1974 Brazil borrowed 91% of its total government borrowing from DAC countries, whereas only 7.4% came from the East Bloc countries. For additional information regarding the aid programs of each member of the DAC countries, see OECD (1973). Loans from the USSR and Eastern Europe are almost entirely bilateral. They are heavily project-oriented, and technical assistance for the project usually comes with the loan. Typically such loans carry a low interest rate of 2.5% but have shorter maturities.

8. It may be noted that the share of suppliers' credits in the debt structures of Mexico and India was only 4% and 2%, respectively, for 1975.

9. For detailed understanding of the concept of resource transfer, see Avramović (1970: 134-136) and Garg (1977: 95-96).

10. An average resource transfer of 54% for Brazil is somewhat in line with the data calculated by this author for 86 developing countries. The average of resources for 86 developing countries was 55% from 1967-1974. See Garg (1977: 96).

11. The maturity structure for Colombia, another coffee-exporting country, at the end of 1974 called for 51% of the total debt to be repaid in less than ten years, and only 26% to be repaid in less than five years (IBRD, 1976b: 51). This situation made Colombian debt maturity structure more favorable as compared to that of Brazil.

## REFERENCES

AVRAMOVIC, D. (1970) "Latin American external debt." J. of World Trade Law (March-April): 121-154.

Economic Commission for Latin America [ECLA] (1976) Economic Survey of Latin America, 1974. New York: United Nations.

GARG, R. C. (1977) "Debt problems of developing countries." Intereconomics, Rev. of Int. Trade and Development (March-April): 93-96.

IBRD (1977) World Debt Tables, Vols. I and II (September 2). Washington, DC: World Bank.

——— (1976a) Summary Proceedings: 1976 Annual Meetings World Bank IFC/IDA. Washington, DC: World Bank.

——— (1976b) World Debt Tables, Vols. I and II (October 31). Washington, DC: World Bank.

International Monetary Fund (1977) IMF Survey (June 6). Washington, DC: IMF.

Morgan Guaranty Trust Company (1977) World Financial Markets (June). New York: Morgan Guaranty Trust Co.

New York Times (1977) "Mountain of debt pile up as banks push foreign loans." May 15, Sec. 3.

OECD (1973) Flow of Resources to Developing Countries. Pairs: OECD.

U.S. Senate (1977) "International debt, the banks, and U.S. foreign policy." Staff report prepared for the use of the Subcommittee on Foreign Economic Policy of the Committee on Foreign Relations (August). Washington, DC: Government Printing Office.

Wall Street Journal (1977) "Developing debts: poor countries face test of their ability to repay bank loans." April 14.

*Ramesh C. Garg is Associate Professor of Finance in the School of Business of the Philadelphia College of Textiles and Science. During the summer of 1971 he conducted research in Latin America on the external debt problems of Brazil, Chile, Colombia, and Argentina. In addition to having delivered papers on external debt problems of developing countries at various professional meetings, he is the author of "Debt Problems of Developing Countries" (March/April, 1977,* Intereconomics, Review of International Trade and Development, *Hamburg).*

# Advertising Supplement:

# Journal of Interamerican Studies and World Affairs

This supplement has been prepared especially for our readers to bring them information and announcements of professional interest. By placing advertisements in the pages of this journal, our advertisers have indicated a desire to communicate with our readers. We hope our readers will acknowledge their indirect support of the journal and its purposes by mentioning the journal in correspondence with advertisers.

# LATIN AMERICA AND WORLD ECONOMY: A Changing International Order

edited by **JOSEPH GRUNWALD**

How do nations of Latin America interact with other countries in the world community? This anthology approaches the region's relations with the outside world from both an economic and a political perspective, examining Latin America's desire to integrate with the world economy, as well as its struggle for self-reliance. Latin American and non-Latin American contributors discuss a range of subjects including the character of the "special relationship" between Latin America and the United States, and the ambiguous nature of Latin America's relations with other countries of the Third World.

**CONTENTS**


Preface

1. Reflections on Latin America in the World Economy, JOSEPH BRUNWALD

**Part I. Economic Relations with Industrial Countries**

2. The Mature Neighbor Policy: A Proposal for A United States Economic Policy for Latin America, ALBERT FISHLOW
3. Britain's Economic Relations with Latin America, LAURENCE WHITEHEAD
4. The Economic Relations between Germany and Latin America and the significance of the European Community, ALBRECHT von GLEICH
5. Latin America's Opening to the Pacific, CLAUDIO VELEZ

**Part II. Mexico and Brazil**

6. The External Sector of the Mexican Economy, LEOPOLDO SOLIS
7. The Determinants of Brazil's Foreign Economic Policy, WERNER BAER, CARLOS von DOELLINGER

**Part III. Regional Integration and Economic Relations with the Third World**

8. The Andean Pact: A Model of Economic Integration for Developing Countries, RICARDO FFRENCH-DAVIS
9. Fissures in the Volcano? Centeral American Economic Prospects, CLARK W. REYNOLDS
10. Latin America and the Third World, FELIPE HERRERA

**Part IV. Two Major Issues: Financing Development and the Multinational Corporation**

11. Problems of External Financing in Latin America, LUIS ESCOBAR
12. Mexico and Multinational Corporations: An Explanation of State Action, DOUGLAS BENNETT, MORRIS J. BLACHMAN, KENNETH SHARPE

**Part V. Commentary**

**The Good Neighbor Policy Revisite**

**Part V. Commentary**

The Good Neighbor Policy Revisited, BRYCE WOOD

Notes on SELA, GABRIEL VALDES S.




*"As long as the notion persists that Latin America is unimportant for the United States and other developed countries, it will be difficult to persuade Latin American countries that they are living in an interdependent world. One-sided importance creates a one-sided dependency relationship. Such a perseption results in demands, not cooperation. Cooperation for development becomes meaningful only when there is a recognition of interdependence on both sides of the North-South relationship."*

*— from Chapter 1*


Latin American International Affairs, Volume 2

| | | | |
|---|---|---|---|
| April 1978 | ISBN 0-8039-0864-4 | hardcover | $18.50 |
| 320 pages | ISBN 0-8039-0966-7 | softcover | $ 7.95 |

**SAGE** Publications, Inc.
275 South Beverly Drive
Beverly Hills, California 90212

**SAGE** Publications Ltd
28 Banner Street
London EC1Y 8QE

Vol. 20 No. 4
November 1978

# JOURNAL OF INTERAMERICAN STUDIES

# and WORLD AFFAIRS

A Publication of the Center for Advanced International Studies,
The University of Miami

SAGE PUBLICATIONS

*Journal of INTERAMERICAN STUDIES and WORLD AFFAIRS*



The editors and publisher wish to acknowledge with gratitude the assistance and encouragement of the Center for Advanced International Studies, University of Miami, in providing ancillary services and support for this journal.

*Journal of*
INTERAMERICAN
STUDIES
*and* WORLD AFFAIRS

Vol. 20
No. 4
November
1978

# CONTENTS

*Rural Poverty in Twentieth-Century Colombia*
ALBERT BERRY 355

*The Wisdom of Salomon: Myth or Reality?*
DAVID NICHOLLS 377

*Regional Party Voting in Jamaica (1959-1976)*
CARL STONE 393

*The American Revolution and Latin America: An Essay in Imagery, Perceptions, and Ideological Influence*
ROBERT FREEMAN SMITH 421

**REVIEW ESSAYS**

*Political Power in Contemporary Costa Rica*
JOHN PATRICK BELL 443

*Characteristics of Contemporary Latin American International Relations*
JAMES D. COCHRANE 455

**BOOKS RECEIVED** 469

**INDEX** 477

SAGE PUBLICATIONS / *Beverly Hills* *London*

**POLICY: THE JOURNAL OF INTERAMERICAN STUDIES AND WORLD AFFAIRS** reflects the interests of the scholarly community and interested public concerned with the social, economic, political, and cultural aspects of life in Latin America (including the Caribbean); particularly in those instances where the subject is of concern to more than one of the traditional disciplines. As these concerns change, so will the content of the journal.

**ARTICLES** which have special relevance for interrelationships between American nations and of those nations with the rest of the world will be given special consideration. An effort will be made to include occasional articles that state an unusual or even discordant position on a subject of broad interest to be supplemented by critical comments of authorities representing differing positions on the topic. The editors continue to welcome articles by scholars from all parts of the world.

**MANUSCRIPTS** should be submitted in duplicate to: Editor, JOURNAL OF INTERAMERICAN STUDIES AND WORLD AFFAIRS, Box 24-8134, University of Miami, Coral Gables, Florida 33124. Manuscripts should be typewritten, double-spaced, with footnotes, references, tables, and charts on separate pages, and should follow the current journal style. A brief biographical paragraph describing each author's current affiliation, research interests, and recent publications should accompany the manuscript.

**CORRESPONDENCE** regarding book reviews should be sent directly to: Book Review Editor, JOURNAL OF INTERAMERICAN STUDIES AND WORLD AFFAIRS, Box 24-8134, University of Miami, Coral Gables, Florida 33124.

---

**JOURNAL OF INTERAMERICAN STUDIES AND WORLD AFFAIRS** is published four times annually—in February, May, August, and November. 

**Subscriptions:** Regular institutional rate $28.00. Individuals may subscribe at a one-year rate of $15.00. Add $1.00 per year for subscriptions outside the United States. Orders from U.K., Europe, the Middle East, and Africa should be sent to the London office (address below). Noninstitutional orders **must** be paid by personal check.

Second-class postage paid at Beverly Hills, California.

**Inquiries:** Address all correspondence and permissions requests to SAGE PUBLICATIONS, INC., 275 South Beverly Drive, Beverly Hills, California 90212. Inquiries and subscriptions from U.K., Europe, the Middle East, and Africa should be sent to SAGE PUBLICATIONS LTD, 28 Banner Street, London EC1Y 8QE, England. Other orders should be sent to the Beverly Hills office.

**Advertising:** Current rates and specifications may be obtained by writing to the Advertising Manager at the Beverly Hills office (address above).

This journal is abstracted or indexed in **Historical Abstracts, Human Resources Abstracts, Sage Urban Studies Abstracts, International Political Science Abstracts, Public Affairs Information Service, Current Contents, Social Sciences Citation Index, Social Sciences Index, ABC POL SCI and United States Political Science Documents.**

**Back Issues:** Information about availability and prices of back issues may be obtained from the publisher's order department (address above). Write to London office for sterling prices.

**Claims for undelivered copies** must be made no later than three months following month of publication. The publisher will supply missing copies when losses have been sustained in transit and where the reserve stock will permit.

---

**Change of Address:** Six weeks' advance notice must be given when notifying of change of address. Please send old address label along with the new address to insure proper identification. Please specify name of journal.

**ALBERT BERRY**
*Department of Political Economy*
*University of Toronto*
*100 St. George Street*
*Toronto, Canada M5S 1A1*

# *RURAL POVERTY IN TWENTIETH-CENTURY COLOMBIA*

Until recently Colombia has been a mainly rural and agricultural country. At the turn of the century probably 65% to 75% of the labor force was in agriculture; by 1951 this share had fallen to about 55% and in 1975 to about 35%. The share of population in rural areas was a little higher. In 1900 perhaps 50% to 55% of output came from agriculture; though it remains the main producing sector, its share had fallen to 25% by 1974.

Colombia has always had a highly unequal distribution of income, the major historical cause being an extremely unequal distribution of land. Over the years economic policy could be fairly described as "urban biased," so that the group to whose welfare public policy has contributed the least are the landless agricultural workers, including a good number of migrant workers.

This paper addresses itself to the character and the severity of rural poverty in Colombia during this century, with particular focus on whether it has been substantially alleviated by the growth and development of the economy during this period. Available evidence, while scattered, does permit some judgments on both counts. Poverty has, of course, its material aspect and any attempted quantifications of it refer to that aspect. However, other aspects of living patterns may be equally, or more, important to the welfare of a group. The position of materially poor people in the social system, the insecurity of material and nonmaterial welfare in the future, and the levels of internal conflict are all pertinent. In both the material and the less tangible

Journal of Interamerican Studies and World Affairs, Vol. 20 No. 4, November 1978

aspects, it is important in looking at rural Colombia to distinguish different groups: small farmers from landless workers, the poorest regions from less poor ones, women from men, one cultural group from another (e.g., Indian groups from black or white groups). Lack of information precludes a discussion of poverty which gives due account to the varying life styles and contexts of these groups. Rather, we attempt to illustrate the relevance of such distinctions while generalizing to the extent possible.

## *I. Living Conditions in Rural Areas in the First Half of the Twentieth Century*

Colombia's period of most rapid structural change began in the 1920s and accelerated in later decades. There was, most notably, a large decline in the share of the population living in rural areas, although the absolute number of rural people continued to increase until recently. In the first decades of this century rural life was, for most people, decidedly traditional and decidedly sparse in most respects.

As of the late 1930s, although rural income levels were very low, inequality was probably less extreme than now. Most of the poorer rural families were engaged mainly in farming (their own or other's land) or as hired agricultural workers—frequently a combination of the two. Probably about 10% to 15% of family heads were paid employees (CIDA, 1966: 133), though nearly one-half of the labor force were. With land less scarce than later, and mechanization little advanced, labor's share of value added (including imputed labor income of the self-employed) appears to have been over 50%—much higher than it is now (Berry and Urrutia, 1976: 68). Typical rates in the various departments ranged between 50 and 80 centavos per day (i.e., about 30 to 50 U.S. cents).[1] Poverty was most severe in the long-settled Andean departments of Nariño, Cauca, Boyacá, and Cundinamarca, although no department escaped exiguity.

Poverty meant low levels of consumption and nutrition, high mortality rates and low life expectancy, little education of inferior quality, and virtually no prospect of substantial advance in economic or social terms. In most of the main cultural variants found in Colombia, the occupation of farmer or agricultural worker was of low social prestige.[2] For nonwhites, this occupational inferiority was often combined with a racial inferiority taught by the dominant culture and leading to widespread repressed resentment and hostility to it. Work was hard and long. The role of women was especially difficult; they bore large families, worked hard, suffered frequent abuse from their husbands, and were virtual servants (Gutiérrez de Pineda, 1963; Ortiz, 1973).

Some of these aspects of poverty can be quantified. We have estimated that in 1960, 30% of the income-earning agricultural labor force (this excludes unpaid family workers) got less than 1,500 pesos per year (about U.S. $240) and 60% got less than 2,000 pesos (about U.S. $300). Family incomes would be somewhat higher. For these low income groups, the big majority of their income (probably 70% to 80%) came from paid labor (Berry and Urrutia, 1976: 56).

The percentage of income spent on food (and more generally the overall composition) is a useful indicator of income levels. In Caldas, Cundinamarca, Nariño, Santander, and Valle in the 1950s and 1960s, small farmers were found to use more than 70% of their total expenditures (including home consumption) on food (Berry, n.d.: Table I-7). Comité Interamericano de Desarrollo Agrícola's [CIDA] (1966) family expenditure questionnaire (taken about 1962) indicated that almost all the hired workers spent more than one-half of their monetary incomes for food and often as much as 80% to 90%. The share of food expenditures on animal products is low. In 1962 farmers in the Río Suárez region spent relatively less this way than did *obreros* (blue-collar workers) in six of the seven cities in which the 1953 consumer survey was carried out, even less than the bottom fifth of those obrero families whose incomes fell in the range of 100-200 pesos per month (Reyes, et al., 1965: 233-236; Controlor General de la República, 1955). The share of expenditures on tubers and roots, higher than for any of the urban groups cited, is also indicative of low income, and further confirms the conclusion that most of Colombia's grinding poverty has traditionally been found in the rural areas.

Rural housing is distinctly inferior to urban. Houses tend to be small; in the late 1940s average size was estimated as 20 square meters—larger in the highlands, smaller in the lowlands—and the ratio of persons per room was estimated at two or more (IBRD, 1950: 232, 234). They do not have windows; light is provided by candles. Furnishings are very sparse; boxes or trunks typically serve as chairs. In 1951, 67% of the houses had earthen floors (DANE, 1954-1955). Electricity, sanitary facilities, and running water are absent.

Life expectancy was probably about 36 in rural areas as of the late 1930s. Infant mortality was very high (perhaps 200 per 1000 live births); life expectancy at age five was considerably higher, perhaps around 50.[3] Completed family size was large (probably six to eight surviving children on average); the number of births per woman was substantially larger since the infant mortality rate was so high.

A series of nutritional surveys found that about 46% of the families showed too low caloric consumption and about 48% too low protein consumption (Ministerio de Salud Pública, 1963). The figures would probably be even higher for rural areas alone. Often the diet is not well balanced. Many Colombians (especially rural) unfortunately have held beliefs which unnecessarily decreased the quality of their intake. Vegetables, for example, are commonly believed to be food for rabbits; citrus fruits are thought to be bad because they "cortan la sangre," and so on (Ministerio de Salud Pública, 1963: 20).

Heavy spending on alcohol by adult males exacerbates nutritional problems when it reduces consumption by children and women. Alcoholism has long been a serious problem in parts of rural Colombia (Bejarano, 1924). Drinking is often related to machismo and face-saving (Fals Borda, 1955) and to abuse of family.

The physical stature of the farmers, particularly in the highland areas, is indicative of nutritional problems. Smith et al. (1945) noted that as of 1945 the average height of males was

5 feet and of females 4 feet 6 inches. Impressionistic evidence would suggest that statures have risen since then.

The lack of potable water in most rural areas is a cause of many digestive tract diseases and, along with malnutrition, contributes to the high level of infant mortality, lying within the 125-175 range as of the mid-1960s and above 200 in the 1930s.

Government performance in the field of rural public health has been unimpressive. In a recent study of national health conditions (Ministerio de Salud Pública, 1967) the prevalence of self-perceived illness extended to a little over 40% of the population sampled (rural and urban); only eight percent of this group received medical care, with an almost equal number being treated by pharmacists, "curers," and others. These ratios vary with income levels and are worse (incidence of sickness somewhat worse and lack of treatment much worse) in rural than in urban areas (Zschock, 1968: 222).

Literacy and educational levels have always been low in the rural areas. In 1918 the literacy rate of persons 14 years and up (as recorded in the population census) may have been about 35%; in 1938, 47%; in 1964, 59%; and in 1973, 65%. Of those persons living in rural areas in 1964 and of primary school age in the late 1930s, 46% reported having finished grade two and 55% having finished grade one. Less than two percent finished the first year of secondary.[4]

The major deterrent to higher levels of rural education appears to have been the lack of facilities. In 1941, for example, only 30% of rural schools went beyond grade two. Quality is also a serious problem. As late as 1967 only about one-quarter of rural primary school teachers had any kind of diploma (though this was indeed a substantial improvement over the corresponding figure of nine percent in 1932). More strikingly, as of 1967 about 15% had no education beyond the primary level themselves.

Rural education has been a victim of official disinterest, as reflected in salary scales, facilities, and the like (Havens, 1965). Schools have typically been located in old dilapidated houses; frequently, the only teaching material present was a map of Colombia. As of 1970, more public funds were being spent on the

23,000 students attending the national universities than on the 1.35 million primary and secondary school age children in rural areas (Ministerio de Educación Nacional, 1973). Less than 10% of the primary school budget went to rural areas (Arnove, 1978), although at that time about 40% of public primary enrollment was in rural areas.

> A Paez family is up by four o'clock in the morning. In the semi-darkness one can hear them march down the road probably going to work in a field far from their houses. A man is accompanied by his wife and children, walking fast and silently without greeting, as they pass the house of a friend. They do not return until sunset. After a long day's work visiting is rare, unless the families live next door to each other and are very good friends. This working schedule continues indefinitely without any patterned break [Ortiz, 1973: 65].

Much of the paid labor force is made up of individuals who have their own small plot and divide their time between that plot and other work. There are relatively few permanent hired workers —i.e., employed full-time by one employer (probably under 15% of the agricultural labor force). Seasonal and occasional workers may or may not have their own land. A substantial portion of this group are migrant workers. The standard of living of these workers is often abysmally low; frequently they have to sleep outdoors; they may lack decent water (Ruíz, 1973: 48). They have to be on the move frequently in search of work. Sometimes the camps of such migrant workers are extremely violent.

For persons starting low on the economic scale, rapid upward mobility is difficult. What with pressures for social spending and the small margin of income above subsistence, saving is difficult for most of the rural poor.[5] The capital markets in rural areas do not facilitate capital accumulation by the small operator or the landless worker. Apart from land and agricultural capital (livestock and so on), there are no assets which in the average decade will even maintain their real value, let alone increase in value. Thus, the landless worker is likely to accumulate only if he can buy land or livestock, difficult because of the need for a minimum savings level (e.g., to buy a small farm) or the unwillingness of other people to make such arrangements (employers may fear losing a worker). The small operator suffers from the same constraints, though in lesser degree.

While social patterns may not promote savings and growth, they do provide elements of protection against calamity (Vautier and Fals Borda, 1958). In Saucío (Cundinamarca) Fals Borda (1955) noted the solidarity of the people, the considerable amount of economic cooperation (e.g., production in partnership and so on), and lending of money and tools.

Lack of political influence has been a notable feature in the life of the rural poor. Under Colombia's two-party system, the tradition in most parts of the country has been that a large farmer's tenants and workers are expected to vote as he tells them. Since local governments are weak and in any case partly appointed from above, and since rural areas are not administered separately from the country towns, the total political clout of the rural poor has been minimal. The lack of self-determination in politics in much of the rural population has not, paradoxically, made politics an unemotional aspect of life. Rather, political violence has been all too characteristic in Colombia and was a scourge during the late 1940s and early 1950s, the famous period of *La Violencia,* when close to perhaps 200,000 persons were killed in the rural areas. Most rural Colombians have borne great costs while receiving almost no benefits from political participation.

Unequal distribution of political power creates many other problems for the small farmers, tenants, and landless workers. Land conflict has been frequent in some areas and the poor are usually losers in such conflicts. One knowledgeable observer told me he knew of few large farms whose expansion (often gradual over long periods) had not involved some taking advantage of weaker claimants to land. Sometimes small farmers are in conflict among themselves (Ortiz, 1973: 90-91). Both types of situations can arise easily when land titles are vague and boundaries are not defined unambiguously.

## *II. Trends in Rural Poverty*

The twentieth century in general and the last several decades in particular have witnessed a considerable increase in income per capita in Colombia, in both rural and urban sectors. This raises the question of whether poverty and the difficulty of life have been alleviated in the rural areas as a result.

Agricultural output has grown at a modest rate over the twentieth century. The first engine of that growth (and of Colombia's overall development) was the expansion of coffee in the late nineteenth and early twentieth centuries. Area expansion in a variety of products was the main source of output growth through mid-century, after which technological improvement began to take on greater importance. In the last three decades labor-saving mechanization has made its appearance.

Output of the nonagricultural sector has grown at an average rate of over six percent since 1925, as compared with 3.3% for agriculture. But the terms of trade have moved in favor of agriculture over that period, due both to the increase in coffee prices determined at the world level and to an improvement in relative price of other agricultural products vis-à-vis nonagricultural output. Therefore, income generated in agriculture has risen at around four percent per year.

Low rural incomes are and have been the result of (a) a high supply of workers with agricultural skills but little opportunity outside agriculture, and (b) inequality in the distribution of the other income earning assets, land and capital. Given the latter characteristic, the higher the labor share of income generated in agriculture, the more equal rural income distribution is likely to be. From the mid-1930s on (when it became possible to make rough estimates), that share has trended substantially down. Mainly on the basis of this development, Berry and Urrutia (1976: ch. 3) have argued that income distribution in the agricultural sector is now worse than in the 1930s. During the early 1970s, when stagnant or falling real wages have characterized many agricultural and nonagricultural jobs, a major factor has probably been the rapid and accelerating inflation. Other factors may have been at work over a longer period, though their influence cannot yet be pinned down. During the 1960s there appears to have been a rapid decline in tenanted land, possibly due to the expansion of large-scale commercialized agriculture. This may have been part of a general pattern whereby the increasing capital intensity and the changing size composition of producing units were curtailing the demand for labor and holding down the equilibrium wage.

*INCOME DATA*

Data permits one to judge trends in some aspects of rural living standards, based partly on income data and partly on information about housing, health, and education. On the income side, only one piece of evidence is available over a considerable period of time—the daily wage rate as reported by DANE, based on reports from contacts in each municipality. These data are particularly relevant for the poorer rural families, most of whom earn the majority of their income working for wages. Unfortunately, there is no information on trends in days worked per year. Still the trend of the real daily wage rate is unlikely to be inversely related to that of real annual earnings of workers. Table 1 presents a national wage series, based on data from the departments, weighted by number of wage workers in each. The series indicates that wages rose between the early 1940s and the late 1960s. It seems probable that by the mid-1960s they had risen by one-third or thereabouts above the level of the mid-1920s.[6]

The next decade (1965-1975), however, saw a sharp downward trend with the 1973-1975 estimate 17% below the high reached in 1964-1967. At least part of this decline may be attributed to the accelerating inflation of the 1971-1975 period, but not all of it. Real wages appear to have started down in the late 1960s under price stability and rapid output growth. DANE's new series beginning in 1976 suggests an increase since 1970—if the data are comparable with the earlier series. This remains to be seen.

Even accepting that its twentieth-century trend has been upward, it is clear that the agricultural wage has risen more slowly

TABLE 1
Index of Agricultural Real Wages by Climatic Zone, 1935-1937 to 1973-1975 (1963 - 100)

| PERIOD | HOT CLIMATE ZONES | COLD CLIMATE ZONES | COLOMBIA |
|---|---|---|---|
| 1938–1939 | 84.3 | 91.4 | 87.9 |
| 1940–1944 | 77.2 | 82.0 | 80.1 |
| 1945–1949 | 78.5 | 73.6 | 79.5 |
| 1950–1954 | 83.5 | 84.3 | 84.0 |
| 1955–1959 | 81.9 | 87.7 | 85.1 |
| 1960–1963 | 94.7 | 98.3 | 96.5 |
| 1964–1967 | 96.2 | 97.6 | 96.8 |
| 1968–1970 | – | – | 93.2 |
| 1971–1972 | – | – | 93.6 |
| 1973–1975 | – | – | 85.0 |

SOURCES: For 1935-1937 to 1964-1967 (Berry and Urrutia, 1976: 66-67); for 1968-1970, unpublished calculations by the author from the same data series. The estimates for 1971-1972 and 1973-1975 are based on data on the wage rates of affiliates of the social security system, a very small share of all agricultural workers with above average salaries (Instituto Colombiano de Seguros Sociales, n.d.). They correspond to median monthly incomes and are spliced to the previous series in 1969-1970.

than has income per capita in the sector.[7] Families relying solely on paid employment have thus been losing ground relative to other persons engaged in agriculture, and to the economy as a whole.

Income of small farmers usually consists of some wage income (more, the smaller the farm) and some income from the farm. Land productivity has probably risen only modestly on such farms since the 1930s although the higher coffee prices which have prevailed during most of the last 25 years have improved the terms of trade for coffee farmers.

For increasing farm incomes to contribute to the income of the poorer operator families, it not only is necessary that small farms become more productive (in value terms) but also that their land base not be reduced. Land has always been distributed unequally in Colombia with 10%-15% of families operating none

TABLE 2
Land Concentration, 1960 and 1970-1971

| PERCENTAGE OF LAND HELD BY: | 1960 | 1970-1971 |
|---|---|---|
| Smallest 20% of Operators | 0.31 | 0.327 |
| 2nd 20% " | 1.12 | 1.003 |
| 3rd 20% " | 2.58 | 2.47 |
| 4th 20% " | 6.50 | 6.61 |
| 5th 20% " | 89.49 | 89.59 |
| Top 10% | 81.16 | 80.44 |

SOURCE: DANE (1964, 1974).

at all. The total agricultural labor force continued to grow until quite recently amid the breakup of some large farms into small ones, of small farms into smaller ones, consolidation of some small units into larger ones, opening up of new lands, and so on.[8] Until two agricultural censuses had been taken in 1960 and 1970-1971 (DANE, 1964, 1974), there was no means of judging the net effect of these changes on land distribution.

Even with respect to this intercensal period, it is still too early to judge how the distribution of land among farm operators may have changed. The number of farms reported was a shade (about three percent) lower in 1970-1971, with the number having less than 10 hectares falling by over six percent and the number having more than that rising by over 10% (DANE, 1974). The share of land managed by an administrator rose from one-third in 1960 to 40% in 1970-1971. Small rented and share-cropped farms became much less numerous; those under 10 hectares decreased from about 238,000 in 1960 to 138,000 in 1970-1971.[9] Among farm operators, the distribution of land remained about the same between the two censuses (see Table 2).

Had the agricultural labor force been growing, a decline in the number of farms would indicate that an increasing share of families were landless. But a reasonable guess is that either it was constant or a slight decline of less than five percent occurred. So in short, this evidence suggests little change in the ratio of farms to agricultural labor force.[10]

It is harder to judge whether, and how, the distribution of land by owner may have shifted. Between 1960 and 1970-1971, the number of owner-operators rose by 7.1%, and the share of land in their farms rose from 72.4% to 74.5% (DANE, 1974: 28-29). What is more relevant is that of the 20% smallest farms in 1960, over 63% were fully owned and probably 67% at least partly owned (adding to the fully owned category those under "more than one tenure farm") and in 1970-1971, over 71% were fully owned and about 73% at least partly owned. A similar increase also occurred for the next quintile of farms. This would suggest some increase in the share of income generated on small farms and staying with the farmer.

The only attempt at an overall measure of change over time in the real per capita income of the small farm sector (excluding coffee) is that of Thirsk (1972: 159) referring to the 1951-1964 intercensal period, a period in which the national agricultural wage index rose by about 15% or a trifle over one percent per year. Thirsk concludes that output per worker (measured in 1958 pesos) probably fell five to ten percent between the two end years —years which do not appear to have been far off the trend line. However, a real price increase of the small farm bundle of perhaps 15% seems to have taken place over the period. If all produce was sold and the output bundle did not change over the period, these output and price estimates would suggest a five to ten percent increase in real income per person. In fact, not all of the produce is sold, and production could have shifted toward the products with rising prices. This data does suggest the definite possibility that a substantial segment of these producers had little improvement or even suffered income declines over this period. More recently, they may have done better if we judge by the increasing average size of small farms (as of all farms), some probable increase in land productivity, and the unchanged or increased relative price of their output over the period 1964-1975.

### *HOUSING*

Available data suggest a gradual improvement in rural housing conditions over the last four decades. Between 1938 and 1973 the share of dwellings outside municipal seats (approximately equivalent to "rural") with electric lights rose from 2.2% to 13.2%; the share with running water (inside or outside the dwelling) rose from 1.3% to 28.5%; and the share with sewage disposal system rose from 0.5% to 6.5% (Dirección Nacional de Estadística, 1942: 185; DANE, 1977). Such data, however, provide little help in adducing the income changes of the bottom one-third of the population. Those people moving into the category with electric lights, running water, toilets, and so on are in the upper 10% or 20% in terms of housing conditions.[11] In 1964, those moving into the category with nonearthern floors, brick, cement or wooden walls, or roofs of anything but thatch were at least in the middle of the income distribution. The percentage of houses with earth floors fell from 67% to 57% between 1951 and 1964; the percentage with brick, cement or wooden walls rose from 16.5% to 24.6% (see Table 3); and the percentage with thatched roofs fell from 51% to 42%. Perhaps the best indicators for the poorest farms would be the percentage of houses without windows and percentage below a certain size, but data are not available. All departments shared gains, and in a few, the move to nonearthern floors reached the last quintile of the rural dwellings (Table 4).

On a cross-sectional basis, housing conditions appear to correspond in general to other measures of welfare, although the absolute levels of the two variables are difficult to compare across departments because of the implications of different climates for housing needs.

### *HEALTH*

Overall improvements in life expectancy over the last three to four decades have probably been shared to some extent in the rural areas, though as late as 1965 it appeared that the infant/child mortality levels may have still been very high. If life expectancy was about 35 years in the late 1930s, it had probably risen to about 50 to 55 by 1970.[12] Earlier in this century, an improvement occurred when yellow fever was brought largely under control.

TABLE 3
Building Materials of Rural Houses, 1951 and 1964[1]
(Percentage of Houses Using the Indicated Input)

| MATERIALS | 1951 | 1964 |
|---|---|---|
| Floors | | |
| Wood | 24.1 | 24.7 |
| Tile (tego) | n.a. | 1.8 |
| Cement | 3.6 | 23.3 |
| Brick | 2.2 | 1.4 |
| Earth | 66.9 | 57.1 |
| Synthetic materials | n.a. | 0.1 |
| Other | 3.2 | 1.6 |
| Walls | | |
| Brick | 1.6 | 4.8 |
| Cement Block | 0.4 | 2.4 |
| Adobe | n.a. | 10.8 |
| Waste materials | n.a. | 0.2 |
| Wood | 14.5 | 17.4 |
| Bahareque | 76.2 | 48.4 |
| Packed earth | n.a. | 12.1 |
| Other | 7.4 | 3.8 |
| Roofs | | |
| Earthen tile | 27.0 | 31.5 |
| Asbestos-cement tile | 1.3 | 4.1 |
| Metal | 6.3 | 17.8 |
| Cement | n.a. | 0.2 |
| Thatch & similar | 51.0 | 42.1 |
| Wood | n.a. | 3.1 |
| Waste materials | n.a. | 0.2 |
| Other | 5.5 | 1.0 |

SOURCE: DANE (1954-1955, 1968).
1. "Resto de los municipios," the category to which our figures here refer, include all of the municipios except the county seat. They therefore include some small villages.

TABLE 4
Some Characteristics of Rural Housing by Departments: 1938, 1951, and 1964

| | PERCENTAGE OF HOUSES | | | | | | |
|---|---|---|---|---|---|---|---|
| | WITH EARTH FLOOR | | WITH RUNNING WATER | | | WITH THATCHED ROOFS | |
| DEPARTMENT | 1964 | 1951 | 1964 | 1951 | 1938 | 1964 | 1951 |
| Antioquia | 43.6 | 52.2 | 29.8 | 16.7 | 3.4 | 25.9 | 33.6 |
| Atlántico | 51.9 | 71.9 | 12.6 | 6.0 | n.a. | 58.1 | 77.7 |
| Bolívar | 88.9 | | | | | 90.0 | |
| Bolívar & Córdoba | 89.2 | 95.9 | 7.4 | 2.7 | 0.5 | 92.0(±) | 95.2 |
| Boyocá | 83.2 | 94.1 | 8.9 | 0.6 | 0.2 | 41.6 | 73.0 |
| Caldas | 11.0 | 15.6 | 10.1 | 21.6 | 3.1 | 6.7 | 16.3 |
| Cauca | 67.7 | 73.4 | 6.8 | 1.6 | 0.3 | 48.2 | 71.0 |
| Cundinamarca (incl. Bogotá) | 59.1 | 75.4 | 17.6 | 6.3 | 1.1 | 25.7 | 60.6 |
| Chocó | 4.7 | 2.8 | 2.9 | 2.0 | 0.3 | 85.5 | 84.1 |
| Huila | 54.3 | 72.5 | 7.1 | 1.6 | 0.3 | 38.0 | 70.4 |
| Magdalena | 73.7 | 88.7 | 10.7 | 4.8 | 0.2 | 68.0 | 89.8 |
| Nariño | 56.6 | 68.1 | 6.0 | 0.9 | 0.3 | 59.7 | 75.1 |
| Norte de Santander | 65.1 | 81.4 | 21.6 | 5.2 | 0.8 | 42.8 | 72.0 |
| Santander | 71.3 | 86.3 | 14.6 | 3.1 | 2.2 | 36.8 | 62.9 |
| Tolima | 39.9 | 58.8 | 12.0 | 11.1 | 1.7 | 37.8 | 65.9 |
| Valle | 24.8 | 35.8 | 13.8 | 10.9 | 1.6 | 16.5 | 34.3 |
| Meta | 67.4 | 75.6 | | | | 36.0 | 44.5 |
| Córdoba | 89.7 | | | | | 95.4 | |
| Bogotá | 39.4 | | | | | 11.6 | |

SOURCES: Dirección Nacional de Estadística (1942), DANE (1954-1955, 1968).

Beginning in 1958 an extensive program of malaria eradication was initiated in cooperation with PAHO and UNICEF with additional bilateral, technical, and financial assistance from the United States. A survey conducted at that time indicated that nearly eight percent of the population was infected and that it was the fourth highest cause of illness in the country, producing an annual economic loss estimated in the range of Col $58 million.

> As a result of the application of modern case finding methods in the field, it is now believed that less than 3 per 1,000 of the population harbor malaria plasmodia, a significant reduction in the foci and sources of infection which were estimated to approach about 80 per 1,000 about ten years earlier [World Bank, 1972: 439].

The mortality rate from tuberculosis, another disease affecting a high share of the rural population in earlier times, has followed a steadily downward trend.

Physical stature appears to have been increasing, and the acceptance of modern medicine seems to be more widespread as education and communications improve.

## EDUCATION

Although some rural children still do not attend elementary school at all, and a considerable proportion do not go beyond the second year, it is true that the access of rural children to education has improved substantially over the recent decades with the addition of new schools (many of these built by the Acción Comunal groups).

Table 5 indicates that the percentage of rural children in the age group 7 to 11 enrolled in rural elementary schools has risen from about 30% in the early 1930s to about 60% in the late 1960s (enrollment figures overstate attendance figures, however). The percentage of children who reach school and successfully complete grade one has increased significantly over the period, from probably 35% to 40% in the early 1930s to about 75% to 80% in the mid-1960s (Berry, n.d.: ch. VI). As many rural schools provide only two years of education, there is naturally a heavy dropoff between the second and third years. The percentage of children ever entering the third year of primary school is estimated to have reached 30% only in the late 1960s, after a dramatic increase in that decade. The increased share of children attending school has been due to the increased share who enter, not to any dent in the attrition problem (at least not until the mid- or late-1960s). The small degree of success achieved in decreasing the rate of attrition of children once they are in school seems to be explained principally by the simple lack of schools providing more years. In the 1960s, however, the share of schools with more than two years, and with boys and girls together rather than alternating (i.e., boys attending one day and girls the next) started to increase fairly quickly (see Table 6).

There is also evidence of improvements during the 1960s in some of the qualitative aspects of rural education. Teachers'

TABLE 5
Enrollment Ratio, Rural Children 7-11 Years, 1932-1968[a]

| YEAR | RATIO |
|---|---|
| 1932-1934 | 34.2 |
| 1935-1939 | 36.1 |
| 1940-1944 | 35.3 |
| 1945-1949 | 35.8 |
| 1950-1954 | 39.5 |
| 1955-1959 | 46.5 |
| 1960-1964 | 55.0 |
| 1965-1968 | 62.4 |

SOURCE: Berry, n.d.: Table VI-13.
a. The population figures used in these calculations are adjusted up from the census data to take account of demographers' estimates of relative undernumeration by age and the relative completeness of the three different censuses on which the series is based; 1938, 1951, 1964. Enrollment figures are adjusted up from those presented in DANE, *Anuario General de Estadística,* various years, to take account of the fact that some municipios did not report in certain years.

salaries rose in real terms and payment was more regular. However, the gap between rural and urban educational opportunities obviously has not narrowed. Reform plans have outrun achievements by a wide margin. A case in point are the Rural Development Centers proposed in 1971, which not only added grades six through nine, but also provided various health, nutritional, agricultural extension, credit, and adult education services. Progress has been slow, and political expediency has played a large role in determining their loction; inauguration has often been ill-planned (Arnove, 1978: 27).

*EMIGRATION FROM RURAL AREAS*

It could be argued that comparisons of rural income and welfare made over a period of time should take into account the large outflow of rural people to urban areas. From the natural increase in population in rural areas a gradually increasing portion has left for urban areas or has gone abroad. This exodus increased from approximately one-third of the natural increase

TABLE 6
Rural Official Schools by Years Available
and Whether Unisex, Alternating, or Mixed

| YEAR | YEAR: ONE | TWO | THREE | FOUR | FIVE | TOTAL | SEX: BOYS ONLY | GIRLS ONLY | ALTERNATING | MIXED |
|---|---|---|---|---|---|---|---|---|---|---|
| 1941 | 303 | 3,839 | 1,451 | 279 | | 5,872 | 685 | 644 | 3,618 | 925 |
| % | 5.16 | 65.38 | 24.71 | 4.75 | | | 11.67 | 10.97 | 61.61 | 15.75 |
| | | | 29.46 (three + four) | | | | | | | |
| 1949 | 580 | 6,239 | 1,081 | 137 | | 8,037 | 917 | 878 | 4,856 | 1,386 |
| % | 7.22 | 77.63 | 13.45 | 1.70 | | | 11.41 | 10.92 | 60.42 | 17.25 |
| | | | 15.55 (three + four) | | | | | | | |
| 1938 | 844 | 8,760 | 1,578 | 527 | 112 | 11,861 | 1,471 | 1,370 | 7,664 | 1,356 |
| % | 7.45 | 73.86 | 13.30 | 4.44 | 0.94 | | 12.40 | 11.55 | 64.62 | 11.43 |
| | | | 18.68 (three + four) | | | | | | | |
| 1962 | 1,070 | 10,382 | 2,393 | 837 | 324 | 15,006 | 1,850 | 1,809 | 8,087 | 3,260 |
| % | 7.13 | 69.19 | 15.95 | 5.58 | 2.16 | | 12.33 | 12.05 | 53.89 | 21.72 |
| | | | 23.69 (three + four) | | | | | | | |
| 1967 | 779 | 9,073 | 3,915 | 1,758 | 1,052 | 16,577 | 1,650 | 1,579 | 3,380 | 9,968 |
| % | 4.70 | 54.73 | 23.62 | 10,61 | 6.35 | | 9.95 | 9.52 | 20.39 | 60.13 |
| | | | 40.58 (three + four) | | | | | | | |

SOURCE: DANE, *Anuario General de Estadística,* respective years.

earlier in this century to approximately 100% at the present time. If, as is generally true, these emigrants fare better economically than those left behind, then the incidence of poverty would decline more rapidly for people born in rural areas than for those living in rural areas. It could be argued, too, that the opportunity to leave for an urban job helps to curtail and soften some of the nastier aspects of rural life. Work in domestic service creates an alternative for many rural girls—rural-urban migration is particularly intense for girls less than 20 years old. Although their lot in the city is often a very difficult one, it is arguably better than the rural alternative. Young men too become more independent of their parents when job opportunities are available elsewhere. Sometimes tenants are less easily exploited by owners when they can find an urban job. An important problem in dealing with migration relates to whether the act itself (and its contemplation) involves important costs and/or benefits. In general the ex post evidence shows the typical migrant gains in income from the move. But the costs or benefits of that act of shifting may be equally important—and on these costs or benefits little or no information is available.

*Overview*

The incidence of poverty—whether defined strictly in terms of income or more broadly in terms of such other factors as housing, education, health, and range of opportunities—is higher in rural than in urban areas of Colombia. Income distribution is highly unequal in both, and the accompanying social structure and attitudes emphasize class differences. Many people have had no choice with respect to their state in life. Both physically and socially life has been hard; often it has been short.

The last several decades taken as a whole do, however, appear to have witnessed modest but gradual improvement in some of these respects, including more measurable aspects like income level, education, and health. The hierarchical political and social structure has begun to erode and the opportunities to escape from a bleak future by migrating away have improved as compared to the first decades of this century. The present situation remains very bad in many respects, and the indication of wage stagnation, possibly even decline, over the last 10 years is worrisome. The rapid expansion of rural primary education in the last couple of decades, on the other hand, is encouraging.

The relationship between rising rural incomes and the evolution of rural social structure is too imperfectly understood at present to permit much in the way of speculation as to whether or how fast that structure is moving away from the class consciousness and undemocratic nature which has characterized it in the past. Some developments give grounds for modest optimism. The recent development of Acción Comunal and the Usuarios movement—both partially grass-roots organizations of small farmers—go well beyond any previous initiatives of that sort. Education should reduce the inferiority feelings of many rural people, and make them more confident in their dealings with outsiders and with landowners. The decreasing conservatism of the Church will presumably show through gradually in the rural areas. Optimistically, one might anticipate some improvement in the role of women as education and health services expand and as the urban demand for domestic servants increases.

## NOTES

1. Converting at the contemporary exchange rate of 1.75 pesos per dollar.

2. Although this attitude, coming from the dominant white culture, pertained to the large number of persons involved primarily in Indian, black or mestizo subcultures, sometimes it was tempered by differing traditional views.

3. Based on estimates for rural and urban together of 38 and 52 years, respectively.

4. Calculations by the author on the basis of the 1964 population census.

5. Some social norms make it more difficult to get ahead economically. Purchasing beer for the neighbors is in many regions a social commitment necessary to maintain one's friends (Fals Borda, 1955).

6. Wage series which do go back beyond the mid-thirties—when that for agriculture starts—tend to show temporary, and presumably in some sense, artificial, increases in the real wage rate as prices fell in the early 1930s and wage rates—at least the ones recorded—fell less rapidly. The wage levels presumably moved back down to their equilibrium levels again after inflation began in the late 1930s.

Over a longer period, data presented by McGreevey (1971) suggest that the purchasing power of the wage in terms of four major wage goods was higher by 45% in 1962 than in 1892.

7. This is also true of the wage rate for other relatively unskilled occupations, e.g., construction workers (Berry, 1975).

8. In some individual municipios, studies have indicated that farm breakup has been serious, but there is no reason to believe that these municipios provide a representative sample of the country as a whole. Increasing minifundism was the main feature cited by Haney (1968) in his analysis of Fomeque, Cundinamarca.

9. Simultaneously, there was a sharp increase in the number of farms listed as "other farms," though not enough to nearly offset the decline just mentioned, even if it included mostly cases of "rental."

10. One anomaly in the data should be noted. Between 1964 and 1973, the population census indicated a sharp reduction of from 42.4% to 27.7% in the share of the occupational category "farmers et al.," who were employers or independent workers, and a rise from 39.7% to 61.4% of those who were classified as blue-collar workers. Such a shift would be expected to correspond to a decreasing ratio of farms to labor force.

It is possible that in practice, categories were defined differently in 1973, an argument given some support by the fact that DANE's 1970 and 1971 household surveys found the job position breakdown very similar to that of 1964.

11. Or they are the village dwellers; in either case, the figures would not cast light on the bulk of the people in agriculture.

12. Based on the estimates of demographers that expectancy was about 61 years around 1970 for Colombia (Potter el al., 1976: 518). This would suggest at least 50 in the rural areas.

## REFERENCES


ARNOVE, R. (1978) "Education policies of the national front," in A. Berry, R. Hellman, and M. Solaún (eds.) The Politics of Coalition: Essays on the Colombian National Front. New Brunswick, NJ: Transaction Books.

BEJARANO, J. (1924) El Alcoholismo en Colombia. Bogotá: Editorial M. Casis.

BERRY, A. (n.d.) "The development of the agricultural sector in Colombia." (mimeo)

——— (1975) "Changing income distribution under development: Colombia." Rev. of Income and Wealth 20: 289-316.

——— and M. URRUTIA (1976) Income Distribution in Colombia. New Haven, CT: Yale Univ. Press.

CIDA [Comité Interamericano de Desarrollo Agrícola] (1966) Tenencia de la Tierra y Desarrollo Socio-Económico del Sector Agrícola: Colombia. Washington, DC: Unión Panamericano.

Controlor General de la República (1955) Economía y Estadística 85. Bogotá.

DANE [Departamento Administrativo Nacional de Estadística] (1977) Boletín Mensual de Estadística 309. Bogotá: DANE.

——— (1974) Censo Nacional Agropecuario: Valle, Cauca, Nariño, 1970-1971. Bogotá: DANE.

——— (1968) II Censo Nacional de Edificos y Viviendas (Julio 15 de 1964) Resumen General. Bogotá: DANE.

——— (1967) XIII Censo Nacional de Población (Julio 15 de 1964) Resumen General. Bogotá: DANE.

——— (1964) Directorio Nacional de Explotaciones Agropecuarias (Censo Agropecuario) 1960: Resumen Nacional (Segunda Parte). Bogotá: DANE.

——— (1954-1955) 1951 Censo de Edificios y Viviendas, various departments. Bogotá: DANE.

——— (1954) Censo de Población de Colombia, 1951. Resumen. Bogotá: DANE.

Dirección Nacional de Estadística, Controleria General de la República (1942) Censo General de Población, 5 de julio 1938: Resumen General del País. Bogotá: Imprenta Nacional.

FALS BORDA, O. (1955) Peasant Society in the Colombian Andes. Gainesville: Univ. of Florida Press.

GUITIERREZ DE PINEDA, V. (1963) La Familia en Colombia, Vol. 1. Bogotá: Universidad Nacional de Colombia, Facultad de Sociología.

HANEY, E. (1968) The Minifundio Dilemma: A Colombian Case. Madison: University of Wisconsin, Land Tenure Center.

HAVENS, A. E. (1965) Education in Rural Colombia: An Investment in Human Resources. Madison: University of Wisconsin, Land Tenure Center.

IBRD [International Bank for Reconstruction and Development] (1950) The Basis for a Development Program for Colombia. Baltimore: IBRD.

Instituto Colombiano de Seguros Sociales (n.d.) Series Estadísticas, Años 1949-1975. Bogotá: ICSS.

McGREEVEY, W. P. (1971) An Economic History of Colombia, 1845-1930. Cambridge, England: Cambridge Univ. Press.

Ministerio de Educación Nacional (1973) La Educación Ante el Congreso. Bogotá: Ministerio de Educación Nacional.

Ministerio de Salud Pública (1963) Informe de Colombia a la Reunión Técnica Latinoamericana Sobre Encuestas Alimenticias. Bogotá: Ministerio de Salud Pública, Servicio-Cooperativo Interamericano de Salud Pública, Instituto Nacional de Nutrición.

Ministerio de Salud Pública y Asociación Colombiana de Facultades de Medicina (1967) Estudio de Recursos Humanos para la Salud y Educación Médica en Colombia, Investigación Nacional de Morbilidad. Bogotá: Ministerio de Salud Pública.

de ORTIZ, S. (1973) Uncertainties in Peasant Farming: A Colombian Case. London: Athlone Press.

POTTER, J., M. ORDONEZ G., and R. MEASHAM (1976) "The rapid decline in Colombian fertility." Population and Development Rev. 2, 3, and 4: 509-528.

REYES, M., R. PRIETO, and B. HANNESON (1965) Estudio Agroeconómico de la Hoya del Río Suárez. Bogotá: CEDE, Universidad de Los Andes and CAR.

RUIZ, S. (1973) La Fuerza de Trabajo en la Producción de Arroz y Algodón, Tomo I: Algodón. Bogotá: DANE.

SMITH, T. L., J. DIAZ RODRIGUEZ, and L. ROBERTO GARCIA (1945) Tabio. A Study in Rural Social Organization. Washington, DC: Office of Foreign Agricultural Relations, Department of Agriculture.

THIRSK, W. (1972) "The economics of farm mechanization in Colombia." Ph.D. dissertation, Yale University. (unpublished)

World Bank (1972) Economic Growth of Colombia: Problems and Prospects. Baltimore: Johns Hopkins Univ. Press.

VAUTIER, E. and O. FALS BORDA (1958) La Vereda de Chambimbal: Estudio y Acción en Vivienda Rural. Bogotá: Centro Interamericano de Vivienda y Planamiento.

ZSCHOCK, D. K. (1968) "Economic aspects of health needs in Colombia." Milbank Memorial Fund Q. 46: Part 2.

*Albert Berry, Professor of Political Economy at the University of Toronto, has coauthored* Income Distribution in Colombia *with Miguel Urrutia. His other publications and ongoing research interests are largely concerned with the economic development of Colombia.*

**DAVID NICHOLLS**
*1, Walton Crescent, Oxford*
*OX1 3DP England*

# *THE WISDOM OF SALOMON*
## *Myth or Reality?*

History is written by the winners," wrote Orwell (1970: 110); he went on to suggest that a totalitarian government "claims to control the past as well as the future." Yet such a concern with controlling the past is not a distinguishing feature of totalitarianism; many examples of an ideological or legendary version of the past receiving government sanction can be found in non-totalitarian countries. While few governments or political parties can afford to ignore the past completely, it is undoubtedly the case that in some countries a "correct" interpretation of the past is of more pressing concern to contemporary politicians than it is in others. Since the early days of independence, Haitians have shown an absorbing interest in their past—not a dead "historical" past, but a living ideological past. The position which a Haitian has taken with respect to the past has been closely connected to his political commitments in the present, and rival parties have elaborated competing legends which function as legitimations of their current policies and interests.

Elsewhere (Nicholls, 1974a) I have discussed the development of a mulatto legend of the Haitian past, which grew up during the regimes of Pétion (1806-1818) and Boyer (1818-1843), and which received detailed elaboration in the period from 1847 to 1867. In these years mulatto ideologists including Beaubrun Ardouin, Joseph Saint Rémy, Emile Nau, and Beauvais Lespinasse, presented a picture of the Haitian past in which the heroes were Ogé and Chavannes, rather than Toussaint; Pétion and Boyer rather than Dessalines and Christophe. It was, I suggested, a legend calculated to establish and reinforce the mulatto hegemony

Journal of Interamerican Studies and World Affairs, Vol. 20 No. 4, November 1978

in Haiti. A correct view of Dessalines was particularly important in the mulatto legend. The black leader was undoubtedly one of heroes of Haitian independence—and the mulattoes were as nationalistic as the next man—but he was also seen as a barbarous tyrant whose oppressive rule was deservedly ended by his assassination.

With the fall, in 1843, of Jean Pierre Boyer, black discontent manifested itself in a number of ways. One aspect of the black revival was an attempt to rehabilitate Dessalines. A leading spokesman of this movement was Louis Etienne Lysius Felicité Salomon *jeune*. In a memorial service for the emperor in 1845 at the cathedral in Les Cayes, Salomon (1845) declared that Ogé and Chavannes, the mulatto rebels against the French colonial administration, "misconceived their mission, betrayed their mandate," by claiming rights for the relatively small number of *affranchis* only, and ignoring the situation of the slaves. Toussaint was the "new Sparticus" who emerged to right these wrongs. But it was Dessalines who completed the work:

> Honor, hommage and glory to Dessalines. Before him, as after him, no one has done more for the sons of Africa. In making Haiti a free sovereign and independent state, he assured to black and colored men of all countries a piece of land where they could preserve all the dignity of their being.

Dessalines's slaughter of the remaining French planters in 1804 was "an action grand and terrible, no doubt, but necessary: it consolidated the revolution."[1]

Salomon was, then, instrumental in establishing a revised view of the Haitian past—a "black legend," as we may call it—which was later to receive elaboration in the writings of Louis Joseph Janvier, Alcius Charmant, Antoine Michel, and in the modern period of Arthur Holly, Lorimer Denis, François Duvalier, and Leslie Manigat. In the latter versions of the black legend Salomon appears as one of the principal characters, and it is the purpose of this article to examine some of the claims made on behalf of Salomon by a number of present-day *noiriste* writers.

## *Salomon and the Black Legend*

Salomon jeune was born in Les Cayes on 30 June 1815, of a black landowning family. Together with other members of his family he led a rising of peasant irregulars, known as *piquets,* in 1843-1844. This movement demanded, among other things, an end to the mulatto domination of the country. Salomon became Minister of Finance under Soulouque (1847-1859), but went into exile soon after Geffrard (1859-1867) came to power. Two of his brothers and other members of his family were put to death by Geffrard, and in 1865 he himself was expelled by the British from Jamaica where he had been living in exile. Under Salnave (1867-1869) he represented his country as a diplomat in Europe. He returned to Haiti under Domingue (1874-1876) but, because of hostile demonstrations against him, he had to take refuge in the British consulate and once more left for Jamaica. He again went back to Haiti for a short while under Boisrond Canal (1876-1879). Salomon was elected President of the republic in 1879 after the victory of the predominantly black National Party in the elections of that year. His regime lasted until 1888, when it was overthrown by a rising in the North. Salomon died a few months later in France.

The principal claims made on Salomon's behalf by present-day noiriste writers are that he was a proletarian class leader who regrouped the blacks into a viable political force; also that he was a fervent nationalist and a prophet of *négritude.* The most clearly legendary writing on Salomon in recent years comes from Antoine, a member of the *Griots* group and for many years a minister under Francois Duvalier. *Salomon jeune: martyr volontaire de sa classe* is introduced by Duvalier, who points out the importance of a correct understanding of the past. The present, he continued,

> can be built only if we bind it to the great spiritual forces of the national and ethnic past [Antoine, 1968: xxxiv].

Ulrich Saint Louis, a duvalierist of long standing, spoke of Duvalier himself as a synthesis of dessalinism and salomonism

(République d'Haïti, 1966: 33; see also Pierre Louis, 1965: 22), and Duvalier himself (1966a: 152 and 1967: 94) frequently referred to Salomon in his political speeches, seeing himself as continuing the work of this black predecessor. He wrote in 1946:

> The great Salomon, by his energy and his clear sight, regrouped the black forces in order to secure a rational organization of the class [Duvalier, 1966b: 312].

Duvalier used his influence in 1957 to ensure that the presidential election of that year should be held on 22 September, the anniversary of the day when Salomon allowed the Port au Prince mob to burn and pillage the houses and business premises of the elite.[2] This date later became *le jour de la souveraineté nationale.*

Manigat and Saint Louis make further claims on behalf of Salomon and the National Party. Manigat (1957: 30) suggests that the Nationals were characterized by their "proud jealousy of national independence" and that they "desired to work for a blossoming of a new black civilization by valuing the African foundation of our national culture."[3] This latter claim is reiterated by Saint Louis (1970: 108), when he writes: "The National Party advocated the reconnecting of Haiti to a black civilization, in other words, the return of Haiti to Africa."

## *A Return to Africa?*

A careful reading of Salomon's writings and of National Party propaganda gives not the slightest support to the claim that these men were oriented toward Africa in their cultural ideas. There is, in fact, no sense in which they can be said to have advocated a "return to Africa." With their Liberal Party rivals, the National writers accepted the fact that, biologically speaking, Haitians belonged to the black or African race, but this had no implications in the cultural field for them. For them civilization in the nineteenth century was European civilization. Some of them argued that the origin of civilization was in Africa, but they did not use this as an argument for the development in Haiti of a specifically African civilization.[4] Laroche (1885: 119) denounced Salomon for being "the official protector" of the voodoo religion, but this was a familiar accusation in Haitian politics and not to be taken as evidence that Salomon was involved in the cult. As we have seen (note 3) Laroche also accused the National Party of wishing to ensure the isolation of Haiti in a black civilization, but this again must be seen as an attempt to slander his political opponents.[5] The truth is quite the opposite. In 1867 Demesvar Delorme, a leader of the Nationals, wrote to Salomon

> We have the hope and the sincere intention of building on the ruins which we displace, a regular and new order of things, on the model of the civilizations which exist in Europe [PRO, 1867].

In his address to the electorate in Haiti, written from Paris, Delorme (1874) referred to the forests of Central Africa as places where "indolent people, reclining in ignorance, sleep, protected by the deserts." His own novels were set in Europe and give no indication of any interest in Africa, nor indeed in Haiti.[6]

Janvier (1884a: 25-26), one of the spokesmen of the extreme wing of the National Party, known as "ultranationals" insisted that the Haitian youths of his day were familiar with the latest literary and scientific trends in Europe. Haitian literature was, he maintained, but a daughter of the French, claiming in Auguste et al., (1882: 27) that French was the ordinary language of Haiti, which was as untrue then as it is now. Janvier (1883a: 94) denied the very existence of voodoo in the Haiti of his day, and in later years declared that Haitians should copy the British and the French rather than the Africans in their legal and constitutional practice (Janvier, 1907a: 54, 1907b). With respect to the voodoo religion, the Nationals were no less hostile than were their political opponents. It was not until the U.S. occupation (1915-1934) that sympathy for voodoo became a badge of noirisme. The National Party journal *l'Oeil* (23 juillet 1881) declared how

> it is important to obstruct the progress of the voodoo cult, whose adepts practice it in a way which is thoughtless and harmful to all

> people trying to shake off (as ours are) the heavy burden of their origin in order to walk in the path of progress.

Noiristes later in the century maintained this attack upon voodoo. J. F. Thalès Manigat (1897: 1) assailed those who practiced the rites of "this abominable sect which our ancestors introduced into the country."[7]

There is thus no evidence to suggest that Salomon and the National Party were in favor of Haiti moving in the direction of African culture. In fact, Salomon's government was resolutely francophile in its foreign policy, as we shall see, and this orientation was partly inspired by the belief that Haiti was a country which had a predominantly French culture. Salomon's wife was French and this, no doubt, reflected his favorable attitude toward that nation. He voiced these sentiments in a conversation with the French minister in Port au Prince:

> Our origin, our language, our instincts incline us towards you; it is France—honest, loyal and generous—whom we prefer to all the other nations (AAE, 1883b).[8]

In a "Proclamation" on Independence Day of 1882 (République d'Haïti, 1882a: 2), Salomon urged his fellow countrymen to prove "by a prompt and intelligent assimilation" that civilization was not the exclusive possession of one race. Salomon's policy of encouraging French teachers to work in Haiti, which is recognized by Leslie Manigat (1973: 147), was hardly calculated to facilitate the development of a black civilization based upon Haiti's African roots.

*National Independence*

If there is no truth in the claim that Salomon and the Nationals were the prophets of a "return to Africa," can it properly be said that they were outstanding defenders of national independence? This is a more difficult question to settle. There is little to suggest that during his period as Finance Minister under Soulouque, Salomon manifested an unusual degree of concern for national independence. He established certain government monopolies, but this was principally in order to raise public funds. Soulouque's regime was generally favorable to foreign, and particularly to British, interests (St John, 1889: 97), and Salomon himself was described by the British vice consul in 1859 (PRO, 1859) as "a very quiet and inoffensive person." It is true that Soulouque was very much concerned about reconquering the eastern part of the island which had declared independence in 1844, and that this was due mainly to his fears that Haitian independence might in the future be threatened by some foreign power establishing itself in the East. His policy on this matter has frequently been misunderstood as MacLeod (1970) has pointed out. Nevertheless, the claims that the National Party and their leader were fierce defenders of national independence must be tested principally in the period of Salomon's presidency.

Since the days of its independence, Haiti had found itself isolated in a world of white nations and peculiarly vulnerable to foreign intervention in its affairs. Britain, France, the United States, and Germany all had interests in the country during the nineteenth century—if not economic and commercial, then strategic. Haitian leaders became aware at an early stage that independence could be maintained only by playing off one power against another, and much Haitian foreign policy must be seen as a consequence of this realization. On the other hand, however, political divisions among Haitians which were closely connected to color distinction have frequently been so deep that successive leaders have been willing to seek foreign support and thereby invite foreign intervention rather than allowing their rivals to gain power.[9] It is difficult to decide which of these intentions played the major role in the policy of successive Haitian governments, as it is frequently possible to explain their involvement with foreign governments in terms of either intention. President Boyer's alleged willingness to accept French protection is regarded by noiriste writers as a means of his strengthening the mulatto hegemony and as conclusive proof of his betrayal of Haitian independence (Manigat, 1954), while Salomon's requests for a similar protection is explained as the consequence of a proper desire to counterbalance the growing menace of British intervention and thereby, to preserve independence. This is not the place to discuss Boyer's policy; but what is to be said of Salomon?

The British government was certainly opposed to Salomon, partly owing to his francophile policies and to his unwillingness to settle the Maunder claims. These are complicated claims for compensation by the Maunder family for damage done to their property in the isle of La Tortue and for wrongful arrest. The Maunders had suffered under Salnave, had been compensated by Nissage (1870-1874), and dispossessed under Domingue. Boisrond Canal had agreed to compensate the family, but the matter was not finally settled when Salomon came to power.[10] Salomon's government told the Americans that the British were likely to seize the isle of La Tortue (Preston to Frelinghuysen, 11 January 1883, quoted in Logan, 1941: 373), which was probably not the case. It also claimed (PRO, 1883c), rightly, that the British were implicated in the invasion of Miragoâne, when a number of Salomon's Liberal Party opponents landed in the South of Haiti in March 1883 (Chancy, 1890; Mars, 1948). The British had allowed the invading party to leave Jamaica and had probably assisted them in other ways.

Salomon turned for support to France and to the United States. In a private talk to the U.S. minister in Port au Prince in May 1883, Salomon stated that he wished to put his country "in such relations, positive and practical, with the Government of the United States of America that the protection of such Government would be assured us" (Langston to Frelinghuysen, 30 May 1883, quoted in Logan, 1941: 374). The U.S. government's reply was unfavorable, and the President approached the French. Burdel, the French minister in Haiti, reported his confidential discussion with Salomon on the question:

> After a pause of some moments, during which he seemed absorbed in a melancholy meditation, he resumed with determination: "Would the Government of the French Republic accept the protectorate of the Republic of Haiti?" [AAE, 1883b].

Salomon's minister, Fouchard, had already written to the Haitian minister in Paris urging him to support these efforts to secure a protectorate, pointing out that in order to resist British plots it was necessary to have an alliance with France, "toward whom everything leads us" or to arrange a *marriage de raison* with the United States (Fouchard à Villevaleix, 3 novembre 1883, quoted in Logan, 1941: 375). The French response to these overtures was not encouraging (AAE, 1883b), and Salomon went back to the Americans with an offer of the Môle Saint Nicolas or the isle of La Tortue in exchange for protecting Haiti and providing financial, military, and diplomatic assistance (Langston to Frelinghuysen, 19 November 1883, quoted in Logan, 1941: 376). This offer was again rejected. Throughout the ensuing two years it was Salomon's aim to secure the protection of one of these two powers. Was this merely to resist British intervention, or was there more to it? Everything about the situation suggests that one of the purposes of such protection was to secure his own position against his Liberal opponents. In a letter to General François Manigat (PRO, 1884), the President put the position clearly:

> With the support of France we have no need to fear any other power which threatens us or any enterprise of what remains of the Liberal faction. What an advantage for us to know that at the least movement by exiles a French warship will oppose their attempt.

It appears that Salomon's government was thus prepared to sacrifice—or to risk the sacrifice of—Haitian independence partly in order to prevent his opponents from gaining power, and that resistance to the British threat was not the only reason why these men sought foreign protection.

All this is not, however, to say that Salomon was any worse than his opponents in this matter, for many of them were busily approaching the British minister in Port au Prince with requests for a similar protection (PRO, 1883a). These were principally "light coloured Haitians, who belong to the best educated class of Natives. . . . The Haitians," he went on, "who wish for a protectorate are principally the owners of property and the traders."

Such a move would, however, be opposed by the majority of blacks, "who have been taught by their leaders to regard white people as their bitter enemies." It is sad to think that these very leaders were in the process of attempting to sell national independence to the French or the Americans.

With respect to the question of whether Salomon was an outstanding defender of national independence there are two further considerations. In the first place, the founding of the Banque Nationale in 1880-1881 with French capital led to increased foreign intervention in the life of the country. In Salomon's defense it might be argued that his intention was to undermine the small foreign lending agencies in Haiti by founding a strong central bank, over which the government might at least have some control. Whatever his intentions, however, the long-term consequences were disastrous. The takeover of the bank by U.S. interests in 1911 was a decisive step toward the occupation of the country by American marines in July 1915 (Manigat, 1967). The prognostications of Salomon's leading Liberal opponents were realized. "Salomon, the apostle of evil," wrote Boyer Bazelais, "in decreeing the Bank, has delivered our country to the whites!" (*L'Avant Garde,* 12 avril 1883). Paul (1880: 62) likened the bank to a Trojan horse which would introduce into the country foreigners bent on annexation.

## *Foreign Ownership and the Agrarian Law*

The second way in which Salomon's government might be said to have risked national independence is on the question of the agrarian law of 1883. The first constitution of independent Haiti had stipulated in 1805 that no "white" should be allowed to own landed property in the country. This provision (with slight modification) remained in force until the constitution of 1918, which was, in the words of Warren Harding (quoted in Millspaugh, 1931: 96n), jammed down the throats of the Haitians "at the points of bayonets borne by United States marines." The prohibition was a continual matter of contention in Haiti throughout the nineteenth century (Nicholls, 1974b).[11] On one side it was argued that the provision was necessary in order to maintain an effective independence; on the other, it was claimed that the law should be changed in order to attract much-needed capital. Positions taken on this issue cut across party and color lines. While many National Party spokesmen, particularly Janvier and Pinckombe, were fierce defenders of the prohibition, Salomon himself and Delorme were noticeably noncommittal. Before his election to the presidency, the former told his political friends that the time was not ripe for a change in the law, and he denounced those who campaigned for such a change (Michel, 1913: 159-160). The black leader knew that the mass of the people would oppose such a reform. Yet Salomon made it clear in private that he favored a change. He wrote to François Manigat (PRO, 1884) that it was impossible to repeal the prohibition but that it should be possible to secure some modification in the law. "Public opinion," he stated, "proclaims itself against larger concessions."[12] The British minister in Port au Prince reported to London:

> President Salomon assured me that he was fully aware of the pernicious effect of Art. 6 of the Constitution, and that he intended to change it as soon as he was able to overcome the prejudice of the Haitians to Foreigners holding land [PRO, 1882].

In reply to the French minister's questions on the same subject, Salomon admitted (AAE, 1883c) that it would be difficult to change the constitution, "but that which cannot be attacked head-on, may be secretly undermined." The question arises whether these comments made to diplomats were merely sweet words designed to foster good relations or whether they represent a genuine reflection of the President's ideas. One might be tempted to think that the former was the case, if the legislature had not been in the process of passing a law that had precisely the effect of undermining the prohibition. The celebrated agrarian law of 1883 not only provided for a distribution of state lands to those who would grow crops for export, but it also contained the less celebrated but equally significant article 5, which reads:

> The factories founded for the processing of the said products, the limited companies . . . will enjoy, as moral persons, the privileges of nationality (*Le Moniteur,* 1 mars 1883).[13]

The law which had been prepared by François Manigat, the minister of agriculture, received criticism in the Senate. One senator, Stewart, raised the issue of the foreign ownership of land which would be facilitated by article 5. Another senator, Riboul, explicitly defended it on these grounds. The Senate committee which recommended approval of the bill included Jeantel Manigat (*Le Moniteur,* 8 mars 1883), and a committee of the House of Representatives, of which Guillaume Manigat was president, made the following comment:

> The appeal made to foreign capital by the establishment of factories of all kinds for the processing of our products will achieve the economic revolution which must revive our unhappy country (*Le Moniteur,* 29 mars 1883).

It is curious to read Janvier—who had elsewhere warned of the dangers of foreign investment and foreign ownership and had urged his fellow citizens to develop the country with local capital (Nicholls, 1974b: 21f)—praising Salomon as "the first Haitian head of state to have seriously opened his country to French capital" (Janvier, 1883b, 1884b: 46).

In his public pronouncements Salomon laid considerable emphasis upon the importance of economic dependence as likely to undermine the effective political independence of the country, and we have no reason to doubt his good faith on this matter. Salomon (1882) listed some of the imported products which Haitians could very well manufacture for themselves. "Must we for ever remain tributory to the foreigner, and even at his mercy, for our food?" he demanded. In a speech to the legislature (Salomon, 1883), he ascribed the troubles of Haiti to its isolation and to internal dissensions that

> have diverted our attention from the growing danger to which our political independence was exposed by the material dependence

> into which we have allowed ourselves to fall with respect to the foreigner.

Yet a politician cannot be judged solely by his intentions. There can be no doubt that the founding of the Banque Nationale, article 5 of the agrarian law, and the search for U.S. and French protection together represent the most significant invitation to foreign intervention in nineteenth-century Haiti and contributed in a major way to create the conditions which made the U.S. invasion of 1915 possible. Whatever Salomon's intentions, the consequences of his regime by no means enable us to describe him as a fierce defender of national independence.

*Color and Class*

The further two claims about Salomon, as the man who regrouped the blacks into an effective party and as the proletarian class leader, can be dealt with more briefly. There is no doubt that he was associated with the cause of the blacks from 1843 onward. The National Party, of which he was the recognized head, was predominantly black in its composition and leadership (though like its rival, the predominantly mulatto Liberal Party, it contained leading members of the other color). Salomon was generally known as "*mangeur des mulâtres,*" but it was an epithet that he rejected, pointing out that his own children were mulattoes. Although the National Party was composed principally of blacks, it was an elite party, representing the interests of a rural black landowning class and of a small black elite in Cap Haïtien. Divisions developed between the different elements in this alliance after the defeat of the Liberal invasion, and Salomon's regime was eventually overthrown by a black group from the North. He can hardly therefore be said to have effectively consolidated the blacks in any permanent way, nor can it properly be said that he was a proletarian leader. The class which he led in the risings of 1843-1844 was composed of middle and small landowners, and while he had support from the masses in the capital from time to time, this was only because he was marginally less arrogant and exclusive than were his mulatto opponents.

It will therefore fairly be concluded that the claims made on behalf of Salomon and the National Party by present-day noiriste writers are not substantiated by a study of the evidence which is available. While it is no doubt important for the politician to propound legends of the past in order to reinforce his claims in the present, it is at least part of the historian's work to question these stylized accounts and, where appropriate, to demolish them.

## NOTES

1. For Salomon's *noirisme* see also Salomon (1861).

2. On the events of 22-23 September 1883 the British minister wrote (PRO, 1883b), "It was quite a war of colour, the blacks massacring the coloured people."

3. These claims made by Manigat are based on statements by the notorious mulatto ideologist Laroche (1885: 91). I should in fairness add that Manigat's writings on Haiti are very much more significant and perceptive than those of the other *noiriste* writers mentioned. I have myself benefited greatly from his insights and from his friendly criticisms of my earlier writings. No one who is concerned with understanding the Haitian past can ignore his important contributions.

4. This position was also maintained by Liberals like Firmin (1885) and Price (1900).

5. Nord Alexis, for example, was later denounced by the *noiriste* Charmant (1905: 266) as "ce grand pontife du Vaudoutisme."

6. For a critique of Delorme see Trouillot (1968) and Mars (1954: 190).

7. See also "Le diabolisme et le Vaudoux," in the *noiriste* journal *L'Impartial* (10 septembre 1896) and Charmant (1905: 266).

8. The instructions, in the hand of Fénélon Faubert, Salomon's secretary, which were sent to Haitian minister in Paris, Stéphen Preston, read: "que la nature, la communauté d'origine, de langue, de loi nous destiner a servir de point d'appui à la politique française dans la Golfe de Mexique" (PRO, 1885a).

9. This is one of the major themes in my forthcoming book on *Race, Colour and Independence in Haiti, from Dessalines to Duvalier.*

10. There is a brief account from J.B.W. Maunder's point of view (PRO, 1885b). The Haitian government's position is stated in République d'Haiti (1882b).

11. This provision had, however, been omitted from Christophe's constitutions of 1807 and 1811.

12. Delorme also viewed the prohibition as "un mesure transitoire" (in Pinkckombe, 1874: 53). "Pinckombe" is sometimes spelled "Pinkcombe," and there is no consistency even in his own publications.

13. L. F. Manigat (1973: 147) refers to "la loi agraire Manigat-Cameau," but fails to note article 5.

# REFERENCES

AAE [Les Archives du Ministere des Affaires Etrangères, Quai d'Orsay, Paris] (1883a) Ferry à Burdel, 15 novembre, Correspondance Politique Haïti 33/198.

——— (1883b) Burdel à Challemel-Lacour, 5 octobre, Correspondance Politique Haïti 33/107.

——— (1883c) Burdel à Challemel-Lacour, 5 mars, Correspondance Politique Haïti 33/54.

ANTOINE, M. A. (1968) Salomon *jeune*, martyr volontaire de sa classe. Port au Prince: the author.

AUGUSTE, J., C. DENIS, A. BOWLER, J. DEVOT, and L. J. JANVIER (1882) Les detracteurs de la race noire et de la république d'Haïti. Paris: Marpon et Flammarion.

CHANCY, E. (1890) Pour l'histoire. Port au Prince: the author.

CHARMANT, A. (1905) Haïti: vivra-t-elle? Le Havre: Le Roy.

DELORME, D. (1874) Adresse: au citoyens de la république d'Haïti. Paris: the author.

DUVALIER, F. (1967) Oeuvres essentielle iii: La révolution au pouvoir. Port au Prince: the author.

——— (1966a) Ouevres essentielle ii: La marche à la présidence. Port au Prince: the author.

——— (1966b) Oeuvres essentielle i: Eléments d'une doctrine. Port au Prince: the author.

FIRMIN, J. A. (1885) L'égalité des races humaines. Paris: Pichon.

JANVIER, L. J. (1907a) Humble adresse aux electeurs de la commune de Port au Prince. Port au Prince: the author.

——— (1907b) "Notre république." Haïti Littéraire et Sociale (Port au Prince) 5 janvier.

——— (1884a) L'égalité des races. Paris: Rougier.

——— 91884b) Les antinationaux. Paris: Rougier.

——— (1883a) La république d'Haïti et ses visiteurs 1840-1882. Paris: Marpon et FLammarion.

——— (1883b) "La république radicale." L'Oeil (Port au Prince) 17 novembre.

LAROCHE, L. (1885) Haïti: une page d'histoire. Paris: Rousseau.

LOGAN, R. W. (1941) The Diplomatic Relations of the United States with Haïti, 1776-1891. Chapel Hill: Univ. of North Carolina Press.

MacLEOD, M. (1970) "The Soulouque regime in Haïti, 1847-1859: a reevaluation." Caribbean Studies (Rio Piedras) 10 (October): 35-48.

MANIGAT, J.F.T. (1897) Conférance for the vaudoux. Cap Haitien: the author.

MANIGAT, L. F. (1973) L'Amérique latine au XXe siècle, 1889-1929. Paris: Richelieu.

——— (1967) "La substitution de la prépondérance américaine a la prépodérance francaise en Haïti au début du XXe siècle: la conjoncture de 1910-11." Revue d'Histoire Moderne et Contemporaine (Paris) 14 Octobre—Decembre): 321-355.

——— (1957) Un fait historique: l'avenèment à la présidence d'Haïti du général Salomon. Port au Prince: the author.

——— (1954) Le délicat problème de la critique historique. Port au Prince: the author.

MARS, J. P. (1954) Ainsi parla l'oncle. New York: Parapsychology Foundation.

——— (1948) Jean-Pierre Bâyer Bazelais et la drâme de Miragone. Port au Prince: the author.

MICHEL, A. (1913)Salomon *jeune* et l'affaire Louis Tanis. Port au Prince: the author.

MILLSPAUGH, A. (1931) Haïti under American Control, 1915-1930. Boston: World Peace Foundation.

NICHOLLS, D. (1974a) "A work of combat: mulatto historians and the Haitian past, 1847-1867." J. of Interamerican Studies and World Affairs 16 (February): 15-38.
——— (1974b) Economic Dependence and Political Autonomy, the Haitian Experience. Montreal: McGill University, Centre for Developing Area Studies.
ORWELL, G. (1970) "As I please," in the Collected Essays Journalism and Letters of George Orwell. Harmondsworth, England: Penguin.
PAUL, E. (1880) Haïti au soleil de 1880. No place recorded; the author.
PIERRE LOUIS, U. (1965) La révolution duvaliériste. Port au Prince: the author.
PINCKOMBE, E. (1874) L'article 7: lettre à D. Delorme. Paris: Alcan-Levy.
PRICE, H. (1900) De la réhabilitation de la race noire por la république d'Haïti. Port au Prince: the author.
PRO [Public Record Office, London] (1885a) Wyndham to Granville, 22 April, FO 35/125.
——— (1885b) Maunder to Granville, 9 January, FO 35/125.
——— (1884) Salomon à Manigat, 24 juin, FO 35/125.
——— (1883a) Hunt to Granville, 24 December, FO 35/118.
——— (1883b) Hunt to Granville, 26 September, FO 35/118.
——— (1883c) Fouchard à Villevaleix, 9 septembre, FO 35/120.
——— (1882) Hunt to Granville, 13 December, FO 35/115.
——— (1867) Delorme à Salomon, 4 juillet, FO 35/71.
——— (1859) Byron to Malmesbury, 26 February, FO 35/53.
Republique d'Haïti (1966) Ouverture solennelle de la 6ème et dernière session de la 39ème législature, 18 avril. Port au Prince. République d'Haïti.
——— (1882a) Bulletin des Lois, No. 13. Port au Prince: République d'Haïti.
——— (1882b) Documents diplomatiques, relations extérieures, affaire Maunder. Paris: République d'Haïti.
SAINT LOUIS, R. A. (1970) La présociologie haïtienne. Ottawa:
SAINT LOUIS, R. A. (1970) La présociologie haitienne. Ottawa: Lemeac.
ST. JOHN, S. (1889) Hayti: or the Black Republic. London: Smith Elder.
SALOMON *jeune,* L.E.L.F. (1883) Discours de S.E. le Président de la République, session extraordinaire. Port au Prince: Republique d'Haïti.
——— (1882) Circulaire, 18 fevrier. Port au Prince: République d'Haïti.
——— (1861) Une defense. Brussels: Labrou et Martens.
——— (1845) "Discours," 29 octobre. Proces verbal. Aux Cayes: No publisher stated.
TROUILLOT, H. (1968) Demesvar Delorme, ou introduction à une sociologie de la littérature haïtienne. Port au Prince: the author.

*David Nicholls of Oxford University has written on political theory, modern religious thought, Caribbean history, and politics. He is the author of* The Pluralist *State (London, Macmillan, 1975),* Three Varieties of Pluralism (London, Macmillan, 1974) and two chapters in the forthcoming centenary volume Newman and Gladstone *(Dublin, Veritas), as well as a monograph and numerous articles in the field of Caribbean studies. His forthcoming book* Race, Colour and Independence in Haiti *will be published by Cambridge University Press in their Latin American Studies Series in early 1979.*

CARL STONE
*Department of Government*
*University of the West Indies*
*Mona, Kingston 7, Jamaica*

# *REGIONAL PARTY VOTING IN JAMAICA (1959-1976)*

The analysis of voting behavior patterns from electoral statistics aggregated by regions and urban and rural districts has a long and rich tradition (Lipset and Rokkan, 1967). This mode of electoral analysis has, however, declined in usage due to the emergence of the sample survey method, which allows for a more detailed analysis of individual voting choices and the related social and attitudinal factors which influence them.

It is often forgotten, however, that aggregate analysis of area or geographically defined voting statistics is a low-cost research method when compared to the exclusive and much more expensive sample survey research method. Aggregate analysis can be applied effectively with careful adaptation to most of the areas of electoral analysis, particularly so in societies in which community and residential patterns are structured according to clear socio-economic and stratification variables such as income, status, and occupation. This applies as well to societies in which regional and territorial divisions are more than just administrative units but represent focal points of local identities and loyalties.

Additionally, using the sample survey technique the study of aggregate voting statistics is ideally suited for analyzing the impact of "regionalism" and "localism" in voting behavior where exceptionally large samples or operationally difficult longitudinal

---

AUTHOR'S NOTE: The data used in this article are part of a larger study of local level voting in Jamaica. Invaluable assistance was received from the Institute of Social and Economic Research in preparing and coding the data.

Journal of Interamerican Studies and World Affairs, Vol. 20 No. 4, November 1978

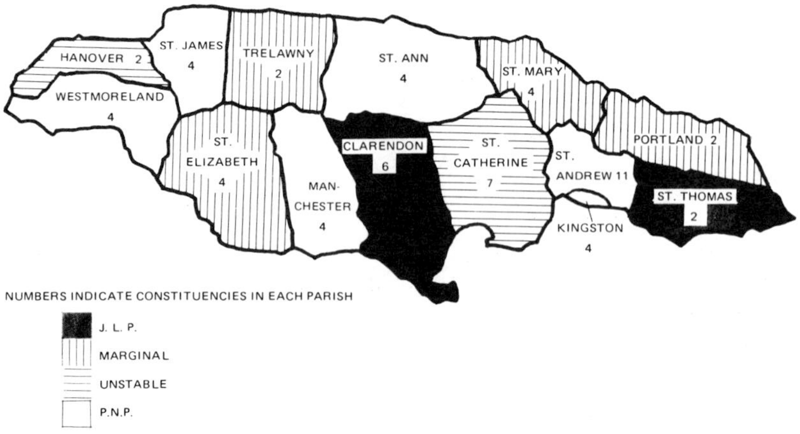


**Figure 1: Parishes of Jamaica**

panel samples are required. The method, moreover, is irreplaceable if voting trends and patterns over reasonably long periods of time are to be analyzed in countries in which the sample survey technique has been recently applied to electoral analysis.

The author initiated the first series of sample survey studies of voting behavior in Jamaica between 1970 and 1976 (Stone, 1973, 1974, 1978). The picture they portray needs to be filled out by connecting the trends they reveal with earlier voting patterns, so that these more recent electoral developments can be put into perspective.

In Jamaica the competing political parties—the Jamaica Labour Party and Peoples National Party—each seek to establish hegemony over defined political territory or areas. Violence, intimidation, bribery, patronage, victimization, rehousing, and restrictive voter registration of known supporters of the competing party by the governing party are all used to establish party hegemony in areas of growing, established or potential voting strength. These party pressures act to reinforce the more informal local community and class pressures that seek to force one of the available party and candidate choices on the individual.

While individuals attempt to resist these pressures, the weight of local level pressures indicates distinct patterns of regional and community voting trends discoverable by aggregate analysis of regional and community voting statistics.

An earlier survey study established that Jamaicans have developed a modern sense of national identity and consciousness. This national identity has, however, been superimposed on an earlier mass identity with the local community and the parish. In the period before the postwar modernization of society, the development of mass parties and trade unions, emergence of national media, and the local village and the parish or other administrative area in which it was located, provided a strong focal point of territorial identity. In the 12 more rural parishes that lie outside the Urban Metropolitan Area of Kingston and St. Andrew, the parish and local district still serve as reference points for territorial identity. Parishes as well as established and recognized local areas or regions within them can therefore be expected to show distinct patterns of voting choice and party-voting traditions discoverable from aggregate analysis of parish level and intraparish regional electoral statistics. In the Urban Metropolitan Area of Kingston and St. Andrew, territorial identity with local community is very strong.

Both urban and rural communities and regions in Jamaica are stratified according to measurable socioeconomic variables which have been shown in earlier survey studies to influence voting patterns. In the Urban Metropolitan Area of Kingston and St. Andrew, communities of residence range from inner-city slums and suburban squatter settlements with concentrations of the subproletariat, the unemployed, and the poorest strata of the working class, to exclusive and luxurious upper-middle-class areas with the professional and business elite. In between these two extremes are other communities[1] representing various levels of the stratification system differentiated by income, occupation and educational levels. Manual wage labor, the unemployed, and self-employed workers make up the majority of the electorate.

The areas and communities in the rural parishes represent gradations of urbanization and modernization ranging from small isolated farming villages in the remote and hilly interior to towns with most of the social and physical infrastructure of urban life. In addition, regions within these rural parishes are also differentiated by varied concentrations of economic activity, including small, domestic, peasant agriculture and large sugar plantations producing for export. In these areas where local residents are highly dependent on a single pattern of income generation tied to one of these economic activities, comparisons can be made of voting patterns over time to establish the impact of these economic parameters on electoral behavior.

The study of electoral data ordered by geographical units involves more than aggregating voting choices by area and correlating these with socioeconomic variables. Electoral systems such as Jamaica's which are based on "the first past the post" plurality system rather than on proportional representation, seek to give parliamentary representation to geographical areas (Rae, 1967). This fact is often lost in the focus on popular vote patterns which merely aggregate votes and emphasize numbers of voters biased in favor of urban areas with large population concentrations. In addition to analyzing party strength in popular vote terms, both nationally and regionally, it is also necessary to examine the spatial or geographical strength of parties to establish the territorial spread of party support.

Voting and party competition in Jamaica represent a relatively unique pattern of party competitiveness. Since the first electoral contest based on universal adult suffrage in 1944 the two major parties, the Jamaica Labour Party (JLP) and the People's National Party (PNP), have alternated in office at two-term intervals over a series of eight parliamentary elections. The pattern of electoral victories is shown in Table 1.

This unique pattern of two-party competitiveness is based partly on the slender margins of party majorities within a large proportion of the electoral constituencies and on the relative magnitude of the vote swings that occur at every second election to unseat the governing party.

Part of the objective of this study is, therefore, to discover the regional and community voting patterns which support this high

TABLE 1
Distribution of Votes and Seats, 1944-1976

| Elections | Parliamentary Seats | | Popular Vote | |
|---|---|---|---|---|
| | JLP | PNP | JLP | PNP |
| 1944 | 22 | 5 | 41.4 | 23.5 |
| 1949 | 17 | 13 | 42.7 | 43.5 |
| 1955 | 14 | 18 | 39.0 | 50.5 |
| 1959 | 16 | 29 | 44.3 | 54.8 |
| 1962 | 26 | 19 | 50.0 | 49.6 |
| 1967 | 33 | 20 | 50.7 | 49.1 |
| 1972 | 17 | 36* | 43.2 | 56.1 |
| 1976 | 13 | 47 | 43.2 | 56.8 |

*Adjusted from 16-36 after a successful JLP petition and judicial recount.

level of interparty competitiveness at the national level. In other words, the strained attempts at party hegemony outlined earlier operate within what is clearly one of the most competitive of two-party systems. The discovery of the regional and local voting patterns that lie behind this highly competitive electoral system is therefore the central task of this study.

## *The Data*

The data used for this study consist of three time series representing regional and community levels of voting. The first data set consists of voting statistics measuring the percentage distribution of the party vote between the two parties, the JLP and the PNP, for 825 areas in the 14 parishes. In the 12 more rural parishes the areas consist of traditional and established local rural communities[2] based on boundaries defined by knowledgeable local residents and community notables, as well as well-defined urban centers of varying size and population concentration. The towns in the rural parishes and the Urban Metropolitan Area of Kingston and St. Andrew have also been included. These urban areas are not disaggregated into local communities, although the parish boundary is used to separate and distinguish Kingston from urban St. Andrew.

The voting data in this first data set cover the period 1959 to 1976, which includes five parliamentary elections. Each unit of analysis is classified in terms of the following six-point scale of urbanization: (1) less than 3,000; (2) 3,000 to 5,000; (3) 5,000 to 9,000; (4) 10,000 to 19,000; (5) 20,000 to 99,000; (6) 100,000 and more.

The respective party shares or percentages of the vote are calculated as proportions of the total number of registered voters rather than proportions of the total number of actual voters. This is done in order to minimize likely statistical distortions due to extreme values which could exaggerate in a positive or negative direction mean or average measures of party tendencies and correlation coefficients over the period under study. The scale of party voting is based on a classification of five ranges of party percentage majorities of the registered electorate. These ranges are set out below.

| *Code Categories* | *Ranges of Percentage Majorities* | |
|---|---|---|
| 1 | 20% and more JLP majority | (STRONG JLP) |
| 2 | 10%-19% JLP majority | (WEAK JLP) |
| 3 | less than 10% JLP or PNP | (MARGINAL) |
| 4 | 10%-19% PNP majority | (WEAK PNP) |
| 5 | 20% and more PNP | (STRONG PNP) |

The second data set comprises popular vote standings for each of the 14 parishes over the period of five elections between 1959 and 1976. Parish boundaries have remained constant in the electoral system, while constituency boundaries have been changed three times since the 1950s. As was done in the case of the first data set, the raw percentage scores are converted to an identical five-point scale of party strength.

For both data sets, 1959 is chosen as the baseline election for data collection because it is the first parliamentary election in which the third parties and independent candidates received only a trivial fraction of the votes cast in all constituencies and parishes.

The third data set consists partly of voting data for 46 groups or clusters of polling divisions, each representing relatively homogeneous socioeconomic zones or subareas of larger communities in the urban area of Kingston and St. Andrew. These 46 areas are grouped into the following five categories representing differing levels of the stratification system of the Urban Metropolitan Area of Kingston and St. Andrew.

(1) Lower Class (or very poor Working Class): at least 80% manual labor, more than 50% unskilled labor, and less than 20% with more than primary education.
(2) Working Class: at least 80% manual labor, more than 50% skilled and semi-skilled labor, and between 20% and 35% with more than primary education.
(3) Lower Middle Class: at least 80% made up of skilled and white-collar labor (and at least 40% from each category), and between 36% and 50% with more than primary education.
(4) Middle Class: at least 80% of nonmanual occupations, with at least 80% with more than primary education.
(5) Upper Middle Class: at least 80% nonmanual occupations, with at least 50% representing elite professions, managerial occupations, and owners of business, and at least 80% with more than primary education.

The voting data are restricted to the 1967, 1972, and 1976 elections due to high levels of population mobility in the urban area and the recency of certain important housing and residential community developments that fall in the sample of areas studied.

In order to facilitate comparison with other socioeconomic communities and classes, similar clusters of polling divisions are grouped for the following identifiable socioeconomic strata in 12 more rural parishes: (1) sugar estate workers (or the agroproletariat); (2) urban wage labor in the towns of the more rural parishes; and (3) small peasant communities producing mainly mixed crops for the domestic market and for their own subsistence.

Each community so classified had at least 51% of the labor force falling in the small peasant, agroproletariat, and urban wage labor categories.

The voting data also covered the 1967, 1972, and 1976 elections. All electoral data sets are coded in terms of the five-point scale of party tendencies outlined earlier for each of the three elections.

*Party Strength by Parish*

It seems quite evident that with the PNP's popular vote varying over the years between 57% and 49%, and the JLP's vote between 51% and 43%, that the PNP is the stronger of the two parties, in spite of the fact that neither party has been able so far to break through the cycle of party government changes at intervals of every two elections or after every two successive electoral victories. The first question to be answered is precisely how the superior strength of the PNP is reflected in the parish vote.

Table 2 classifies the 14 parishes in terms of their party tendencies over the period of five elections between 1959 and 1976. The classification was based on the following schema of aggregate party vote scores for the five elections: (1) JLP, 5-11 points (average between weak and strong JLP); (2) PNP, 19-25 points (average between weak and strong PNP); (3) MARGINAL, 12-18 points (average lower than weak PNP and more than weak JLP); and (4) UNSTABLE, with both JLP and PNP majorities of at least 10% and more.

The aggregates are computed by adding the party vote scores for each parish for each of the five elections. The geographical dominance of the PNP is most apparent in terms of the spread of parish party-vote tendencies.

Six parishes indicate consistent PNP party tendencies with St. Ann being the leading PNP parish. In five out of the six parishes

TABLE 2
Party Tendencies by Parish, 1959-1976

| Parish | Tendency | Aggregate Scale Score | Mean PNP % Vote | No. of PNP Vote Majorities |
|---|---|---|---|---|
| St. Ann | PNP | 23 | 62 | 5 |
| Manchester | PNP | 21 | 58 | 5 |
| St. Andrew | PNP | 21 | 58 | 5 |
| Kingston | PNP | 20 | 57 | 5 |
| Westmoreland | PNP | 20 | 57 | 5 |
| St. James | PNP | 20 | 56 | 4 |
| St. Elizabeth | Marginal | 17 | 54 | 4 |
| St. Mary | Marginal | 16 | 52 | 4 |
| Trelawny | Marginal | 16 | 51 | 4 |
| Portland | Marginal | 14 | 50 | 3 |
| St. Catherine | Unstable | 17 | 49 | 1 |
| Hanover | Unstable | 13 | 48 | 3 |
| Clarendon | JLP | 10 | 42 | 1 |
| St. Thomas | JLP | 9 | 42 | 1 |

the JLP failed to win any parish popular vote majorities even during its period of ascendency in the 1962 to 1967 period. Among the four marginal parishes which show no strong tendency in either party direction, the trend favors the PNP, as can be seen from the fact that only in Portland did the JLP win two out of five popular vote majorities over the period. Most significant is the fact that only two parishes are classified as JLP, and in either case, the PNP has won at least one popular vote majority during its period of ascendancy.

Even if one takes into account the fact that the data series is biased slightly in favor of the PNP, since it includes three elections won by the PNP and two by the JLP, the greater parish strength of the PNP is still very evident. Although the JLP won two of the five elections, only in five of the 14 parishes did it win at least two popular vote majorities in the five elections. This balance of

TABLE 3
Aggregate and Mean Party Vote Scores by Elections

| Scores | 1959 | 1962 | 1967 | 1972 | 1976 |
|---|---|---|---|---|---|
| Aggregate Score | 52 | 41 | 41 | 53 | 54 |
| Mean Score* | 3.71 | 2.93 | 2.93 | 3.79 | 3.86 |

*Mean Score: 1 = Strong JLP; 2 = Weak JPL; 3 = Marginal; 4 = Weak PNP; 5 = Strong PNP.

parish party strength is reflected in the fact that the PNP won 50, or 71% of the 70 parish popular votes over the period.

One result of this greater parish spread of PNP voter strength is that when the PNP wins an election, it does so in almost all of the parishes, while the JLP margin of parish majorities is closer to one-half of the total number of 14 parishes. In the 1959, 1972, and 1976 elections, the PNP won in 11, 12, and 13 parishes, respectively, indicating a possible trend toward greater uniformity in parish voting patterns. The JLP, on the other hand, won vote majorities in eight parishes in 1962 and six parishes in 1967. In addition, when the PNP wins elections, the mean parish majorities tend to be somewhat larger compared to the majorities in the elections won by the JLP. This is reflected in the aggregate and average scores of partisan tendencies for each of the five elections as shown in Table 3.

Table 3 indicates that average parish voting in JLP-won elections tends toward marginal scores (or an average party vote majority of less than 10%), while the average tendencies in PNP-won elections are toward a weak PNP score (or an average PNP party vote majority of 10% to 19%).

Given this clear evidence of PNP parish vote superiority, the question remains as to what generates the extraordinary competitiveness of the vote pattern which has unseated governing parties at approximately ten-year intervals.

TABLE 4
Mean Swings by Parish Type

| Parish Type | Mean Swing or Net Percentage Change in Party Strength 1959-1976 |
|---|---|
| PNP (6) | 5.42% |
| Marginal (4) | 4.75% |
| Unstable (2) | 7.38% |
| JLP (2) | 7.25% |

The first contributing factor is the six parishes which fall in the grouping of marginal and unstable parishes. Among the four marginal parishes, Portland, St. Mary, Trelawny and St. Elizabeth, the small size of popular vote margins means that relatively small voter swings or net changes in party support between elections can wipe out majorities at both the parish and constituency levels. The two unstable parishes, St. Catherine and Hanover, are characterized by both small popular vote margins generally and larger-than-average tendencies for swings in voter support between elections.

Ignoring the direction of vote swings over the period, the average swing per parish over the five elections is a 5.7% net change in relative party strength. Table 4 indicates that both the JLP and the unstable parishes show larger-than-average swing patterns, while the PNP parishes and marginal parishes are more stable in their level of party voting. Although the comparative differences in swing magnitude seem to favor the PNP given the relatively greater stability of the PNP parishes compared to the JLP parishes, the advantage is not as great as it seems. Clearly the concentration of PNP majorities in six parishes where the average PNP vote over the five elections is 58% guarantees that party a certain number of seats where the average swing or net percentage change is approximately 5%. Of the 6 PNP parishes, only St. James with a very high average swing of nine percent (the highest among the parishes) departs from this general pattern of relative stability. However among the eight remaining non-PNP parishes, the size of swing pattern relative to their popular vote margins guarantees that voter swings between elections can give either of the two parties a sufficiently increased parish vote to win majorities in the overall distribution of parliamentary seats.

A central issue, therefore, is the distribution of seats within the parishes and how the balance of this distribution is spread between the more competitive and less competitive parishes as regards vote swings and the respective popular vote margins. A precise measure of vote competitiveness at the parish level is the average popular vote safety margin divided by the average swing or net change of percentage party strength over the period of five elections. The resulting index measures the likelihood of average swings disturbing the parish popular vote party majorities. The parish safety margin is computed by calculating the net difference between the percentage vote for the majority party for each election and 50%. The smaller or lower the index score, the greater is the vote competitiveness of the parish. Indices falling below or equal to unity are highly competitive, while those appreciably exceeding unity are not competitive. Those marginally above unity are considered moderately competitive.

Table 5 ranks the parishes in terms of their respective scores on the "Index of Competitiveness." The six highly competitive parishes include the four marginal parishes (Portland, St. Mary, Trelawny, and St. Elizabeth), one of the unstable parishes (Hanover), and one of the PNP parishes (St. James). These six competitive parishes are, therefore, critical parishes relative to the change process that produces electoral victories for opposition parties. Four of them fall in the group of the five geographically contigous parishes in the western end of the island which make up the county of Cornwall.

Five of these six highly competitive parishes (excluding St. James) include those parishes which, in terms of a ranking of 1960 wage income data, constitute the poorest of the 14 Jamaican parishes.[3] If one excludes the tourist center of Montego Bay, which is the capital and main urban center in St. James, rural

TABLE 5
Ranking of Parish by Indices of Voter Competitiveness and Poverty

| Parishes | Poverty Index* | Voter Competitiveness Index | Degree of Competitiveness |
|---|---|---|---|
| Hanover | 75 ( 1) | .79 | High |
| St. Elizabeth | 70 ( 2) | .81 | High |
| Portland | 64 ( 5) | .93 | High |
| St. James | 55 (10) | .97 | High |
| St. Mary | 66 ( 3) | 1.00 | High |
| Trelawny | 64 ( 4) | 1.00 | High |
| Clarendon | 56 ( 9) | 1.23 | Moderate |
| St. Catherine | 49 (12) | 1.25 | Moderate |
| Kingston | 20 (14) | 1.37 | Moderate |
| Manchester | 61 ( 7) | 1.64 | Low |
| St. Thomas | 60 ( 8) | 1.83 | Low |
| Westmoreland | 62 ( 6) | 1.84 | Low |
| St. Andrew | 24 (13) | 2.63 | Low |
| St. Ann | 55 (11) | 3.40 | Low |

*Index = percent of parish population earning less than $200 per annum, 1960.

St. James fits into this pattern of more entrenched rural poverty than is to be found in the other parishes. Additionally, when the parishes are ranked on a crude index of living standards based on the ratio between concrete and wooden dwellings using 1970 census data, five of the six highly competitive parishes fall in the group of seven parishes with the lowest living standards. High voter competitiveness is related to rural poverty and is therefore not a random factor but expresses cyclical rural voter discontent.

Three parishes are classified as moderately competitive. They include three of the five most urbanized parishes and one each from the categories of JLP, PNP, and unstable parishes. The parishes with the lowest levels of voter competitiveness represent five PNP parishes and one JLP parish.

In spite of the three changes in the intraparish constituency boundaries these have not basically affected the balance of seats

TABLE 6
Distribution of Parliamentary Seats by Parish Competitiveness

| Degree Competitiveness | Percentage of Parliamentary Seats 1959-1962 | 1967-1972 | 1976 |
|---|---|---|---|
| High | 33 | 32 | 30 |
| Moderate | 27 | 25 | 28 |
| Low | 40 | 43 | 42 |
| | 100 | 100 | 100 |

between the three parish levels of voter competitiveness. As can be seen from Table 6, the majority of the seats have consistently been located in the moderately and highly competitive parishes. This distribution of seats in which the majority fall in the more competitive parishes is clearly one of the major factors contributing to the competitiveness of the Jamaican two-party system.[4]

The pattern of electoral victories indicates that there are two main types of elections. The first consists of "realigning" elections in which the opposition party comes to power, and the second, the "stablizing" election that follows, in which the governing party maintains its seat and popular vote majority. Both types of elections are distinguishable by a number of important features.

First of all, in the realigning elections the size of the average net changes in party standing across the 14 parishes is much larger. It will be noted from Table 7 that the average parish swings in the 1967 and the 1976 elections, which were stabilizing elections (won respectively by the JLP and the PNP), are much lower than those which occurred in the realigning elections of 1962 and 1972.

In addition to the magnitude of the cross-parish swings, the two main types of elections are also distinguishable in that in the realigning elections, interparish swings tend toward conformity of direction in favor of the winning party. In the stabilizing elections, the cross-parish swing pattern tends in both party directions and therefore cancels out the effects on the relative standing

TABLE 7
Size of Average Swings by Elections

| | 1962 | 1967 | 1972 | 1976 |
|---|---|---|---|---|
| TYPE | Realigning | Stabilizing | Realigning | Stabilizing |
| WINNING PARTY | JLP | JLP | PNP | PNP |
| MEAN PARISH SWING (Ignoring Direction) | 6.8% | 3.9% | 7.1% | 4.9% |
| NET CHANGE IN NATIONAL POPULAR VOTE MARGIN | 6.01% | .06% | 7.27% | .30% |

of the parties. The result of this canceling effect is that there is no significant net change in the relative national popular vote strength of the parties in stabilizing elections. In the stabilizing election in 1967, eight parishes swung to the opposition party, the PNP, and in 1976, seven parishes to the JLP. In the 1962 and 1972 elections the direction of the parish swings are all uniformly toward the winning parties, the JLP and the PNP, respectively. The details of the interparish swings are set out in Table 8.

A most intriguing discovery from these data in Table 8 is the degree to which clusters of parishes that are geographically contiguous tend to swing in the same direction regardless of the type of election involved. Five main parish groupings or clusters are identified.

The first cluster of parishes lies in the southeastern end of the island and comprises the Urban Metropolitan Area of Kingston and St. Andrew, together with St. Thomas, which borders on both urban parishes. The second cluster is located in the northeast and consists of the two adjacent parishes of St. Mary and Portland. The third group is in the south central zone of the island, comprising the very large and contiguous parishes of Clarendon and St. Catherine. The fourth group lies across the center of the island and extends into the southwest. It includes

TABLE 8
Patterns of Swing by Parish, 1962-1976

| Groups of Adjacent Parishes | Interelection Swings 1959-62 | 1962-67 | 1967-72 | 1976-76 |
|---|---|---|---|---|
| GROUP 1 | | | | |
| Kingston | - 4 | - 7 | + 3 | + 7 |
| St. Andrew | - 1 | - 4 | + 9 | + 2 |
| St. Thomas | - 6 | - 1 | + 8 | + 8 |
| GROUP 2 | | | | |
| Portland | - 6 | + 2 | + 4 | + 3 |
| St. Mary | - 7 | + 5 | + 2 | + 5 |
| GROUP 3 | | | | |
| Clarendon | - 7 | + 7 | +13 | - 4 |
| St. Catherine | - 5 | + 3 | + 5 | +11* |
| GROUP 4 | | | | |
| St. Elizabeth | - 8 | - 3 | +10 | - 6 |
| Manchester | - 7 | - 4 | + 7 | - 3 |
| St. Ann | - 4 | - 5 | + 5 | - 3 |
| GROUP 5 | | | | |
| Trelawny | - 5 | + 5 | + 2 | + 3* |
| St. James | -12 | + 3 | +13 | - 6 |
| Hanover | -11 | + 4 | +13 | - 5 |
| Westmoreland | - 9 | + 2 | + 6 | - 2 |

"+" = Swing to PNP; "–" = Swing to JLP.
*Two deviant swings.

St. Elizabeth and adjacent Manchester as well as St. Ann, which touches on the Manchester border. The fifth grouping or cluster of contiguous parishes is to be found in the extreme northwestern end of the island. It comprises the largest grouping of four parishes in the western county of Cornwall, joined by adjacent borders.

With the exception of two out of a total of 56 parish swings over the five election periods, all the swing directions are consistent and uniform within the five groupings of parishes. The magnitude of the swings, of course, differs in many cases, but the remarkable uniformity of direction for the groupings in the stabilizing elections of 1976 and 1967, when the overall cross-parish swings are in both party directions, testifies to the impact of regionalism on voting trends. This is in spite of the fact that clusters are not similar with respect to overall partisan tendencies. In other words, the common vote trends within the clusters are limited to floating voters and new voters who have been shown in earlier survey analyses (Stone, 1974) to account for most of the interelection swings. This clearly means that the degree of party influences on these critical minorities who determine election outcomes is not a function of the overall partisan tendency in the parish, but reflects region-wide trends within the clusters or groups of parishes.

Although the patterns aggregated at the parish level clearly point to these sharp differences between "realigning" and "stabilizing" elections, it remains to be established if these patterns hold for the 825 mainly intraparish regions.

One area of difference between the two main types of elections is subject to detailed analysis on a parish by parish basis for the rural parishes. This concerned the unidirectional trends of swings in realigning elections and the two-party swing trends found in stabilizing elections at the parish level. Table 9 sets out the proportion of the intraparish regions which swung to the JLP and the PNP, respectively, for the 1962, 1967, and 1972 elections. While the swing directions are not uniform for the individual parish areas in the "realigning" elections, in all cases the majority of areas show swings toward the winning party. There are some deviant cases where fairly substantial minority areas show swing trends toward the losing party. These include St. Thomas in 1962 and Portland and Trelawny in 1972. As expected, the stabilizing election of 1967 shows less of a unidirectional tendency in swing trends within the parish, but the difference is not very great. As far as the intraregional swing patterns go, it seems that for both types of elections the majority of the areas in most parishes tend to show swings in one party direction, although the one-party swing tendency is stronger in realigning elections than in stabilizing elections.

The data on aggregated cross-parish voting emphasize the

TABLE 9
Direction of Internal Regional Swings
by Rural Parishes for Three Elections

| Parishes | Swing Directions by Party Percentages 1962 JLP | 1962 PNP | 1967 JLP | 1967 PNP | 1972 JLP | 1972 PNP | Number Parish Regions |
|---|---|---|---|---|---|---|---|
| St. Thomas | 64 | 36 | 57 | 43 | 16 | 84 | 61 |
| Portland | 74 | 26 | 46 | 54 | 37 | 63 | 54 |
| St. Mary | 72 | 28 | 21 | 79 | 14 | 86 | 76 |
| St. Ann | 72 | 28 | 26 | 74 | 20 | 80 | 89 |
| Trelawny | 78 | 22 | 30 | 70 | 42 | 58 | 69 |
| St. James | 95 | 5 | 25 | 75 | 11 | 89 | 57 |
| Hanover | 63 | 37 | 35 | 65 | 6 | 94 | 34 |
| Westmoreland | 71 | 29 | 37 | 63 | 13 | 87 | 88 |
| St. Elizabeth | 64 | 36 | 35 | 65 | 3 | 97 | 90 |
| Manchester | 80 | 20 | 50 | 50 | 8 | 92 | 66 |
| Clarendon | 80 | 20 | 32 | 68 | 6 | 94 | 98 |
| St. Catherine | 78 | 22 | 29 | 71 | 25 | 75 | 102 |

superiority of the PNP over the JLP in the parish spread of the vote in Jamaica. The data also point to the patterns of parish competitiveness in party voting which have maintained an evenly balanced two-party system up to 1976 in spite of the majority strength of the PNP. The demonstrated effect of regionalism in influencing interelection swings at the parish level and the outlined patterns of differences between realigning and stabilizing elections serve to define some of the parameters within which the two parties compete for hegemony. It remains now to examine the effects of socioeconomic variables on the trends of bipartisan support that exist and sustain the two-party system.

*Urbanization, Class, and Party Tendencies*

The two political parties in Jamaica, the JLP and the PNP, emerged as alternate oppositions to the regime of the colonial governors before independence in the early 1940s (Munroe, 1970). The PNP has consistently projected the symbolism and image of a "radical reformist" party in the Democratic Socialist tradition, with leadership dominated by the upper-middle-class intelligentsia. The JLP, on the other hand, has maintained the image of a militant but nevertheless "conservative reform party" with firm beliefs in the free enterprise system. Its leadership came initially from lower-middle-class labor leaders and school teachers supported by a small coalition of planter-merchants.

The JLP's traditional mass image has been shaped largely by its founder-leader, the late Sir Alexander Bustamante, a militant but anticommunist and populist labor leader. Bustamante, in Peronist style of demagogic flamboyance, championed the cause of the lower class against the establishment but with no interest in overturning the system of class domination. The PNP's early mass image was shaped by its founder-leader, the late Norman Manley, an Oxford-trained, intellectual lawyer, who sought to build a party in the image of the British Labor Party. Consequently, the PNP established middle-class status credentials, while pushing an ideological and left-leaning policy thrust which, unlike the JLP's approach, consistently made prescriptions for radical structural changes in economy and society (Stone, 1977).

With the emergence of new leadership in both parties in the 1970s, the party images have changed drastically for new voters and the recently socialized voters. The new PNP leader, Michael Manley, projects a flamboyant populist image in the Bustamante tradition, but this is combined with anticapitalist, antiimperialist, and pro-Third World ideological rhetoric. The JLP's new leaders, Edward Seaga and Labor leader Hugh Shearer, are ideologically right of center but continue the JLP thrust for mass appeal. Seaga, the current leader, is to some extent handicapped by his Lebanese ethnic origin in a mainly Black and increasingly racially conscious society, but he exudes an image of toughness, strength, and intellectual brilliance. Under his leadership, the JLP's strident anticommunist and antisocialist reaction to the PNP and its open identification with conservative class interests has sharply polarized the parties ideologically.

Two central issues, therefore, arise in the analysis of class and community party-vote patterns in Jamaica. The first concerns the discovery of long-term and relatively stable party-vote patterns, which differentiate the divergent socioeconomic communities. The second concerns the nature and direction of the party-vote changes in these socioeconomic communities that accompanied the change toward more ideologically polarized party images which crystallized in 1974.

To analyze the first theme of regional party-vote trends, urbanization was correlated with party-vote tendencies for the 825 mainly intraparish regions for the period 1959 to 1976. Additionally, party-vote trends over the period were correlated to establish the level of party-vote stability for the intraparish regions.

The second theme regarding the shifts in party-vote tendencies due to the ideological polarization of the two parties in the post-1974 period was examined by comparing party-vote trends in the two elections prior to 1976 (1972 and 1967) with those in the 1976 election.

The Pearson R correlation of party-vote trends across the 12 more rural parishes over the two periods, between JLP ascendancy in 1962-1967 and PNP ascendancy in 1972-1976, varied between .7 and .9 for all parishes, thereby indicating a high level of party-vote stability. In the case of the two urban parishes of Kingston and St. Andrew located in the Urban Metropolitan Area making up the country's capital, there was no such stability in party voting. A separate correlation computed for the 46 areas in Urban Metropolitan Kingston and St. Andrew showed a low .2 (Pearson R) coefficient for the party-vote patterns of 1967 and 1976. This would suggest the possibility that this urban center might have been affected to a significant degree by the ideological issues which polarized the parties in 1976.

The data analysis revealed a .5 Pearson R correlation between the six-point scale of urbanization for the 825 regions and the party tendency scores for the five elections aggregated. In other words, there was a moderately high positive association between the PNP tendencies over the period and urbanization, and a corresponding negative relationship between urbanization and JLP party-vote tendencies. This long-term relationship between urbanization and PNP tendencies may indeed account for the dominance of the PNP given the fact that the urban areas are the more rapidly growing sections of the country's population. There is curiously no evidence of a secular decline in PNP tendencies due to the rural to urban population drifts. This suggests that migrants may well be socialized into their host communities due to the strong local party-community pressures of urban life, especially in the poorer districts. This may well be reinforced by the fact that migrants become resocialized politically by the need to seek out local or central government party patronage through local community contacts.

The mean score per area comparing the least urban regions (Category 1) and the five other more urban regions (Categories 2-5) grouped together indicates consistently significant differences (see Table 10). The urban areas as a whole, representing 40% of the electorate, tend toward a weak PNP mean, while the rural areas tend toward a marginal mean. Both show large changes between JLP and PNP periods of ascendancy, although the rural areas indicated a much larger shift toward the PNP tendency. Clearly the rural areas are more competitive than the urban areas. Although the PNP's popular vote in 1976 did not decline over the 1972 level it is evident that ground has been lost in terms of the modest decline in the rural and urban regional averages by area. This is due to the fact that the areas registering PNP gains were the more densely populated rural districts and urban areas. These gains were canceled out in the averaging process by the larger number of less heavily populated urban and rural areas showing gains by the JLP.

The basis of the PNP's greater traditional strength in the urban areas is most likely related to its greater appeal than that of the JLP among the younger, more educated, and upwardly mobile wage laboring majority in the towns and capital city. Any adequate analysis of this inference requires a detailed assessment of the party-vote trends among the various classes identified earlier.

Table 11 sets out the distribution of party-vote tendencies for the various clusters of reasonably homogeneous class communities for the three elections in the 12 more rural parishes. Although it fluctuates, the PNP majority tendency among urban

TABLE 10
Party Vote Tendencies and Urbanization

| Areas | 1967 | 1972 | 1976 |
|---|---|---|---|
| Rural | 2.0 | 3.5 | 3.2 |
| Urban | 3.5 | 4.3 | 4.0 |

1 = Strong JLP; 2 = Weak JLP; 3 = Marginal; 4 = Weak PNP; 5 = Strong PNP.

wage labor remains high even during the 1967 election when the JLP was in the ascendancy. On the contrary, the two rural classes tend toward the JLP in its period of ascendancy, particularly the agroproletariat which approaches a weak JLP average in 1967. Both rural classes show a weakening of the PNP tendency in 1976. This must clearly be a significant factor influencing the regional and national strength of the PNP vote.

In the small peasant areas, a JLP majority in 1967 (in terms of the main tendency in these areas) gives way to a PNP majority in 1972 and the latter declines in 1976, while the JLP tendency increases just short of numerical parity.

In the sugar areas, a large JLP majority area tendency gives way to a smaller PNP area majority in 1972. In 1976 the PNP area majority gives way to a majority showing a marginal party-vote tendency, while the overall JLP tendency remains relatively unchanged.

The Urban Metropolitan Area of Kingston and St. Andrew reveals a fundamentally different picture from the modest change in the post-1972 period among these rural-parish strata of voters. Table 12 reveals that each of the three parliamentary elections portrayed an entirely distinct class-voting pattern. The massiveness of the changes between 1972 and 1976 suggests that ideology played a role in these voter alignments at all class levels, given the degree to which the class responses at either extreme of the urban class structure were sharply polarized.

In 1967 the PNP dominated the middle strata based on its traditional image of respectability and its strong appeal to the middle-class-aspiring upper strata of the working class. This is revealed in the familiar concentrated middle-strata support and weak upper- and lower-class support that confirm the findings from survey studies of that period (Stone, 1973). By 1972 the trend changes fundamentally. With the exception of the lowest strata of the working class that tends toward a marginal party score, the other urban strata embraced the then opposition PNP party and swept it into victory with an all-class coalition.

TABLE 11
Distribution of Party Vote Tendencies

Small Peasant Areas
(N = 78)

| Party Vote | Percentages 1967 | 1972 | 1976 |
|---|---|---|---|
| Strong JLP | 29 | 15 | 19 |
| Weak JLP | 17 | 9 | 13 |
| Marginal | 20 | 26 | 32 |
| Weak PNP | 12 | 15 | 14 |
| Strong PNP | 22 | 35 | 22 |
| | 100 | 100 | 100 |
| Mean Party Vote Scores | 2.7 | 3.5 | 3.3 |

Agroproletarian Areas
(N = 19)

| Party Vote | Percentages 1967 | 1972 | 1976 |
|---|---|---|---|
| Strong JLP | 42 | 11 | 11 |
| Weak JLP | 21 | 5 | 5 |
| Marginal | 26 | 32 | 47 |
| Weak PNP | 5 | 26 | 16 |
| Strong PNP | 5 | 26 | 21 |
| | 100 | 100 | 100 |
| Mean Party Vote Scores | 2.1 | 3.5 | 3.3 |

TABLE 11 (Continued)

Urban Wage Labor (in Large & Medium Sized Towns in the 12 More Rural Parishes) in Areas with Population of 5,000 to 50,000 (N = 24)

| Party Vote | Percentages 1967 | 1972 | 1976 |
|---|---|---|---|
| Strong JLP | 8 | 0 | 4 |
| Weak JLP | 8 | 9 | 4 |
| Marginal | 21 | 16 | 21 |
| Weak PNP | 21 | 9 | 13 |
| Strong PNP | 42 | 66 | 58 |
| | 100 | 100 | 100 |
| Mean Party Vote Score | 3.8 | 4.3 | 4.2 |

The ideological party polarization of 1976 pulled the poorest strata of the working class out of the traditional JLP tendency, while pushing the middle and upper-middle class in the JLP direction. The lower-middle-class PNP support as well as that of the better-off working-class voters also moved toward the JLP slightly but remained clearly in the orbit of PNP dominance. A residue of middle-class traditional PNP loyalty restrained the shift to the JLP and restricted its movement somewhat short of a JLP tendency. The unstable upper-middle class moved with a massive shift into a strong JLP tendency.

The new party images and symbols evidently had a major impact on these sharp urban voter realignments between 1972 and 1976. The instability of these Urban Metropolitan Area voter trends over the period suggests that future basic changes in party styles, images, ideology, and class perspectives are not unlikely to disturb the present curve of class voting tendencies. In view of the fact that the survey findings suggest that the middle and upper strata changes and realignment are primarily ideological (Stone, 1978) and the lower strata voter shifts have responded mainly to

TABLE 12
Party Vote Tendencies* of Socioeconomic Strata in Urban Metropolitan Area

| Elections | Lower Class 1 | Working Class 2 | Lower Middle Class 3 | Middle Class 4 | Upper Middle Class 5 |
|---|---|---|---|---|---|
| 1967 | 2.0 | 3.5 | 5.0 | 4.5 | 2.0 |
| 1972 | 2.8 | 4.8 | 5.0 | 5.0 | 5.0 |
| 1976 | 4.6 | 4.3 | 4.3 | 3.4 | 1.0 |

* 1 = Strong JLP; 2 = Weak JLP; 3 = Marginal; 4 = Weak PNP; 5 = Strong PNP.

expectations for positive material gain from government's policies, a dual pattern of change could occur in the future. Continued decline of the Jamaican economy, and failure of the PNP government to solve basic socioeconomic problems and revitalize an economy experiencing by 1977 four successive years of zero and negative growth, will mean a further shift of working-class and lower-middle-class voting toward the JLP, and a movement of the vote of the poorer strata of the working class in that direction. On the other hand, the PNP is unlikely to modify its ideological image which indicates further erosion of PNP middle- and upper-middle-class voter support but for different reasons.

In order to assess more precisely the effect of the regional parish patterns outlined earlier on voting trends at the micro-community level, the socioeconomic communities in the 12 more rural parishes were grouped according to main types of parishes. The latter include the PNP dominant and the JLP dominant.

Small peasant, agroproletarian, and urban wage labor communities drawn from the 12 more rural parishes were compared across these two types of parish party tendencies. Table 13 sets out the mean party tendency scores for these socioeconomic communities stratified by parish type.

The data shown in Table 13 indicates that for similar socioeconomic areas, the PNP parishes show higher levels of PNP voting than the JLP parishes, with the sole exception of the sugar areas in 1976. The residual effect of parish regionalism is stronger

TABLE 13
Party Vote Tendency by Socioeconomic Areas Stratified by Parish Type

| Parish Type | Party Vote Tendency JLP | PNP | PNP-JLP |
|---|---|---|---|
| Small Peasant | | | |
| 1967 | 2.3 | 3.4 | 1.1 |
| 1972 | 3.3 | 3.4 | .1 |
| 1976 | 2.9 | 3.5 | .6 |
| Agroproletariat | | | |
| 1967 | 1.7 | 2.9 | 1.2 |
| 1972 | 3.3 | 4.6 | 1.3 |
| 1976 | 3.4 | 3.3 | - .1 |
| Urban Wage Labor in Parish Towns | | | |
| 1967 | 2.7 | 4.3 | 1.6 |
| 1972 | 3.7 | 4.9 | 1.2 |
| 1976 | 3.0 | 4.5 | 1.5 |

1 = Strong JLP; 2 = Weak JLP; 3 = Marginal; 4 = Weak PNP; 5 = Strong PNP.

in the urban areas than in the more rural parishes where the differences are more consistent and much larger. This parish regionalism accounts for some of the weakening of the link between urbanization and party-vote tendency, as PNP vote strength is consequently lowered in the urban areas in the JLP parishes. Also, the party-vote tendency is considerably more unstable in the JLP parish areas of urban wage labor compared to those in the PNP parishes.

This comparison of party-vote trends in similar socioeconomic areas of JLP and PNP parishes confirms the existence of parish regionalism in Jamaican voting patterns. The data point clearly to the fact that identifiable territorial party-vote traditions operate as a separate influence of voting in Jamaica over and above the evident independent impact of class.

## *Conclusion*

This paper has identified a number of important patterns in party-vote trends in the Jamaican two-party system. These include regionalism and class effects in parish and community party-vote trends, interparish regionalism in swing patterns, and high levels of two-party competitiveness in most regions of the country. The data presented document the geographical superiority of the PNP, which complements its national popular vote superiority, and point to the fact that these PNP advantages of superior strength over the JLP are counterbalanced by highly competitive voting trends in rural areas, which sustain a balance of power between the two parties and form the basis of the changes in party government at roughly ten-year intervals.

## NOTES

1. These community class types are revealed in the 67 census divisions mapped and demarcated by the Department of Statistics for the Urban Metropolitan Area of Kingston and St. Andrew. The areas proved too large in many cases and too heterogeneous in socioeconomic composition to provide an adequate basis for isolating the class voting patterns in the Urban Metropolitan Area.

2. These intraparish boundaries, grouping areas in the 12 more rural parishes, were initially obtained from one of the parties and were subsequently refined by reference to long-standing local area residents in each parish.

3. The per capita wage levels for the respective parish tends, however, to be mainly measuring wage income, since the income flows to the self-employed of petty commodity production, especially in agriculture, have not been accurately measured in census data.

4. The stability of this ratio is all the more surprising given the strident local accusations of gerrymandering of electoral boundaries.

## REFERENCES

LIPSET, S. and S. ROKKAN (1967) Party Systems and Voter Alignments—Cross National Perspectives. New York: Free Press.

MUNROE, T. (1970) Political Change and Constitutional Development in Jamaica. Kingston: University of the West Indies, ISER.

RAE, D. (1967) The Political Consequences of Electoral Laws. New Haven, CT: Yale Univ. Press.

STONE, C. (1978) "Class and status voting in Jamaica." Social and Economic Studies 26: 279-293.

——— (1977) "Class and the institutionalization of two-party politics in Jamaica." J. of Commonwealth and Comparative Studies 14: 177-196.

——— (1974) Electoral Behaviour and Public Opinion in Jamaica. Kingston: University of the West Indies, ISER.

——— (1973) Class, Race and Political Behaviour in Urban Jamaica. Kingston: University of the West Indies, ISER.

*Carl Stone, a Reader in Political Sociology at the University of the West Indies, did his graduate work at the University of Michigan. He is the author of two books on political behavior in Jamaica and numerous articles on the sociology of Jamaican politics, as well as on Latin America. He is currently writing a book on the political economy of electoral politics in Jamaica.*

ROBERT FREEMAN SMITH
*Department of History*
*The University of Toledo*
*Toledo, Ohio 43606*

# *THE AMERICAN REVOLUTION AND LATIN AMERICA*

## *An Essay in Imagery, Perceptions, and Ideological Influence*

In 1929 the British scholar, Cecil Jane, published his classic, *Liberty and Despotism in Spanish America.* In it he wrote:

> The War of Independence was neither anti-Spanish nor non-Spanish. It was not the outcome of the spread of ideas recently imported from Europe or of some sudden awakening of political life, produced by the reception of eighteenth-century philosophic theories or by such events as the successful revolt of the English colonies in North America and the French Revolution [Jane, 1966: 81].

Instead, Jane (1966: 79) argued that the War of Independence was an attempt to realize the most deeply felt ideals, "which were derived not from any external sources, but from the very hearts of the people." Similarly he argued that the political conceptions of Spanish Americans were (and continued to be) Spanish, not Anglo-Saxon, and he strongly suggested that the example of the British North Americans exerted little if any influence on the Spanish Americans of the nineteenth century. Jane (1966: 111-112, 168-172) also attacked with thinly veiled contempt the idea that the salvation of Latin America lay in emulating England or the United States.

Journal of Interamerican Studies and World Affairs, Vol. 20 No. 4, November 1978

Jane's argument ran counter to the prevailing academic interpretations of the role of the revoluntionary experience of North America in the independence movements of Latin America, and of the nature of Latin American culture. Haring (1930: 179) clearly revealed the emotions such scholarly controversies could stir when he wrote that Jane's argument was eloquently presented but its "willfulness and trifling ingenuity, the gratuitous assumptions . . . leave the reader in a state of dazed exasperation."[1] This interpretive controversy has been renewed periodically, and the celebration of the Bicentennial in the United States has provided the setting for another round of argument concerning this problem of historical influence.

The study of national and cultural influences is a tricky and ambiguous task especially when one is considering ideals, ideas, and national examples. Some limited aspects of economic influence (such as trade patterns and investments) can be readily measured, but it is difficult to find empirical data for "higher" forms of influence relating to revolutionary causality, political values, or institutional change. North American commentators on U.S. influence in Latin America generally have been divided into two groups: externalists and internalists. Since the late nineteenth century the externalists have been overwhelmingly predominant in both academic and governmental circles although scholars have been more divided than other groups. Believing that the United States has played a major role in shaping Latin American developments, the externalists have created historical models and models for U.S. foreign policy. Ironically, this belief unites the "New Left" in both the United States and Latin America (Galeano, 1973) with such Americans as General Leonard Wood and Stephen Bonsal (1913). Depending on the ideology of the externalist commentator, the United States is either hero or scapegoat, nation builder or imperialist monster.

On the other hand, the internalists have stressed the idea that the United States has exercised a minimal role in shaping the internal political, economic, social, and ideological conditions in Latin America. Utilizing arguments similar to those of Hartz (1955) in his studies of U.S. history, the internalists have emphasized cultural factors and internal, historical processes. They have recognized the role played by the United States (and Great Britain) in this historical process, and the fact that some North Americans have tried to influence and "Americanize" Latin America. But they have pointed out that many North Americans have vastly exaggerated the ability of the United States to shape the ideas, systems, and institutions of the nations to the south.

The internalist-externalist debate is of major significance in any attempt to assess the impact of the American Revolution on Latin America. For the most part, externalists have believed that the United States and Latin America basically share a common cultural tradition, or at least a common sphere (the New World) which produces similar ideals and aspirations. And they stress that from the Wars for Independence onward, Latin America has been following (or attempting to follow) the path laid out by the United States. To many orthodox externalists the American Revolution (with its associated ideas, ideals, and institutions) has been of some significance in the "good" aspects of Latin American development, although its influence has been hampered by a combination of factors such as corrupt forces, poverty, lack of "political maturity," European influences, and traditional institutions. Within this scenario, the central question is: "what has gone wrong in Latin America?" The "New Left," with its dependency model of "perverted" development, reverses the morality, but asks the same question.

To the internalist, this question is irrelevant due to the basic dissimilarities of the cultures involved. As historian Morse (1964a: 107) has stated:

> The heart of the matter is that here are two cultures whose historic spiritual trajectories are not merely different . . . but diametrically opposed.

Space does not permit me to give more than a sketch of the arguments of the internalists. Those who are interested should consult the works of such scholars as Morse (1964a, 1964b), Pike (1974), Wiarda (1974), Dealy (1968), Veliz (1967), Moreno (1970), and Smith (1974). These scholars (with some variations) stress the dominant Hispanic-Catholic (Portuguese in the case of Brazil) value structure of most Latin American nations, "embodying a dominant form of socio-political organization that is similarly hierarchical, elitist, authoritarian, bureaucratic, Catholic, patrimonial, and corporatist to its core" (Wiarda, 1974: 6). Within this cultural-institutional framework, the American Revolution has had a limited impact, and its influence must be understood in a peculiarly Latin American context. In the last analysis, Latin American perceptions of the American Revolution have been more important than any overpowering dynamic of the event or the ideas.

The following analysis of the impact of the American Revolution will consider three types of influence.

(1) The direct example of the North American war for independence and revolutionary imagery on the ideas and actions of Latin Americans.
(2) The direct (intellectual/rational) influence of the dominant ideas and ideals of the American Revolution as embodied in the Declaration of Independence, the Constitution, and other works of the period.
(3) The symbolic influence of the United States as a society with institutions and ideals worthy of respect, admiration, and emulation.

These types of influence emanated from both dimensions of the American War for Independence-American Revolution. At one level the war in North America was a struggle of colonies, first to change the imperial system, and (when that was rejected) to strike for complete independence. Out of this conflict emerged a set of political, economic, and social principles which not only justified independence but also the establishment of institutions and systems for the governing and guidance of the new nation. Thus, at another level the Revolution was a war to establish the political structures of ideas and ideals. Although to the

British colonists these two dimensions were so intertwined as to be almost inseparable, outside observers could more readily pick and choose the part of the North American experience they saw as most applicable to their own situation.

Between 1777 and 1810, the literature of the American Revolution and the new republic circulated among the discontented Creole intellectuals of the Spanish and Portuguese empires in the Western Hemisphere. The Declaration of Independence, the Federalist Papers, the Constitution, Washington's Farewell Address, and the writings of Thomas Paine, Thomas Jefferson, and Benjamin Franklin were translated and read by at least a few intellectuals in every region. A few Yankee merchants and diplomatic agents helped to promulgate this material. For example, the merchant David Curtis DeForrest gave a copy of the Farewell Address to the Argentinian Manuel Belgrano in 1805, and donated some works of the French Philosphes to the Buenos Aires public library. Belgrano translated and published the Farewell Address in 1813 (Burns, 1972: 69).

The Creole intellectuals were already well-read in the works of Locke, Adam Smith, Rousseau, Raynal, Voltaire, Montesquieu, and other European philosophers. Undoubtedly this literature, combined with the successful North American struggle for self-determination, influenced some of the Creole elite who were interested in imperial reform. Burns (1972: 71) has written that the economic societies, the academies, and the clandestine Masonic Lodges provide considerable evidence for this influence. He notes that some of the most prevalent ideas among these groups were "the equality of all men before the law, the need to open the ports to world trade, the hardships worked by monopolies and restrictions on trade and production, the desirability of expanding educational facilities and opportunities, the benefits of a free press, and the necessity of establishing justice as an independent branch of government." The ideas of North Americans and Europeans provided intellectual ammunition and inspiration for those Creoles who wished to change certain aspects of the imperial system in order to advance their own interests and develop what they hoped would be a more progressive society. But, until about 1808 only a minority of the Creole elite actively associated these ideas with independence and revolution.

Of course, conservative Spanish officials and clerics considered these works to be "seditious literature," especially those from the former British colonies. A Chilean priest, Fray Melchor Martínez, wrote:

> The Boston republic isolated and surrounded by many peoples desiring to imitate its ideas of liberty, recognizes and at the same time fears the weaknesses of its existence, and for this reason is making its greatest efforts to enlarge its boundaries and to extend its system, as the only method of providing for its stability and maintenance. To this end it puts into action all imaginable means, without hesitating at the most iniquitous and immoral, in order to attract the Spanish colonists to its depraved designs. The freedom of conscience and the freedom of the press assist it in publishing and spreading subversive and seditious principles and maxims, which always find reception with the majority of men, ruled by ignorance and malice [Moses, 1966: 39-40].

Martínez considered the "Bostonese" to be a subversive, conspiratorial movement. He charged these Yankees with infiltrating the principal families, the government, and even the Catholic Church in order to promote sedition and the overthrow of royal authority (Moses, 1966: 41). A few North Americans, such as Captain William Shaler, were trying to encourage the secession of parts of the empire, but for the most part the good padre's charges were vastly overdrawn (Nichols, 1956: 83-102).

From the later 1770s on, a small group of disaffected Creoles (located for the most part in New Grenada) not only obtained literature regarding the independence struggle to the north, but also hoped to emulate it. In 1780-1781 some of the leaders of the *comunero* uprisings in New Granada paid tribute to the North American example. Some of the broadsides of the *comuneros* mentioned "the example of the North American colonies," and one called for self-governing republics. At this stage, however, most of the participants were more interested in local issues than in independence. By 1777 Joseph Ignacio

Moreno (Caracas) had obtained the 1774-1775 proclamations of the Continental Congress and had prepared a manuscript containing these proclamations. Moreno was later implicated in the 1797 plot led by Juan Picornell, Manuel Gual, and José María España. These conspirators cited the inspiration of the republicanism of the United States. Antonio Nariño was also implicated in this plot, and he had purchased a library in 1791 which contained "a compilation of the constitutive laws of the United States." The library had been sold by the Creole *corregidor* of Zipaquirá (and a member of Nariño's literary society) to finance a trip to the United States to seek aid for an independence movement (Liss, 1975: 8, 20-33).[2]

The small group of Creole agitators made some noise during the 1790s, but with very little effect. This situation prompted the anti-Spanish, Jesuit priest, Pablo Vizcardo, to chide the Spanish colonials in 1799:

> The valor with which the English Colonies of America fought for liberty, which they now gloriously enjoy, covers our indolence with shame. . . . That valor indicts our apathy [Johnson, 1968: 124].

This statement was part of a tract which Madariaga has called "the first clear statement advocating the independence of the New World" (Madariaga, 1963: 260; Robertson, 1969: 60-109). Published in Philadelphia 16 years after the end of the American Revolution, the tract was circulated throughout Latin America by one of the original advocates of independence, Francisco de Miranda.

Miranda had been influenced by the North American example. After conversing with him, John Quincy Adams commented that Miranda knew more about the American War for Independence than most American leaders. Serving as an officer in the Spanish army during the American Revolution, he had personally received the surrender of the British garrison at Pensacola. At that time he was secretly corresponding with a few disgruntled Creoles in Caracas such as Juan V. Bolívar (father of Simón) about the necessity for independence (Nicholson, 1968: 60-61). But, he realized the vast obstacles in the way and the gap between secret correspondence and active involvement. He later referred to his sentiments in 1781:

> When I realized on receiving the capitulations of Sipaquira (June 8th, 1781) how simple and inexperienced the [Spanish] Americans were and on the other hand how astute and perfidious the Spanish agents had proved, I thought it best to suffer for a time in patience till the Anglo-American colonies achieved their independence, which was bound to be in the future the infallible preliminary of ours [Madariaga, 1963: 279].[3]

The obstacles to independence were greater than even Miranda realized, and he spent the next 25 years trying to stir up independence sentiment in what later became Venezuela and to obtain military support from Great Britain, the United States, France, and even Russia. With the assistance of private citizens in North America, Miranda finally outfitted the ship Leander in 1806 and launched the first expedition against the royalists in South America. In spite of growing discontent among the Creoles, Miranda did not find any real support and the attempt failed.

A significant number of Creoles moved for independence only after Napoleon's interference in the Spanish government produced an imperial crisis. Basically, many members of the Creole elite were conservative in matters of social change and feared the possible consequences of a revolution. To such men, the word revolution produced visions of the bloody slave revolt in St. Domingue (Haiti) and the reign of terror of the French Revolution. Both of these events of the 1790s had created a cautious approach toward independence, which was overcome only by the drastic shift of power in Spain. Even a staunch supporter of independence such as Miranda was shaken by these events. In 1798 he wrote:

> I confess to you that just as much as I desire the liberty and independence of the New World, I fear the anarchy of a revolu-

> tionary system. God forbid that these beautiful countries become, as did St. Domingue, a theatre of blood and of crime under the pretext of establishing liberty. Let them rather remain if necessary one century more under the barbarous and imbecile oppression of Spain [Madariaga, 1963: 295].

It is in the years after 1808 that some Creole leaders began to point (with varying degrees of enthusiasm) to the American Revolution as an example to follow. Miranda had been the precursor in this regard also as he wrote in 1799, "Two great examples lie before our eyes: the American Revolution and the French Revolution. Let us discreetly imitate the first; let us most carefully avoid the disastrous effects of the second" (Madariaga, 1963: 296).

The ideas of the French philosophes still produced intellectual excitement for some. But, it was the example of the American Revolution and the success of the young republic which finally convinced enough Creole leaders that one could espouse liberal political and economic ideas, support independence, and still prevent social upheaval and slave insurrections. Madariaga (1963: 295) summarized the mood:

> The misgivings of the Creoles were laid at rest by the spectacle of men such as Washington and Jefferson, living like patriarchs in comfortable wealth among their slaves. It pleased them to know that Jefferson, the enlightened, well-off lawyer at Monticello was the author of those ringing phrases of the Declaration of Independence and yet lived none the worse.

A Latin American historian recently has observed, "The American Revolution, while unequivocally republican, scarcely appeared to be a revolution to those Latin American contemporaries who were unaware that it had roused any opposition among the local inhabitants" (Halperin-Donghi, 1973: 113).

As the enthusiasm for independence spread after 1810, the North American example became a popular theme in some parts of Latin America. The "immortal Washington" was extolled by journalists and revolutionary leaders, and some even named their sons after him. Journals such as *La Aurora de Chile* (the first peridical to be published there) reprinted Fourth of July orations and speeches by Washington, Jefferson, and President James Madison (Moses, 1966: 100-103). The impact in Brazil of the American example came during the period 1828-1838 (especially after 1831). Important newspapers cited the United States as a model of prosperity, moderation, and independence from Europe. A few even suggested a federation with the United States (Wright, 1975). In Mexico, in contrast, this enthusiasm arose after March 1823 when the Creole emperor Augustín de Iturbide was ousted.

But, as the wars for independence progressed, this feeling toward the United States seems to have diminished. In part, this was due to the noncommittal attitudes and policies of the U.S. government. As Simon Bolívar bitterly complained in 1815, "Not only the Europeans but even our own brothers to the North have remained indifferent spectators of this conflict, which by its very nature is a most just one" (Zea, 1969: 55).[4]

Some citizens and political leaders in the United States did view the wars for independence in Latin America as logical extensions of the American Revolution and urged an active policy of support for these struggles. Most American leaders, for a variety of reasons, did not want the United States to become involved, and as a result the country continued to be a spectator. The exception was the U.S. assertion of the neutral rights doctrine to break San Martín's blockade of royalist forces on the west coast of South America. Many North American leaders were not at all sure that the principles of the American Revolution were applicable to Latin America. John Quincy Adams bluntly stated, "there is no community of interests or of principles between North and South America" (Whitaker, 1964: 148). And Thomas Jefferson observed that:

> The issue of its struggles, as they respect Spain, is no longer a matter of doubt. As it respects their own liberty, peace and happiness, we cannot be quite so certain. Whether the blinds of bigotry, the shackles of the priesthood, and the fascinating

> glare of rank and wealth, give fair play to the common sense of the mass of their people, so far as to qualify them for self-government, is what we do not know. Perhaps our wishes may be stronger than our hopes [Koch and Peden, 1944: 681].

Henry Clay and others argued that the liberation of Latin America from European despotism was an ongoing aspect of the American Revolution. But, in a test vote in the House of Representatives in 1818 on the possible recognition of the United Provinces of the Rio de la Plata, the Clay forces lost by a vote of 115 to 45 (Whitaker, 1964: 245). In response to the successes of the Wars for Independence after 1820, official U.S. opinion shifted. Adams now asserted that the independence of Latin America spelled the end of the European mercantilistic system of commercial restrictions and the victory of commercial freedom and the principle of complete commercial reciprocity. He hoped that the establishment of economic freedom would lead to political and religious freedom as well. The belated U.S. commitment to Latin American independence still was conditioned by various factors, and did not apply unconditionally to the Caribbean (Setser, 1937: 244; La Feber, 1965: 122-126).

In a different context, the American Revolution may have had some influence in the early stages of the revolution which swept St. Domingue (Haiti) in the 1790s. Mulatto soldiers from the island served with the French army in North America during the Revolution, and a few black slaves were involved as servants of French officers. Vandercook (1952: 10-11, 23) has argued that this exposure to revolution and ideas about liberty had some effect on the hopes and dreams of these men when they returned home. The French Revolution, of course, had the most direct and explosive effect in St. Domingue, but the spark may have been kindled for some in North America. Henry Christophe, a twelve-year-old slave serving a French naval officer, first heard of revolution and independence from the mulatto volunteers. He joined the army of Toussaint L'Ouverture in 1794, rose to second in command seven years later, and finished his career as Emperor of Haiti (Vandercook, 1952: 10-11, 23). But, if his introduction to ideas of liberty came from North America, his concept of government seems to have been derived from Napoleon.

In considering the Creole leaders of the Wars for Independence, one must ask, to what extent did they actually internalize the ideas and ideals of the American Revolution? How many were fully converted to the ideas of republican government and individual freedom? The answer is mixed and ambiguous. Some Creole intellectuals did become authentic republicans, and tried to effect the related ideas and ideals. But, Bolívar believed that for most Creoles the conversion to republicanism was more emotional than intellectual, and that their republicanism waned somewhat when they were faced with the problems of governing and functioning politically in a Hispanic-Catholic environment (Johnson, 1968: 87). The Liberator himself admired the ideas of the American Revolution, and played with the idea of republicanism for a time. But, he wrote, "I think it would be better for South America to adopt the Koran rather than the United States' form of government, although the latter is the best in the world." (Johnson, 1968: 86). Bolívar believed that the North American system was not compatible with the culture and internal conditions of South America, and he advocated a version of the British constitutional monarchy as the most suitable model (Nicholson, 1968: 208-209;Lynch, 1973: 214-215, 284-285).[4] San Martín also advocated the adoption of the British system, and even expressed a desire for a British prince (Metford, 1971: 144-147).

Many of those members of the Creole elite who could be classified as nineteenth-century liberals seem to have adopted the ideas and ideals of the American Revolution in varying degrees, but their application of these was conditioned to a significant extent by the traditional value system. This has been well-documented by Dealy's (1968: 37-58) study of the constitutions of Spanish America from the independence period to the present. Dealy notes that most of the original constitutions copied portions of the U.S. Constitution and even established similar institutions (in some cases). But, he stresses that there were "quite different assumptions underlying each constitutional system." For example, politics was perceived as the achievement of the common good in the tradition of St. Thomas Aquinas, not the "satisfaction of interests in the style of Locke." In addition, these constitutions interpreted "rights" in a somewhat different manner than the U.S. Constitution. Most of the bills of rights in these constitutions established Catholicism as the state religion, prohibited, or limited, the free exercise of other "cults," and abridged freedom of the press and speech. Even the present day constitutions, Dealy notes, deny the proposition of "unalienable rights" and proclaim "necessity of state" as a recognized doctrine.

In the case of Mexico, Hale (1968: 195), in his study of Mexican liberalism, discusses the enthusiasm for the U.S. model of republicanism during the 1820s. But he concludes:

> In effect, the overt acknowledgment of imitation by the Mexicans in 1824 reveals the superficial engagement of the American model in Mexican constitutional liberalism. The American form was adopted enthusiastically in large part because it was the *symbol* of liberal progress. . . . Yet in matters such as the organization of municipal governments, the judicial system, and the procedure for elections, the point of reference for the deputies was French and particularly Spanish liberal experience.

The Latin American Creole's perception of republicanism can also be observed in two prominent liberals of the period. Francisco de Miranda attended several meetings of the legislative assembly in Massachusetts and commented that power had been given to men of ignorance rather than men with principles and education. He was astounded to see a former tailor, a caulker, an innkeeper, and a smith sitting in the assembly. To this Creole republican these men did not possess the maturity or virtue required for good government. And, Miranda was very critical of the American version of republicanism for emphasizing property (interests) rather than virtue; the latter element an undefined spiritual trait obviously not possessed by caulkers and smiths (Madariaga, 1963: 319). This view was aristocratic in the extreme, and well-grounded in the traditional culture. Mariano Moreno of Buenos Aires translated and printed Rousseau's *Social Contract,* but deleted the sections on religion. Moreno also wrote in a tract that the masses of the people should be given "complete liberty to speak on any matter." But, the sentence concluded, "as long as it is not in opposition to the holy truths of our august religion and the decisions of the government, which are always worthy of our greatest respect (Kinsbruner, 1973: 76-77). Thus, when the ideas and ideals of the American Revolution were translated into political reality in Latin America, the results were naturally different.

But, there were results, and from independence to the present, Latin American liberals have stood and fought for the various freedoms associated with the American Revolution. They have not been in the majority in ruling circles, and they have enjoyed more success during periods of economic boom than in times of diminished prosperity (Pike, 1974: 156-157). Yet, any analysis of liberal thought in Latin America should mention such men as Juan Batista Alberdi (Argentina), Domingo Faustino Sarmiento (Argentina), Benito Juárez (Mexico), José Victorino Lastarría (Chile), Francisco Bilbao (Chile), José Martí (Cuba), Luis Quintanilla (Mexico), Ezequiel Padilla (Mexico), José Figueres (Costa Rica), and Rómulo Betancourt (Venezuela). These men, and others, have acknowledged their relationship to the ideas and ideals of the American Revolution, and whatever direct impact these have had since the early years of the republics has been due largely to their efforts. (Crawford, 1961; Martí, 1953; Quintanilla, 1943; Padilla, 1943).

Historically, the image and influence of the United States probably has been related more closely to its economic policies and system than to its political institutions. In this context the ideals of economic liberalism of the men who made the American Revolution have had a direct relationship not only to Latin American conceptions of political and economic progress but also to inter-American relations. The preamble to the Franco-American Commercial Treaty of 1778 (based on the Model Treaty drafted by the Continental Congress in 1776) elaborated the liberal principles of "the most perfect equality and reciprocity" and the "founding of the advantages of commerce solely upon reciprocal utility and the just rules of free intercourse" (Gilbert, 1961: 50-56). Writing in 1823, John Quincy Adams declared that this preamble "was to the foundation of our commercial intercourse with the rest of mankind, what the Declaration of Independence was to that of our internal government" (Moore, 1918: 161-162). To the founding fathers of the American republic, these principles not only challenged the mercantilist (or statist) economic systems of Europe (and especially Britain), but also presented the hope of a peaceful open world order based on equality of treatment and the free flow of ships and goods.

These ideals and principles of the American Revolution helped to shape the official U.S. attitudes and policies toward the newly independent Latin American republics. John Quincy Adams stressed this in 1822 when he informed Stratford Canning that the "liberation of the Spanish colonies would mean the end of exclusive commercial policies everywhere" (Setser, 1937: 244). The Latin American policy of the Monroe and Adams administrations was aimed at establishing reciprocity as a key element in inter-American relations, and preventing the reestablishment of the old colonial order of economic mercantilism and political authoritarianism. As Secretary of State Adams noted in May 1823, American policy should be designed, "to counteract the efforts which it cannot be doubted European negotiations will continue to make in the furtherance of their monarchical and monopolizing contemplations." To promote these goals Adams hoped to negotiate treaties with the new republics which would be based upon, "the broad and liberal principles of *independence, equal favors,* and *reciprocity.*" And, he hoped that the principle of complete national treatment of foreigners would be established in the hemisphere. (La Feber, 1965: 123).

To Adams and Monroe the open world was to be established first in the Western Hemisphere. The Monroe Doctrine was, in part, a general declaration of these aspirations. Commercial freedom was an important part of the American rivalry with the European system, but the authors of the Monroe Doctrine envisioned the "American System" in a broader sense. As Adams pointed out in his policy statement of May 1823, "Civil, political, commercial, and religious liberty, are but the various modifications of one great principle, founded in the unalienable rights of human nature, and before the universal application of which the colonial domination of Europe over the American hemisphere has fallen" (La Feber, 1965: 124). Thus, the anti-colonial, open-world elements of the original Monroe Doctrine were rooted in the ideas and principles of the American Revolution.

Many Latin American Creoles viewed the economic liberalism of the United States with much enthusiasm, and during the 1780s and 1790s there was more Creole support for commercial liberalization than for independence. Of course, the Wars for Independence were fought by both liberal and conservative Creoles, and in the years after the establishment of the republics, economic liberalism had a mixed and ambiguous existence, based on the success of liberal or conservative parties. Véliz (1967: 10) has written that the ruling groups in this era were prosperous enough to depart from their traditional institutions and emulate "the culture of wealth, progress, prosperity." To these groups, he notes, the evidence was abundant that

> free-trading liberalism and the export of primary commodities resulted in vast and immediate wealth while every protectionist measure diminished this wealth and "taxed the worker" in the name of an illusory future development of national industries which, even if they were ever formed, would not be able to face competition from European manufactures without protection [Lynch, 1973: 337].

During the 1820s the United States signed treaties embodying commercial reciprocity with Colombia and Brazil. But the latter nation insisted on retaining preferential status for Protugal, and U.S. commercial negotiations with several other states (including Mexico) were not too productive due to their desire to retain some restrictive trade practices (Setser, 1937: 246-251). After the 1820s, the Western world, led by Great Britain, entered a period of widespread commercial liberalism, and this limited the development of mercantilist policies in Latin America and gave support to the open-world aspects of the Monroe Doctrine.

Many Latin American Creoles viewed the American Revolution as essentially conservative in regard to radical changes in society. This factor, which attracted the nineteenth-century Creole elite, has made the American Revolution much less of a model for twentieth-century revolutionaries who have derived some of their inspiration and guidance from those European ideas and examples which have stressed the destruction of capitalism and the elimination of various socioeconomic groups. Yet, one must be careful with this type of analysis. The successful revoluntionaries of the twentieth century have been rooted more in indigenous examples and in basic cultural values than in foreign elements. Fidel Castro, for example, won support by linking his movement to José Martí; Karl Marx came in later after Castro had consolidated his power. Soviet-oriented communist parties have had no success in winning power on their own in Latin America. In general, the CP has achieved some degree of political influence only when allied with groups much more oriented to indigenous values.

Some modern revolutionaries have cited the U.S. role in pioneering self-determination, and have quoted the sentiments of Jefferson and Paine about the rights of man. In his speech to the court after the abortive attack on the Moncada Barracks (1953), Castro cited both of these men in defense of revolution, as well as the first paragraph of the Declaration of Independence. And, he told a U.S. reporter in 1958 that burning cane fields was the equivalent of the Boston Tea Party (Bonachea and Valdes, 1972: 218, 369-370). But I do not believe that the American Revolution had much influence on Castro or other modern revolutionaries except in very general, symbolic terms. One reason for this has been that many of these revolutionaries have viewed the powerful United States as the enemy in their struggle for self-determination. Whatever the merits of this belief—and there are legitimate arguments on both sides—the United States since the nineteenth century has been seen by most revolutionaries as Goliath and not David. Also, messianic revolutionaries require "The Enemy," and since the 1950s, the United States has been the only real target. Before that, the British, French, and Germans shared the shooting gallery.

However, there is another factor which separates modern Latin American revolutionaries from the American Revolution. This has been, and is, the American revoluntionary ideal of individual freedom: political, economic, and religious. In the perspective of world history this was, and is, a rather radical doctrine. Latin American revolutionaries of the twentieth century, with their collectivist/statist orientation, have consciously rejected the most radical aspect of the American Revolution, and in so doing they are rather similar to many of the Creoles of the early nineteenth century. When Fidel Castro told the Cuban people in 1970, "Today the citizen feels that the state should solve his problems. And he is right," one hears echos of the Incas, the Roman Emperors, and the "Divine Right" monarchs. Perhaps this "reactionary" element (rooted in the culture) in modern revolutionary thought and practice is as important in separating Latin American revolutionaries from the American Revolution as the actions of the U.S. government.

Paradoxically, some believe that in the twentieth century the United States still exudes some revoluntary tendencies. For example, Pike (1974: 138-141, 165-169) has argued that throughout the twentieth century the Latin American ruling elites have "feared that penetration of its [United States] cultural values would herald social revolution." In other words, these elites have feared the spread of the "individualistic, competitive, bourgeois ethic" to the lower echelon of the "two-culture, corporate society." If so, perhaps what some have labeled the "revolution of rising expectations" is partly due to the introduction of these acquisitive values through the auspices of U.S. enterprises, consumer goods, and services.

The twentieth-century elites may have exaggerated the cultural influence of the United States is much the same way that Fray Melchor Martínez overestimated the influence of the Bostonese in the early nineteenth century. But, it is understandable that the intellectual sons of Ariel would see the dark presence of Caliban behind every McDonald's *Hamburguesa* or Colonel Sander's Kentucky *Pollo Frito* (Rodó, 1922). Of course, the revoluntionary influence of U.S. cultural factors in this century is just as difficult to measure as those ideas, images, and examples produced by the American Revolution. But, these cultural factors provide new grist for the mills of historical interpretation.

History cannot be understood in an "either-or" context; the past is complex and filled with competing factors. Hopefully we are moving into a less emotional-ideological period of scholarship where internalists and externalists may work out a synthesis somewhere between the extremes of Cecil Jane, Stephen Bonsal, and Eduardo Galeano.

## NOTES

1. The book was generally praised in British journals and in nonacademic publications in the United States. A number can be found in the 1930 edition of the Book Review Digest.

2. I would like to thank Dr. Liss for sharing this material with me. It will be part of a forthcoming book on the subject.

3. Bolívar was referring to the declarations made by the *comuneros* during the uprising of 1780-1781.

4. Bolívar's Bolivian Constitution provided for a lifetime president with power to name his successor.

## REFERENCES

BONACHEA, R. and N. VALDES, [eds.] (1972) Revolutionary Struggle, 1947-1958. Cambridge, MA: MIT.

BONSAL, S. (1913) The American Mediterranean. New York: Moffat, Yard.

BURNS, E. B. (1972) Latin America: A Concise Interpretive History. Englewood Cliffs, NJ: Prentice-Hall.

CRAWFORD, W. R. (1961) [reprint of 1944 ed.] A Century of Latin American Thought. New York: Praeger.

DEALY, G. (1968) "Prolegoma on the Spanish American political tradition." Hispanic Amer. Historical Rev. 48 (February): 37-58.

GALEANO, E. (1973) The Open Veins of Latin America: Five Centuries of the Pillage of a Continent. New York: Monthly Review.

GILBERT, F. (1961) To the Farewell Address: Ideas of Early American Foreign Policy. Princeton, NJ: Princeton University.

HALE, C. (1968) Mexican Liberalism in the Age of Mora. New Haven, CT: Yale University.

HALPERIN-DONGHI, T. (1973) The Aftermath of Revolution in Latin America. New York: Harper & Row.

HARING, C. (1930) "Review of liberty and despotism in Spanish America." Amer. Historical Rev. 36 (October): 179.

HARTZ, L. (1955) The Liberal Tradition in America. New York: :Harcourt Brace Jovanovich.

JANE, C. (1966) [reprint of 1929 ed.] Liberty and Despotism in Spanish America. New York: Cooper Square Publishers.

JOHNSON, J. J. (1968) Simón Bolívar and Spanish American Independence, 1783-1830. Princeton, NJ: Van Nostrand.

KINSBRUNER, J. (1973) The Spanish American Independence Movement. New York: Dryden.

KOCH, A. and W. PEDEN [eds.] (1944) The Life and Selected Writings of Thomas Jefferson. New York: Random House.

La FEBER, W. [ed.] (1965) John Quincy Adams and American Continental Empire. Chicago: Quadrangle.

LISS, P. K. (1975) "The United States Declaration of Independence and Latin America, 1776-1808." Paper presented at the Fourth International Conference on the Enlightenment, Yale University.

LYNCH, J. (1973) The Spanish-American Revolutions, 1808-1826. New York: W. W. Norton.

MADARIAGA, S. (1963) [reprint of 1947 ed.] The Fall of the Spanish American Empire. New York: Collier.

MARTI, J. (1953) The America of José Martí: Selected Writings: New York: Noonday.

METFORD, J.C.J. (1971) [reprint of 1950 ed.] San Martín the Liberator. Westport, CT: Greenwood.

MOORE, J. B. (1918) The Principles of American Diplomacy. New York: Harper & Row.

MORENO, F. J. (1970) "Justice and law in Latin America: a Cuban example." J. of Inter-American Studies and World Affairs 12 (July): 367-378.

MORSE, R. M. (1964a) "The strange career of 'Latin American studies'." Annals of the Amer. Academy of Pol. and Social Sci. 356 (November): 107.

——— (1964b) "The heritage of Latin America," pp. 123-177 in L. Hartz (ed.) The Founding of New Societies: Studies in the History of the United States, Latin America, South Africa, Canada, and Australia. New York: Harcourt Brace Jovanovich.

MOSES, B. (1966) [reprint of 1926 ed.] The Intellectual Background of the Revolutions in South America, 1810-1824. New York: Russell & Russell.

NICHOLS, R. F. (1956) Advance Agents of American Destiny. Philadelphia: University of Pennsylvania.

NICHOLSON, I. (1968) The Liberators; A Study of Independence Movements in Spanish America. New York: Praeger.

PADILLA, E. (1943) Free Men of America. Plainview, NY: Books for Libraries.

PIKE, F. B. (1974) "Corporatism and Latin American United States relations," pp. 132-170 in F. B. Pike and T. Stritch (eds.) The New Corporatism: Social-Political Structures in the Iberian World. Notre Dame, IN: University of Notre Dame.

QUINTANILLA, L. (1943) A Latin American Speaks. New York: Macmillan.

ROBERTSON, W. S. (1969) [reprint of 1932 ed.] Hispanic-American Relations with the United States: New York: Kraus Reprint.

RODO, J. E. (1922) Ariel. Boston: Houghton Mifflin.

SETSER, V. (1937) The Commercial Reciprocity Policy of the United States, 1774-1829. Philadelphia: University of Pennsylvania.

SMITH, P. H. (1974) "Political Legitimacy in Spanish America," pp. 225-256 in R. Graham and P. H. Smith (eds.) New Approaches to Latin American History. Austin: University of Texas.

VANDERCOOK, J. W. (1952) [reprint of 1928 ed.] Black Majesty. New York: Pocket Books.

VELIZ, C. (1967) "Introduction," pp. 10-13 in C. Véliz [ed.] The Politics of Conformity in Latin America. London: Oxford University.

WHITAKER, A. P. (1964) [reprint of 1941 ed.] The United States and the Independence of Latin America, 1800-1830. New York: W. W. Norton.

WIARDA, H. J. (1974) "Corporation and development in the Iberic-Latin world: persistent strains and new variations," pp. 3-33 in F. B. Pike and T. Stritch (eds.) The New Corporatism: Social-Political Structures in the Iberian World. Notre Dame, IN: University of Notre Dame.

WRIGHT, F. (1975) "The impact of the American independence movement in Brazil." Paper presented at the New World Conference of Americanists, San Antonio, Texas.

ZEA, L. (1969) Latin America and the World. Norman: University of Oklahoma.

*Robert Freeman Smith is Professor of History at the University of Toledo. He is the author of* The United States and Revolutionary Nationalism in Mexico, 1916-1932 *(1972) and currently is working on the Latin American policies of the Truman Administration.*

# REVIEW ESSAY

## *POLITICAL POWER IN CONTEMPORARY COSTA RICA*

*Arias Sanchez, Oscar. ¡QUIEN GOBIERNA EN COSTA RICA?. San José, Costa Rica: Editorial Universitaria Centroamericana (EDUCA), 1976.*

*Cerdas Cruz, Rodolfo. LA CRISIS DE LA DEMOCRACIA LIBERAL EN COSTA RICA. San José, Costa Rica: Editorial Universitaria Centroamericana (EDUCA), 1975.*

*Stone Zemurray, Samuel. LA DINASTIA DE LOS CONQUISTADORES. San José, Costa Rica: Editorial Universitaria Centroamericana (EDUCA), 1976.*

The three books under review attempt with considerable success but with different approaches to analyze the political situation in contemporary Costa Rica. None of the three, however, in and of itself fully explains the forces which have led Costa Rica to a critical point in its evolution as Latin America's most enduring democracy.

Each presents one particular facet of the current scene. In varying degrees the authors tend to see Costa Rican society as increasingly incapable of coping with the problems of the coming generation.

The significance of the authors' points of view lies as much in their merited prestige as in the weight of their arguments as formulated in the works under consideration. All of the authors teach or have taught in the School of Political Science at the University of Costa Rica and fall in varying degrees within the fecund Latin American tradition of *pensadores,* who at the same time are deeply and actively involved men of affairs and academicians. Although still young men, all have wide experience outside academia as well as within, holding earned doctorates from European universities.

Although their themes and approaches are quite different, the three authors have several important characteristics in common. All belong to a new generation of national leadership; although long active in national affairs they had no direct participation in the traumatic events of the 1948 revolution and the enduring divisions produced during that epoch of violent political change. All have traveled extensively in the first, second, and third worlds. All indicate inquietude for their country's future and the particular juncture in which the nation finds itself. As either the title or the subtitle of each implies, the historic moment carries with it the implicit dangers of a period of transition. The time frame of all reaches back to 1948 and in the cases of Stone and Cerdas far beyond that. The authors published before the 1977-1978 electoral campaign.

Cerdas and Stone, in sharply contrasting approaches, write broad-gauged revisionist interpretations of the Costa Rican past in order to buttress their interpretation of the present. Both are rich in novel use of material and new insights from a sociopolitical vantage point into the still largely underresearched past of this uniquely tranquil and progressive democracy.

Cerdas's work reflects his basic ideological position as an independent Marxist nurtured within Costa Rican communism. However, as a mature academic, he broke with the party to pursue a more nationalistic path. His father, Jaime Cerdas Mora, helped organize the Communist Party in Costa Rica during the 1930s and suffered imprisonment for his political beliefs in 1948 during the de facto government of José Figueres. Cerdas Cruz grew up in San José within the ambience of the clandestine Popular Vanguard Party (PVP) tolerated by the dominant national Liberation Party (PLN). After taking a law degree at the University of Costa Rica, Cerdas did postgraduate studies in the Soviet Union and later received a doctorate in political science in France. The PVP expelled him for his growing dissidence from party doctrine and discipline. Cerdas, while continuing his research and teaching, initiated his political career as an independent Marxist, being elected a deputy to the National Assembly from San José province in February 1978.

In his *La Crisis de la Democracia Liberal en Costa Rica,* Cerdas began to enunciate his own political position as well as analyze the Costa Rican past from a Marxist point of view. He divides his work into four parts, the last two of which are of particular interest to us in our consideration of political power in contemporary Costa Rica.

The first two parts deal with "The Formation of the Nation State" and the "Consolidation of the Agro-Exporter and Mercantile-Exporter Bloc." They serve mainly to set the stage for the second two chapters which analyze the present and project into future national needs.

In the first part he adds to the growing body of research which clearly demonstrates that colonial Costa Rica enjoyed far less social equality than was long thought and in attenuated form suffered many of the nondemocratic ills which beset most European colonies elsewhere such as slavery, racial discrimination, exploitation of the indigenous people, and sharp class distinctions. He sees the formation of Costa Rica as a nation state coming during the consolidating dictatorship of Braulio Carrillo (1835-1842), which confirmed the ascendency of classical liberalism over conservatism, and of San José, the new capital, over Cartago, the old colonial capital.

In the second part he deals with the rise of the coffee culture and the formation of the *cafetaleros,* an elite formed around coffee processing, and the greatly expanded rule of international trade in the Costa Rican economy. The "liberal democracy" which the author sees in crisis evolved under the aegis of the coffee elite, responding to the needs of that group.

This narrow approach to liberal democracy constitutes a major weakness of the volume, for the crisis which Cerdas analyzes and which is central to his interpretation could more aptly be viewed as the shortcomings within a democracy dominated too long by the narrow interests of an economic elite tied to the cultivation and exportation of a single crop. This domination resulted in structural aberrations which obstructed the full implementation of liberal democracy. What we are suggesting is that the turmoil which the author traces results from the efforts of an increasingly complex and better-educated society to expand democratic participation and break the hold of the old elite, an effort which in no way negates the viability of liberal democracy nor its passing but rather confirms its vitality and ability to perfect itself. In fact, the aberrant form of a liberal democracy dominated by a tightly knit elite passed through a crisis stage during the revolutionary decade, 1940-1950, and now finds itself moribund. What followed and continues is, in political terms, a more authentic rendering of liberal democracy with much broader and more effective participation by the citizenry in national affairs. Cerdas, as does Stone, sees ominous signs in the breakup of the old order. Arias clearly demonstrates that Costa Rican democracy has responded favorably during the last generation.

Cerdas, however, simply sets the stage in the first two chapters for the third, which carries the true thrust of his analysis. This chapter occupies well over one-half of the entire volume; in it he really defines the nature and dimensions of a national crisis. His analysis goes far beyond the question of the stability of liberal democracy in Costa Rica to question, at least implicitly, the viability of the Costa Rican state unless radical restructuring takes place. He offers a brief outline of what is needed in his fourth and final chapter.

His analysis in the third chapter focuses on the results and implications of Central American integration. He sees economic integration as an aggravation of the problems of underdevelopment and dependency because U.S. interests dominate the growth sectors of the economy. It is in this context that Cerdas makes a telling critique of interfaced phenomena in contemporary Costa Rican society which does indeed relate directly to the vitality of liberal democracy, i.e., the increasingly potent managerial class and a "pseudo-aristocracy" in the ranks of labor. These groups both owe their ascendancy to foreign investment attracted by the incentives offered by the Central American Common Market. Both can prosper only if foreign investment does. In turn, this will also foster a greater degree of dependency which will weaken the fabric of Costa Rican democracy and, if carried to its ultimate ramifications, lead to a loss of sovereignty. Cerdas, therefore, sees these favored few laborers and managers conceding their primary loyalty to their firms rather than to any national entity. Their fundamental weakness derives from their not being authentically national. He relates their ascendancy to the debilitation of political parties and to official indifference to agrarian problems and the acute problems of poverty.

The inability of the traditional political parties to respond to these new forces in a manner consistent with national sovereignty will force the nation into a crisis of its socioeconomic and institutional structures. The author's conclusions in his all-important third chapter lead us to conclude that the crisis he is most concerned about is that of the very survival of the Costa Rican state itself. Although the forces that he notes present some thorny questions for Costa Rica, we feel safe in asserting that its democracy remains sufficiently resilient and dynamic to cope with them and not only survive, but thrive. However, to substantiate the above assertion would require a volume of equal proportions and scholarship with that under review.

Cerdas himself, in his fourth chapter, also indicates that the process of decay is reversible. He seems to suggest that a perfected version of the existing political democracy coupled to an economy which is neither socialist nor capitalist and within a heightened sense of nationalism will bring Costa Rica out of the alleged "crisis of liberal democracy." However, he does not define his solution in positive terms, only in negative ones that constitute a critique of the policies and leadership of existing political parties. One can expect that Cerdas will define his "new democracy" in both theory and practice now that he has been elected to the National Assembly as the only deputy of his new party, the Costa Rican Popular Front.

Stone, a colleague of Cerdas's in a recently formed private research and training institute called CIAPA (Centro de Investigación y Adiestramiento Político-Administrativo), differs markedly from Cerdas both in his interpretation of the Costa Rican past and in his analysis of the contemporary crisis. They are, nonetheless, in agreement that their nation has entered into a crisis as evidenced by Stone's subtitle "La Crisis del Poder en la Costa Rica Contemporánea."

Stone, a naturalized Costa Rican of British and American parents, studied in Costa Rica, the United States, and, like Cerdas, received his doctorate in France. While in France he also served as his nation's representative to UNESCO and as cultural attaché to the Costa Rican Embassy in Paris. As a direct descendant of the founder of the Cuyamel Fruit Company, his childhood in Costa Rica differed significantly from Cerdas's.

His work closely follows the ground broken by his mentor, François Bourricaud (1967), in the political sociology of Latin American elites. His basic thesis is that certain families in Costa Rica, descendants of the *hidalgos* of the colonial period, have controlled the governmental and production apparatus from colonial times until the 1940s. For proof of his hypothesis, the author relies heavily on elaborate sets of geneological tables and charts which appear as extensive (167 pages) appendices at the end of the volume. His arguments and conclusions based on these tables and charts make up the first of three parts into which the book is divided. Stone sees a lineal development of a social elite from the colonial period, whose descendants through their social and economic predominance have controlled national politics until recent times.

The erosion of the power of the elite constitutes for Stone the "Crisis of Power in Contemporary Costa Rica." Again, as in Cerdas's "crisis," the case is overstated; in this instance on the one hand Stone suggests that gradual diminution of the elite's political power constitutes a crisis, and on the other, he indicates that power has become more dispersed but that no real vacuum exists. The expanded state bureaucracies, including those of the autonomous institutions, exercise power; a new class of industrialists drawn in part from the old elite but more importantly from the ranks of foreigners and the near-eastern minorities, Jewish and Lebanese, exerts strong influence on national decision-making; sectors of the middle class organized along professional lines manifest ever-increasing political clout. Stone demonstrates the passing of an era of dominance by the coffee-growing elite but again as in Cerdas this too has the semblance of wishful thinking because by almost any measure—economic, social, political, or educational development—Costa Rica does very well indeed.

Despite the vast scholarship and erudition that he amply demonstrates, Stone's hypothesis that the Costa Rican elite descended directly from the colonial hidalgos strains his evidence beyond the breaking point. He maintains its validity only by the analytical device of including in *la clase* not only foreigners and nationals who intermarry with its members, but also individuals who gain acceptance by one means or another into la clase or are even closely associated with it. Although there is a high degree of correlation between Stone's thesis and that developed by Hall (1977) regarding the nature and origin of the *cafetaleros* or coffee-processing class, Hall's is the more convincing. Stone interprets the cafetaleros as a class made up of descendants of la clase which incorporate some foreigners into its ranks, thus making these foreigners and their descendants members of la clase. According to Hall's analysis, however, the cafetaleros represent an essentially new class formed in response to the economic opportunities provided by the coffee boom of the second half of the nineteenth century. Foreigners and nonelite Costa Ricans play very prominent roles in the formation of this new group of successful entrepreneurs dedicated to all phases of coffee production for the international market. This new class attains dominance and remains the arbiter of the national destiny until the revolutionary changes of the 1940s.

Even though Stone strains his data in order to prove his hypothesis of the continuity of power of an elite descended from the conquerors and the exaggeration implicit in his subtitle, Stone's *La Dinastía de los Conquistadores* is one of the most important works in Costa Rican social science literature. There is no other work of comparable scope or depth (for example, nowhere else will one find discussions of the development of important minority groups). Since our concern is political power in contemporary Costa Rica, we have touched on only a few aspects of this work pertinent to this essay and not on the myriad facets of the Costa Rican past and present which Stone so ably researched and articulates. There is hardly a significant aspect of Costa Rican national life on which he does not make a contribution. For our purposes, the truly salient element is that the dominance of the cafetaleros is definitively broken by the revolutionary changes of the 1940s and that subsequent to that, there are new contenders for power which have rendered the Costa Rican political scene all the more fascinating and certainly more democratic. One can no longer identify the players with a program based on the hidalgo families, but that hardly constitutes "a crisis of power."

Arias's work on who governs in Costa Rica nicely complements Stone's work with its sharp focus on the period from 1940 forward and particularly on the period since 1948. It is one of the most scientific and useful studies on Costa Rica to date.

Arias, unlike Stone and Cerdas, and despite his relative youth, has already served at the ministerial level in the past two governments. He is a lineal descendant of one of the non-hidalgo cafetaleros. Along with Cerdas, Arias won election to the National Assembly in February 1978; he has already taken the initiative in calling the National Liberation Party (PLN) to a process of democratization and rejuvenation following its surprisingly resounding defeat at the polls in February.

Arias's work does not attempt to deal with the question of the informal structure of power, or the power(s) behind the throne, or the implications of long-maturing tendencies in the broad sweep of Costa Rican history (as do Stone and Cerdas). He sets out to investigate the socioeconomic characteristics of the national formal elite and changes therein during the period 1948-1974. For his data the author relied on 368 interviews and questionnaires administered to members of the three powers—the executive, legislative, and judicial—and to the managerial level of the autonomous institutions.

His findings at times surprise and consistently fill the need for quantitative analysis in Costa Rican political science, suggesting and providing bases for many future studies.

Among the major unexpected results, given the postrevolutionary period covered, are: (1) that "no changes over time in the composition of the elite were found in regard to social stratum, education, rural and urban origin"; (2) that the legislators of the post-1948 period consistently have had a higher average age than those of the period 1940-

1948; and (3) that there is little upward vertical mobility among office-holders, i.e., that the way to the top is to be born at or near the top; one does not work his way up through the party or through local political office to ministerial positions.

This study is a virtual storehouse of information and analysis about the Costa Rican political process and present-day Costa Rica in general. One finds, for example, statistical evidence that the small farmers, formerly the backbone of the republic, continue to lose ground as their farms are absorbed by large-scale holdings. The reader will also discover that in 1974 the lowest 20% of the population received a slightly lower proportion of national income than in 1948 and that a significant redistribution of income from the upper classes to the middle classes occurred during the same period. In this respect both Stone and Arias are rich lodes of otherwise unavailable information.

Caution should be exercised in evaluating Arias's definition of the upper class because he categorizes all professionals as members of that class. Although this may have been a valid criterium in early generations, Costa Rican higher education has exploded during the last generation and other criteria need to be applied to discern if a professional belongs to the upper or middle classes. Taking this factor into consideration, one should surely find a somewhat higher degree of middle-class participation than the author indicates. In addition, this would affect his conclusions in that one would find not only an increased level of middle-class participation in the executive branch, but also an additional avenue of social mobility from the middle to upper class through office-holding in executive offices.

The composite obtained from the three books under review leaves one with the sensation that Costa Rica has entered into a new crisis responding to the twentieth-century pattern of a crisis every 30 years: the Tinoco dictatorship from 1917-1919; the 1948 civil war; and now 1978. Yet by almost any measure Costa Rica must be considered one of the few unquestionable success stories of the post-World War II era.

Despite the lack of significant mineral resources and left principally to the exploitation of rich lands, hard work, and ready wits, Costa Rica has developed socially, economically, and politically throughout the national period in a consistently positive manner with very few down-turns and those of a transitory nature. Starting with the presidential inauguration of Dr. Rafael Angel Calderón Guardia in May 1940, national development accelerated. The Junta Fundadora de la Segunda República consolidated the social advances of the previous two administrations and oriented future Costa Rican development along social democratic lines.

A good case could be made that Costa Rican society has reached a political consensus which espouses social and economic development within the context of social democracy. There were several indications of this in the recently past political campaign. The three major candidates—Rodrigo Carazo, the new president; Luis Alberto Monge, his nearest rival; and Rodrigo Gutiérrez—were all either present (Monge) or former members of the PLN which has since its beginnings professed a social democratic ideology. Carazo's Unidad, although manifestly adhering to a social-Christian ideological position, did not campaign on a platform which differed in any substantial way from the PLN's historic program. In fact, in some instances—as in the case of eliminating the executive presidencies from the autonomous institutions—Carazo's programs sounded more like one of a PLN purist who urged a return to that party's origins. Gutiérrez, Pueblo Unido's (a coalition of Marxist parties which included the communist Vanguardia Popular) candidate, spoke theoretically of radical restructuring of Costa Rican society. However, his immediate program sounded very similar to that of the PLN. This consensus does not in any way preclude a crisis within the PLN, beset by internal frictions which contributed to its defeat at the polls; what seems more important for the nation is that the progress of the past generation can continue within a political context of fine tuning of the ideological vehicle of state, a largely successful system, with no perceived need of even a major overhaul, let alone a change of model.

The past generation of Costa Ricans has accomplished prodigies in many areas. It would be inappropriate to try to do any more than suggest the variety and depth of these achievements in this essay.

The most thorough and fundamental change has been effected in the political sphere. The electoral mechanism developed since 1947 leaves virtually no phase of the process open to fraud. The citizenry recognizes the completeness of the electoral system and trusts its results even though they predictively violate the hopes of a sizable proportion of the electorate (those who voted for defeated candidates). Permanent political parties have replaced the transient grouping around caudillos, as the increasingly better-educated electorate applies more sophisticated criteria in its choice of candidates. Personal liberties and human rights are respected in Costa Rica as in no other Latin American nation and as in few nations of the world. No greater proof could be given than the recent national elections in which the government party, PLN, was decisively defeated, losing the presidency, the legislature, and a majority of the municipalities. Yet there is no doubt that the PLN respects the unfavorable verdict and girds itself for four years as the major opposition party.

Freed since 1948 of the economic millstone of a military establishment, Costa Rican leaders have channeled governmental income into more productive pursuits. A handful of secondary schools in the major cities have expanded into a national system of free public high schools. The nascent University of Costa Rica, founded in 1940, has grown into a prestigious self-governing institution of over 30,000 students and four regional centers. There are now four additional institutions of higher education striving to complement the U.C.R.'s efforts. The transportation infrastructure of roads, port facilities, and airports has been expanded into a truly national system. Autonomous institutions have been founded or expanded to provide essential public services, potable water, electricity, telecommunications, housing, railroads, and insurance.

During the past generation the nation has enjoyed a sustained high rate of economic growth and increasing per capita income (even though now declining, population growth rates reached four percent in the mid-1960s). Costa Rica progressed from a middling position among Latin American nations to a leading position with one of the highest living standards in the region.

The range of progress is immense: from the universalization of the medical delivery system under social security to the effective incorporation of the national territory into the national economy; agricultural technification and diversification; assertion of national ownership over basic public services; a new dynamism in the performing arts and letters; and the more diverse opportunities for Costa Ricans in all spheres of endeavor.

The "crisis" for the present generation is how to sustain this record of accomplishment and adapt national institutions to new realities. For example, how will this generation modify political institutions to provide for greater democratic participation and adequate representation to newly populated areas such as San Carlos, Coto Brus, and Pérez Zeledón? How will Costa Ricans divert industrial development from the *meseta central* before their heartland goes the way of the valleys of Mexico City and Caracas? How will they break the cycle of poverty which Arias's findings revealed? Can the labor movement regain its dynamism of the 1940s?

As the society becomes ever more complex, Costa Ricans can expect the problems to become equally complex, and it will become increasingly difficult to maintain the optimum "mixture" in their mixed economy. The task no longer revolves around how to exploit obviously unused resources, but rather to identify and even create new ones.

The critical approach and the sound methodology demonstrated by these authors indicate that success is predictable if not assured. The authors, in fact, largely answer their own queries. The crisis to which Cerdas addresses himself seems well on the way to solution by the gradual substitution of social democracy for liberal democracy, as he uses the term. Stone's crisis of power requires adjustments to the passing of the old order dominated by the cafetaleros, but he, Cerdas, and Arias mention groups that have not only moved to fill the void but eagerly helped create it. The new managerial class, the industrialists, the independent banana producers, the newly potent professional and business organizations, and the political parties themselves, independently worked to gain a greater voice in national affairs. Their creative and responsible use of it should insure that there will be no power vacuum.

Once the reader gets by the ominous aspects of the titles or subtitles of these works, their substance reflects the very solid and creative scholarship of the authors and the increasing sophistication of social science research in Costa Rica. In that context the authors as scholars are critical, in the best sense of the word, of their own society, and, in the case of Arias, of his own political party as well. Yet as men of affairs and part of a rising generation of leaders, they view their nation's future somewhat with alarm not because Costa Rica has accomplished so little but because they want, and I suspect fully expect, that it will achieve much more in the future if it avoids complacency and maintains the keen awareness of its own shortcomings as revealed in these critical studies.

*—John Patrick Bell*

## REFERENCES

BOURRICAUD, F. (1967) Pouvoir et Societé dans le Perou Contemporain. Paris: Colin.

HALL, C. (1976) El Café y el Desarrollo Histórico-Geográfico de Costa Rica. San José: Editorial Costa Rica.

*John Patrick Bell is Associate Professor of History at Indiana University, Fort Wayne. He recently returned from two years as Visiting Professor at the University of Costa Rica, where he offered advanced seminars in the contemporary history of Latin America, Central America, and Costa Rica, as well as a lecture course in United States history. He previously taught at the College of William and Mary and Tulane University. His* Crisis in Costa Rica *(Texas, 1971) was translated by EDUCA under the title* Guerra Civil en Costa Rica *in 1976.*

# REVIEW ESSAY

## *CHARACTERISTICS OF CONTEMPORARY LATIN AMERICAN INTERNATIONAL RELATIONS*

*Atkins, G. P. LATIN AMERICA IN THE INTERNATIONAL POLITICAL SYSTEM. New York: Free Press, 1977. $11.95.*

*Davis, H. E. and L. C. Wilson, eds. LATIN AMERICAN FOREIGN POLICIES: AN ANALYSIS. Baltimore: Johns Hopkins University Press, 1975. Hardcover, $18.00; Paperback, $5.95.*

*FONTAINE, R. W. and J. D. Theberge, eds. LATIN AMERICA'S NEW INTERNATIONALISM: THE END OF HEMISPHERIC ISOLATION. New York: Praeger, 1976. $22.50.*

*Fox, A. B. THE POLITICS OF ATTRACTION: FOUR MIDDLE POWERS AND THE UNITED STATES. New York: Columbia University Press, 1977. $15.00.*

*Hellman, R. G. and H. J. Rosenbaum, eds. LATIN AMERICA: THE SEARCH FOR A NEW INTERNATIONAL ROLE. Volume 1, Latin American International Affairs Series. New York: Halsted Press (A Sage Publications Book), 1975. $17.50.*

*Schneider, R. M. BRAZIL: FOREIGN POLICY OF A FUTURE WORLD POWER. Boulder, CO: Westview Press, 1976. $16.50.*

During World War II and for roughly two decades after, the international relations and foreign policy of most Latin American countries (except, of course, of Argentina, and to a lesser extent Chile during the war, and Cuba after Castro aligned that country with the Soviet Union) were very largely dominated by their interactions with the United States. Since the latter 1960s, that has been less true for most of the

Journal of Interamerican Studies and World Affairs, Vol. 20 No. 4, November 1978

countries. The change, which is more one of degree than kind for the United States, continues to be an important factor—often the single most important factor—in the international relations of the Latin American countries. It was facilitated by changes external to the region—the decline in global-level bipolarity, the emergence of detente, the rise of multipolarity, and the lessening of Washington's concern with and involvement in Latin America.

During the same period of time there was a change in the nature and extent of scholarly concern in the United States with Latin American international relations and foreign policy. For the greater part of the post-world War II period, U.S. researchers largely ignored the subjects, save for one facet—U.S.-Latin American relations. Stimulated at least in part by the shifts that were taking place in the substance of the international behavior of Latin American countries, that situation began to change at the outset of the present decade. Since then, a growing number of studies exploring contemporary Latin American international relations and foreign policy have been published in the United States.

## *Main Characteristics*

The books covered in this essay are a noteworthy part of this body of literature. From them the reader/observer can identify at least the main characteristics of the contemporary international relations and foreign policy of the more than 20 Latin American countries.

### *GAINING INDEPENDENCE*

Without exception, each of the Latin American countries is seeking to establish itself and to be recognized as an independent, sovereign actor in fact as well as in international legal theory. That objective, however unattainable in an increasingly interdependent world, is a natural outgrowth of several historical and contemporary phenomena—the decades of economic, political, military, and social/cultural penetration and even domination by more powerful countries (first European ones and, more recently, the United States), the intervention of more powerful countries, the emergence of a strong feeling of economic nationalism (on this sentiment, see Swansbrough, 1976), and the anticolonialism that is a strong current in Latin America and throughout the entire Third World. Atkins (1977: 49) aptly characterizes the quest for independence as both difficult and paradoxical. He writes:

> Latin American states want to achieve . . . independence in their international actions, but to do so they must be strong in relation to the outside world; to become strong they must obtain some sort of assistance from the outside world toward which they wish to be independent, thus increasing the chances for a dependent relationship. Latin America's continuing dilemma, then, is this: how are nations to improve their capability position and modernize their societies while preventing inordinate influence in their economies and political systems?

The course selected by most Latin American decision makers (a notable exception being those in Cuba) is that of diversification of dependence. That is, they are endeavoring to reduce their dependence on a single larger country (the United States) by expanding their international contacts. This is being accomplished by securing export markets in a number of countries; acquiring imports from vaiious supplier-countries; and attracting development assistance from various countries, development financing agencies, and private investors in as large a number of countries as possible instead of looking mainly to the United States. The diversification of dependence is not, however, the only means that is being employed to promote a more independent status in the international system. Of the several other means, two stand out. One is the increasingly frequent practice of multilateral action—the countries of Latin America joining together (and increasingly often combining with other developing countries) to make demands felt, to exert leverage, and to extract concessions. The other is the imposition of various restrictions and control on foreign investors in order to gain a greater degree of domestic economic control. There is, of course, great variation among the countries of Latin America regarding the degree of independence so far realized and the potential for realizing a greater degree. In general, however, it is the larger, already more developed countries that have achieved most autonomy; it is the same countries that have most in the way of potential for achieving more. For the other Latin American countries, a more independent status is an illusive end.

## *BROADENING OF INTERNATIONAL CONTACTS*

Among other things, the quest for independent status entails a broadening or expansion of international contacts, and most Latin American countries have been doing this on a substantial scale since the late 1960s and early 1970s by expanding contacts, particularly economic contacts, with the member-countries of the European Community, other European countries (Eastern and Western), Canada, and Japan. Most of the Latin American countries have expanded their military relationships, now obtaining large portions of their arms imports from Western Europe and a few other supplier-countries instead of relying exclusively or almost so on the United States as was the case for the first two decades of the post-World War II era. Diplomatic/political contacts, too, have been broadened. There has been an intensification of existing diplomatic relationships, and there has been an initiation of many new ones—most notably with communist counties, new nations in Africa and Asia, and with other Latin American countries. The broadening has gone sufficiently far in a few Latin American countries so that for them the United States is an important—indeed, perhaps, the single most important non-Latin American actor—but no longer a dominant or preeminent actor. The expansion of international contacts has made a tangible contribution to the achievement of independent status; equally important if not actually more important, it has contributed psychologically, enhancing the feeling of independence.

Significant variations, as is to be expected, exist among the Latin American countries as to how most contacts have been broadened. In addition, there are variations among the countries in capacity to expand further contacts with others. Those Latin American countries with something to offer—e.g., large internal markets, attractive investment opportunities, needed raw materials, demand for foreign manufactured goods, political support to offer, and the like—are in the most favorable position to establish new international relationships of a beneficial sort or to intensify existing relationships. Not all of the expanded contacts, it should be noted, are balanced ones. Those between Latin American countries and many developed ones, for example, those between Latin America as a whole and the European Community (Krause, 1976) are asymetrical, more favorable to the other party or parties than to those in Latin America.

*VARIATION IN POWER AND CAPABILITY*

A country's level of power and capability contribute very greatly toward defining what goals it can reasonably pursue in its international relationships; as well, its level of power and capability establish the means that can reasonably be employed to gain objectives. From a global perspective, all of the Latin American countries are lesser ranking ones in terms of power and capability to act in the international system. (For a global ranking of countries according to level of power, see Spiegel, 1972: 93-128.) Within Latin America there is, as on most other counts, diversity, great diversity, in power and capability to act. At one extreme is Brazil, a country "on the make" which is unquestionably the most powerful Latin American country, with both the desire and the potential to in time move into the major world power ranks. At the other extreme are the countries of Central America and the Caribbean (again, excepting Cuba) that are virtually powerless and all but wholly lacking in capability, barely describable as viable political entities. Between these extremes are a number of different gradations of power among the Latin American countries.

Level of power and capability possessed by the majority of countries in Latin America dictates that they pursue foreign policy objectives of a more or less limited, modest nature and requires them to concentrate on matters of immediate and fundamental concern. So far as means go, Atkins (1977: 48) reports that most of the Latin American countries employ

> the same means chosen by most small states in the world, exerting influence as they can through such tactics as (1) playing active roles in international organizations, (2) promoting international law and supporting such principles and procedures as non-intervention and peaceful settlement of disputes, (3) appealing to humanitarian sentiments and moral principles, (4) exploiting the rivalries of greater powers while remaining as noncommital as possible themselves, and (5) bargaining with their markets and natural resources.

While there are many sources of the weakness that marks most countries of Latin America in their global international relations, two are of particular importance. One is the lesser degree of their economic development; the other is that many non-Latin American countries do not regard most of the countries in the Latin American region as important to them and do not have interests that depend on the responsiveness of countries in the region.

It is important, however, not to exaggerate the lesser power position of most of the countries. As Fox (1977: 3) puts it: "If power lies in not having to give in, it may be exerted in a particular situation somewhat independently of the ranking of two contending governments in someone's power calculations." When power is conceived of in this way, it becomes apparent that on occasion some, and perhaps all or almost all, Latin American countries are endowed with some measure of power that objective calculations do not reveal. The ability not to give in or to say no helps to explain how a country such as Panama was able to induce the United States government to conclude an agreement with it to transfer the canal to Panamanian jurisdiction; similarly, it helps to explain Brazil's ability to disregard U.S. protests about the South American giant's nuclear power agreement with the Federal Republic of Germany. Obviously, the ability not to give in is a technique that is appropriate and exploitable in only some relational situations, not all. An additional factor to be taken into account in assessing the power and capability of the countries of Latin America is the growing ability of many, through accumulation of knowledge and skill, to assert control over external actors—particularly external economic actors (Moran, 1974; Tugwell, 1975)—that have long dominated aspects of Latin American society.

## *BLENDING OF FOREIGN AND DOMESTIC POLICY*

In the Latin American countries today, as in most other countries of the world, there is no sharp distinction between foreign and domestic policy. Instead, in Latin America a country's international relations are regarded as one means of attaining various domestic objectives or, more correctly, one means of attaining objectives that are catgorized as neither foreign nor domestic, but simply as national objectives—especially national economic objectives. Schneider (1976: 40) reports that in Brazil "foreign policy is generally viewed in terms of its possible contribution to internal economic development." On this count, it appears that what is true of Brazil is also true of the other countries in the region.

*OBJECTIVES*

The Latin American countries are a very diverse collection of states, differing in many ways that bear directly or indirectly on both foreign policy and international behavior. These include level of economic development, degree of political development, historical experiences in the international arena, political ideology, skills and perceptions of political leaders, political and economic resources, to name only a few. Yet, despite these points of difference which suggest that about all the countries of Latin America have in common is the continent they occupy, there is considerable similarity among them with regard to the objectives they seek to advance through their global international relations. Indeed, the editors (Davis and Wilson, 1975: 445) of one study which explores the foreign policy of each of the countries conclude that "on the whole, the most striking fact emerging from this brief survey of the foreign policies of the Latin American republics is that they share many policy objectives and that on many major questions their policies have been virtually identical." Security and survival are two common objectives; many, although by no means all, others have to do in one way or another with development—political and economic—and the achieving of independent status in the international system. In point of fact, security and survival, economic and political development, and independent status are not regarded by Latin American decision makers and international affairs commentators as separate categories of objectives; rather, they are regarded as closely interrelated components of a single objective. In his analysis of Latin American perspectives on international affairs, Milenky (1975: 103) writes that "development is linked to national power and the achievement of meaningful national sovereignty and autonomy. . . . Development will lead to sovereignty if it is autonomous."

The existence of many very similar and even identical objectives in no way means that all or even most Latin American countries constitute a "united front" or always cohesive collection of states in the global international arena—and certainly not in the Latin American region. While objectives are identical, or at least very similar, policies and approaches not always are. International policies and approaches are not identical in the area of economic development and development assistance (Davis and Wilson, 1975) nor are policies and approaches identical in the law of the sea area (Brown, 1975), to mention only two international issue areas where objectives are either identical or similar.

There are any number of reasons why the countries are not an always cohesive grouping of states. Some stand out. First, only within the last few years have institutionalized mechanisms, as opposed to ad hoc ones, existed for Latin American consultation on international issues and for nonbinding coordination of policy. Second, when consultation and coordination do occur, they are not in all instances carried through or given effect. Several cases in point are to be found in the economic area.

> On paper the policy picture gives a strong impression of agreement. The Alliance for Progress, LAFTA, CACM, the Andean Group, the Caribbean Free Trade Association, various agreements of the presidents (e.g., that of 1966 for the achievement of a Latin American Common Market by 1985), commodity agreements, and the Consensus of Viña del Mar are encouraging aspirations, but little has been done to implement them in national foreign policies [Davis and Wilson, 1975: 447-448].

Third, there are not infrequently country-to-country differences in decision makers' philosophy about how to pursue objectives that are common. Fourth, in some foreign policy issue areas the countries have competing, and even conflicting, interests.

### *FOREIGN POLICY-MAKING*

Foreign policy-making and the conduct of international relations in all of the Latin American countries are in the domain of the chief executive. However, the making of foreign policy and the conduct of international relations are not, regardless of the form of government, fields of governmental activity in which the chief executive and only the chief executive is involved just as in domestic politics, regardless of the form of government, the chief executive is not the only actor involved. Although its exact composition varies from country to country and from one time to another within countries, there is in each Latin American country a constellation of actors that comprise what may be described as a foreign affairs community or constituency. These actors are individuals and groups, both governmental and private sector, that have some formal responsibility for the making and/or carrying out of foreign policy. Included in this category are foreign ministers, foreign ministry staff, diplomats, intelligence services, legislatures and legislative committees in democratic countries and occasionally in some authoritarian countries, as well as national security agencies or those with a vested interest in the country's foreign policy and international relatoins, or merely interested observers. The latter includes government agencies dealing with economic affairs, business groups, and individual businessmen. Also in this foreign affairs constituency are intellectuals, members of the press, and foreign interests. Their number varies in degree depending on the country. The more open the political system, the more actors in the foreign policy community. However, in none does public opinion have more than a very limited impact on foreign policy or in the conduct of international relations, although it may operate as some sort of constraint by establishing the outer limits of permissibility. (That, and all other aspects of foreign policy-making in Latin America, is an area where much more research is needed.)

The extent of influence that each actor in the foreign affair community has is unclear. However, very limited evidence suggests that none, with the exception of the armed forces in issue areas they deem vital to national security, has anything approaching the clout that a number of elements of the U.S. community have (for a degree of insight, in this instance that of joining LAFTA and the Andean group, respectively, see Schmitter and Haas, 1964; Avery, 1976). In the past—even the very recent past and in a few countries at present—foreign actors, most notably foreign governments, but in more than one instance foreign investors, had and still may have a veto.

In all of the Latin American countries the armed forces are usually major members of the foreign affairs community. However, even in the case of military and military-controlled governments, as a general rule the armed forces do not dominate all aspects of the making of foreign policy and conduct of international relations. But, in military and military-controlled governments, the armed forces do set the broad outlines of foreign policy. The armed forces take a leading, if not dominant, role in any matter of foreign policy or international relations that has to do with national security or with the armed forces themselves. At least, that is the case in Brazil's military-dominated government (Schneider, 1976: 68-77). On the surface it seems likely to characterize other countries with a simliar type of government.

### *PERCEPTIONS*

A substantial influence on the country's international aspirations and behavior is exerted by decision makers and how they view the world, their country's position in it, their country's capabilities, and what is possible. Although officials' public rhetoric before domestic audiences and in international forums might suggest otherwise, most Latin American decision makers have moderate, even modest, and very pragmatic perceptions of their countries' place in the world, objectives, capability, and what is possible. Milenky (1975: 107) states:

> It is possible to conclude that some consensus exists in Latin America on the future of the region and its individual nations in world affairs. Generally, Latin Americans see themselves as members of weak, externally penetrated societies in which great powers, multinational corporations, and international economic relationships play important roles. As a result nation-states in the classic sense of impervious units . . . do not exist. Latin American governments are seen as mediators between indigenous and nonindigenous actors and forces. These conditions are the product of underdevelopment and the low power position of Latin American nations in the world.

Aspirations, as the same author goes on to say, are equally moderate and pragmatic. He reports that "with the exception of some Brazilians and Argentines, most Latin Americans would accept regional international roles, or minimally, a sense of national autonomy. Collective bargaining may produce some limited improvements, but most expect to stay under substantial United States influence." Other authors (Schneider, 1976; Fortin, 1975) also mention pragmatism as a characteristic of both Latin American perceptions and behavior in the global international arena.

## *INTRA-LATIN AMERICAN CONTACTS*

Traditionally, intra-Latin American contacts have been limited. But, since the 1960s those contacts have been expanding, intensifying, and increasing in importance. Intraregional cooperation is seen by some in Latin America, and elsewhere, as a way of countering U.S. influence and asserting independence (Swansbrough, 1975). It is also viewed as a way to advance other ends. However, nationalism, competition among countries, and the heavy hand of tradition all work against intraregional cooperation becoming the dominant element in contacts among the Latin American countries. But, although it may become more pronounced as the level of intra-Latin American contact continues to increase (see Ronfeldt and Einaudi, 1974), it appears unlikely that conflict will, at least in the forseeable future, become the dominant element in intra-Latin American relations, or that frequent and/or large-scale war (as distinct from minor incidents or small-scale fighting) will become common. Barros (1975) discusses several potential sources of intense interstate animosities and the mix of them most likely to spill over to armed combat.

> By themselves neither commercial competition nor the traditional rivalries of South American countries would be a sufficient reason for active aggression. A more serious problem may be the ideological differences between governments. Any of these reasons alone is unlikely to generate war, but if these are adequately mixed, the likelihood of war may very will increase. My hypothesis is that ideological differences coupled with traditional rivalries are the ingredients that make war acceptable. If one of these conditions is absent, countries are much more likely to try to solve their problems by nonmilitary methods.

In contemporary Latin America some ideological differences do exist (e.g., Brazil and Peru, Peru and Chile, Venezuela and Cuba). But, the main interstate rivalries are of the traditional sort. Another factor mitigating against large-scale war is the restraint of decision makers, even those of rival countries. Decision makers appear to view war, because of its disruption of the development effort, as an all but unthinkable policy instrument—unless survival of the state is in question.

## *Need for Further Research*

The research on Latin American international relations and foreign policy that has been done to this point by scholars in the United States is welcome and much needed. It represents a beginning, but a small, and, for the most part, tentative beginning. No facet of the subject matter has been adequately studied nor does the existing literature provide the basis for constructing a theory or even a pretheory of Latin American international relations. Needed is a series of comprehensive, in-depth studies of the numerous facets of international relations and foreign policy, both contemporary and historical, of each of the countries of Latin America. Research of that scope and intensity would, first provide greater insight into and understanding of each country as an international actor, and, second, would provide the groundwork necessary for theory construction.

*—James D. Cochrane*

## REFERENCES

AVERY, W. P. (1976) "Oil, politics, and economics policy making: Venezuelan and Andean Common Market." International Organization 30 (Autumn): 541-571.

BARROS, A.S.C. (1975) "The diplomacy of a national security: South American international relations in a defrosting world," p. 142 in R. G. Hellman and H. J. Rosenbaum (eds.) Latin America: The Search for a New International Role. New York: Halsted Press (A Sage Publications Book).

BROWN, E. D. (1975) "Latin America and the international law of the sea," pp. 247-270 in R. G. Hellman and H. J. Rosenbaum (eds.) Latin America: The Search for a New International Role. New York: Halsted Press (A Sage Publications Book).

FORTIN, C. (1975) "Principled pragmatism in the face of external pressure: the foreign policy of the Allende government," pp. 217-245 in R. G. Hellman and H. J. Rosenbaum (eds.) Latin America: The Search for a New International Role. New York: Halsted Press (A Sage Publications Book).

KRAUSE, L. B. (1976) "Latin American economic relations with Western Europe," pp. 143-156 in R. W. Fontaine and J. D. Theberge (eds.) Latin America's New Internationalism: The End of Hemispheric Isolation. New York: Praeger.

MILENKY, E. (1975) "Problems, perspectives, and modes of analysis. Understanding Latin American approaches to world affairs," in R. G. Hellman and H. J. Rosenbaum (eds.) Latin America: The Search for a New International Role. New York: Halsted Press (A Sage Publications Book).

MORAN, T. H. (1974) Multinational Corporations and the Politics of Dependence. Princeton: Princeton Univ. Press.

RONFELDT, D. F. and L. R. EINAUDI (1974) "Conflict and cooperation among Latin American states," pp. 185-200 in L. R. Einaudi (ed.) Beyond Cuba: Latin America Takes Charge of Its Future. New York: Crane, Russak.

SCHMITTER, P. C. and E. B. HAAS (1964) Mexico and Latin American Economic Integration. Berkeley: Institute of International Studies, University of California.

SPEIGEL, S. L. (1972) Dominance and Diversity: The International Hierarchy. Boston: Little, Brown.

SWANSBROUGH, R. H. (1976) The Embattled Colossus: Economic Nationalism and the United States Investors in Latin America. Gainesville: Univ. of Florida Press.

——— (1975) "Peru's diplomatic offensive: solidarity for Latin American independence," pp. 115-130 in R. G. Hellman and H. J. Rosenbaum (eds.) Latin America: The Search for a New International Role. New York: Halsted Press (A Sage Publications Book).

TUGWELL, F. (1975) The Politics of Oil in Venezuela. Stanford: Stanford Univ. Press.

*James D. Cochrane is Professor of Political Science at Tulane University. His current research is focused on the international relations of the countries of Latin America.*

# BOOKS RECEIVED

## *GENERAL AND LATIN AMERICA*

Benjamin, Jules Robert. THE UNITED STATES AND CUBA: HEGEMONY AND DEPENDENT DEVELOPMENT, 1880-1934. Pittsburgh, PA: University of Pittsburgh Press, 1977. Notes, bibliography, index. xii, 266 pp. $14.95.

Camp, Roderic Ai. THE ROLE OF ECONOMISTS IN POLICY-MAKING: A COMPARATIVE CASE STUDY OF MEXICO AND THE UNITED STATES. Tucson: Institute of Government Research, University of Arizona Press, 1977. Notes, appendix, selective bibliography, index. 78 pp. (paper).

Cornelius, Wayne A. and Robert V. Kemper, eds. METROPOLITAN LATIN AMERICA: THE CHALLENGE AND THE RESPONSE. Latin American Urban Research, Vol. 6. Beverly Hills: Sage Publications, Inc., 1978. Bibliography, recent urban studies on Latin America, 1974-1976, and about the editors and contributors. 346 pp. $18.50 (cloth), $7.95 (paper).

Duncan, Kenneth and Ian Rutledge, eds., with the collaboration of Colin Harding. LAND AND LABOUR IN LATIN AMERICA: ESSAYS ON THE DEVELOPMENT OF AGRARIAN CAPITALISM IN THE NINETEENTH AND TWENTIETH CENTURIES. New York: Cambridge University Press, 1978. Glossary of Spanish and Portuguese terms, weights and measures, notes on contributors, subject and author indexes. Tables, figures and maps. xxiii, 535 pp. $29.95.

Francis, Michael J. THE LIMITS OF HEGEMONY: UNITED STATES RELATIONS WITH ARGENTINA AND CHILE DURING WORLD WAR II. Notre Dame, IN: University of Notre Dame Press, 1977. International Studies of the Committee on International Relations, University of Notre Dame. Conclusion, notes, index. xii, 292 pp.

Gianaris, Nicholas V. ECONOMIC DEVELOPMENT: THOUGHT AND PROBLEMS. North Quincy, MA: Christopher Publishing House, 1978. Name and subject index. 364 pp. $14.95.

Grunwald, Joseph, ed. LATIN AMERICA AND WORLD ECONOMY: A CHANGING INTERNATIONAL ORDER. Latin American International Affairs Series, Vol. 2. Beverly Hills: Sage Publications, Inc., 1978. Index, about the Center and series, notes on editors and contributors. 323 pp. $18.50 (cloth), $8.95 (paper).

Hardoy, Jorge E. and Richard P. Schaedel, compiladores. ASENTAMIENTOS URBANOS Y ORGANIZACION SOCIOPRODUCTIVA EN LA HISTORIA DE AMERICA LATINA. Buenos Aires: Ediciones SIAP, 1977. 385 pp. (paper).

Hardoy, Jorge E. and Richard P. Schaedel, compiladores. LAS CIUDADES DE AMERICA LATINA Y SUS AREAS DE INFLUENCIA A TRAVES DE LA HISTORIA. Buenos Aires: Ediciones SIAP, 1975. 451 pp. (paper).

Hughes, Barry B. THE DOMESTIC CONTEXT OF AMERICAN FOREIGN POLICY. San Francisco: W. H. Freeman, 1978. Index. xii, 240 pp.

Inter-American Development Bank. BIBLIOGRAPHY ON NEW FORMS OF POST-SECONDARY EDUCATION: LATIN AMERICAN MEETING ON NEW FORMS OF POST-SECONDARY EDUCATION AND SEMINAR ON OPEN LEARNING SYSTEMS. Washington, DC: IDB, Economic and Social Development Department, 1977. 282 pp. (paper).

Irish, Donald P., ed. MULTINATIONAL CORPORATIONS IN LATIN AMERICA: PRIVATE RIGHTS—PUBLIC RESPONSIBILITIES. Edited proceedings of five symposia. Associated Colleges of the Twin Cities, February 18-March 17, 1976. Papers in International Studies, Latin America Series No. 2. Athens: Ohio University Center for International Studies, 1978. $5.50 (paper).

Lechner, Norbert. LA CRISIS DEL ESTADO EN AMERICA LATINA. Caracas: El Cid Editor, S.R.L., 1977. Colección Estudios Interdisciplinarios / 6. 160 pp. (paper).

Lernoux, Penny. NOTES ON A REVOLUTIONARY CHURCH: HUMAN RIGHTS IN LATIN AMERICA. New York: Alicia Patterson Foundation, 1978. 91 pp. (paper).

Loveman, Brian and Thomas M. Davies, Jr. THE POLITICS OF ANTIPOLITICS. THE MILITARY IN LATIN AMERICA. Lincoln: University of Nebraska Press, 1978. vii, 309 pp. $19.95 (cloth), $5.95 (paper).

Mesa-Lago, Carmelo. MODELOS DE SEGURIDAD SOCIAL EN AMERICA LATINA. Estudio comparativo. Buenos Aires: Ediciones SIAP-Planteos, 1977. 221 pp. (paper).

Molineu, Harold, ed. MULTINATIONAL CORPORATIONS AND INTERNATIONAL INVESTMENT IN LATIN AMERICA: A SELECTED AND ANNOTATED BIBLIOGRAPHY WITH AN ANNOTATED FILM BIBLIOGRAPHY. Papers in International Studies, Latin America Series No. 3. Athens: Ohio University Center for International Studies, 1978. Indexes. vii, 98 pp. $5.00 (paper).

Ross, Stanley R., ed. VIEWS ACROSS THE BORDER: THE UNITED STATES AND MEXICO. Appendixes, bibliography, index. xiv, 456 pp. $5.95 (paper).

Saulniers, Suzanne Smith and Cathy A. Rakowski. WOMEN IN THE DEVELOPMENT PROCESS: A SELECT BIBLIOGRAPHY ON WOMEN IN SUB-SAHARAN AFRICA AND LATIN AMERICA. Austin: Institute of Latin American Studies, University of Texas Press, 1977. Appendixes, 287 pp. $6.95 (paper).

Spalding, Hobart A., Jr. ORGANIZED LABOR IN LATIN AMERICA: HISTORICAL CASE STUDIES OF WORKERS IN DEPENDENT SOCIETIES. New York: New York University Press, 1977. Postscript, index, xv, 297 pp. $15.00 (cloth), $5.95 (paper).

Walbek, Norman V. and Sidney Weintraub, eds. CONFLICT, ORDER AND PEACE IN THE AMERICAS. Part I: Dialogues on the Central Issues. Austin: Lyndon B. Johnson School of Public Affairs, The University of Texas Press, 1978. 125 pp. (paper).

Wayland-Smith, Giles. THE CATHOLIC CHURCH AND SOCIAL CHANGE: A RESEARCH NOTE AND SOME PRELIMINARY FINDINGS ON THE ARCHDIOCESE OF YUCATAN. Monograph No. 5. Erie: Mercyhurst College, Institute for Latin American Studies of Northwestern Pennsylvania, 1977. Appendixes. 34 pp. (paper).

Wilkie, James W., ed. MONEY AND POLITICS IN LATIN AMERICA. Statistical Abstract of Latin America Supplement 7. Los Angeles: UCLA Latin American Center Publications, University of California, 1977. Tables, charts, symbols used in tables. xix, 91 pp. (paper).

Wilkie, James W. and Kenneth Ruddle, eds. QUANTITATIVE LATIN AMERICAN STUDIES: METHODS AND FINDINGS. Statistical Abstract of Latin America Supplement 6. Los Angeles: UCLA Latin American Center Publications, University of California, 1977. Tables, figures, symbols used in tables. xiv, 92 pp. (paper).

Wilkie, James W., ed., and Peter Reich, coeditor. STATISTICAL ABSTRACT OF LATIN AMERICA, Vol. 18 (1977). Statistical abstract of Latin America series. Los Angeles: UCLA Latin American Center, 1977. Maps, tables, explanation of terms, index, xxii, 449 pp.

*ARGENTINA*

Milenky, Edward S. ARGENTINA'S FOREIGN POLICIES. Boulder, CO: Westview Press, Westview Replica Edition, 1978. List of tables and figures, select bibliography, note on sources, list of acronyms. xvii, 345 pp. $20.00.

*BRAZIL*

Basseches, Bruno. A BIBLIOGRAPHY ON BRAZILIAN BIBLIOGRAPHIES/ BIBLIOGRAFIA DAS BIBLIOGRAFIAS BRASILEIRAS. Detroit: Blaine Ethridge, 1978. Preface by José Honorio Rodrigues. Index. Front matter in English and Portuguese. viii, 185 pp. $14.00.

Erickson, Kenneth Paul. THE BRAZILIAN CORPORATIVE STATE AND WORKING-CLASS POLITICS. Berkeley: University of California Press, 1978. List of tables, glossary of Portuguese terms, bibliography, index. xvii, 242 pp. $ 14.00.

Goldman, Frank Perry and Demarisee Machado Goldman. PROBLEMAS BRASILEIROS: ALGUNS ASPECTOS SOBRE O PROCESSO DE ENVELHECER. Piracicabo, S. P., Brazil: Editoria Franciscana do Lar Franciscano de Menores, 1977. Notas bibliográficas, livros consultados, legislação consultada, outras fontes.

Levine, Robert M. PERNAMBUCO IN THE BRAZILIAN FEDERATION, 1889-1937. Stanford, CA: Stanford University Press, 1978. Appendixes, notes, bibliography, index, xxii, 236 pp. $17.50.

*CARIBBEAN REGION*

INTEC. Documentos I. Presentación de relaciones internas. Santo Domingo, D. R.: Instituto Tecnológicoi de Santo Domingo, INTEC, 1976. 122 pp. (paper).

Latorre, Eduardo. POLITICA DOMINICANA CONTEMPORANEA. Santo Domingo, D. R.: Ediciones INTEC, 1975. Tablas, bibliografía. xi, 407 pp. (paper).

Lent, John A. THIRD WORLD MASS MEDIA AND THEIR SEARCH FOR MODERNITY: THE CASE OF COMMONWEALTH CARIBBEAN, 1717-1976. Cranbury, NJ: Buckness University Press, 1977. List of tables, appendixes, bibliography. 405 pp. $22.50.

Llerena, Mario. THE UNSUSPECTED REVOLUTION: THE BIRTH AND RISE OF CASTROISM. Ithaca, NY: Cornell University Press, 1978. Illustrations, chronology of Cuban revolution, figures of the Castro movement, appendixes, notes, index. 324 pp. $12.50.

Malagón Barceló, Javier. EL DISTRITO DE LA AUDIENCIA DE SANTO DOMINGO EN LOS SIGLOS XIV A XIX. Second edition. First edition, 1942. Text, basic documents (1511-11861), catalog of Archivo de la Real Audiencia de Santo Domingo, now in Cuba (1708-1788). Santiago, R. D. : Universidad Católica Madre y Maestra, 1977. Indice. 302 pp. (paper).

Mesa-Lago, Carmelo. CUBA IN THE 1970s: PRAGMATISM AND INSTITUTIONALIZATION. Revised edition. Albuquerque: University of New Mexico Press, 1978. Notes, index, list of tables. xv, 187 pp. $9.95 (cloth), $4.95 (paper).

*CENTRAL AMERICA*

Rodríguez, Mario. THE CADIZ EXPERIMENT IN CENTRAL AMERICA, 1808 TO 1826. Berkeley: University of California Press, 1978. Notes, glossary, bibliography, index, maps. xii, 316 pp. $18.00.

Rodríguez Becerra, Salvador. ENCOMIENDA Y CONQUISTA: LOS INICIOS DE LA COLONIZACION EN GUATEMALA. Sevilla, Spain: Publicaciones del Seminario de Antropología Americana, Universidad de Sevilla, 1977. Documentos, bibliografía, índice. 202 pp. (paper).

*CHILE*

Alexander, Robert J. ARTURO ALESSANDRI: A BIOGRAPHY. Two volumes. Ann Arbor, MI: University Microfilms International, 1977. Unedited facsimile of the author's typescript. xvii, 986 pp. $59.50 (cloth), U.S.A.; $65.50, Canada and Mexico; elsewhere, $68.50.

Drake, Paul W. SOCIALISM AND POPULISM IN CHILE, 1932-1952. Urbana: University of Illinois Press, 1978. Epilogue, appendixes, bibliography, index, list of tables. xii, 418 pp.

Informe, Cinda. EL SISTEMA DE DESARROLLO CIENTIFCO TECNOLOGICO EN LA SUBREGION ANDINA. Santiago, Chile: CPU (Corporación de Promoción Universitaria), 1977. 141 pp. (paper).

Sigmund, Paul E. THE OVERTHROW OF ALLENDE AND THE POLITICS OF CHILE, 1964-1976. Pittsburgh, PA: University of Pittsburgh Press, 1977. List of illustrations, notes, index. xiii, 326 pp. $14.95 (cloth), $5.50 (paper).

*COLOMBIA*

Lavados, Ivan, ed. UNIVERSIDAD Y DESARROLLO. Santiago, Chile: CPU, 1976. 152 pp. (paper).

Rodríguez F., Jaime. LAS TRANSFORMACIONES DEL SISTEMA EDUCATIVO Y SU REPERCUSION SOBRE LA UNIVERSIDAD DE LA DECADA DEL 80 EN COLOMBIA. Bogotá, Colombia: ICFES, 1977. Anexos, bibliografía. 88 pp. (paper).

Sharpless, Richard E. GAITAN OF COLOMBIA: A POLITICAL BIOGRAPHY. Pittsburgh, PA: University of Pittsburgh Press, 1978. Notes, bibliography, index. xii, 229 pp. $11.95.

*MEXICO*

Alba, Francisco. LA POBLACION DE MEXICO: EVOLUCION Y DILEMAS. México, D. F.: El Colegio de México, 1977. Lista de referencias, índices de cuadros y gráficas. 187 pp. (paper).

Anna, Timothy E. THE FALL OF THE ROYAL GOVERNMENT IN MEXICO CITY. Lincoln: University of Nebraska Press, 1978. Notes, selected bibliography, acknowledgments, index. xix, 289 pp. $15.00.

Camp, Roderic Ai. MEXICAN POLITICAL BIOGRAPHIES, 1935-1975. Tucson: University of Arizona Press, 1976. Selected bibliographic essay, how persons were selected for inclusion, source abbreviations, abbreviations, biographies. xxvii, 468 pp. (paper).

Centro de Estudios Internacionales. LA VIDA POLITICA EN MEXICO 1970-1973. México, D. F.: El Colegio de México, Colección Centro de Estudios Internacionales X, 1974. 187 pp. (paper).

Centro de Estudios Internacionales. LAS FRONTERAS DEL CONTROL DEL ESTADO MEXICANO. México, D. F.: El Colegio de México, Colección de Estudios Internacionales, XVI, 1976. 175 pp. (paper).

Chance, John K. RACE AND CLASS IN COLONIAL OAXACA. Stanford, CA: Stanford University Press, 1978. Appendixes, notes, bibliography, index. xvi, 250 pp. $14.00.

Figueroa, José (translated, with an introduction and notes by C. Alan Hutchinson). A MANIFEST TO THE MEXICAN REPUBLIC, which Brigadier General José Figueroa, Commandant and Political Chief of Upper California, presents on his conduct and of that of José María de Hijar and José María Padrés as Directors of Colonization in 1834 and 1835. Berkeley: University of California Press, 1978. Bibliography, index, 165 pp. $15.75.

González Navarro, Moises. ANATOMIA DEL PODER EN MEXICO (1848-1853). México, D. F.: El Colegio de México, Centro de Estudios Históricos colección, Neuva series 23. Epílogo, fuentes, índice analítico. 498 pp. (paper).

Grabendorff, Wolf, BESTIMMUNGSFAKSTOREN UND DIMENSIONEN DER AUSSENPOLITIK MEXIKOS. Ebenhausen, West Germany: Stiftung Wissenschaft und Politik, Forschungsinstitut für Internationale Politik und Sicherheit, 1977. 183 pp. (paper).

Hart, John M. ANARCHISM AND THE MEXICAN WORKING CLASS, 1860-1931. Austin: University of Texas Press, 1978. Notes, bibliography, bibliographic note, index. x, 249 pp. $14.95.

Hellman, Judith Adler, MEXICO IN CRISIS. New York: Holmes & Meier Publishers, Inc., 1978. Notes, bibliography, index, vi, 229 pp. $15.75 (cloth), $7.95 (paper).

Herrera Canales, Index. EL COMERCIO EXTERIOR DE MEXICO, 1821-1875.

México, D. F.: El Colegio de Mexico, Centro de Estudios Históricos, Neuva series 25, 1977. Fuentes, bibliografía, anexos, índices de cuadros, gráficas, mapas. 193 pp. (paper).

Krauze, Enrique, con la colaboración de Jean Meyer and Cayetano Reyes. LA RECONSTRUCTION ECONOMICA. Historia de la Revolución Mexicana, Período 1924-1928, No. 10. México, D. F.: El Colegio de México, 1977. Index. 323 pp. (paper).

Martínez, Oscar J. BORDER BOOM TOWN: CIUDAD JUAREZ SINCE 1848. Austin: University of Texas Press, 1978. Summary and conclusion, appendix, notes, bibliography, index, list of illustrations and tables, notes on terms and symbols. xvi, 231 pp. $12.95.

Meyer, Lorenzo. EL CONFLICTO SOCIAL Y LOS GOBIERNOS DEL MAXIMATO. Historia de la Revolucion Mexicana, Período 1928-1934, No. 13. México, D. F.: El Colegio de México, 1978. Bibliografía, índice analítico. vii, 335 pp. (paper).

Nadal Egea, Alejandro. INSTRUMENTOS DE POLITICA CIENTIFICA Y TECNOLOGICA EN MEXICO. México, D. F.: El Colegio de México, Colección Centro de Estudios Econónicos y Demograáficos V, 1977. Indice de caudros. 309 pp. (paper).

Pellicer de Brody, Olga and Esteban L. Mancilla. EL ENTENDIMIENTO CON LOS ESTADOS UNIDOS Y LA GESTACION DEL DESARROLLO ESTABILIZADOR. Historia de la Revolución Mexicana, Período 1952-1960, No. 23. México, D.F.: El Colegio de México, 1978. Epílogo, bibliografía, índice onomástico. ix, 299 pp. (paper).

Pellicer de Brody, Olga and José Luis Reyna. EL AFIANZAMIENTO DE LA ESTABILIDAD POLITICA. Historia de la Revolución Mexicana, Período 1952-1960, No. 22. México, D.F.: El Colegio de México, 1978. Epílogo, bibliografía citada, índice de nombres. x, 222 pp. (paper).

Ross, Stanley R. FRANCISCO I. MADERO: APOSTOL DE LA DEMOCRACIA MEXICANA. Versión española de Edelberto Torres. This is a second Spanish edition of a book originally published in 1955 by Columbia University Press. México, D.F.: Editorial Griajalbo, 1977. Abreviaturas, bibliografía, índice de nombres. 407 pp. (paper).

Whitaker, Irwin and Emily. A POTTER'S MEXICO. Albuquerque: University of New Mexico press, 1978. Glossary of Mexican Pottery terms, bibliography, index. xvi, 136 pp. $17.50.

*PERU*

Ballon Echegaray, Eduardo, César Pezo del Pino, Luis Peirana Falconi, and Gilberto Váldex Herrera. EDUCACION BASICA LABORAL: PROCESO A UN PROCESO. Praxis No. 9. Lima: DESCO, 1978. 142 pp. (paper).

Cabieses, Hugo and Carlos Otero. ECONOMIA PERUANA: UN ENSAYO DE INTERPRETACION. Lima: DESCO, 1978. Anexos. 221 pp. (paper).

Esculies Larrabure, Oscar. Marcial Rubio Correa, and Veronica González del Castillo. COMERCIALIZACION DE ALIMENTOS: QUIENES GANAN, QUIENES PAGAN, QUIENES PIERDEN. Praxis No. 8. Lima: DESCO, 1977. Fuentes consultadas. 190 pp. (paper).

Pease Garcia, Henry and Alfredo Filomeno. PERU 1976 CHRONOLOGIA POLITICA, Tomo V. Lima: DESCO, 1978. Indice, 2389 pp. (paper).

Peirano, Louis, Eduardo Ballon, Leyla Bartet, and Gilberto Valdex. PRENSA:

APERTURA Y LIMITES. Lima: DESCO, 1978. Anexos, xix, 241 pp. (paper).

Sánchez León, Abelardo, Julio Calderón Cockburn, and Raúl Guerrero de los Ricos. PARADERO. FINAL? EL TRANSPORTE PUBLICO EN LIMA METROPOLITANA. Lima: DEXCO, 1978. Anexos, bibliografía. 217 pp. (paper).

*VENEZUELA*

Bond, Robert D., ed. CONTEMPORARY VENEZUELA AND ITS ROLE IN INTERNATIONAL AFFAIRS. A Council on Foreign Relations Book. New York: New York University Press, 1977. Index. x, 267 pp. $15.00 (cloth), $6.95 (paper).

Concejo Municipal del Distrito Federal. ARTE DE VENEZUELA. Caracas: Concejo Municipal, 1977. 159 pp.

Herrera de Weishaar, María Luisa, María Leonar Ferreira Ferreira, y Carlos Nestor Albarez Cabrera. PARROQUIA LA BEGA: ESTUDIO MICRO-HISTORICO. Caracas: Concejo Municipal del Distrito Federal, 1977. Sección documental, fuentes consultadas, mapas. 176 pp. (paper).

MONTALBAN NO. 7. Caracas: Facultad de Humanidades y Educación, Instituto Humanísticos de Investigación, Universidad Católica Andrés Bello, 1977. Index. 985 pp. (paper).

Moron, Guillermo. HISTORIA DE LA PROVINCIA DE VENEZUELA. Caracas: Concejo Municipal del Distrito Federal, 1977. 390 pp. (paper).

Salas, Carlos. LA FIESTA BRAVA EN CARACAS. CUATRO SIGLOS DE HISTORIA. Caracas: Concejo Municipal del Distrito Federal, 1978. Biblioteca y Hemeroteca Taurinas, Indice Onomástico. 356 pp.

*MISCELLANEOUS*

Altback, Philip G. and Gail P. Kelly. EDUCATION AND COLONIALISM. New York: Longman, Inc., 1978. Select bibliography, index. vii, 372 pp. $6.95 (paper).

Bartley, Russell H. IMPERIAL RUSSIA AND THE STRUGGLE FOR LATIN AMERICA INDEPENDENCE 1808-1828. Austin: Institute of Latin American Studies. University of Texas, 1978. List of tables, illustrations, notes, bibliography, index, transliteration table. xvi, 236 pp. $14.95 (cloth), $5.95 (paper).

Langer, William L. IN AND OUT OF THE IVORY TOWER: THE AUTOBIOGRAPHY OF WILLIAM L. LANGER. New York: Neale Watson Academic Publications, Inc., 1978. Index. x, 268 pp. $15.00.

Lucio, A., Ricardo, ed. ESTUDIOS DE POBLACION. Two volumes. Bogotá, Colombia: ACEP (Asociación Colombiana para el Estudio de la Población), 1976. Vol. 1, 383 pp.; Vol. 2, 305 pp. (paper).

# INDEX

to

# JOURNAL OF INTERAMERICAN STUDIES

# AND WORLD AFFAIRS

VOLUME 20

Number 1 (February 1978) pp. 1-104
Number 2 (May 1978) pp. 105-224
Number 3 (August 1978) pp. 225-352.
Number 4 (November 1978) pp. 353-480

## Authors:

BELL, JOHN PATRICK, "Political Power in Contemporary Costa Rica" [Review Essay], 443.
BERG, RONALD H. and FREDERICK STIRTON WEAVER, "Toward a Reinterpretation of Political Change in Peru During the First Century of Independence," 69.
BERRY, ALBERT, "Rural Poverty in Twentieth-Century Colombia," 355.
BROOKENS, BENOIT OTIS, "Diplomatic Protection of Foreign Economic Interests: The Changing Structure of International Law in the New International Economic Order," 37.
CIRIA, ALBERTO, "Argentina at the Crossroads" [Review Essay], 211.
COCHRANE, JAMES D., "Characteristics of Contemporary Latin American International Relations" [Review Essay], 455.
CRAIG, RICHARD B., "La Campaña Permanente: Mexico's Antidrug Campagin," 107.
DEMAS, WILLIAM G., "The Caribbean and the New International Economic Order," 229.

FERRER, ALDO, "Latin America and the World Economy: Some Observations on External Indebtedness and the International Monetary System," 321.
GARG, RAMESH C., "Brazilian External Debt: A Study in Capital Flows and Transfer of Resources," 341.
GIBBS, WILLIAM E., "Diaz' Executive Agents and United States Foreign Policy," 165.
GRABENDORFF, WOLF, "Mexico's Foreign Policy—Indeed a Foreign Policy?" [Review Essay], 85.
JAMES, DANIEL, "Power and Politics in Peronist Trade Unions," 3.
JINGUITO, ROBERTO, "Latin America and the Primary Product Trade," 297.
MAMALAKIS, MARKOS, "The New International Economic Order: Centerpiece Venezuela," 265.
NICHOLLS, DAVID, "The Wisdom of Salomon: Myth or Reality?" 377.
PREMDAS, RALPH R., "Guyana: Socialist Reconstruction or Political Opportunism?" 133.
SMITH, ROBERT FREEMAN, "The American Revolution and Latin America: An Essay in Imagery, Perceptions, and Ideological Influences," 421.
STONE, CARL, "Regional Party Voting in Jamaica (1959-1976)" 393.
VANDEN, HARRY E., "The Peasants as a Revolutionary Class: An Early Latin American View," 191.
VON LAZAR, ARPAD, "On the Virtues of Total Submersion: An Essay on the Trials and Tribulations of Development Literature Through the Bright Light of a New Product" [Review Essay], 93.
WEAVER, FREDERICK STIRTON, see Berg, Ronald H.

## Articles:

"The American Revolution and Latin America: An Essay In Imagery, Perceptions, and Ideological Influence," Smith, 421.
"Brazilian External Debt: A Study in Capital Flows and Transfer of Resources," Garg, 341.
"La Campaña Permanente: Mexico's Antidrug Campaign," Craig, 107.
"The Caribbean and the New International Economic Order," Demas, 229.
"Diaz' Executive Agents and United States Foreign Policy," Gibbs, 165.
"Diplomatic Protection of Foreign Economic Interests: The Changing Structure of International Law in the New International Economic Order," Brookens, 37.
"Guyana: Socialist Reconstruction or Political Opportunism?" Premdas, 133.
"Introductory Note," 227.
"Latin America and the Primary Product Trade," Jinguito, 297.
"Latin America and the World Economy: Some Observations on External Indebtedness and the International Monetary System," Ferrer, 321.
"The New International Economic Order: Centerpiece Venezuela," Mamalakis, 265.
"The Peasants as a Revolutionary Class: An Early Latin American View," Vanden, 191.
"Power and Politics in Peronist Trade Unions," James, 3.
"Regional Party Voting in Jamaica (1959-1976)" Stone, 393.
"Rural Poverty in Twentieth-Century Colombia," Berry, 355.
"Toward a Reinterpretation of Political Change in Peru During the First Century of Independence," Berg and Weaver, 69.
"The Wisdom of Salomon: Myth or Reality?" Nicholls, 377.

## Review Essays:

"Argentina at the Crossroads," Ciria, 211.
"Characteristics of Contemporary Latin American International Relations," Cochrane, 455.
"Mexico's Foreign Policy—Indeed a Foreign Policy?" Grabendorff, 85.
"On the Virtues of Total Submersion: An Essay on the Trials and Tribulations of Development Literature Through the Bright Light of a New Product," von Lazar, 93.
"Political Power in Contemporary Costa Rica," Bell, 443.

## Books Received:

99, 221, 469.